Christian Ethics
and the Church

Christian Ethics and the Church

Ecclesial Foundations
for Moral Thought and Practice

PHILIP TURNER

Baker Academic
a division of Baker Publishing Group
Grand Rapids, Michigan

© 2015 by Philip Turner

Published by Baker Academic
a division of Baker Publishing Group
P.O. Box 6287, Grand Rapids, MI 49516-6287
www.bakeracademic.com

Printed in the United States of America

All rights reserved. No part of this publication may be reproduced, stored in a retrieval system, or transmitted in any form or by any means—for example, electronic, photocopy, recording—without the prior written permission of the publisher. The only exception is brief quotations in printed reviews.

Library of Congress Cataloging-in-Publication Data
Turner, Philip, 1935–
    Christian ethics and the church : ecclesial foundations for moral thought and practice / Philip Turner.
       pages cm
    Includes bibliographical references and index.
    ISBN 978-0-8010-9707-2 (pbk.)
    1. Christian ethics. 2. Theology, Doctrinal. I. Title.
BJ1261.T875 2015
241—dc23
                                                                           2015005960

Scripture quotations are from the Revised Standard Version of the Bible, copyright 1952 [2nd edition, 1971] by the Division of Christian Education of the National Council of the Churches of Christ in the United States of America. Used by permission. All rights reserved.

15 16 17 18 19 20 21   7 6 5 4 3 2 1

In keeping with biblical principles of creation stewardship, Baker Publishing Group advocates the responsible use of our natural resources. As a member of the Green Press Initiative, our company uses recycled paper when possible. The text paper of this book is composed in part of post-consumer waste.

It will be the task of our generation, not to "seek great things," but to save and promote our souls out of the chaos, and to realize that it is the only thing we can carry as a "prize" from the burning building. . . . We shall have to keep our lives rather than shape them, to hope rather than plan, to hold out rather than march forward. . . . It will not be difficult for us to renounce privileges, recognizing the justice of history.

Dietrich Bonhoeffer

Grant, O merciful God, that your Church, being gathered together in unity by your Holy Spirit, may show forth your power among all peoples, to the glory of your Name; through Jesus Christ our Lord, who lives and reigns with you and the Holy Spirit, one God, for ever and ever. Amen.

Book of Common Prayer

Contents

Preface ix
Introduction xiv

Part 1 The Focus of Christian Ethics: Three Accounts

1. John Cassian's Ethic of Individual Sanctification 3
2. Walter Rauschenbusch's Ethic of Social Redemption 19
3. John Howard Yoder's Ethic of Communal Witness 38

Part 2 A Prismatic Case: The Epistle to the Ephesians

4. The Goal and Basis of Life Together in Christ: *A Reading of the Epistle to the Ephesians (Part One)* 61
5. The Character of Life Together in Christ: *A Reading of the Epistle to the Ephesians (Part Two)* 77

Part 3 Possible Exceptions

6. Possible Exceptions: *The Self* 107
7. Possible Exceptions: *Society* 125

Part 4 The Shape of an Ecclesial Ethic

8. The Goal, Basis, and Character of an Ecclesial Ethic 153
9. The Ecclesial Setting of a Devout and Holy Life 176

10. An Ecclesial View of Life in Civil Society   198
11. An Ecclesial View of Life within Political Society *(Part One)*   218
12. An Ecclesial View of Life within Political Society *(Part Two)*   245

Afterword   267

Bibliography   270

Scripture Index   277

Author Index   283

Subject Index   285

Preface

This book has taken shape over the last decade, but its origin lies even further back in time. From 1961 to 1971 I served as a missionary of the Episcopal Church assigned to the Church of Uganda. During that time I spent a year in the bush learning to speak one of the twenty-eight languages found within Uganda's borders. I taught for several years in a Church of Uganda seminary located in a little village near the capital, Kampala. I took a year out to study social anthropology at Oxford University and returned to teach in the Department of Religious Studies at Makerere University. During this decade, I worked closely with the African leadership that came into office with Uganda's independence. In particular, I came to know Archbishop Janani Luwum, who was killed by Idi Amin. My many conversations with him and my experience of the life of the Church of Uganda led me to change my view of the calling of the church and the nature of its relation to society.

In my case the change was marked. A seminary professor of mine once said of me, "Where you come from [in my case Virginia], being an Episcopalian is something that happens in certain families." His observation was on the mark. I was born into a family whose members had been Episcopalian since colonial times. I went to an Episcopal school, and the Episcopal Church financed my graduate education.

The church into which I was born and in which I grew up prided itself on its cultural position, its influence, and its openness to new learning. It understood its mission as being the religious and moral tutor of an educated and Christian society. The school I attended taught my fellow students and me that our privilege carried with it a responsibility to serve society and live an exemplary life. The Episcopal Church was part of a far wider coalition of liberal Protestant churches that saw their mission in much the same way. They were to encourage tolerance and justice in society and provide its religious foundation.

That is my background, but I lived outside of the United States for a decade—from 1961 to 1971. I missed the 1960s in America, but I observed my country from afar, and I came to realize that the world in which I had been raised was passing away. More importantly, I came to realize that the churches in the United States were being pushed to the social margins in a manner similar to the way in which the churches in Europe in an earlier period had lost their dominant social position. I came to believe that the churches in the United States were addressing their changed circumstances in exactly the wrong way. They were expending enormous energies to maintain their social position, and in so doing they failed to realize the extent to which their previous attachment to social position and cultural relevance had actually compromised their integrity. I came to believe that the most immediate calling of the churches is to form a culture in which Christ is taking form rather than to transform a culture.

These perceptions came about in part because I was immersed in the life of a church that was as different from mine as night is different from day. To be sure, the Church of Uganda was not without its own social ambitions. It had been the church of the colonial power that made Uganda a protectorate. The Church Missionary Society, whose successes were not unrelated to the British Raj, had evangelized it. The Church of Uganda had benefited from a close association not only with the ruling colonial power but also with Uganda's ruling class. It is not surprising that, following the lead of the Church of England, it somewhat pretentiously took the name "the Church of Uganda."

That said, it was not the lay and clerical leadership that supplied the dynamism of the Church of Uganda. The East African Revival supplied the energy. Its members stressed the importance of sudden and dramatic conversion, and they placed great emphasis on the marked changes in "lifestyle" that were to accompany conversion. They also stressed the necessity of public witness on the part of every Christian. They required participation in "fellowship meetings," at which sins were publically confessed, backsliders challenged, and people in doubt counseled.

The ways of this church were strange to me—even a little off-putting. Personal testimony was frowned upon within Episcopal circles, and what appeared to me a harsh moralism frequently surfaced within the attitudes and actions of "the brethren" (as they termed themselves). Nevertheless, I could not get away from the fact that the common life of the Church of Uganda lay far closer to that of the church of the New Testament than did that of the Episcopal Church (and for that matter most of the other churches in the United States). Over time I was compelled to ask if I did not have something of great importance to learn from this church—something about the calling of the church and the character of its common life that was missing in the churches I knew about in North America.

The reason for my change of mind and heart can best be explained by recounting an experience I had one Friday afternoon in 1962. On that day, I attended the "fellowship meeting" held by the brethren who worked for or lived near the tea estate on which I was living. On that day, a young couple asked the members of the fellowship to help them with what appeared to them to be an irresolvable conflict between their newly found faith and the advice they were getting from the husband's fellow employees at Texaco (where he had recently been employed). His new employment meant that he would have to move from the countryside into the city of Kampala. There, he had been told, he would need to take out an insurance policy on his property because of the rampant thievery present in the city. He was also told that he would need to procure a watchdog that was willing to attack because the thieves were violent and often killed their victims.

These two suggestions seemed contrary to the couple's newfound belief and way of life. Had not Jesus commanded his disciples to take no thought for the morrow, and had he not told them, when attacked, to turn the other cheek? It seemed to them that an insurance policy hardly presented the world with people who took no thought for the morrow, and a watchdog hardly seemed a way of turning the other cheek. They wondered if their newfound faith allowed for them to take this new and quite lucrative job. They asked the fellowship for advice that might set their conscience at rest.

As might be expected, the discussion of these issues among the brethren soon surfaced a "pro-watchdog party" and an "anti-watchdog party." Similar divisions appeared when it came to buying insurance. After a lengthy discussion, the elders told the rest of us to pray while they withdrew to seek the Lord's will. About a half an hour later, they returned and rendered their judgment. That judgment literally stunned me. They said that the couple could take out an insurance policy because, should they be robbed, they would no longer be living among the people who would take care of them. On the other hand, they should not procure a watchdog because Christ died for his enemies. To defend themselves with a watchdog trained to attack would compromise their witness to Christ's death for his enemies. The congregation accepted this judgment, sang a hymn, and went home.

I say the judgment of the elders stunned me because it seemed then, and still seems, a judgment of remarkable depth—one that I could not imagine a congregation I knew in America capable of. Permission to buy an insurance policy was based on a fact of this congregation's common life. Among them there was no needy person. That was their assumption, and it controlled what they said about the possible losses of the couple. On the other hand, procurement of a dangerous watchdog was forbidden because acceptance of death at the hands of his enemies was central to Christ's work of reconciliation. To arm themselves was, in the mind of this congregation, a betrayal of the gospel.

To this day, I do not agree with their judgment about the watchdog, and the body of the text that follows will make clear why. What stunned me was not the decision itself but rather the extent to which this congregation's understanding of its calling and its common life shaped the pastoral care it provided its members. From that moment, I said to myself, I have to rethink everything I thought I knew. When I returned from Africa, I began the study of Christian ethics. My experience in Africa soon lodged a question in my mind. Do the figures I am studying pay enough attention to the relation between Christian ethics and the common life of the church?

This is how the question that led to this volume came to be. It took me a long time to state my thoughts on this matter with any degree of clarity. There are, however, a few people who have helped me along the way, and I would like to thank them. Sadly, the first of them is now dead. Janani Luwum was shot by Idi Amin in Luzira prison just outside the city limits of Kampala. Archbishop Luwum spoke with me at length about the radical changes that faith in Christ had required of him. He also spoke of the need for the church to present Christ to the world through its way of life. In a way that I have found quite prescient, he also said that he thought that the churches in the West faced an even more difficult challenge. It is more difficult, he said, to present the gospel of Christ to a culture that once honored him than it is to one that has as yet not really heard of him. I have come to believe that his observation was correct.

A few people in this country, too, have helped me enormously during this project. I first must mention John Howard Yoder (sadly now deceased) and Stanley Hauerwas, whose work questions the easy fit between Christian belief and the present culture of liberal democracies. These men call for a change of focus on the part of the churches—one that shifts attention from the formation of a Christian society to the formation of a faithful community. It was their work that first gave me a glimpse of the direction in which my scholarly work had to go.

As this project progressed I turned frequently to three colleagues who talked with me about the project and gave of their time and effort to provide a critical reading of what I had written. The three are Professor Gene Outka of Yale University, Professor Gilbert Meilaender of Valparaiso University, and Professor Timothy Sedgwick of Virginia Theological Seminary. Their encouragement and advice have been invaluable. The errors of this book are all mine. Its strengths, however, are in no small measure due to their insightful comments, suggestions, and critical reading. I also owe a depth of gratitude to three of my colleagues at the Anglican Communion Institute—Christopher Seitz, Ephraim Radner, and Mark McCall. Christopher Seitz made me aware that my project required a reading of Holy Scripture that relied not on odd quotations but on a coherent reading of its overall sense. Ephraim Radner's work in ecclesiology made me aware of the central importance of church unity and the role that ethics plays in sustaining that unity and restoring it when it is broken. Mark McCall taught me more than I thought I would ever know about the history of my own church and about the relevance of that history to this project. It is rare to have colleagues with whom one shares so much, and I would like to thank them publicly for their companionship. I also wish to thank Ted Wardlaw, president of Austin Presbyterian Theological Seminary, who invited me to deliver the seminary's MidWinter Lectures on a topic of my choice. I welcomed his invitation for a number of reasons. The invitation gave me an opportunity to test the ideas that had been brewing for some time. It was also the case that H. Richard Niebuhr had delivered the same lectures. They were later published as *Christ and Culture*, a book with which I was in constant conversation as I thought through what I had to say on a related topic. President Wardlaw's invitation seemed more than fortuitous.

I would also like to thank the editors of *Pro Ecclesia: A Journal of Catholic and Evangelical Theology* for permission to publish the chapter of this book that treats the work of John Cassian. An earlier version of this chapter appeared in *Pro Ecclesia* under the title of "John Cassian and the Desert Fathers: Sources for Christian Spirituality?"

Finally, I must mention my wife Elizabeth. Many spousal tributes mention patience and long-suffering during the course of a given project. I can certainly testify to patience and long-suffering in abundance, but recognition of these admirable qualities does not capture her real importance. She is an Episcopal priest who is rector of a parish here in Austin, Texas. Watching her lead this congregation anchored what I was trying to say in a living, breathing body of Christians. Time and again she provided a concrete example of what I was searching for.

Austin, Texas
January 28, 2014

Introduction

On one level, the chapters that follow compose a book on the nature and calling of the Christian church. As such, *Christian Ethics and the Church* is a book about the theological subject of ecclesiology. Yet, on another level, these chapters contain arguments both about the significance of what is now called Christian ethics for understanding that nature and calling, and, more broadly, about the relation between Christian theology on the one hand and Christian ethics on the other. Too frequently in this age, theology and ethics, though acknowledged to have overlapping concerns, are treated as separate subjects. Indeed, the separation of these subjects has become so common that one can easily find examples of Christian ethics that have little theological content and even more examples of theological works that have no ethical content whatever. This separation of "faith and morals" has not always been either so distinct or so pervasive, and it is to no small degree the object of this study both to suggest the baleful results of their separation and to map a way toward their reunification.

To follow that way, I believe, requires a shift in understanding—one that focuses Christian moral thought on the common life of the church rather than on the inner life of the believer or the general state of society. Contrary to common opinion, the following argument contends that the first concern of Christian ethics is properly how Christians are to live with one another rather than how they are to progress in personal holiness or how they are to relate to a surrounding social and political order.

This is not to say that those who think about the ways in which Christians ought to live should not concern themselves with these personal and/or broadly social questions. These are vital questions that demand attention. I am not asking that they be ignored. I believe, however, that we need to ask again what the "focus" of Christian moral thought ought to be. I have chosen the word "focus" very carefully. To have a focus does not mean that one has no peripheral vision. It means only that one's line of sight is centered on a particular spot. Thus, to say that I believe the focus of Christian ethics is properly the common life of the church does not mean that the life of the soul and the life of society are not matters of concern for Christians. It is to say only that what might be called "the originating locus" of Christian ethics lies properly within the interior life of the church rather than in the interior life of the soul or the moral state of society.

In taking this position, I knowingly enter into a conversation with the most influential book in Christian ethics to have appeared in the last century—H. Richard Niebuhr's *Christ and Culture*. Niebuhr was presciently aware of the importance of the common life of the churches, and indeed distinguished his concerns from those of his brother, Reinhold Niebuhr. H. Richard Niebuhr insisted that his brother's project had more to do with the reform of culture, while his own addressed the reformation of the church.[1] Be that as it may, his readers showed more interest in his work *Christ and Culture* than they did in his broad concerns about ecclesiology. His defining legacy was a concern not for reform of the internal life of the church but for the relation of the churches to the society in which they might be located. His five-part typology framed Christian moral discussion in North America for several generations. Christ against culture, Christ of culture, Christ above culture, Christ and culture in paradox, and Christ the transformer of culture became the common coin of moral discourse, at least among liberal Protestants. Of the five types, he and his liberal Protestant readers clearly favored the view that Christ is most adequately understood as "the transformer of culture."

Given the nature of the times, it is not surprising that this position was so widely shared. His was a period in which mainline Protestantism was a vital social force—one that saw the transformation of a society as its mission. The World Council of Churches and the National Council of Churches, along with the various denominations in America, were taken up with the question of what it was for a nation to be a Christian society. None of these organizations now occupy the social position they once did. It is easy to forget what a different time it was. The mainline denominations were riding high on the bubble of American civil religion. One could choose one's denominational brand with full confidence that the choice would not place one outside the mainstream of American life.

---

1. William Werpehowski, *American Protestant Ethics and the Legacy of H. Richard Niebuhr* (Washington, DC: Georgetown University Press, 2002), 15.

However, there is increasing recognition that the denominations in America suffered from what can now be recognized as a fatal flaw. America's civil religion grew out of the soil of the Enlightenment from which emerged a religious settlement that looked something like the following. According to enlightened reason, it is important for a society to have religious foundations, but those foundations ought not to be dogmatically restrictive. The moral fiber of society is to be sustained by religion, but that religion is to be thinly defined with a focus on love of God and love of neighbor rather than on complex and hotly debated matters of doctrine. These matters are thought to have their place, but that place lies within the various denominations. The particularities of belief and practice are to be sustained not by established religions but by individual denominations wherein what can be called a "thick" construal of theology and ethics can be advocated and passed on without causing destructive social conflict. America's religious culture is to be devotedly pluralistic.

What has happened, however, is that the broad umbrella of civil religion has not, as intended, protected the particularities of doctrine. Rather, these thick construals of Christian belief and practice have been sucked into the bath of pluralist culture and diluted so as to fit the minimalist dogmatic pattern of civil religion. The result within the denominations is pervasive theological and ethical vacuity. The decline of the social position of the denominations has been accompanied by, perhaps even occasioned by, the evisceration of robust accounts of Christian theology and ethics.

In a cultural situation like that described above, ethics moves in one of two directions, and on occasion in both directions at the same time. On the one hand, Christian ethics becomes a charter myth for equal access to coveted social goods, and its moral vocabulary shrinks to that of "rights." On the other hand, Christian ethics moves inward toward "spirituality." Spirituality is the inward expression of what is outwardly sought by the struggle for equal rights. That is, as one struggles outwardly for the social recognition of one's identity group, so also one struggles inwardly to find one's own personal identity.

It is in this context that I have posed the question of the focus of Christian ethics. Ought we to focus, as did the readers of H. Richard Niebuhr, on the transformation of culture; or do we go inward toward the realm of personal meaning in a way traced by Robert Bellah and his colleagues in *Habits of the Heart*?[2] Or do John Howard Yoder and Stanley Hauerwas have it right when they insist that we turn our attention to the common life of the church?

---

2. Robert Bellah, Richard Madsen, William Sullivan, Ann Swidler, and Stephen M. Tipton, *Habits of the Heart: Individualism and Commitment in American Life* (Berkeley: University of California Press, 1996).

These are the three options (the life of the soul, the life of society, or the life of the church) that have appeared not only within the religious history of America but in fact throughout the course of Christian history. Accordingly, I have begun this study by analyzing an example of each possible focus. I have sought to display the particular focus of each example by posing three diagnostic questions: What is the goal of life in Christ? What is the basis of life in Christ? What is the character or shape of life in Christ? These questions can be posed in any order. No matter what the order chosen, however, the answers given clarify the focus of any given account of Christian living.

I have posed these questions to three authors—John Cassian, a central figure in Western monasticism; Walter Rauschenbusch, the great advocate in America of the social gospel; and John Howard Yoder, who, along with Stanley Hauerwas, in recent years has called the churches to form what Hauerwas has called "a community of character."[3] The analysis of each option is reasonably lengthy because I have wanted to show how fruitful these questions can be not only in identifying the focus of any given account of the Christian life but also in providing a full and critical presentation of what a given writer might have to say. In asking these questions as a means of identifying the focus of a given account of Christian living, I have also had a methodological concern. I have not only desired to identify the focus of any account of the Christian life; I have also wanted to find a method of analysis that puts on display the full scope and adequacy of that account.

Finding the right example of each type has proved a taxing assignment because I wanted to locate not only a helpful example of each but also examples that come from various periods in the intellectual and social history of the churches of the West. In the end, I decided upon what at first might seem an odd assortment. The first example, John Cassian, is decidedly *premodern*. Cassian was an early monastic heavily influenced by Neoplatonism. As might be expected, his account of the Christian life focuses on the sanctification of the individual soul. A second exemplary figure is Walter Rauschenbusch. His rendition of Christian living is precisely the reverse of that of John Cassian. His account is as *modern* as Cassian's is *premodern*. It reflects the Enlightenment perspectives of both Schleiermacher and Kant and, not unexpectedly, focuses on the redemption of the social order rather than the sanctification of the individual soul. The third example is John Howard Yoder. His ethical writings are thoroughly *postmodern*, insisting that, in respect to Christian ethics, there is no "scratch," no sure starting point or foundation—be it in a

3. Stanley Hauerwas, *A Community of Character: Toward a Constructive Christian Social Ethic* (Notre Dame, IN: University of Notre Dame Press, 1988).

heavenly realm of archetypes or in an earthly one of reason and/or experience. He insists that Christian living is grounded in the particulars of the person and work of Christ. Christian ethics are first a matter of witness by means of the imitation of Jesus's life on the part of a faithful community firmly located within the course of history.

Admittedly, these three figures have been chosen merely as examples of three options or types. Use of isolated examples, separated as these are by both time and circumstance, in no way captures the subtle differences that appear in more extended historical studies. However, these examples do serve well to display both major foci of Christian ethics and the differing intellectual and social climates in which these accounts appeared.

Whether I have chosen wisely will become apparent only over time. Whatever the case may be, however, these studies have led me to believe that the proper focus for an account of life in Christ is the common life of the church. I have also come to believe that the current move toward "spirituality" represents a pervasive form of narcissism that seeks to treat the primary disease of an overly individualistic culture not by the production of antibodies but by massive injections of the sickness from which it suffers. I believe also that Robert Wilken's criticism of H. Richard Niebuhr's ethic of cultural transformation is essentially correct.[4] Wilkin charges that the transformation of culture is more an idea than an incarnated reality. Niebuhr and his latter-day followers have never addressed the basic question. That question is not how Christ transforms culture but how Christ forms a culture and how that "Christianly" formed culture penetrates the wider culture in the first place.

If one asks this question, it becomes apparent that Christ is present in the church in a way that forms a culture that in some ways is quite distinct from the larger one in which it is taking root. If the issue is posed in this way, the first question becomes how Christ forms a culture, and only then how that culture is to relate to the one in which it has taken root. If the formation of a culture "in Christ" is the first issue, the relation between those who live in Christ and their host culture becomes a derivative one. The question becomes, how does a body that has a culture (and so also an ethic) sort out the relation between its common life and that of its host culture?

How then will this argument about the nature and calling of the church and the focus of Christian ethics be developed? If one is to make a convincing case for holding that ecclesiology is an aspect of theology as well as ethics, one must at least show that such linkages accord with the way in which the Bible presents the nature and calling of the church. Failing this, if such a view

---

4. Robert Wilken, "Amo, Amas, Amat: Christianity and Culture," in *Reflections* 7 (2003).

does not accord with the biblical witness, Christians at least must ask if there are other reasons for holding it.

Accordingly, the argument that follows finds its center in its second part. That part contains an extended reading of the Epistle to the Ephesians. The reading I have presented is intended (by means of a single yet, one hopes, well-chosen example) to establish a link between the nature and calling of the church and the way of life that is to be lived therein. In the course of making this case, it will become apparent that I believe it to be a mistake to view the nature of the church as it exists in the course of history in purely essentialist terms such as "the body of Christ" or the "communion of saints." Venerable, common, and indeed necessary as these terms may be, they do not, on their own and apart from a larger narrative context, do justice to the fact that the church may, like ancient Israel, exist in a state of defection as well as obedience. Accordingly, in the course of history, the nature of the church as a "communion" or as a "body" does not appear in a steady state but as a reality that comes to be in the midst of conflict and disobedience under the providence of God. To put the matter another way, the nature of the church as "the body of Christ" or as a "communion of saints" becomes manifest in the midst of conflict with forces within its own life that are directly contrary to such a nature. For this reason, it is important to grasp that any essential qualities that might belong to the church do not exist as a possession of the church per se but as aspects of God's sovereign administration of the church's life. In the course of that administration, these qualities may well be punctual and partial in respect to their appearance within the actual life of the church. To put the matter in yet another way, it is as important to think of the church as a fractured body that may well find itself subject to divine judgment as it is to think of it as the body of Christ or the fellowship of the Holy Spirit.

It is in large measure because the nature of the church within history is conflicted as well as peaceful, unfaithful as well as faithful, that ethics is best considered in the first instance as an aspect of theology in general and of ecclesiology in particular. It is in fact in the very midst of these conflicts and defections that the significance of Christian ethics is displayed most vividly, not as an addendum to theology. It is also in the midst of these conflicts that the importance of ethics for the present search for "Christian identity" on the part of the denominations is best understood. Indeed, America's denominations are in search of identity, and in this respect, their position is not unlike those of the Western church at the end of the first period of Christian history. Robert Markus says this of the church at what he calls "the end of ancient Christianity": "Very early in its history the Christian community was forced to ask itself what it was."⁵ Changes in circumstance forced the church to ask some very difficult questions. Chief among them was, "What was essential to Christianity, and what was indifferent, merely linked with the particular form of the society in which it was embodied?"⁶

The change in social location of the churches in America has pressed questions like this one upon them. They have been sent in search of an understanding of their nature and calling that makes sense in these altered circumstances. It is not surprising that the doctrine of the church has become a topic of intense interest among the clerical and lay leadership of America's denominations. Since the mainline Protestant churches no longer enjoy the social charter that once was theirs, and since it is unlikely that a similar charter will in any foreseeable future be conferred on any other denomination or group of denominations, the question of how Christians ought to view the nature and calling of their various denominations becomes urgent. In part, the chapters that follow constitute an attempt to answer this question—by calling the denominations away from concerns about their loss of social position and "market share" and toward a common vision of their calling under God.

At crucial times in Christian history the church has been forced to ask just what it is. We surely exist in such a time. The triumph of Constantine forced the church to reassess its relation to society. In like manner, with the decline of their social position and political strength, the churches are being forced to ask that question again—this time from a position of social weakness rather than social strength. It is my conviction that Christian identity is the question for this time and that the question is being posed more by moral than by theological questions.

By emphasizing Christian identity and in particular the way in which Christian ethics, as an aspect of the interior life of the church, plays a central role in forging that identity, I have no intention of presenting a "sectarian" ecclesiology. I do not believe that Christians ought to think of themselves and their common life as being entirely "over against" the cultures into which they are born and in the midst of which they are socialized. A project of this sort would prove both impossible and destructive. Neither do I believe the primary calling of the churches is to become a vanguard for social reform. By contending that the originating focus of Christian ethics is in fact the common life of the church rather than personal holiness or social reform, I speak only of a focus and not of an exclusive concern. My contention is only that

---

5. Robert Markus, *The End of Ancient Christianity* (Cambridge: Cambridge University Press, 1997), 1.
6. Ibid.

the churches will once more discover their identity and calling under God, not in a retreat to pietism and spirituality, nor in attempts to recover general social influence, but in the reconstitution of their common life. I believe also that an undertaking of this sort will provide not only a basis for growth in personal holiness that escapes the narcissism of the presently fashionable interest in "spirituality" but also an alternative to current social opinion and practice that will have profound effects upon the social matrix in which the churches exist.

What then will it take to make a project of this sort credible? To do so, three additional questions will have to be answered. First, is the focus of Christian ethics present in the Epistle to the Ephesians, and so central to this argument, idiosyncratic, or supported by other books of the Bible? Second, if the Bible does indeed focus its account of life in Christ on the common life of the church, what is the overall shape of this account of life in Christ? That is, what account is to be given of the basis, goal, and character of such an ethic? Third, if America's denominations were to shift the focus of their attention to the common life of the church, what account might be given of the life of the soul and the churches' relationship to the larger societies and political structures of which they are a part?

Finally, I feel called upon to comment on three matters of great importance—one concerns terminology, and the other two are important subjects that do not receive adequate treatment in this book. In respect to terminology, the account of the character or the identifying marks of Christian ethics I have given includes a discussion of both moral virtues (like patience or kindness) and moral practices (like marriage or sharing wealth). In respect to "virtues," I have chosen to use the term "graces" rather than "virtues." I have done so in order to make clear that these powers of soul and capacities for action, though certainly in part the products of human instruction and discipline, are best understood within Christian ethics as gifts of Christ. Through the Spirit he subjects or orders them to love of God and neighbor and so toward the fulfillment of God's purposes for the world.

The first matter not discussed is the moral witness of the Old Testament. To adequately establish the ecclesial focus of the biblical account of Christian living, it would be necessary to show that the various writings contained in the Old Testament have the same focus on the common life of God's people as do those of the New Testament. I have not undertaken this task, necessary as it is, for the simple reason that the present project would have become too long and too diffuse. I believe, however, that it is simply the case that the moral focus of the Law and the Prophets is on the common life of Israel both as a testimony to God's graciousness to his people and as a witness to the nations.

Given the constraints of the present project, I will have to let that statement stand and make its way on its own.

The second matter not discussed is church governance. If the focus of Christian ethics is properly the common life of the church, and if that common life manifests throughout time a conflict between what God intends for it to be and its own defections from God's will and purpose, then church governance must become an aspect of Christian ethics. If the common life of the church, even if imperfectly, is to manifest the unity to which God calls his creation and for which he brought it into being, then one must ask how Christians are to order their life together so as to encourage peace, manage conflict, and maintain order. In short, "polity" must be moved from the fringes of moral concern and be relocated toward its center.

It may seem strange to place the study of church polity and Christian ethics in the same room, but a moment's thought will show that the move is not strange at all. Plato, Aristotle, St. Augustine, John Calvin, Richard Hooker, Thomas Hobbes, and John Locke, to mention but a few, would have thought that the question of governance should never be separated from the question of how we ought to live our lives. Societies find their identity in common purposes and values, and their forms of governance are constructed so as to protect and further those purposes and values. What is true of society in general is true of the church as well. The church has been placed in history to serve a certain goal, proclaim a certain truth, and live a certain sort of life. Given the changes and chances of history, and given its own imperfections, it cannot possibly serve the end for which it exists apart from the graces and practices of its members, but neither can it serve that end by means of a panoply of graces and practices alone. If one is to place the focus of Christian ethics on the common life of the church, the way in which that life is to be maintained and ordered in a less-than-perfect world must, like the graces and practices that mark the character of its members, become a normal aspect of moral discourse. For these reasons, I had originally intended to include a discussion of church governance in this volume, but I soon realized that the issues were sufficiently complex to require a separate treatment. That discussion will have to wait for another time.

This work has been a long time in the making, and I do not wish to delay its appearance further. The struggles of my own denomination to come to terms with its new social location and to find its identity in the midst of change and conflict have again and again taken me away from this particular task. Nevertheless, the delays and detours have only strengthened my original conviction that the mission of the churches in America is no longer to serve as the chaplain to society but as a witness to another form of life that has a very different goal, basis, and character from that of mainstream America. If that witness is to be made, more than words are required. Another form of life must be on display as well.

For a change of this sort to occur, it will be necessary to change the focus of Christian ethics in ways that move it away from personal holiness and social reform and redirect it toward the reform and renewal of the common life of the churches. As this study makes plain, there will also have to be an accompanying renewal of trinitarian theology. If the focus of Christian living is to center on how Christians live one with another, and from that perspective speak in new ways about the life of the soul and the relation of believers to American culture, then the burning questions before the churches will have to change. It will be necessary to ask theological questions as well as ethical ones. What is the goal of creation set by God the Father? How is that end lived out and brought near by God the Son? And how are we drawn into the end for which the world was made through the Son and in the Spirit? The answer to these questions will lead to ones about how we are to live together, how we are to live a holy life as individuals, and how we as the body of Christ are to live within the various societies and political structures of which we are a part.

PART ONE

The Focus of Christian Ethics

THREE ACCOUNTS

JOHN CASSIAN,
WALTER RAUSCHENBUSCH,
AND JOHN HOWARD YODER

1

John Cassian's Ethic of Individual Sanctification

Introduction

John Cassian was one of the founders of Western monasticism. He was born circa 360 CE. His parents were wealthy Christians who provided him with a fine education that rendered him fluent in both Greek and Latin. His theological perspective was shaped by both Evagrius Ponticus and Origen. John Chrysostom ordained him circa 399. Prior to that, sometime between 378 and 380, with his friend Germanus, he entered a monastery near the Church of the Nativity in Bethlehem. Soon, he and his friend left for the Egyptian desert to learn from the desert fathers. There, he collected the wisdom of these spiritual guides and later presented their views, along with his own, in two works, *The Conferences*[1] and *The Institutes*.[2] Together these works contain Cassian's moral theology along with an account of the exercises he believed necessary for spiritual progress. Both concern that form of life known in the ancient world as *philosophia*. The parallels between these two works and other renditions of spiritual practice common to the period are marked.

1. John Cassian, *The Conferences*, Ancient Christian Writers Series 57 (Mahwah, NJ: Newman Press, 1997). Hereafter cited as *C*.
2. John Cassian, *The Institutes*, Ancient Christian Writers Series 58 (Mahwah, NJ: Newman Press, 2000). Hereafter cited as *I*.

Pierre Hadot has argued rightly that, in contrast to modern notions, ancient philosophy was before all else a way of life.[3] Spiritual exercises lay at the heart of the practice of philosophy, and their goal was self-improvement that moved the practitioner toward the perfection of human nature and *eudaimonia*, a form of well-being in which "unhappy disquiet" is overcome and a whole new way of life undertaken. People often overlook the fact that Christian theologians like Cassian, Basil, Gregory of Nyssa, Gregory of Nazianzus, and Origen thought of the way in which they lived in Christ as *philosophia*. By this term they meant more than philosophical argument and speculation. They had in mind a way of life in which thought and spiritual practice are part of a single enterprise, the end of which is knowledge of God and human fulfillment.

The extraordinary parallels between the accounts these men gave of life in Christ and the prescriptions for living espoused by the various philosophical schools are often overlooked. Nevertheless, these parallels, once mentioned, are apparent. The goal of *philosophia* was escape from what Pierre Hadot has nicely termed "a state of unhappy disquiet" in which one is overwhelmed by worry and torn by passions that lead to a way of life that, in the end, proves contrary to both reason and human nature.[4] The goal of *philosophia* also was to learn a new form of life that conforms not to human prejudices and social conventions (which are in fact products of the passions) but to the demands of reason and the basic nature of humankind. All schools believed in the power of reason and the will to overcome ignorance and the power of the passions to distort one's view of life.

The practices advocated by the philosophical schools all have their parallels in the writings of Cassian and other church fathers. Like the philosophers of the schools, the early fathers saw life in Christ as a form of exercise analogous to the physical exercises of athletes. Like the exercises of the philosophers, those advocated by the church fathers involved constant meditation, close attention to oneself, and triumph over the passions with a view to living life as nature intends or as God wills.

Into these exercises, however, Cassian and others introduced certain particularly Christian elements. In this respect, what the fathers had to say about what is now called "sexuality" is of particular importance. Peter Brown has noted that in their presentation of ascetical practices, the early fathers of the church gave considerable attention to the renunciation of sexual activity.[5]

3. See Pierre Hadot, "Spiritual Exercises," in Pierre Hadot, *Philosophy as a Way of Life*, ed. Arnold I. Davidson (Oxford: Blackwell, 1995), 82–83.
4. Ibid., 101.
5. Peter Brown, *The Body and Society: Men, Women, and Sexual Renunciation in Early Christianity* (New York: Columbia University Press, 1988), 31–36.

Control of sexual desire was also a concern of the schools, but for reasons other than those that concerned the fathers of the church. In contrast to the thought and practice of the schools, the issue for the fathers was not a balanced life in which the appetites are controlled and moderated by reason. Their concern was rather purity of heart and body that signaled the fact that Christians belong entirely to another realm of being. Sexual purity was in fact a trope for an utterly different form of life. Thus, Christian ascesis did not seek the successful control of daily social life. Rather, it sought to transfer the practitioner into a heavenly world and, in so doing, cut altogether his or her ties with the normal mechanisms of daily living.

Another important difference between the fathers and the schools appears in the common admonition to imitate a paradigmatic life. All the schools of philosophy emphasized imitation of figures who had gone before. One finds the same focus in the writings of the fathers. Christians are urged to take Christ as their model. Nevertheless, in undertaking to imitate Christ, a significant difference between the thought and practice of the fathers and that of the schools appears. According to the fathers, will and intellect alone are inadequate to the imitative task. Successful imitation is dependent to one degree or another upon grace; because of this dependence, humility, patience, and obedience are essential companions of self-knowledge and self-control. The significance attached to human weakness and the consequent valorization of the virtues of humility and patience give a distinctive profile to the accounts of *philosophia* advocated by the fathers and John Cassian.

The Goal and Basis of Life in Christ according to John Cassian

The Goal of Life Together in Christ

The best way to identify the focus of any account of life in Christ is to ask first of all how the goal of that life is construed. How, in his *philosophia*, does John Cassian portray that goal? In the first book of *The Conferences*, Abba Moses remarks: "All the arts and disciplines have a certain *scopos* or goal, and a *telos*, which is the end that is proper to them, on which the lover of any art sets his gaze and for which he calmly and gladly endures every labor and danger and expense."[6] He then goes on to say: "The end or *telos* of our profession . . . is the kingdom of God, or the kingdom of heaven; but the goal or *scopos* is purity of heart, without which it is impossible for anyone to reach that end."[7]

6. C 1.2.1.
7. C 1.4.3.

Though Aristotle used the terms *telos* and *scopos* interchangeably, the Stoics made a distinction between the two that one sees present in the remarks of Abba Moses. According to the Stoics, the *telos* refers to an agent doing or obtaining something and it is expressed by verbs. On the other hand, *scopos* refers to the thing done or obtained, and is expressed by nouns. The Stoic Arius distinguished the difference in this way: "A *scopos* is the target to be hit, like a shield for archers; a *telos* is the hitting of the target."[8] Put another way, the *scopos* is the end aimed at and the *telos* is the act of obtaining that particular end.

For Cassian the end to be *aimed* at (*scopos*) is purity of heart or "perfection."[9] Perfection is (negatively) a state in which one is free from the distorting thoughts that take the mind and heart away from God and (positively) a state in which one's mind and heart are focused without interruption upon God. This is the target at which one is to aim and to which one is to direct all attention and effort. The *telos*, that which is obtained when the target is hit, is living in the kingdom of God, or enjoying eternal life.[10] The point Cassian wishes to make is that by fixing one's eyes upon the proper *scopos*, one reaches the *telos* of a practice in the quickest way. Thus, all one's effort is to be directed to obtaining purity of heart that will, in turn, allow one to contemplate and enjoy God without interruption.

It is this *scopos* and this *telos* that are to claim all one's attention and energy. In a word, they are to "trump" any other concerns or obligations. Good works, for example, are of secondary importance to "*theoria*," or divine contemplation.[11] The story of Mary and Martha shows "that the Lord considered the chief good to reside in *theoria* alone—that is in divine contemplation."[12] All other virtues, though necessary and good, are secondary. Even good works, necessary though they may be, are so only because people have taken for their own what God meant to be shared by all. There are poor people in the world because of the presence of avarice, but one day God will rid the world of both vice and poverty. Thus, in the kingdom of heaven, good works will no longer be needed. Only contemplation will remain.[13]

The monk thus seeks to take heaven by storm. For those who search for knowledge, good deeds are but necessary interruptions in a more interior task.

---

8. Cited by Julia Annas in *The Morality of Happiness* (Oxford: Oxford University Press, 1993), 34.
9. C 1.6.
10. C 1.5.2.
11. See esp. C 5.24.
12. C 1.8.1, emphasis added.
13. C 1.10.4–5.

The overwhelming priority of seeking purity of heart and the kingdom of heaven is perhaps best illustrated by Cassian's treatment of broken promises. The issue arose because, when leaving the monks in Bethlehem for those of Egypt, Cassian and his friend Germanus promised to return. They became convinced, however, that remaining in Egypt served better to promote their quest for perfection.

The Seventeenth Conference with Abba Joseph is best understood as Cassian's attempt to resolve the moral issue of his broken promise. Thus, Abba Joseph remarks that one is justified in breaking a promise if it serves the greater good of purity of heart. It is, he holds, the inner aspect of the act rather than the act itself that has moral weight. In this case, the inner aspect served to promote purity of heart, and for this reason the broken promise was not morally culpable. In this account of Christian living, the moral character of any action or event is determined univocally by whether or not it "leads us by sincere faith to divine realities and makes us cling unceasingly to the unchangeable good."[14]

The Basis of Life Together in Christ

The same relentless focus on individual sanctification is apparent also in the basis Cassian provides for life in Christ, and it can be seen particularly in the ruthless quality of this version of Christian ethics. To be sure, ruthlessness is a quality that is not without support in the writings of the New Testament. Both Matthew and Luke report that Christ told his disciples that loyalty to him was to take precedence even over obligations to one's own family (Matt. 10:35; Luke 12:53; 14:26). Cassian and other monastic writers might admit that there is a certain degree of ruthlessness about their prescriptions. Nevertheless, they would insist that such ruthlessness has its basis in Christ's own life and teaching. They would point first of all to Christ's command in the Sermon on the Mount (Matt. 5:48)—namely, that those who would follow him must be "perfect" as their heavenly Father is "perfect."

As rendered by John Cassian, the basis of his account of life in Christ is, in an almost univocal sense, the teaching and example of Jesus himself. One does not find in his writings the broader trinitarian basis for Christian living that appears, for example, in Paul and the Gospels. As we shall see, for these New Testament authors, holy living is rooted in the original will of God the Father, made manifest in the life, death, resurrection, and ascension of the Son, and revealed and established through the presence of the Holy Spirit.

14. C 6.3.1–2.

There are echoes of this trinitarian base in the writings of Cassian, but they are faint. The demand of Christ to be perfect overshadows all else, and this demand is interpreted through a narrowly focused lens—in the first instance through Christ's sacrificial death.

It is not the details of Christ's life (as, say, in the case of Ignatius Loyola) that most interest Cassian. It is the overall pattern of that life. For the monk, imitation of this pattern requires the sacrifice of everything in pursuit of the *scopos* and *telos* of life in Christ. Above all else, Christ's life displays a pattern of "renunciation," and this pattern is to be imitated by anyone seeking perfection. Thus, in *The Institutes* renunciation is the first step a monk is to take. The matter is stated with clarity in chapter 34 of book 4 of *The Institutes*, where Cassian notes for the benefit of prospective monks, "Renunciation is nothing else than a manifestation of the cross and of a dying. Therefore you should know that on this day you have died to the world and to its deeds and desires and that, according to the Apostle, you have been crucified to this world and this world to you." He concludes, "We ourselves then must pass our time in this life with the deportment and aspect of him who hung upon the gibbet for us." Abba Paphnutius is recorded as saying that no one understands this call to renunciation that has not seen life through the eyes of their teacher, Christ. It is Christ who turns the eyes of his followers away from present things so that those things are seen as already over—indeed as dissolving into nothing.[15]

The pattern of Christ's renunciation is indeed total. Furthermore, the pattern of renunciation is to be a matter of constant meditation, to such an extent that it makes one blind and deaf to anything that deflects from the march toward perfection. The pattern of Christ's renunciation is to shield monks against all things that divert them from the *scopos* and *telos* of their calling. Abba Pinufius advises that one who seeks perfection should "set out as one who is deaf and mute and blind, so that, apart from looking upon him whom you have chosen to imitate by reason of his perfection, whatever you might see that is less than edifying you will not see."[16]

The importance of Christ's life is, in a word, rooted in the example he provides, an example of renunciation that calls one away from ordinary life and shows the way toward another form of life that takes place in an entirely different realm—the kingdom of heaven, wherein the contemplation of God is one's sole activity and *eudaimonia* is one's only state of being.[17] The parallel between the *philosophia* of Cassian and that of the schools could not be clearer

---

15. C 3.7.4.
16. I 4.41.1.
17. See especially the discussion of sinlessness in C 23, wherein *theoria* is depicted as the chief good in the light of which all other goods and virtues grow pale.

than in the central importance both assign to the imitation of a life. As Arnold Davidson notes, the importance of "biography" (perhaps better, hagiography) for the schools lay in its capacity to display the superiority of a way of life.[18]

So for Cassian, Christ above all else shows a superior form of life. Christ is important because he teaches a pattern of life that leads from one form to another. Contemplation of the form of life manifest in Christ is to be a constant occupation. Through contemplation and imitation the monk unites his life with that of Christ. To depart from these activities for a moment is "fornication." It is further to place one's soul in danger, because only contemplation of the cross will give one understanding of the various temptations that assault one seeking to follow Christ. One is called upon to weigh or assess the various thoughts that cross one's mind, and the cross of Christ—his renunciation of all worldly goods—is to guide the mind as it makes judgments in respect to good and evil.[19] Thus, as Henry Chadwick notes, contemplation of the life of Christ "leads through temptation, teaches the way of prayer, guides the judgment of elders, restrains and conquers the demons, bestows continual grace."[20]

The primary emphasis in Cassian's account of the basis of life in Christ is most certainly "imitation." Christ provides the pattern the Christian is to follow toward purity of heart and the kingdom of heaven. However, Cassian also presents Christ as one who enables the believer to emerge victorious from the struggle for perfection. As one grows in holiness, the assaults of the demons become more terrible. One cannot prevail in this struggle without the aid of Christ, who is, on occasion, presented not only as a model but also as a companion along the way. So Cassian notes that, as the struggle for perfection intensifies, one would not be able to prevail "were it not for the fact that Christ, the most merciful arbiter and the overseer who presides over our struggle, balances out the strength of the contestants, repels and restrains their fierce attacks, and with the trial provides a way out, so that we are able to endure."[21]

The basis of life in Christ is first the pattern of Christ's renunciation, and second, to a lesser extent, the help of Christ as "arbiter and overseer" of the struggle to follow that pattern. Cassian's account of the grace provided by Christ in the midst of the struggle for perfection is not, however, the radical one offered by St. Augustine, and perhaps for this reason he has little to say about the work of the Holy Spirit. To be sure, in the famous Thirteenth Conference with Abba Chaeremon, "On God's Protection," Cassian insists upon the importance of prevenient grace and of what might be called "assisting

---

18. Arnold Davidson, introduction to Hadot, *Philosophy as a Way of Life*, 28.
19. C 1.33.2.
20. Owen Chadwick, *John Cassian* (Cambridge: Cambridge University Press, 1968), 108–9.
21. C 7.20.2.

grace." One can make no progress along the road to perfection without them. The necessity of grace is given even stronger emphasis in book 12 of *The Institutes*. There God himself gives the victory over the vices that infect the soul. Cassian writes,

> For no affliction of this body and no contrition of heart could be sufficient to lay hold of the true chastity of the inner man so as to be able to acquire by bare human effort—that is, without God's help—the great virtue of purity, which is natural to angels alone and native to heaven, since the accomplishment of every good thing comes from the grace of the one who, out of his manifold generosity, has bestowed everlasting blessedness and immeasurable glory on our slender willing and our brief and paltry running.[22]

Human willing may, as he says, be "slender" and human running "paltry," but in his account of the process of sanctification, the operations of grace are insistently brought into relation both with human effort and with a natural goodness that sin may have weakened but not destroyed.[23] It is in his treatment of grace and freedom that Cassian separates himself from Augustine. Grace in all its forms is an aid to human will and the residual goodness that may be weakened and distorted but never destroyed. Cassian's soteriology, in contrast to that of St. Augustine, is without question a form of synergism.

Christ as exemplar and helper lies at the base of Cassian's account of life in Christ. So also does the figure of Adam—the original embodiment of created human nature. Given the residual importance that human will and created nature have for life in Christ, it is not surprising that the figure of Adam hovers, if not in the foreground, then certainly in the background of Cassian's account. Christ's victory over temptation is pictured as a reversal of the fall of Adam.[24] Thus, like Adam, Christ is tempted by gluttony, vainglory, and pride, and he overcomes these temptations not in the garden but in the wilderness. He does not have to face the temptations offered by the other vices because these are attendant upon the original ones. They were not part of the original temptation in the garden. Christ is then a second Adam who reverses the fall and returns human nature to its pristine state. In keeping with this line of thought, the ascetic practices of the desert fathers (particularly that of fasting) were intended to undo the sin of Adam (he saw that the fruit of the tree was good to eat) and return the body to a pristine state.[25] For Cassian, the pristine

22. *I* 12.11.
23. *I* 12.11.
24. *C* 5.5.1–3.
25. Brown, *Body and Society*, 220–21.

state of Adam included the virtues. These were the original inhabitants of the soul, but invading vices dislodged them. Abba Serapion, in his discussion of the eight principle vices, says this:

> For the will of the Lord did not assign by nature the possession of our heart to the vices but to the virtues. After the fall of Adam they were thrust out of their own region by the vices that had grown insolent—that is, by the Canaanite peoples; and when they have been restored to it by the grace of God and by our diligence and effort, they must be believed not so much to have occupied foreign territory as to have received back their own.[26]

There is, to be sure, a good deal of rhetorical overstatement in this passage. Cassian cannot without inconsistency insist both that the virtues have been entirely driven out and that they are to be restored with the cooperation of human effort. The very notion of effective human effort implies the presence of some degree of virtue. The matter of importance at this juncture, however, is not the quarrel between Augustine and Cassian but the belief on Cassian's part that life in Christ serves, through imitation, to undo Adam's fall and return human nature to its original goodness. In other words, the pattern of Christ's life charts the way to an original state—a state that is to be found in Christ's own life and that, as a result, forms an aspect of the basis of the life to which believers are called.

To anticipate future development of the argument, it may prove helpful at this point to note how this account of the basis of life in Christ compares to the writings of the New Testament. As with the goal of life in Christ, so also in respect to its basis there appears a narrowing of conception. The full scope of God's providential history depicted in Holy Scripture has faded into the background. One is not called upon to contemplate the vast scope of divine providence. One is asked instead to focus on the life of a single exemplary figure. This more narrowly focused object of attention is in turn viewed through an even smaller lens than any of those presented in the New Testament. Christ is not so much a redeemer and reconciler who gives his life in obedience to God's purpose for the creation as he is an example to be followed by individuals who wish to escape the disquiet of their lives and find *eudaimonia*. A tradition has been brought forward but construed in terms drawn from *philosophia*. A certain domestication of the biblical witness has occurred—one that confines that witness within the concern for individual salvation that so occupied the minds and hearts of those who inhabited Hellenistic culture. If one asks why this change has occurred, it may well prove

26. C 5.24.2.

the case that a Platonic division between a heavenly world of changelessness and atemporality and an earthly one of temporality and change has been substituted for a biblical eschatology that sees all creation taken up into a resurrected form of life in which creation and so also time and change are both redeemed and perfected rather than transcended.

The Character of Life in Christ according to John Cassian

A shift in eschatology of this sort may well explain a similar narrowing in Cassian's depiction of the character of life in Christ. If one is in search of an image that displays most fully Cassian's characterization of this life, that of an athlete being tested in the Olympic Games comes most readily to mind. Once more, Cassian's similarity to the philosophical schools emerges. His focus is ever on the training and discipline needed to emerge victorious in a contest with one's own vices and with the demons that manipulate these weaknesses for their own purposes. Thus, in his discussion of the need to overcome the vice of gluttony, Cassian remarks,

> This is our first . . . trial in the Olympic Games—the extinguishing of the belly's desire to gormandize out of a yearning for perfection. To this end not only must a superfluous appetite for food be trampled upon by the contemplation of virtue, but even what is necessary for nature itself must be eaten with anxious heart, as being contrary to chastity. Only thus is our life's course to be laid out, so that there is no longer any time wherein we may feel that we are being diverted from spiritual pursuits beyond that which compels us to descend to the necessary care of the body, on account of its fragility.[27]

In the fourth book of *The Institutes*, one finds an epitome of the character of the training and testing that one who seeks perfection must undergo.[28] At this point, Cassian's portrayal of the contest takes on a particularly Christian stamp. The process begins with the fear of the Lord that is the beginning of wisdom. Fear drives one to conversion and the search for perfection. The search requires that one develop contempt for worldly things through renunciation, including family and possessions. Renunciation leads in turn to the virtue of humility, which results in the death of desire, and when desire has died, the vices are uprooted and wither away. With the expulsion of the vices, virtue begins to grow and bear fruit. When virtue is abundant, purity of heart is acquired, and with purity of heart, the kingdom of heaven.

27. *I* 5.3.
28. *I* 4.39, 4.43.

The importance that renunciation holds for Cassian has been established. Humility, however, is renunciation's close companion and as such provides the distinguishing mark by which a life in quest of perfection is to be recognized. Humility, Cassian says, can be recognized by its (1) effort to put to death all desires, (2) refusal to conceal anything from the Abba, (3) willingness to leave all judgment to the Abba, (4) obedience and patience, (5) refusal to bring harm to others and unwillingness to be saddened when injury occurs to oneself, (6) refusal to depart from the example of the saints who have gone before, (7) simplicity and sense of unworthiness, (8) willingness to count others as better than oneself, (9) discretion in speech, and (10) sobriety.

Scanning this epitome, one can see that the chief characteristics of life in Christ are the fear of the Lord, renunciation, humility, obedience, and patience. These qualities are those of the crucified Christ and so also of anyone who desires to be crucified with Christ. Their chief fruit is apostolic love, understood primarily as love of God. It is the first rather than the second commandment that dominates this account of sanctification. Love, however, is the fruit of right knowledge. Indeed, right knowledge rather than love dominates Cassian's account of the character of life in Christ. In the Fourteenth Conference, Abba Nestoros speaks of the nature of spiritual knowledge. It is of two sorts—*practikē* and *theōretikē*. The former (practical knowledge) is essential for the latter (theoretical knowledge); nevertheless, they are not linked in an ascending order as was typical of the time. For Cassian, the two forms of knowledge constantly feed one another.[29] Practical knowledge requires both that one come to understand the working of the vices and that one have a mind formed in accord with the virtues. Theoretical knowledge, like practical knowledge, is also of two sorts. Both pertain to the knowledge of Holy Scripture, but they differ in degrees of complexity and importance. There is, first of all, the literal or historical meaning of the text. This more primitive knowledge opens the door for a second degree of understanding—spiritual knowledge. Spiritual knowledge is of three sorts: allegorical (knowledge that pertains to Christ, the church, and the sacraments), tropological (moral knowledge), and anagogical (knowledge of invisible, eternal, and heavenly matters).

Anagogical knowledge is clearly the goal to which one is to aspire. Meditation on the Holy Scriptures is indispensable for its acquisition, and so meditation on the sacred writings is to be the monk's constant occupation. Nevertheless, the Holy Scriptures will not yield the spiritual knowledge they mediate apart from *practikē*—the work of stilling the passions and acquiring the virtues. Consequently, the character of life in Christ as presented by

---

29. Markus, *End of Ancient Christianity*, 184–89.

Cassian has as its most distinguishing feature the virtue of discretion. Citing St. Anthony, Abba Moses says, "Discretion is the begetter, guardian, and moderator of all the virtues."[30] Love of God may indeed be the chief fruit (and mark) of life in Christ, but its character is built neither upon charitable works nor upon what might be called "God intoxication."[31] Rather, love's character rests upon an intellectual virtue that allows the monk to discern the way in which the demons manipulate the vices that cloud the mind and so prevent true knowledge of God. It may be the case that love of God gives final form to the virtues, but for Cassian, the intellectual virtue of discretion is a mark of character apart from which both the virtues and the love of God remain but a distant hope. Indeed, he elevates discretion above fasts, vigils, contempt of the world, and even love and hospitality, and insists that apart from discretion the good of all these practices and virtues will most certainly be lost.[32] A lack of discretion can ruin all virtues.[33] In his valorization of an intellectual virtue, Cassian places knowledge in the forefront of the practice of *philosophia* and so, at yet another point, links his way of salvation to that of the schools. Right knowledge is the key to perfection, and perfection opens the way for eternal life, which is to be understood through the term *eudaimonia*.

By tracing what Cassian has to say about the acquisition of discretion (rather than love), one can display the lineaments of his presentation of the character of life in Christ. From his teacher Evagrius, Cassian took over a classification of the eight (not seven) chief vices that infest the soul and cause disquiet.[34] These are gluttony, fornication, avarice, anger, sadness, acedia (anxiety or weariness of heart), vainglory, and pride. These vices present themselves in the form of "thoughts" that trouble the mind.[35] Thoughts, however, have three sources—God, the devil, or the self.[36] With effort, thoughts can be accepted or rejected as either profitable or unprofitable.[37] If one's relation to thoughts is to be profitable, however, one must weigh them as a moneychanger weighs coins to test for value.[38] That is, one must, by the use of "wise discretion," trace their origin, cause, and authorship so as to

---

30. C 2.4.4.
31. I owe this phrase to my friend Gene Outka. See Gene Outka, "Theocentric Love and the Augustinian Legacy, Honoring Differences and Likenesses between God and Ourselves," *Journal of the Society of Christian Ethics* 22 (2002): 97–114.
32. C 2.2.1–4.
33. C 2.2.4.
34. For Cassian's most sustained discussion of the vices, see I 5–12 and C 5.
35. C 1.17.1.
36. C 1.19.1.
37. C 1.17.1.
38. C 1.20.2.

understand, in the light of who is making the suggestion and what its quality is, how best to approach them.[39]

How does Cassian understand the nature of discretion? He uses Anthony's definition that has been summarized by Boniface Ramsey in this way: "Discretion is the judgment whereby a person discerns what is correct and, in particular, avoids excess of any kind, even of the apparent good."[40] This summary is adequate only to a point, for discretion as understood by Cassian can be adequately grasped only if linked to three accompanying graces apart from which it cannot be acquired—humility, obedience, and patience.[41]

Cassian's ten-point account of the nature of humility suggests the close connection he sees between discretion and these graces. Humility requires not only that one reveal all to one's Abba but also that one do all he says and live patiently through the trials obedience may require. Beginners obtain discretion only by submission to elders.[42] They can learn discretion only from one who has walked the path beforehand and learned from the example of forebearers. True discretion lies embedded in a tradition of discernment that must be learned from others, hence the importance of obedience. So also patience is important. One learns discretion only over time and in the midst of trial so that one learns both to discern rightly and to wait patiently for the visitation of the Holy Spirit.[43]

According to Cassian, discretion, humility, obedience, and patience display the chief characteristics of life in Christ. These graces are, however, obtained in the context of certain practices that also give distinctive form to life in Christ. Chief among these practices are fasting, work, meditation upon Holy Scripture, and prayer. Fasting is a necessary first step in the struggle for perfection. Gluttony is the most rudimentary of the vices, and one cannot begin to undertake the struggles of the inner person unless the demands of the belly have been conquered.[44] Work also serves to turn one from the vices and direct one's attention to the contemplation of God. When attacked by "thoughts" that depress the spirit and turn one away from God, one should focus on one's work. One should continue to read the Holy Scriptures as well and meditate upon the example of Christ.

One should also rush to prayer. The mind is naturally light and, if not weighed down by vices, moves naturally toward God.[45] Ascetic practice is designed to still the vices and give birth to the virtues. Prayer is the central

---

39. C 1.20.1
40. Boniface Ramsey, introduction to John Cassian, *The Conferences*, ed. and trans. by Boniface Ramsey, OP (New York: Paulist Press, 1997), 78.
41. C 4.36.
42. C 2.10.1–3.
43. C 4.4.1–3.
44. I 5.11–16.
45. C 7.4.3, 9.4.2.

practice that crushes the weight of vice and liberates the mind. As one struggles toward perfection, prayer takes a variety of forms. The forms may be compared to the rungs of a ladder. Confession of sin and petition for pardon and help constitute the first rung.[46] The second rung is one on which something is offered to God.[47] The third is that of intercession on behalf of loved ones and for the peace of the world.[48] The fourth is that of thanksgiving whereby "the mind, whether recalling God's past benefits, contemplating his present ones, or foreseeing what great things God has prepared for those who love him, offers to the Lord [thanksgivings] in unspeakable ecstasies."[49]

There is finally a fifth rung, which Cassian terms "fiery prayer." Fiery prayer is a state in which all forms of prayer are engaged in simultaneously. Such prayer is the work of the Holy Spirit and comes only to those who are firmly rooted in purity of heart. It takes place in a state of ecstasy wherein one neither knows nor remembers what is said or thought.[50] Fiery prayer is the highest form of prayer, but prayer in all its forms produces a sublime and exalted condition wherein one contemplates God, comes to love him, and learns to speak with him familiarly as "Father."[51] Fiery prayers thus spring from the *scopos* of Christian living (purity of heart) and provide a partial realization of its goal (the kingdom of God).

How then does Cassian understand the character of life in Christ? How is it acquired, and what are its features? Life in Christ may be compared to the life of an athlete training for the Olympic Games. The prize to be won is eternal life. The means to the prize is acquisition of purity of heart. To acquire purity of heart, one must learn to imitate Christ, the teacher who shows the way to gain the prize. Imitation begins with renunciation. If renunciation is to produce its desired result, however, one must learn discretion, an intellectual virtue or grace that allows one to discern what is truly good in the midst of countless presentations by the mind. Discretion, however, requires a particular sort of training. One must learn humility, obedience, and patience. These graces allow one to benefit from the wisdom of sages who have walked the path to purity of heart beforehand. Renunciation, discretion, humility, obedience, and patience accompanied by grace allow one to fight off the deceptions of the demons. These deceptions cloud the mind and so both deflect one from the true goal of life and rob one of its rewards.

46. C 9.11.1.
47. C 9.12.1
48. C 9.13.
49. C 9.14.
50. C 9.15.2.
51. C 9.18.1.

Acquisition of these graces requires single-mindedness. To borrow a phrase from Søren Kierkegaard and to put the matter in a different way, purity of heart requires that one will one thing—to focus completely on the quest for perfection.[52] Such steadiness of attention is aided by certain practices in the midst of which one acquires the graces mentioned above. The chief of these practices are fasting, work, meditation upon Holy Scripture, and prayer. Fasting helps subdue the most primitive vices. Work focuses the mind and wards off the demons. Meditation upon Holy Scripture presents the mind with the truth about God and one's own life. Prayer places one's life with all its light and shadow in the presence of God. From this presence one receives aid in the struggle for perfection, and in this presence one anticipates the prize for which one longs.

Concluding Comments

Before moving on to a second and quite contrary example of the focus of Christian ethics, let us pause for a moment and take stock. How is one to evaluate this account of life in Christ? Let it be said first that Cassian's account along with his borrowings, conscious or unconscious, from the concerns of the philosophical schools of his day, has made a contribution of fundamental importance to what in the present era is often termed "spirituality." From Cassian comes a full catalog and accurate description of the great enemies of human life, the vices. From him also come disciplines and practices that aid individuals in their life with God. One must not underestimate the significance of this contribution to what Jeremy Taylor later was to call "holy living."[53] Here, in the works of John Cassian, is solid food for anyone seeking to grow in the knowledge and love of God.

It should be noted, however, that Cassian has narrowed his focus from that found in Holy Scripture. In centering on the sanctification of the individual, Cassian has in fact reduced the scope of the rich account of the character of life in Christ found not only in the Pauline corpus but also in the Gospels and Pastorals. In Cassian's hands, the battle with forces that preside over a fallen world is reduced to a skirmish in the life of a single pilgrim. As noted previously, just as the goal of the Christian life has shifted from the manifestation of the mystery of God to the entire creation to the perfection of an individual seeker, and just as the basis of life in Christ has shifted from the full economy of God—Father, Son, and Holy Spirit—to the example of God's Son, so now

---

52. Søren Kierkegaard, *Purity of Heart Is to Will One Thing* (New York: Harper, 2009).
53. Jeremy Taylor, *Holy Living and Dying*, Kindle ed.

it is to be noted that the character of that life also has become more narrowly conceived. Though, as Robert Markus notes,[54] in his more mature thought Cassian places the contest in which the monk is engaged more firmly within a community of monks, it remains the case that the community engendering and preserving graces of lowliness, gentleness, patience, forbearance, truthfulness, kindness, tenderheartedness, forgiveness, and love (to be found, for example, in Ephesians) has been replaced by the self-perfecting graces of renunciation, humility, obedience, and patience. The narrowing of vision one sees in the works of John Cassian appears to be the result of substituting a Platonic worldview for the eschatological vision contained in the full sweep of the biblical narrative and from filtering a full account of the Christian life through the reducing mesh of Hellenism's search for an escape from disquietude. The result, despite many fundamental insights about holy living, is a diluted and distorted account not only of God's purpose but also of the scope of Christian obedience.

---

54. Markus, *End of Ancient Christianity*, 184–89.

2

Walter Rauschenbusch's Ethic of Social Redemption

John Cassian was in search of a way to address the "unhappy disquiet" characteristic of his age. His search led him on a quest for a transcendent end—one that placed the goal of human life outside and above the vicissitudes of human existence. Walter Rauschenbusch viewed the human condition in a very different way. To his mind, the human problem lay primarily in a corrupt and exploitive social order rather than in a diseased mind and spirit. He sought not escape from a world ruled by false understanding and disordered desire but reform of a world dominated by greed and exploitive practices.

Like John Cassian, Rauschenbusch made the kingdom of God the chief end of both human life and Christian ethics. His account of the kingdom was, however, as earthly as John Cassian's was heavenly. Thus he wrote,

> Our business is to make over an antiquated and immoral economic system; to get rid of laws, customs, maxims, and philosophies inherited from an evil and despotic past; to create just and brotherly relations between groups and classes of society; and thus to lay a social foundation on which modern men individually can live and work in a fashion that will not outrage all the better elements in them. Our inherited Christian faith dealt with individuals; our present task deals with society.[1]

---

1. Walter Rauschenbusch, *Christianizing the Social Order* (New York: Macmillan, 1913), 41–42. Hereafter cited as *CSO*.

He went on to say, "The Christian church in the past has taught us to do our work with our eyes fixed on another world and a life to come. But the business before us is concerned with refashioning this present world, making this earth clean and sweet and habitable."[2]

The very earthly nature of Rauschenbusch's characterization of the goal of Christian ethics is easily understood if one views his work against the backdrop of his age. He was born just four years before the assassination of Abraham Lincoln, and he died in July of 1918, just prior to the armistice that ended the First World War. His life was bounded by the first two modern wars—wars in which technology and industrial capacity both increased the slaughter and decided the outcome. The intervening span of his life may be measured by the Industrial Revolution in America, the ascendancy of the robber barons, and the appearance of a largely urban and often exploited immigrant working class. His primary experience of Christian ministry began in a small congregation of German Baptist laborers who lived in the tenement houses of Hell's Kitchen on New York's Lower West Side. These experiences led him to conclude that the chief enemy of humankind was not some form of innate godlessness but concentrations of wealth and power that corrupted rich and poor alike. It became his goal to redirect the focus of Christian ethics from a concern for personal holiness to the redemption of a corrupt social order.

The ecclesial resources for his views come from his studies of the European Anabaptists. He believed firmly that the church is properly a disciplined, democratic, voluntary association that, by example, can have a direct effect on social institutions.[3] The intellectual resources for this project were derived more from Schleiermacher, Kant, Ritschl, and Harnack than from Marx, whose atheism, despite his valorization of the working class, made him an uncongenial though sometimes intriguing figure for Rauschenbusch.

Rauschenbusch was educated in a German-speaking community in the United States, and abroad at various German universities. Adolf Harnack was one of his teachers. From Harnack he learned to seek a "historical Jesus" who may be discovered behind the accretions found in both the early church fathers and the writings of the New Testament itself. Historical criticism makes plain that the Jesus of history had preached a simple and moral gospel of the coming of the kingdom, a kingdom based upon the universal fatherhood of God and the universal brotherhood of man. From Schleiermacher, he derived the idea that the unique thing about Jesus lay not in the possession of two natures but

---

2. *CSO*, 42.

3. See, e.g., Donovan E. Smucker, *The Origins of Walter Rauschenbusch's Social Ethics* (Montreal: McGill-Queens University Press, 1994), 71.

in his "God-consciousness"—a consciousness Jesus communicated to the community gathered around him. This community, the church, through the spirit of Christ that indwells it, despite many ups and downs remains organically connected to its originating personality. From Kant, and even more from Ritschl, Rauschenbusch derived a notion of the corporate rather than the individual character of salvation. Thus the kingdom of God, the organizing notion of Rauschenbusch's entire theology, was to be understood as a corporate, social fact, which, by the power of moral influence, actually grows through the vicissitudes of history. His commitment to moral and social growth was given further impetus by yet another intellectual trend of the period—namely, the theory of evolution and the progressive development of the human species.

The Goal and Basis of Life in Christ according to Walter Rauschenbusch

The Goal

In the heart and mind of Walter Rauschenbusch, "the social gospel" was the product of this meeting of the German Enlightenment and modern science on the one hand and the abysmal conditions created in America's cities by the Industrial Revolution on the other. Rauschenbusch became the most articulate and well-known spokesman of this gospel in America. In three lengthy works (and in countless articles) he undertook the enormous task of recasting the Christian gospel in social terms. This enterprise led him to restate what he took to be the basic Christian doctrines, including Christology itself, in a way that made their social implications primary. Thus, for example, he exclaimed in *A Theology for the Social Gospel*,

> The speculative problem of Christological dogma *was* how the divine and human natures united in the one person of Christ; the problem of the social gospel *is* how the divine life of Christ can get control of human society. The social gospel is concerned about a *progressive* social incarnation of God.[4]

Even a cursory glance at his three major works, *Christianity and the Social Crisis*,[5] *Christianizing the Social Order*, and *A Theology for the Social Gospel*, makes clear the primary focus of his account of Christian ethics. The full implications of this shift in focus from personal holiness to social

---

4. Walter Rauschenbusch, *A Theology for the Social Gospel* (Nashville: Abingdon, 1945), 148, emphasis added. Hereafter cited as *TSG*.
5. Walter Rauschenbusch, *Christianity and the Social Crisis* (New York: Macmillan, 1913). Hereafter cited as *CSC*.

redemption can be grasped more fully, however, by posing once more the three diagnostic questions used for the analysis of Cassian's work. First, what is the goal of life in Christ? In *Christianity and the Social Crisis*, Rauschenbusch sets out, by means of a study of the prophets of Israel, the life and teachings of Jesus and the dominant tendencies of the early church "to ascertain what was the original and fundamental purpose of the great Christian movement in history."[6] He anticipates his conclusion by saying that the outcome of his historical studies "is that *the essential purpose* of Christianity was to transform human society into the kingdom of God by regenerating all human relations and reconstituting them in accordance with the will of God."[7]

More specifically, how is the goal of the kingdom of God conceived? For John Cassian, the kingdom of God was a state in which the individual, having purified the heart, contemplated God without interruption. To the mind of Rauschenbusch, the view the prophets and Jesus had of the kingdom of God was not inward and transcendental but inner-worldly, social, and quite public. Thus Rauschenbusch seeks to show that for the people of Israel the kingdom of God was a concrete historical expectation that was national and collective in character. It involved the restoration of national sovereignty and the establishment of peace and security for the nation. The coming of the kingdom would bring with it justice, prosperity, and holiness for the nation as a whole. All these things would be accomplished by divine intervention. Israel's enemies would be defeated, and a righteous ruler of the line of David would be placed on the throne.[8]

In his teaching, Jesus transformed this notion, but not in a way that reduced it simply to an inward and individual state. Like the prophets before him, Jesus viewed the kingdom of God as a social reality. So Rauschenbusch wrote that for Jesus, "the kingdom of God is still a collective conception, involving the whole social life of man. It is not a matter of saving human atoms, but of saving the social organism. It is not a matter of getting people into heaven, but of transforming the life on earth into the harmony of heaven."[9] Jesus hoped for the appearance of a very inner-worldly state of affairs. Nevertheless, he repudiated the nationalistic, militaristic, and apocalyptic elements that he believed were so much a part of popular Jewish expectation. Rauschenbusch argued also that, though Jesus indeed envisioned a new social reality, the kingdom he proclaimed was one that included not just Israel but all peoples. Further, Rauschenbusch contended that Jesus's view was that this new social reality would not come by

---

6. *CSC*, xiii.
7. *CSC*, emphasis added.
8. For this account of Israel's expectation, see *CSC*, 56–57. See also *CSO*, 51–53.
9. *CSC*, 65.

political revolt or by sudden (and violent) divine intervention. Violence, as a means of bringing the kingdom, must be renounced.[10] The kingdom will come not by violence but by "organic development."[11] Jesus envisioned the kingdom growing cell by cell, beginning with himself. So Rauschenbusch concludes,

> Jesus worked on individuals and through individuals, but his real end was not individualistic, but social, and in his method he employed strong social forces. He knew that a new view of life would have to be implanted before the new life could be lived and that the new society would have to nucleate around personal centers of renewal. But his end was not the new soul, but the new society; not man but Man.[12]

Belief in organic development led Rauschenbusch to an additional conviction about the nature of the kingdom. If the kingdom is not dependent upon forceful intervention, either human or divine, or upon the reconstitution of the kingdom of Israel, but upon the slow spread of "a new view of life" from person to person and from group to group, then one must say that in a very real sense the kingdom of God is already present. Its consummation may indeed lie in the future, but in a real sense life on earth is already being transformed into "the harmony of heaven."[13]

The appearance of the kingdom of God (and so also the goal of life in Christ) has both a negative and a positive aspect. In a negative sense, it involves the gradual disappearance of what Rauschenbusch often calls "the Kingdom of Evil."[14] The kingdom of evil grows from sin, but sin is not to be understood as an "unvarying racial endowment."[15] Rather, it is a condition that stems from human selfishness. Human selfishness in turn comes not from a "racial endowment" but, as in the works of Kant, from "sensual equipment" that makes people vulnerable to selfish behavior.[16] Sin may thus be defined quite simply as "selfishness;"[17] and selfishness, since it is a manifestation of human weakness rather than an innate fault, is at least partially subject to restraint and correction by human intelligence and will.[18]

That being said, the task of rectification is not an easy one because sin, over time, expresses itself in a social way as what Rauschenbusch (relying upon

10. *CSO*, 59.
11. *CSO*, 59.
12. *CSO*, 60–61.
13. *CSO*, 62.
14. See esp. *TSG*, chap. 9.
15. *TSG*, 43.
16. *TSG*, 46.
17. *TSG*, 47.
18. *TSG*, 43.

Ritschl) calls "the Kingdom of Evil." Selfishness is communicated from generation to generation not by something like genetic transfer but through "channels of social tradition."[19] This social transfer leads to "social idealizations of evil" that falsify the ethical standards of both individuals and communities. In this way, social wrongs are perpetuated by "super-personal forces, or composite personalities."[20] If redemption (that is to say, the kingdom of God) is to come, Christian ethics cannot focus simply on individuals and their particular state before God. In their moral life, Christians must address as well the strength of these superpersonal forces. As he wrote in *A Theology for the Social Gospel*,

> Beyond the feeble and short-lived individual towers the social group as a super-personal entity, dominating the individual, assimilating him to its moral standards, and enforcing them by the social sanctions of approval or disapproval. When these super-personal forces are based on an evil principle, or directed toward an evil purpose, or corrupted by some controlling group, they are sinners of sublimer mould, and they block the way to redemption.[21]

In its negative aspect, the goal of Christian ethics requires overcoming the kingdom of evil. Its positive aspect is most easily seen in Rauschenbusch's discussion of redemption. Redemption must come not only to individuals but also to these superpersonal forces. Redemption brings into being the kingdom of God and occurs when these superpersonal forces, and those whose lives are corrupted and broken by them, come under the law of Christ. This law is understood in the first instance as one of love and mutual service.[22] Wherever this law obtains, the kingdom of God is present. Consequently, as Rauschenbusch says, "The Kingdom of God contains the teleology of the Christian religion."[23] It is to the realization of the kingdom of God that Christians are to direct their moral energy. Thus in *Christianizing the Social Order* he wrote,

> Such a Kingdom of God would be at once the highest good and the highest duty. Its realization is not like other duties, from man to man, but is a duty that the race owes to the race, the duty of realizing its divine destiny. It is a duty so vast that it transcends the powers of man; God alone can bring it to reality. But because we feel the duty, we may conclude that the Ruler of the moral universe is behind it and is cooperating with us, and each of us must work for it as if all depended on himself.[24]

19. *TSG*, 77.
20. *TSG*, 78.
21. *TSG*, 110.
22. *TSG*, 98.
23. *TSG*, 140.
24. *CSO*, 89.

Rauschenbusch contends that it is possible to look back over time and see that this goal has already been partially realized in a number of social institutions. Indeed, he observes that the largest part of the social order is now based in part upon Christian principles.[25] So he notes that familial, ecclesial, educational, and political institutions have moved from despotic regimes to ones based upon love, freedom, democratic equality, and service.[26] These are the primary expressions within the social order of the ethical convictions generally identified with Christ. To be sure, they are not always upheld and acted upon. Rauschenbusch was keenly aware, as were few white males in his time, of the injustices suffered by African Americans and women. Nevertheless, he held that in these matters and in others there were Christian standards to be found in what he was wont to call "a general moral sense," and that public appeal could be made to these standards in cases of injustice. Thus he took the presence of effective, Christian standards of public behavior, despite gross exceptions, as genuine realizations of the kingdom of God on earth. Indeed, he took all those, baptized or not, who worked for those standards as true disciples.[27]

The Christianization of society has progressed over the centuries, but there remains one part of social life that has not been adequately touched—namely, the economic order. The principles that shape this institution do not accord with the general moral sense. The economic order as presently constituted is based in selfishness rather than service. It is in fact the last bastion of autocracy. It divides men into classes. It valorizes profit and competition rather than service and solidarity. He concludes: "Thus, our capitalistic commerce and industry lies along side of the home, the school, the church, and the democratized state as an unregenerate part of the social order, not based on freedom, love, and mutual service, as they are, but on autocracy, antagonism of interests, and exploitation."[28]

The general goal of Christian ethics is the realization of the kingdom of God on earth. There is still work to be done in familial, educational, ecclesial, and political institutions, but given the progress that has been made in these areas of social life, the particular goal of Christian ethics must at the moment become the Christianization of the economic order.[29] At one point he in fact declares, "Money is the root of all evil."[30] Concentrations of wealth corrupt both possessors and

25. CSO, 124.
26. CSO, 128–55, 313, 320–21.
27. Smucker, *Rauschenbusch's Social Ethics*, 46.
28. CSO, 313.
29. CSO, 158.
30. CSO, 321.

dispossessed. Consequently, Christians are to make it their chief moral end to bring about an economic order based on mutual interest, good will, solidarity, cooperation, and service rather than the baser instincts of self-interest, greed, and competition. The presence of the former and the decline of the latter will signal the growth of the kingdom of God and the decline of the kingdom of evil, which together form the negative and the positive goals of Christian living.

The Basis of Life Together in Christ

It is not surprising that Rauschenbusch argues that the basis for the focus he would give Christian ethics is the person and example of Jesus. Of these two, the person of Christ is the most fundamental. As indicated previously, however, he did not construe Christ's person in the traditional terms of one person with two natures. He did not believe that a metaphysical definition of this sort would serve well his desire to reconstruct Christian doctrine in ways that displayed Jesus's most fundamental commitments. In *A Theology for the Social Gospel*, Rauschenbusch noted that one's idea of salvation controls the way in which the person and work of Christ are portrayed.[31] Thus if salvation is understood as a form of knowledge, the emphasis will be on the personality and doctrine of Christ as the complete revelation of God. If salvation is conceived as the expiation of guilt, then emphasis will fall on the work of Christ—on atonement and satisfaction for sins. If, however, salvation is thought of as Jesus thought of it, as the presence and growth of the kingdom of God, then one's concern will be to account for the way in which Christ set in motion the historical forces that gave birth to the kingdom of God and will bring an end to the kingdom of evil.

Rauschenbusch believed that the force that would redeem history was set loose by Jesus's own personality. He held that new life for society "would have to nucleate around personal centers,"[32] that great movements arise from the hearts of a few, and that prophetic minds "condense the longings of the mass of men in concrete experience and thought."[33] Christ is best understood as a *personality* that set loose the forces that would, over the ages, bring to fruition these deep longings. The force of his personality lay in his "consciousness of God" rather than in any metaphysical properties he might possess. So Rauschenbusch writes,

> Jesus had realized the life of God in the soul of man and the life of man in the love of God. That was the real secret of his life, the well-spring of his purity, his

31. *TSG*, 147.
32. *CSC*, 61.
33. *CSO*, 8.

compassion, his unwearied courage, his unquenchable idealism: he knows the Father. But if he had that greatest of all possessions, the real key to the secret of life, it was his highest social duty to share it and help others to gain what he had.[34]

These thoughts were given fuller expression in *A Theology for the Social Gospel*. There he charges traditional theology with a failure to render a Christ who is "truly personal." Thus he seeks to focus on the character and personality rather than the divinity of Christ. He writes, "The social gospel wants to see a personality able to win hearts, dominate situations, able to bind men in loyalty and make them think like himself, and to set revolutionary social forces in motion."[35] Jesus is such a personality. Indeed, the personality "he achieved" is "a new type of humanity," "the primal cell of a new social organism" that carries "new social standards."[36]

This new type of humanity is not to be understood as an "effortless inheritance" bestowed by the Father upon the Son but as an achievement on the part of the man Jesus. What precisely was his achievement? Quoting Fichte with approval, he says, "The consciousness of the absolute unity of the human and the divine life is the profoundest insight possible to man. Before Jesus it did not exist. . . . Jesus evidently had this insight."[37] Rauschenbusch goes on to interpret Jesus's insight in this way. Jesus was the perfect religious personality because his life was "completely filled by the realization of a God who is love" and because he fully absorbed God's basic purpose, the kingdom of God. Because of his God consciousness, he gave that kingdom a meaning that accorded with God's own intentions.[38]

Rauschenbusch concludes that the personality of Jesus calls everyone to a similar consciousness. In this way, Jesus's life becomes a perpetuating force within the history of humankind. However, his fully developed personality, one that is fully conscious of the nature of God and the needs of others, has a concrete identity that is revealed in Jesus's teaching and in his character. Jesus's teaching and character mirror one another. His teaching is to be followed and his character imitated. His teaching requires obedience and his character imitation because the power of his person is communicated through these moral channels. It is consequently not only Jesus's unique consciousness of God but also his teaching and character that form the basis of Christian ethics.

34. *CSO*, 48.
35. *TSG*, 149.
36. *TSG*, 152.
37. *TSG*, 152–53.
38. *TSG*, 154–55.

Jesus's teaching focused on the coming of the kingdom of God and the character of the ethical life that distinguishes the kingdom of God from the kingdom of evil. The salient mark of both Jesus's life and life in the kingdom of God is love. Love, as manifest in Jesus's life, has a distinctive profile. The love one sees in Jesus overcomes selfishness and seeks to stimulate the dormant human faculty of devotion to the common good.[39] Consequently, Jesus was ready to forgive and re-create fellowship when it was broken. Toward this end, he was also willing to take the abuse of others while seeking reconciliation.[40] Jesus's love for others expressed itself as self-sacrifice. Further, since pride is one of the primary expressions of selfishness, the love Jesus showed was accompanied by a form of humility that looked on people as equal before God. The love Jesus had for his fellows sought equality and offered itself as service rather than domination.[41] Selfishness also expresses itself as greed. The love manifest in Jesus's life, therefore, took the form of a passion for justice. It expressed itself in acts of kindness, a special concern for the poor, and in injunctions to share wealth and to abolish rank, along with the badges of social position in which inequality is encrusted.[42]

In sum, the love characteristic of Jesus's life and teaching is directed toward the realization of the kingdom. It has a social thrust toward the common good. It expresses itself as readiness to forgive, willingness to take abuse, a desire for reconciliation, readiness to sacrifice self-interest for the interest of others, humility that looks upon others as equals before God, a desire to see justice done, and a special sympathy for the poor. These are the qualities that are to be imitated both by anyone who wishes to be Jesus's disciple and by the community that claims his name.

Rauschenbusch is convinced that the person, teaching, and character of Jesus were resonant with both divine providence and the deep longings and fundamental moral sense to be found in the human community. Beneath the treble line of adventitious selfishness occasioned by human finitude lay a bass line composed of beneficent divine providence and fundamental human goodness. Christ's fully realized religious personality and exemplary character may compose a new form of humanity, but this new form of humanity corresponds both with the fundamental purposes of God in history and with human nature in its created rather than fallen state. Thus Christian ethics has a basis not only in Christ's person, teaching, and character but in divine providence and human nature as well. In respect to the kingdom of God, the particular

39. CSC, 68.
40. CSC, 68.
41. CSC, 70.
42. CSC, 72–87.

accomplishment of Jesus is not identical with the general purposes of God and the basic character of human nature, but they are compatible.

The themes of divine providence and basic human nature are not pursued in detail as are those connected with the person, character, and teaching of Jesus, but they appear frequently, almost as asides, as Rauschenbusch pursues his basic line of argument. Thus he introduces the concluding chapter of *Christianity and the Social Crisis* by noting that the will of God is revealed not only in Christ but also "in the highest manifestations of the religious spirit," in "the call of human duty," and even in human motives of "self-protection."[43] Jointly, he says, these call people (not all of whom are Christian) "to put their hands to the plough and not to look back till public morality shall be at least as much Christianized as private morality is now."[44] At the beginning of *Christianizing the Social Order* he notes, referring without question to divine providence, that "religious energy is rising from the depth of that infinite spiritual life in which all live and move and have their being."[45] This energy is beginning to awaken America to a "social feeling."[46] So he notes that America stands on the brink of a social renewal because "prophetic minds" can appeal to this energy and in so doing "condense the unconscious longings of the mass of men in concrete experience and thought."[47] These unconscious longings represent a general moral sense that can be attributed to humankind in general. The moral principles that make up this moral sense "find their highest expression in the teaching, the life, and the spirit of Jesus Christ."[48] Jesus incarnates the moral law, and this fact is recognized by both those within and those outside the Christian churches. Jesus is the type of humankind that humankind is meant to be, and he is recognizable as such because of a deep resonance between what he is and what people recognize as their best self.

Here we have, at the conclusion and onset of argument, reference to both providence and human nature. Jointly they provide (once constellated by Christ's person and example) a deep foundation for the social focus of Christian ethics. To these anticipatory developments must be added the voice of the great Hebrew prophets. They represent a special aspect of God's providence—one that introduced the primacy of the kingdom of God and its social character as central to God's purposes. Jesus transforms and expands this prophetic

43. CSC, 343.
44. CSC, 343.
45. CSO, 6.
46. CSO, 5.
47. CSO, 8.
48. CSO, 125.

vision, but his life and teaching represent a correction, fulfillment, and expansion of the divinely guided historical movement of which the prophets speak rather than its repudiation.[49] So it must be said also that, for Rauschenbusch, Christian ethics has a base in a particular form of providence, in the special history God has with his prophets, and, through his prophets, with his chosen people, Israel.

Finally, Christian ethics has a base in a historical force that bears a strong resemblance to the natural forces that have produced ever more complex species of life—namely, evolution. Rauschenbusch never makes it clear whether this force is an expression of some élan within human nature or whether it is the result of divine guidance of the historical process. He does, however, make it clear that something like evolution is at work in human affairs. Thus, in a remarkable statement, he says,

> The spread of evolutionary ideas is another mark of modern religious thought. It has opened a vast historical outlook, backward and forward, and trained us in bold conceptions of the upward climb of the race. There is no denying that this has unsettled the ecclesiastical system of thought, much as the growth of tree roots will burst solid masonry. But it has prepared us for understanding the ideal of a Reign of God toward which all creation is moving. Translate the evolutionary theories into religious faith, and you have the doctrine of the Kingdom of God.[50]

By way of summary, we can say that the basis of Christian ethics is divine providence, manifesting itself quintessentially in the life and teaching of Jesus yet working in cooperation with human nature and the basic élan of the universe.

The Character of Life in Christ according to Walter Rauschenbusch

The way in which Rauschenbusch characterizes life in Christ flows (one wants to say naturally) from the way in which he depicts the goal and basis of Christian ethics. His characterization has both a personal and a communal focus, but (perhaps because of the early influences of pietism and sectarianism on his thought)[51] it is the personal focus that, at the outset of his argument, takes pride of place. In *Christianizing the Social Order*, at the end of his discussion of the steps that must be taken if the economic system of capitalism is to be brought under the law of Christ, he does not, as one might expect, rehearse a reformative legislative program (though indeed he has one). Rather, he states

49. See, e.g., *CSO*, 48–67.
50. *CSO*, 90.
51. Smucker, *Rauschenbusch's Social Ethics*, 21–73.

that the renewal of religion is essential for the renewal of the economic order. By the renewal of religion, however, he does not in the first instance mean the adoption of a progressive or revolutionary social program, as advocated by a number of liberation theologians, or the creation of an exemplary community, as have John Howard Yoder and Stanley Hauerwas recently. Rather, he refers to the responsibility of the churches to be seedbeds for personalities whose "minds have been set free by God and energized by a great purpose."[52] He believes, he says, "in the miraculous power of the human personality."[53] Accordingly, he looks to the churches as places in which powerful personalities—personalities that share that of Christ—can be developed. As he says, "Create a ganglion chain of redeemed personalities in a commonwealth and all things become possible."[54] A belief of this sort in the power of individual personalities to effect social change is quite remarkable in one who saw so clearly the extent to which people are formed (and deformed) by the social order in which they live. Nonetheless, the power of the individual personality was perhaps Rauschenbusch's deepest conviction. The following paragraph states this commitment as strongly as any to be found in his writings.

> The greatest contribution which any man can make to the social movement is the contribution of a regenerated personality, of a will which sets justice above policy and profit, and of an intellect emancipated from falsehood. Such a man will in some measure incarnate the principles of a higher social order in his attitude to all questions and in all his relations to men, and will be a well-spring of regenerating influences.[55]

Here one sees a rather thorough conversion of religion into an ethic that, surprisingly enough, in the first instance at least, is personal. Rauschenbusch is insistent that the ultimate goal of personal virtue is social renewal, but he insists nonetheless that the process of social renewal must begin with righteous individuals. The issue, of course, is what virtues characterize personal holiness or righteousness. Not surprisingly, the virtues Rauschenbusch cites are those he detects in the life of Christ—namely, love expressed as devotion to the common good, forgiveness, humility, service, justice, good faith, kindness, and devotion to the poor and oppressed. These virtues call for imitation on the part of disciples because they manifest a passion for the kingdom of God like that which motivated Jesus.

52. CSO, 460.
53. CSO, 460.
54. CSO, 462.
55. CSC, 351.

To this point, Rauschenbusch's depiction of life in Christ is quite traditional and might easily be confused with the private ethic of personal holiness he is so anxious to criticize. His argument takes a more radical (and perhaps even contradictory) turn, however, when he notes that love, understood simply as a personal virtue, "breaks down" before the enormous task of social renewal. This observation leads him to say that what Christians need in the midst of the present social crisis is a "socialized love."[56] The following statement makes his meaning as clear as possible.

> We can never do without the plain affection of man to man. But what we most need today is not the love that will break its back drawing water for a growing factory town from a well that was meant to supply a village, but a love so large and intelligent that it will persuade an ignorant people to build a system of waterworks up in the hills, and that will get after the thoughtless farmers who contaminate the brooks with typhoid bacilli, and after the lumber concern that is denuding the watershed of its forests. We want a new avatar of love.

These words sound less like those of a traditional moral theologian and more like those of a liberation theologian from Latin America. Love is not cast in terms of personal virtues but in terms of the ideals of the French Revolution—liberty, equality, and fraternity. These are the primary social principles assumed by "a socialized love." The first expression of a socialized love is *liberty*. To be sure, love supports liberty as a personal quality and not just as a social condition. Thus Rauschenbusch insists that though love is the highest Christian quality, it always takes the form of freedom defined as a spontaneous capacity for goodness.[57] Love, however, also supports a social expression of liberty. Jesus, after all, summarized his mission as bringing release to the captives. Love therefore supports a social order in which individuals are freed from the arbitrary constraints that hinder the development of a full personality. Freedom is a fundamental aspect of a Christianized social order, and Rauschenbusch was convinced that a democratic society in which liberty found a prominent place within its basic social institutions was an expression of the kingdom of God. He was convinced that American democracy represented an important step on the road to social redemption because liberty had at long last become a prominent value in the institutions of family, school, church, and state. Only in the economic order had liberty not found its rightful place of honor. Clearly, the next job for socialized love, and therefore for Christians of all stripes, was a struggle to see that liberty is given a place in economic relations similar to the one it enjoys in other dimensions of social life.

56. *CSO*, 43–44.
57. *CSO*, 119.

Similar things must be said about love and *equality*. On a personal level, love expresses itself in forms of humility and accords all people equal value before God. Rauschenbusch argues, however, that a socialized love will express itself in a social vision that opposes all forms of entrenched social privilege. Rauschenbusch is not so naive as to believe in absolute equality, but he does believe that love necessarily opposes inordinate concentrations of wealth and power that create social inequalities of an unacceptable sort. He wants the sort of equality that provides all people access to work, a living wage, education, political activity, and other social goods necessary for a fully developed personality.[58] Once again, at the present time the great enemy of love's social vision is an economic system that establishes privilege and inequality and that, in so doing, robs human beings of liberty and the chance to develop their personalities to the fullest.[59] Love's great ally once more is a democratic political order that opens opportunity to people on an equal basis.

Finally, there is socialized love expressed as *fraternity*. Rauschenbusch notes that both liberty and equality are rather individualistic social virtues. If they are to remain expressions of love, they must be balanced by a dedication to the common good and cooperative effort. Rauschenbusch cites the apostle Paul in support of this interpretation of socialized love.

> In the first century of our era a new social organization spread through the Roman Empire. It had a force of cohesion so strong that it bound men of all races and social classes into a fraternity, resisted the crushing pressure of the Roman despotism, and survived all the shocks and changes of European society for nineteen hundred years. One of the earliest leaders of this remarkable organization formulated its social philosophy from the biology of the human organism. The ideal society, he said, has an unlimited diversity of organs and functions, but a fundamental unity of life, motive and purpose; it is perfect in the measure in which every member has the support and protection of the whole body, and in turn serves the whole in its due place. Paul's philosophy of the Christian Church is the highest possible philosophy of human society. The ideal society is an organism, and the christianizing of the social order must work toward an harmonious cooperation of all individuals for common social ends.[60]

As socialized love, fraternity requires a sense of comradeship and solidarity, a commitment to common enterprise, an ethic of stewardship rather than ownership, and a conviction that there is something like collective wealth and

---

58. For a nice statement of the importance Rauschenbusch attaches to conditions that allow for the fullest possible development of personality, see *TSG*, 142.
59. *CSO*, 365.
60. *CSO*, 366.

so also common ownership of public resources.[61] Once again, the clear and present danger to this socialized expression of love is the capitalistic economic system that emphasizes self-interest and competition rather than cooperation and service.

Socialized love expresses itself first of all in the great ideals of liberty, equality, and fraternity. However, these ideals require support from what Rauschenbusch calls "the simplest and most valuable quality" needed in moral relations—namely, justice.[62] One is not surprised to find that justice is understood primarily as a form of equality that seeks always to do away with privilege. As a virtue, justice sets itself against the inequalities that hinder the full development of human personality, but justice as a virtue requires mechanisms for dispute settlement that support its goal. Hence Rauschenbusch stresses the importance of courts that are protected from undue influence by concentrations of wealth and power.

Rauschenbusch's discussion of justice provides something of a hinge that moves his depiction of the character of life in Christ in what might be called an institutional direction. The growth of the kingdom of God requires certain institutional arrangements—arrangements that serve to promote the great ideals of socialized love. The central importance of democratic institutions has already been noted. Democracy protects liberty, preserves equality, and promotes fraternity. The full realization of its promise, however, requires dramatic alteration of the economic order. He quotes J. S. Mill with approval: "The social problem of the future we consider to be how to unite the greatest individual liberty of action with a common ownership in the raw material of the globe, and an equal participation of all in the benefits of combined labor."[63] Thus he favors public ownership of natural resources. Further, for the full development of personality, people must have a right to work, a just share in the industrial organization of which they are a part, and economic provision for the times and occasions when they are unable to work. These requirements all point to some form of democratic socialism as the political form socialized love must seek. Indeed, socialism is depicted as an expression of that divine providence that moves slowly but relentlessly toward bringing about the kingdom of God in history. Rauschenbusch writes,

> Whatever the sins of individual socialists, and whatever the shortcomings of Socialist organizations, they are tools in the hands of the Almighty. They must serve him whether they will not. . . . Socialism is one of the chief powers of the

---

61. CSO, 365–68.
62. CSO, 332.
63. CSO, 366.

coming age. Its fundamental aims are righteous, not because they are socialistic, but because they are human. They were part of the mission of Christianity before the name of Socialism had been spoken. God had to raise up Socialism because the organized Church was too slow to realize God's ends.[64]

The character of life in Christ as portrayed by Rauschenbusch begins with the power of an individual personality that imitates the personality of Christ, but it moves to a love-inspired commitment to certain social ideals. From there it moves to a resolve to support democratic institutions, oppose the capitalist economic system, and struggle to bring about a new economic order based on public ownership of natural resources, common ownership of the means of production, and common effort for common good. These are the institutional marks of the kingdom of God on earth, and a struggle for their establishment signals a final characteristic of life in Christ.

As mentioned previously, the kingdom of God evolves slowly during the course of history. Life in Christ involves a struggle with the kingdom of evil. In this struggle, progress is slow, but it is certain. In fact, Rauschenbusch believed that in his time progress was marked and rapid, and that extraordinary realizations of the kingdom of God lay within reach. Nevertheless, he did not predict an imminent state of perfection. His eschatology is progressive but not millenarian. Life in Christ requires patient struggle for the ideals of the kingdom, but in that struggle there is genuine hope for improvement of life upon earth. He notes that it is not given to humankind to know the times of seasons of the kingdom's arrival, but he insists that "the ideal of a social life in which the law of Christ shall prevail, and in which its prevalence shall result in peace, justice and a glorious blossoming of human life, is a Christian ideal."[65] He goes on to say,

> Our chief interest in any millennium is the desire for a social order in which the worth and freedom of every last human being will be honored and protected; in which the brotherhood of man will be expressed in the common possession of the economic resources of society; and in which the spiritual good of humanity will be set high above the private profit interest of all materialistic groups. We hope for such an order for humanity as we hope for heaven for ourselves.[66]

He concludes that when it comes to the way in which this great transformation will occur, Christians are to place their hope in development rather than

64. *CSO*, 404.
65. *TSG*, 224.
66. *TSG*, 224.

catastrophic intervention; in this they follow the example of their Lord, who "received the influences of the historical life of the Jewish people through the channels of social tradition, and . . . transmitted the effects of his own life and personality to the future through the same channels."[67]

Concluding Comments

Let us take stock before moving on to a third possible focus for Christian ethics. As John Cassian contributed a remarkably fruitful vocabulary for considering what has come to be called "Christian spirituality," so also has Walter Rauschenbusch provided a vocabulary by means of which Christians are able to address in a Christian voice the social conditions of their times. It is difficult to escape the conclusion that the succeeding contributions of both neoorthodoxy and liberation theology to Christian social ethics would have been slower coming and a good deal less powerful had Rauschenbusch not reinterpreted Christian belief and practice in the way he did. Following on the line of thought pioneered by Kant and later by Ritschl, Rauschenbusch set the scene of God's redemptive purposes firmly within history. Indeed, I chose Rauschenbusch as my example of a socially focused Christian ethics in large measure because his concerns are still so present within the mainline churches of the United States.

Nevertheless, despite a welcome return from the realm of archetypes to that of nature and history, his interpretation of the biblical witness introduces distortions in both belief and practice. Interestingly enough, these distortions, though markedly different from those of John Cassian, nonetheless also stem in large measure from a misreading of Christian eschatology. Whether one reads Paul or Matthew or Revelation, it is difficult to find the notion of progressive social development that is so central to Rauschenbusch's reinterpretation of Christian doctrine. What one finds in the biblical witness is not a progressive view of history based in the slow spread of Jesus's message and example, a belief in social evolution, or confidence in progress that is rooted in an innate moral sense common to humankind as such. What one finds is not belief in an ideal socio-economic political order (democratic socialism) as the goal of history and so also of Christian ethics. What one finds instead is a view of Christ's rule over historical processes that serves to guarantee, in the midst of an ongoing struggle, his triumph and the triumph of those who are faithful to him upon the occasion of a final intervention by God in

---

67. *TSG*, 225.

Christ within both creation and the course of history. What one finds is not the valorization of the march of history or of a given political and social order within its boundaries but a severe limitation of the significance of these matters within the providence of God. What one finds is a certainty that one aeon or qualitative aspect of nature and history will be revealed in the course of and at the culmination of a terrible struggle as vindicated and established by God. What one finds is a view of the risen and ascended Christ as a guarantee that the witness of Christ and his saints in the midst of this struggle will have its effects upon the world, but not that these effects will form part of a progressive march toward the kingdom of God on earth.

Not surprisingly, one also finds in the witness of Holy Scripture a more complete account of the character of Christian living than the one to be found in the works of Rauschenbusch. In these works, love, in its social expression as liberty, equality, and fraternity, is shrunk to a personal and communal virtue. As a result, love appears in a very different guise from the one it assumes, for example, in the Pauline literature that will be examined in part 2 of this study. Within the pages of Rauschenbusch's three great works, love as a personal and community-specific virtue for Christians finds expression primarily as a congeries of socio-political ideals or, in attendant fashion, as a relatively thin list of personal virtues that allow one to persevere and succeed in the struggle for a more just social order.

3

John Howard Yoder's Ethic of Communal Witness

In the work of John Howard Yoder, one finds yet another possible focus for Christian ethics—the common life of the Christian fellowship. In a host of articles and books that began to appear in the mid-1960s, Yoder articulates a view of the goal, basis, and character of Christian ethics that joins theology and ethics and places them first of all in relation to communal identity. Further, in undertaking this project, he explicitly rejects the two options previously considered—what he calls the "theocratic solution" that places the focus of Christian ethics on the institutions of an entire society, and the "spiritualist" position that moves the focus of Christian ethics from society inward to the human heart.[1]

One can track a number of influences that have steered Yoder's thought in the directions it has taken, but three are of particular importance. Among these, Yoder's Anabaptist heritage holds pride of place. Early on, Yoder took a leading role among a group of young Mennonite scholars who worked to reclaim their tradition in a way that allowed Mennonites a critical but constructive relation to both society at large and other churches. He championed a form of the Anabaptist tradition that was not sectarian but thoroughly ecumenical and, in its own way, socially involved. However, the perspective championed

---

1. John H. Yoder, *The Royal Priesthood: Essays Ecclesiological and Ecumenical*, edited by Michael G. Cartwright (Scottdale, PA: Herald, 1998), 71–72. Hereafter cited as *RP*.

by Yoder was not one shaped by traditional ways of presenting the ecumenical and social agenda of the mainline churches. The ecclesial tradition in which he had been raised led him to be quite critical of the usual ways of discussing both the constitution of the church and its relation to society.

In an early collection of articles titled *The Original Revolution*, he called into question the ecumenical usefulness of such notions as the "marks" or "notes" of the church. He argued instead that the real test of whether the church is in fact the church is to be found not in "characteristics which could be measured by looking at the management of the church's liturgy or her business" but at "the point of the relation of church and world."[2] The Mennonite emphasis upon the exemplary importance of a faithful community allowed him to see before many others who now share his perspective that the so-called Constantinian settlement, whereby the life of the church and that of the larger society are conjoined in a mutually supportive relationship, is in a state of advanced decay, if not collapse. Because of this decline, Yoder could argue in ways he had good hope might be ecumenically attractive that the church should seek to become not society's chaplain but an alternative social world, manifesting a different basis and form of life. The Mennonite influence on his social and ecumenical vision is well illustrated by this crucial paragraph.

> What then is the church and what should she be? One source will tell us that she is "one, holy, catholic, and apostolic"; another will tell us that she is to be found "where the sacraments are properly administered and the Word of God is properly preached." Still others would test her by the moral performance or the intensity of piety which can be seen in her individual members. But in our age there is arising with new clarity an understanding that what it means to be the church must be found in a clearer grasp of her relation to what is not the church, namely "the world." For us to say with current ecumenical fashion that the church is a witnessing body, a serving body, and body fellowshipping voluntarily and visibly, is to identify her thrice as not being the same thing as the total surrounding society. This definition demands for the church an existence, a structure, a sociology of her own, independent of the other structures of society.[3]

The structure "independent of the other structures of society" that Yoder advocated in its details stems in large measure from his Mennonite roots. Pacifism has played and continues to play a central role in Mennonite accounts of Christian identity. The pacifism that Yoder advocates rests upon the firm conviction that Christians as a community of disciples are meant to pattern

---

2. John Howard Yoder, "Let the Church Be the Church," in *The Original Revolution* (Scottdale, PA: Herald, 1971), 117. Hereafter cited as OR.
3. Ibid., 114–15.

their lives in a way that imitates the life of Christ. That life, in contradistinction to the view espoused by neoorthodox theologians, is not viewed simply as a noble but unrealizable ideal. Rather, it is seen as a way of life to be followed, even if one's imitation proves an imperfect witness to the original. It is the defining significance of Jesus's life as depicted in the Gospel accounts, a life that does not resist evil with evil, that both lies at the base of Yoder's thought and most clearly signals the formative power of the ecclesial tradition from which he comes.

The work of Karl Barth, with whom Yoder studied as a young man, constitutes a second influence. It is most certainly from Karl Barth that Yoder's postmodern eschewal of theological and moral foundationalism derives. He is fond of saying that, in respect to religious and moral truth, there is no theological or moral "scratch," or foundation, to which generalized appeals can be made.[4] Thus he argues that, because people are fallen, anything read off the world (natural theology and natural law) is bound to reflect the fall and so be twisted. Consequently, human beings, because of their fallen state, are dependent for moral and religious knowledge upon God's self-revelation in Christ. Appropriation of this knowledge depends upon seeking to follow Christ by forms of imitation. These forms, in turn, are to be discerned within the changes and chances of history by communal interpretation of Holy Scripture and communal discipline.

Barth's influence on Yoder can also be seen in the Barth's assessment of the status of the church in the modern world and in his portrayal of its proper constitution. Yoder contends that Barth, in IV/2 of the *Church Dogmatics*, implies that in present circumstances the members of society are not directly addressable in Christian terms.[5] This observation led Barth to speak of church law or constitution as exemplary.[6] The manner in which the church lives its common life in a post-Constantinian world becomes a witness to society of an alternative truth and an alternative way of life. Barth's recognition of the changed social circumstances of the churches, and his view that Christian ethics (rather than apologetics) is best understood as a form of witness, allowed Yoder to join Barth's reprise of Calvinism to his own Anabaptist vision of the nature and calling of the church.

---

4. John Howard Yoder, "Why Ecclesiology Is Social Ethics: The Gospel Ethics versus the Wider Wisdom," in John Howard Yoder, *The Priestly Kingdom: Social Ethics as Gospel* (Notre Dame, IN: University of Notre Dame Press, 1984), 116 (hereafter cited as *PK*); John Howard Yoder, *The Christian Witness to the State,* Institute of Mennonite Studies Series 3 (Newton, KS: Faith and Life Press, 1964), 32–34 (hereafter cited as *CWS*).

5. *PK*, 106.

6. Karl Barth, *Church Dogmatics* IV/2 (Edinburgh: T&T Clark, 1958), 719–26.

A third (this time negative) influence on Yoder is the neoorthodox theology of H. Richard and particularly Reinhold Niebuhr. Reinhold Niebuhr's student Ronald Stone notes that Niebuhr "had learned from Ernst Troeltsch that a final Christian ethic is not achievable" and that "the ideal of love could not be realized in human history."[7] This led Niebuhr to the conclusion that other ethical principles that approximate but do not equal love must be used to govern human social and political relations.

It was at just this point that Yoder challenged the dominant moral stance of neoorthodoxy. In all his works, but particularly in *The Politics of Jesus*, Yoder insists that love has in fact been realized in the life of Jesus.[8] Because of Christ's victory in both his death and resurrection, love is the power that will be revealed as victorious in Christ's final appearance. This victorious love now flows into the life of the church through the power of the Holy Spirit and directs disciples toward the imitation of Christ. In contrast to the "Christian realism" of neoorthodoxy, which in the social arena sees justice as the best love can do, Yoder construes Christian ethics as a call to imitate a life that leads to the formation of an alternative society rooted and grounded in love. Thus he distinguishes between the world "outside the perfection of Christ" and the world "within the perfection of Christ."[9] Within Christ's perfection, following is not an impossible ideal but an immediate call to obedience. As Craig Carter nicely puts it, it is therefore possible, by Yoder's account, "for admittedly sinful and imperfect people to bear a visible witness to the ideal of love, not in their individual piety or goodness, but insofar as they covenant themselves together into an alternative community that lives (and suffers) without resorting to violence."[10]

The Goal and Basis of Life in Christ according to John Howard Yoder

The Goal

The previous quotation displays the ecclesial focus of Yoder's account of Christian ethics. The focus on communal identity is made doubly clear by Yoder's account of the goal or, more accurately, goals of Christian ethics. When his books and articles are taken as a whole, two goals emerge. One is

---

7. Cited by Craig Carter, *The Politics of the Cross: The Theology and Social Ethics of John Howard Yoder* (Grand Rapids: Brazos, 2001), 45.
8. John Howard Yoder, *The Politics of Jesus* (Grand Rapids: Eerdmans, 1992). Hereafter cited as *P of J*.
9. *CWS*, 31.
10. Carter, *Politics of the Cross*, 45.

primary and the other secondary. The secondary goal flows from and is in large measure dependent upon the primary one.

The primary goal is evangelical in character. By living together in a certain way and by relating to the world in a certain way, the moral life of Christians serves as a witness to God's final purposes in history. The secondary goal is socio-political in character. By living together in a certain way, the common life of the church provides society as a whole with a foretaste of the world's destiny, and this preview of human destiny may have demonstrably positive effects upon the social and political life of the environing society in which Christians happen to find themselves.

In his first major publication, *The Christian Witness to the State*, Yoder sets out an understanding of the goal of Christian ethics that he would later amplify but never abandon. As the title suggests, the primary subject matter of *The Christian Witness to the State* is the relation between the community of the church and the political structures under which it must live. His defining question is what the respective roles of state and church ought to be. In respect to the state, he answers in a way very reminiscent of St. Augustine's appraisal of the function of the state within divine providence: "The reign of Christ means for the state the obligation to serve God by encouraging the good and restraining evil; i.e., to serve peace, to preserve the social cohesion in which the leaven of the Gospel can build the church, and also render the old aeon more tolerable."[11]

Of even greater significance, however, is the ultimate purpose of providing a peaceful space. The ultimate purpose is not political but evangelical. By providing an ordered space, political authority makes it possible for the church to proclaim the gospel. The reason for Christian prayer for political authorities is that "God our Savior desires all men to be saved and to come to the knowledge of the truth (1 Tim. 2). The function of the state in maintaining an ordered society is thereby a part of the divine plan for the evangelization of the world."[12] The state serves within divine providence to provide an ordered and relatively peaceful space within which the church can carry out its evangelistic mission.[13] Thus, in contrast to Rauschenbusch, Yoder holds that "the Church is not fundamentally a source of moral stimulus to encourage the development of a better society—though a faithful Church should also have this effect—it is for the sake of the Church's own work that society continues to function. The meaning of history—and so also the significance of the state—lies in the creation and work of the Church."[14]

11. *CWS*, 5.
12. *RP*, 13.
13. *RP*, 10–11.
14. *RP*, 13.

Yoder's account of the goal of the state within divine providence is derived from a previous decision about the goal of Christian ethics. Its most basic purpose is to provide within a fallen world a communal witness to and partial manifestation of "the ultimately triumphant redemptive work of God."[15] As previously noted, in setting this goal for Christian ethics, Yoder self-consciously distinguishes his position from the then-regnant theological liberalism of the Niebuhrs. He insists on distinguishing "the ethics of discipleship" from "an ethic of justice within the limits of relative prudence and self-preservation" that tends to "identify the gospel of the kingdom of God with a plan for social betterment independent of changing men's minds and hearts."[16]

For Yoder, the primary goal of Christian ethics is evangelism by means of witness through a form of common life quite different from that of any society in which Christians may happen to find themselves. This form of life is chiefly characterized by peace, which is the ultimate goal of history.[17] Thus he writes,

> Peace describes the pacifist's hope, the goal in the light of which he acts, the character of his action, the ultimate divine certainty which lets his position make sense; it does not describe the external appearance or the observable results of his behavior. This is what we mean by eschatology: a hope which, defying present frustration, defines a present position in terms of the yet unseen goal which gives it meaning.[18]

In a later collection of essays, *The Priestly Kingdom*, Yoder makes the same point even more clearly. "Although immersed in this world, the church by her way of being represents the promise of another world, which is not somewhere else but which is to come here. That promissory quality of the church's present distinctiveness is the making of peace, as the refusal to make war is her indispensable negative transcendence."[19]

If witness to God's final purpose for history is the first goal of Christian ethics, the provision of a form of social life that can be adopted *in an analogous way* by society at large comprises a secondary goal. It is at this point that Yoder's account of the goal of Christian ethics overlaps that of Rauschenbusch. Like Rauschenbusch, Yoder believes that the imitation of Christ in everyday social life is a practical possibility that carries the promise of positive social

15. CWS, 10.
16. CWS, 23.
17. OR, 56.
18. OR, 56.
19. PK, 94.

results. Unlike Rauschenbusch, however, he posits a much weaker link between the imitation of Christ and social progress. The seed planted by Christ, so Rauschenbusch believes, sprouts within societies inhabited by Christians with a sort of evolutionary necessity. Yoder, on the other hand, sees the possibility but not the necessity of a positive (though limited) connection between Christian discipleship and social betterment. Christian witness may effect positive changes in the social order, but not necessarily. Thus he insists, "We cannot sight down the line of our obedience to the attainment of the ends we seek."[20]

Nonetheless, uncertain though they may be, Yoder is anxious to posit ameliorative social and political effects as a secondary goal for Christian ethics. These ameliorative effects are, on occasion, said (surprisingly enough) to stem not from the power of a specifically Christian witness but simply from the potential social relevance of minority groups that have a "clearly defined life style distinct from that of the crowd."[21] More frequently, however, it is a specifically Christian witness that Yoder has in mind when he speaks of the potential for social good contained in a communal ethic. A central passage of *Christian Witness to the State* makes clear what he means.

> The church is herself a society. Her very existence, the fraternal relations of her members, their ways of dealing with their differences and their needs are, or rather should be, a demonstration of what love means in social relations. This demonstration cannot be transposed directly into non-Christian society, for in the church it functions only on the basis of repentance and faith; yet by analogy certain of its aspects may be instructive as stimuli to the conscience of society.[22]

He goes on immediately to provide a limited number of examples of the power of analogy to have a positive social influence.[23] The diversity of ministries found within the church provides a creative analogy that supports egalitarianism and witnesses against hierarchy. The experience of persecution among Christians warns society as a whole about the temptations of power. The Christian practice of unanimity serves as an example that strengthens communal relations. Christian love for the neighbor demonstrates its influence within schools and hospitals, and the refusal of Christians to assume certain roles in society provides a stimulus for resisting excessive claims to authority on the part of the state. Elsewhere he lists the positive social effects of the exemplary character of the life of the church as brotherhood, honesty, justice, and the

20. *RP*, 203.
21. *P of J*, 39.
22. *CWS*, 17; *PK*, 94.
23. *CWS*, 18.

character of an abundant life.[24] Or again, commenting on the importance of Karl Barth's account of Christian ethics, Yoder lists five ways in which the life of the church can, by analogy, positively influence society. It can promote egalitarianism, socialism, forgiveness as a social virtue, transparency in public life, and recognition of the variety of gifts to be found within society as a whole.[25]

Yoder is always anxious to defend himself against the charge of "sectarianism." Consequently, in an occasionally forced manner, he posits the potential for the church to have a positive influence on both society and government. There is, however, another train of thought in his discussion of the secondary aims of Christian ethics that is less passive in its import. When reasoning in this more aggressive manner, Yoder places a specific moral demand on groups that have a "thick particular identity" to make a conscious and intentional public witness to their alternative way of life. They are morally obligated to engage a larger public. They cannot rest content simply hoping someone notices the benefits of their life together. It is with this more aggressive line of reasoning that Yoder answers the charge that his view of love is irresponsible because it refuses to protect others who may be in harm's way. So he notes that if one defines *agape* by the cross (as Christians do), one warns society (indeed the church is called upon to warn society) of certain moral pitfalls. In order, these are (1) that one's own family, friends, and compatriots are more to be loved than the enemy; (2) that the life of the aggressor is worth less than that of those under attack; (3) that the responsibility to prevent evil is an expression of love when it involves the death of the aggressor; and (4) that letting evil happen is as blameworthy as committing it.[26]

There is yet another way in which Christian witness can have a positive effect upon the social order. In this instance the witness is not that of an alternative community but of individual Christians who can provide a wholesome personal example within civil life. This positive influence is brought about by selective participation in public affairs in ways that do not compromise the exemplary demands of discipleship.[27] Thus, for example, it may well prove compromising for a Christian to seek political office because of the need of politicians to seek power for the sake of power. However, Christians can become journalists or lobbyists and use their position to remind the authorities of their allotted place within God's providence. That is, they can remind those in power that their function under God is to encourage good and restrain evil and in so doing serve peace, preserve social cohesion, and render life in

24. *OR*, 77.
25. *RP*, 28–33.
26. *RP*, 164.
27. *CWS*, 27; *P of J*, 154–55; *PK*, 116–17; *RP*, 164.

a fallen world more tolerable.[28] The witness of individual Christians within the social order can, in short, remind the state of its purpose under God and so also the limits of its authority.

The Basis of Life Together in Christ

The communal focus of Christian ethics is also displayed clearly in Yoder's account of their basis. The historical character of the basis Yoder provides has already been indicated. He is clear that there is no "moral scratch" that can provide an ahistorical foundation for an ethic that may properly be called Christian. All people are historically located, and so he insists upon replacing a phenomenological search for a common morality with a view of morality that roots it in an historical community. The historical root of Christian ethics can only be the particular history of Jesus of Nazareth.[29]

His whole case rests upon a particular Christology: one that links the risen, ascended, and regnant Christ with the presentation of the life of Jesus to be found in the Gospels, particularly in that of St. Luke. The basis of Yoder's communal focus rests, as it were, on two pillars. One is the authority and power of the risen Christ who will come again in victory to judge and redeem. The other is the normative pattern of Jesus's life of suffering and death. As risen and victorious over the powers, Jesus is Lord of history; as normative pattern, he is head of the church.[30]

CHRIST AS LORD OF HISTORY

The goal of Christian ethics requires faithful obedience to Christ's teaching and the pattern of his life, and the essence of such obedience is the quest for peace and the acceptance of suffering. The goal does not allow adjustment to the present form of human society by means of one or another strategy for success. The question naturally arises as to how such a stringent ethic is to be justified, and how it is possible to live its fearful demands. Yoder's answer comes in a trenchant statement to the effect that the Christian witness to peace becomes both plausible and possible when viewed in the light of Christian eschatology.[31]

Yoder argues we now live in two aeons—two overlapping forms of history. In one aeon, the decisive one, Christ rules over the powers that still operate within the other. In Jesus's person and work, God's kingdom is in fact present. In his life, death, and resurrection, the powers that oppose the rule of God are

28. *CWS*, 5.
29. *PK*, 7, 4–44, 53–54.
30. *OR*, 62.
31. For Yoder's most concise statement of this point, see *OR*, 58–76.

defeated. On the cross, God's way of opposing evil becomes both visible and effective. The cross is not a defeat. Christ's death is "crowned by the miracle of resurrection and exaltation."[32] The ascended and glorified Christ now reigns over the powers. He does so not by eliminating them but by restraining their exercise of vengeance in ways that preserve order and give room for the growth and work of the church.

Christ's victory means that an essential change has taken place. The old aeon continues under the restraints imposed by providence, but now the new aeon and its way of life take precedence both in the sense that they are now operative in history and in the sense that they will be vindicated by the total victory of God over the powers when Christ returns in judgment and glory. Thus Yoder contends his ethic of nonresistance "is right in the deepest sense, not because it works, but because it anticipates the triumph of the Lamb that was slain."[33] Yoder makes a similar point in his later collection, *For the Nations*, though the emphasis here is less on the final victory of Christ than on his present ability to constrain the powers.

> It [the New Testament] teaches a coherent (though strange) cosmological vision whereby this world of faithful suffering can be understood. The apostles applied the words of Psalm 110: "The Lord said to my lord, sit at my hand until I make your enemies your footstool," to the ascension of Jesus Christ and his interim rule over the principalities and powers. That means that there are other patterns of power for change than the victory of the good guys. That the Crucified One is now "seated at the right hand of the Father" means that "he has the *whole* world in his hands," without its being in *our* hands. Thereby the apostles testified to their awareness of the patterned quality of the world, which is not a chaos but (even in its fallen state) a cosmos: created although fallen, yet not fallen out of God's hand, and brought under his control precisely by means of the cross.[34]

Christ then is Lord of history in a double sense. He is Lord who orders the powers by making use of their very violence to preserve an order in which the church can fulfill its mission. He is also Lord who will have a final and complete triumph at the second advent. It is this double sense of sovereignty that defines a new aeon and places disciples within what Yoder terms "the perfection of Christ"—a location that both calls and allows for a form of life that, through suffering obedience, bears witness to the victory of God in Christ.[35]

32. OR, 59.
33. OR, 64.
34. John Howard Yoder, *For the Nations: Essays Evangelical and Public* (Grand Rapids: Eerdmans, 1997), 137–38. Hereafter cited as *FN*.
35. CWS, 31–32.

Within "the perfection of Christ," Christians are able to see (and live) history doxologically—that is, in praise and thanksgiving. This doxological stance provides Christ's disciples with certain insights and strengths.[36] In particular, disciples are able to see beyond the limits of the social systems that constrain human ability to follow a different lead—one determined by the world's final destiny rather than the exigencies of the present. For this reason they can see that their role in history is not to control the world's political structures nor pastor the officials who manage them. Their role is "to persevere in celebrating the Lamb's lordship and in building the community shaped by that celebration."[37] In this activity they are to understand that they are participating in God's rule over the cosmos. Thus they know "that action is right which fits the shape of the Kingdom which Jesus announces, not from the righteous state of affairs our action promises to bring about." They know also that "moral being and behaving are primordially proclamation or celebration."[38]

Christ as Lord of the Church

As inhabitants of a new aeon, Christians become disciples of the ascended Lord who, one might say, creates space for faithful rather than compromised living. In this sense, Jesus is Lord of the church. Within the space created by the Lord of history, disciples are subject to the Lord of the church as participants in his suffering yet victorious life. The words "participate" and "participation" are of crucial importance to Yoder. He notes that the New Testament does not discuss the unity of Jesus with his Father in terms of *substance* but in terms of *will and deed*. Thus from the outset the notion of participation is given a moral rather than substantive meaning. At this point, Yoder's project oddly enough bears yet another resemblance to that of Rauschenbusch. In respect to Christology, both are children of the Enlightenment. In his seminary lectures, posthumously published as *Preface to Theology: Christology and Theological Method*, Yoder stresses the fact that we moderns do not think in terms of essence or substance.[39] Rather, we think in terms of history. Accordingly, Christ is best thought of not in metaphysical but in narrative terms—as a man, a social figure, a teacher, a moral exemplar. When, for example, we think of Christ's atoning work, we do well to "seek some relationship between atonement and his [Jesus's] discussions of the kingdom, his forgiving people,

---

36. See *RP*, 129–39.
37. *RP*, 130.
38. *RP*, 136.
39. John Howard Yoder, *Preface to Theology: Christology and Theological Method* (Grand Rapids: Brazos, 2002).

his making of people a church."⁴⁰ For Yoder this means that participatory obedience requires disciples to seek to address human "lostness" as Jesus did—namely, by respecting freedom and showing in their own lives the love of God seen in Jesus. This form of love does not compel but wins the human heart, on the one hand by refusal to meet evil with evil, and on the other by willingness to suffer.⁴¹

In *The Politics of Jesus* Yoder gives his most complete presentation of *participation* in the suffering and glorification of Jesus. In an extended exegesis of St. Luke's Gospel, Yoder seeks to demonstrate that Jesus's ethic was both political and practical and that his life and teaching were intended as examples to be imitated and followed by his disciples within the concrete affairs (political ones included) of daily life. Thus though his presentation of what it involves is quite different, Yoder, like Cassian and Rauschenbusch, offers an account of Christian living that is based upon the *imitation of Christ*.

Yoder presents Jesus as a highly political figure.⁴² At the annunciation of his birth, Jesus is termed both Son of God and Son of David who is to reign over Israel (Luke 1:32–33). Zechariah, father of John the Baptist, announces on behalf of the Holy Spirit that in Jesus God acts to redeem his people and save them from their enemies (1:68–75). Accordingly, Jesus's temptations are all political in nature—he is tempted to take a path marked out by the quest for power rather than the espousal of obedient suffering (4:1–12). Jesus's program is outlined in his first sermon. He is anointed (a term related to his kingship) to preach good news to the poor and proclaim release to the captives and liberty to the oppressed (4:18–19). Yoder contends that the reference in this sermon is to the Jubilee Year—a cyclical event in which the land was to be left fallow, debts remitted, slaves set free, and each person was to return to their family property.

In pursuit of these goals, Jesus calls into being a new social reality. The twelve apostles represent a reconstituted Israel in which distinctions based on power and wealth are to be eliminated (Luke 6:12). In founding this community, Jesus calls people away from family solidarities and into a community of commitment with a distinctive form of life. The feeding of the five thousand, which is coupled with the prediction of the passion, makes clear Jesus's redefinition of both the way of the Messiah and the way of God's people (9:1–22). God's Anointed is not a victorious king but a Suffering Servant who calls his disciples to share in both his service and his suffering.

40. Ibid., 307.
41. Ibid., 310–12.
42. For Yoder's account of Jesus's political significance and his political program, see *P of J*, 24–52.

The new form of life to which Jesus calls his disciples is a threat (in all ages) to the present order of society. Jesus, with full knowledge of what he is doing, nonetheless makes clear in his visit to the temple and his entry into Jerusalem both the nature of his vocation and his claim to authority over Israel (Luke 19:36–46). His last temptation is to renounce this messianic way of suffering and service and follow instead the quest for power (22:24–53). Jesus, however, obeys the voice of his Father in both will and deed. He dies, but he is raised and glorified. Jesus's disciples are called to share or participate in the same fate in both its humiliation and glorification. Yoder provides this summary of his position:

> Jesus was not just a moralist whose teachings had some political implications; he was not primarily a teacher of spirituality whose public ministry unfortunately was seen in a political light; he was not just a sacrificial lamb preparing for his immolation, or a God-Man whose divine status calls us to disregard his humanity. Jesus was, in his divinely mandated . . . prophethood, priesthood, and kingship, the bearer of a new possibility of human social, and therefore political relationships. His baptism is the inauguration and his cross is the culmination of that new regime in which his disciples are called to share.[43]

The call to make manifest the love of God made visible in Christ's life and death implies that, among disciples, unity of practice is as important as unity of faith and worship.[44] Christ is the norm of such communal obedience, but, Yoder goes on to say, the Spirit is the "guarantor of the possibility of discipleship."[45] In making this claim, Yoder adds pneumatology to Christology as a basis for his communal ethic. Christ, it would seem, exercises his lordship over the church in and through the Holy Spirit.

The question, of course, is in what fashion the Spirit facilitates Christ's rule over the common life of the church. Yoder's answer is through a process of dialogue in which unity and so also reconciliation are both sought and found.[46] In this process, the presence of the Holy Spirit is discernable by the presence of certain signs. The community is shaped by a pervasive desire for reconciliation and peace among its members. Every member of the community knows him- or herself to be the bearer of a particular charismatic gift that is to be exercised for the benefit of all. Accordingly, in gatherings of the church, everyone can take the floor and speak. There is to be no fixed order of sub- and

---

43. *P of J*, 52.
44. *RP*, 228.
45. *RP*, 228.
46. *RP*, 316–37.

superordination. In this process, the Holy Spirit guides the community so as to produce a common mind and effect reconciliation between people who might otherwise be divided. This final step Yoder terms "binding and loosing"—a communal act that both charts the common practice of the community and effectively forgives the sins that threaten its unity and integrity.

If one reviews Yoder's corpus, it is clear that there are three elements to his account of Christ as Lord of the church. One is the love of God the Father in sending his Son to reconcile the world to God by the acceptance of suffering and death. Another is the obedient pattern of the Son's life and death in which believers are called to participate. Yet another is the presence of the Holy Spirit within the common life of the church—a presence that makes possible the participation of the church both in the love of the Father and in the obedience of the Son. In a formal sense, therefore, one can say that the basis of Yoder's ecclesial ethic of discipleship is trinitarian.

However, the nature and work of the Father and the Spirit receive scant attention. In contrast to the extensive christological discussion, the nature and work of the First and Third persons of the Trinity become in fact peripheral to Yoder's account of the basis of Christian ethics. As a result, the reader is often left with the impression that, as Jesus is to be understood by will and deed rather than by a substantial relation to God the Father that might come through the presence of the Spirit, so also disciples are to be understood in similar moral terms as people who have aligned their will with that of Jesus. Consequently, their participation in the life of the Son seems at times, in an almost univocal sense, moral. It seems as if "insight" gained through a grasp of Christian eschatology, rather than divine presence in the life of the believer (and that of the church), is what makes discipleship possible. In short, one wonders if, in the end, Yoder's ethic rests not in a trinitarian economy wherein God the Father sends both the Son and the Spirit to reconcile the world but in the intellect and will of believers who have decided to take Jesus as a norm for their behavior.

The Character of Life in Christ according to John Howard Yoder

The procedural nature of Yoder's description of the common life of the church that appears in his account of "binding and loosing" provides a convenient window through which to view his depiction of the character or visible form of Christian ethics. Before that process is described in detail, however, the most dominant themes of Yoder's account of Christian living must be brought to the fore. Not surprisingly, the goal of the process of binding and loosing is one with the goal of Christian living itself—namely, a witness to God's purpose to reconcile all people both to God and to one another. In the Sermon on the Mount, Jesus makes clear that his ethic is one of perfect love that imitates the love of God shown in Christ.[47] Love of this sort is most clearly manifest in the treatment of an enemy. If love for one's enemy is the first characteristic of a Christian ethic, a desire for reconciliation is the second. The Sermon on the Mount above all stresses the duty to seek reconciliation with anyone with whom one may exist in a state of enmity.[48] A desire for reconciliation, if it is genuine, is accompanied by willingness to forgive wrongs done. The duty to seek reconciliation and to forgive stands also behind the next characteristic of Christian living—the prohibition against killing. It is this prohibition that provides both a "mirror and a means" for fellowship with God.[49] Pacifism is a mirror that reflects the way in which God addresses human enmity. It is a means, a way of life, that brings about participation in Christ's life and so his relation with God. Speaking of the Sermon on the Mount, Yoder writes,

> We have only observed the wider framework of Jesus's moral teaching: its dependence on the coming of the kingdom in His person and work; its expectation of novelty, of miracle, of visible witness; its derivation from the unqualified love of God; its unity of motive and deed. Seen in this light the love of neighbor, even the unqualified love of the neighbor, including the enemy, to the point of readiness to suffer unjustly at his hands, appears not only understandable but possible; not only possible but the most appropriate testimony to the nature of God's love and His kingdom.[50]

Yoder insists that all strands of the New Testament, and not the Sermon on the Mount alone, testify to the centrality of suffering and nonviolence for Christians. Indeed, he contends that the "new thing" in the "new aeon" is the rejection of force and self-defense as pragmatic means for ensuring human safety and furthering communal and individual interests.[51] The great temptation that stands before Christians is precisely that which Christ faced—the temptation to meet evil on its own terms.

What then are the chief characteristics of a Christian ethic? Love expressed as a desire for reconciliation with one's enemy, willingness to forgive, and an accompanying renunciation of violence that shows willingness to suffer at the

47. OR, 47–49.
48. OR, 50–51.
49. OR, 50–51.
50. OR, 52.
51. OR, 60–61.

hands of one's enemy for the sake of a faithful witness to God's love and as an expression of one's own love.

Yoder paints Christian ethics as a love ethic modeled after the chief characteristics of Christ's life. These characteristics present believers with several challenges. Love is defined in the first instance rather narrowly as a desire for reconciliation, a willingness to forgive, a renunciation of violence, and a willingness to suffer. These characteristics are to color one's relation to believers and nonbelievers alike. They are of particular significance, however, for defining the relation between one Christian and another. Christians cannot bear credible witness to the peace that God seeks if they do not live at peace among themselves. If they are to be faithful participants in Christ's suffering, they must have in place among themselves a "reconciling process"—one that concludes with what Yoder, following Matthew 18, calls "binding and loosing." In his description of this process, several other characteristics of Yoder's account of Christian living appear.

How, within a voluntary community of disciples, each of whom stands on an equal footing with all others, is peace to be maintained? How are differences of opinion, personal enmities, grudges, and selfishness to be overcome? Only, says Yoder, if the community has in place a reconciling process built upon conversation rather than coercion. Summarizing Matthew 18, he writes,

> The conversation takes place in a context of a commitment to forgive.... The deliberative process begins with only the two parties to the conflict being involved. The conflict is broadened only gradually, and only so far as is needed to achieve reconciliation. The tests of the validity of the process are procedural, having to do with hearing of several witnesses, subject to correction and change over time.[52]

Yoder believes that every element of this procedure for resolving conflict or confronting disobedience is relevant to the way in which the church in all ages ought to form its common life. Neither casuistry nor the application of moral rules can lead on its own to a godly outcome. Rather, the right decision or outcome must be determined in the course of a conversation. It must be placed in a communal context of discernment.

In this process, the various gifts present in the community will come to the fore, each making its own unique contribution to the formation of a common mind and practice. The people having these gifts will become agents of communal unity and peace in various ways.[53] There are those who will appear as "agents of direction." Agents of direction act as prophets who interpret the

---

52. *PK*, 27.
53. *PK*, 28–40.

situation of the community before God. The members of the community in turn refer the prophetic judgments to established communal practice in order to test their adequacy. There are also those who aid the community as "agents of memory." Agents of memory are compared to scribes who interpret Holy Scripture and carry the memory of past acts of faithfulness and failure. In their enterprise of interpretation and memory, "agents of linguistic self-consciousness" also help members of the community. These are people who watch for verbal tricks and feats of rhetoric that might lead people astray. Finally, there are "agents of order and due process." These people serve as "elders" who act to ensure that the deliberations of the community in fact compose an "open process" wherein each member of the community is allowed to contribute to common resolution of the issues confronting its members.

Out of this process of open deliberation comes a communal act of "binding and loosing," a rabbinic term used by Matthew to refer to a decision to withhold fellowship or to forgive, to make something either obligatory or nonobligatory.[54] These judgments can concern either community belief and practice or the particular conduct of an individual. Yoder's summary statement about the process is as follows.

> We have here then a kind of situation ethics, i.e., a procedure for doing practical moral reasoning, in a context of conflict, right in the situation where divergent views are being lived out in such a way as to cause offense. This rejects a rigid automatic casuistic deduction on the one hand and individualism or pluralism on the other. The obedience of the brother or sister is my business. There is no hesitancy in using the word "sin"; yet the intention of the procedure is reconciliation, not exclusion or even reprimand. Out of this utterly personal exchange comes the confirmation (or perchance the modification) of the rules of the community, which can therefore be spoken of, with the technical language of the rabbis, as having "bound" or "loosed."[55]

Analysis of the process leading to binding and loosing reveals another element in Yoder's portrayal of the character of Christian ethics. The process by which the community reaches decisions faithful to the way of Christ displays three additional features of love—truthfulness, equality, and mutual subjection. Love demands that in the process of discernment, each speaks the truth as he or she sees it. Love also demands that there be no fixed hierarchies among God's people, and it requires that God's people become subject one to another in a way that allows them to receive the particular gift of each member of

54. PK, 26; RP, 327.
55. PK, 27.

the community. In these three additional ways, faithful disciples imitate the way of Jesus. He spoke the truth as God gave him to see it, and he subjected himself to the will of his Father and to the welfare of God's people. He also taught that each was to be the servant of his or her brothers and sisters and that, within the kingdom of God, no one was to lord it over another.[56]

One may fairly say by way of summary that the character of the common life of the church is the vehicle for its witness to the world of God's will for the world. Thus Yoder makes this bold statement about the relation between ethics and mission.

> The political novelty that God brings into the world is a community of those who serve instead of ruling, who suffer instead of inflicting suffering, whose fellowship crosses social lines instead of reinforcing them. This new Christian community in which the walls are broken down not by human idealism or democratic legalism but by the work of Christ is not only a vehicle of the gospel, or only a fruit of the gospel; it is the good news.[57]

This paragraph displays the full extent of what he means by participation in the perfection of Christ. The character of the common life of the church is almost an extension of the incarnation, wherein the salvation of the world becomes a synergistic work carried out by both Christ and the church. Yoder is careful to say that such a cooperative venture is made possible only by grace and the presence of the Holy Spirit.[58] Nonetheless, he insists that the power given to the church is "parallel to that given to Jesus."[59] The church is in fact commissioned to act on Jesus's behalf. As the Father sends Jesus, so Jesus sends the church. As the Father gives Jesus authority to forgive sins, so Jesus gives the same authority to the church.

Concluding Comments

To say the least, Yoder's account of Christian ethics is both bold and consistent. The focus of Christian ethics is the common life of the church. This focus is made clear in Yoder's account of the goal, basis, and character of the ethic he depicts. The goal is witness to a new possibility for human life to be found within the perfection of Christ. The basis of this possibility is the life, death, resurrection, and ascension of Jesus, who manifests this new possibility in his

---

56. *FN*, 31–33.
57. *RP*, 91.
58. *RP*, 316–20.
59. *RP*, 330.

life of suffering obedience. The character of Christian ethics is to be found in the form of the church's common life wherein relations are shaped by the imitation of Christ. This imitation is encompassed by love—love that requires a desire for reconciliation, willingness to forgive, willingness to suffer, renunciation of violence, relations based on mutual subjection, and truthful speech.

What is one to make of an account of Christian living that amounts to a frontal attack on the ethical focus of so much contemporary Christian moral thought? Objections will come from all directions. Advocates of "spirituality" will bristle at Yoder's emphasis on communal discipline. Defenders of a more socially involved version of the gospel will criticize his view of the relation between church and society as too accepting of the structures of injustice that now shape public life.

There is indeed room to criticize Yoder's views, but the standard criticisms will, in the end, prove far less effective than many now believe. For one thing, Yoder casts his account of the focus of Christian ethics within an eschatological perspective that has more biblical support than the positions the champions of either virtue ethics or a social gospel can muster. The chief weakness in the writings of John Cassian and Walter Rauschenbusch is a misreading of biblical eschatology. In the case of John Howard Yoder, however, eschatology, despite certain difficulties in his presentation, proves the most convincing part of his work. Christ's victory through suffering and his ascension to the right hand of God both create a space for living an extraordinarily stringent ethic and provide hope for the vindication of suffering obedience despite all indications to the contrary. Further, as will become apparent, his account of the goal of Christian ethics (witness) seems far closer to the biblical witness than either personal sanctification or social reform.

The weaknesses in this account of life in Christ arise, as I have suggested, from an inadequate Christology, an inadequate doctrine of the Trinity, and an incomplete and sometimes distorted account of the character of Christian ethics. His work also suffers from an overdrawn distinction between living within the perfection of Christ and living as a member of civil society. In making a very important point, Yoder creates, I believe, too much distance between the common life of the church and life within the body politic. There are two reasons for saying this.

The first has to do with the relation of believers to divine providence. If life within the perfection of Christ is made possible by the grace and love of God, so also is life within political society. God's love is shed abroad both by preserving life until his purposes for creation are fulfilled and by creating new possibilities for life within the common life of his people. Political order that makes possible civil peace and ecclesial order that provides the setting for new birth and new life are both the work of divine providence. If both are the work of providence and both are expressions of divine love, does the use of force to defend one's neighbor simply cancel out the witness of the church to the new possibilities for life that now exist within "the perfection of Christ"? Supporters of just war theory reasonably and faithfully believe that it does not. They hold that, in cases of armed conflict, life within the perfection of Christ spills over into the political sphere in ways that both allow for defense of their neighbor and limit what can rightly be done in doing so. In short, Christians can reasonably and faithfully hold that both providence and neighbor-love render permeable the membrane that separates life within political society and life within the perfection of Christ.

The second has to do with the characterization of life within political society and life within the perfection of Christ. They are not as different one from another as Yoder suggests. Both are filled with conflict. Both have a need to seek reconciliation between warring parties, and both must resort to disciplinary measures to ensure their integrity and good order. To say that Christians live within the perfection of Christ is an eschatological statement about what will be but is now only imperfectly visible and indeed even possible. Yoder's discussion of "binding and loosing" assumes this to be the case. True, in one instance discipline may involve excommunication and in the other execution. There is indeed a difference, but it is not absolute. St. Paul, for example, may well have believed that expulsion from the church of a man who is sleeping with his father's wife would result in the man's death (1 Cor. 5:1–5, 9–13). For the time being at least, it appears that love's expression is necessarily refracted through the contours of the circumstances in which it is to be expressed. It appears also that the contours of life within and outside the perfection of Christ are more similar than Yoder allows.

These comments bring to an end my presentation of the three foci of Christian ethics. Their presentation, though perhaps in some ways clarifying, nonetheless leaves one with a basic question. How does each of these options in respect to the focus of Christian ethics appear when viewed through the lens of the biblical witness? Of course, each focus is presented as having its basis in the Bible. What requires testing is the adequacy of that presentation.

PART TWO

A Prismatic Case

THE EPISTLE
TO THE EPHESIANS

4

The Goal and Basis of Life Together in Christ

A Reading of the Epistle to the Ephesians (Part One)

The Goal of Life Together in Christ

Does one or another of the three options for the focus of Christian ethics receive the support of Holy Scripture? A close reading of the relevant New Testament texts establishes that the focus is properly the common life of the church rather than the sanctification of individuals or the redemption and reform of a corrupt social order. This contention is based in the first instance upon a reading of a central New Testament text, the Letter to the Ephesians. Once more, the focus of this account of life in Christ becomes clear once one asks, (1) what is the goal of life in Christ, (2) what is the basis of life in Christ, and (3) what is the character of life in Christ?

What is the goal of Christian ethics as portrayed in Ephesians? Ephesians 4:1 provides a key for understanding the letter as a whole. The verse reads: "I, therefore, a prisoner on the Lord's behalf beg you to walk in a way worthy of the calling to which you have been called" (my translation). The question, of course, is what exactly constitutes the calling of the church and what, practically speaking, does that calling imply about the worthiness of believers? As the author of Ephesians sees things, the church is to be the "place" in which

God's purpose for the entire creation begins to come to fruition. Ephesians 1:9–11 speaks with remarkable boldness.

> For he has made known to us the secret of his will in accordance with his purpose which he set forth in him [Christ] for administering [εἰς οἰκονομίαν] the fullness of the ages so as to sum up all things in Christ, things in the heavens and things on the earth in him.[1]

The author's thought can be paraphrased in this way. In Christ, God has made known his eternal purpose for the creation. That purpose is to unify all things (the earth, humankind, and the powers that dwell in the heavens) in Christ, and so bring them under the rule of God. This purpose stands "before" the foundation of the world, but until the present, it has remained a secret. However, at the beginning of the last age, the one ushered in by the life, death, resurrection, and ascension of Christ, it has been made known. Further, God has revealed not only that the last age is ushered in by Christ but also that it is to be "administered" by Christ in a way that makes the summing up, the unity, and the purposes visible.

It should be noted that in presenting the purposes of God in this manner, the author of Ephesians offers an interpretation of God's relation to Israel that is rooted firmly in the Old Testament witness. His interpretation of the Law and the Prophets brings to light what he understands to be their true meaning—a meaning that until the coming of Christ lay hidden within the Holy Scriptures. The true meaning of Israel's existence lies within God's administration of the ages of the world. Israel is to be the people out of all the peoples who belong to God in a special way. Israel is God's portion among the nations and its destiny is to be the people through whom God draws not only the nations, but also the entire creation back to himself. It is Christ who fulfills Israel's destiny, and the life of Christ's body, the church, is continuous with that of Israel.

The goal of the entire creation is unity in God's Son. Given the extraordinary expanse of this purpose, the assertion found in Ephesians 1:22–23 is arresting. The arena in which God's plan for the world now unfolds is small rather than large. It is in God's assembly, the church, rather than in an empire, that Christ's administration of the divine purpose first becomes visible. The primary expression of that administration is depicted in Ephesians 2:11–22, wherein the most basic act of Christ's administration is said to be reconciliation between Jew and gentile. These two solidarities (God's people and the peoples of the earth) comprise the two classes into which all humankind is

---

1. I am in large measure indebted to Andrew Lincoln for this translation. See Andrew Lincoln, *Ephesians*, Word Biblical Commentary 42 (Dallas: Word, 1990), 9–35.

divided. Their unity is the first step toward the unification of all things, both on earth and in heaven. By reconciling Jew and gentile, God establishes his assembly (ἡ ἐκκλησία), the church, in a new way—one in which both Jew and gentile compose God's people. The calling of this people is to be distinguished from that of the rest of humankind, who are not united with Christ (2:3).

The unity of Jew and gentile has been brought about not through the law, which cannot save, but by the sacrifice of Christ, which can (Eph. 2:13, 16). The result of Christ's atoning work is not only that Jew and gentile together have access in the Spirit to one God and Father (2:18) but also that the gentiles, who once lived without access to God's covenants with Israel and so also without the promises that were attached to those covenants, are no longer strangers to God's covenants and promises. They are no longer (at best) foreigners and resident aliens among God's people (2:12). Rather, gentile believers are now united with Jewish believers in such a way that they can be called "fellow citizens" with them and members of the same household—namely, that of the one God who is now Father to them both (2:19). This household can also be described as a structure founded on the apostles and prophets. The capstone of the structure is Christ. The gentiles have, as it were, been built into this structure, and (with their inclusion) the structure has been joined together in such a way that it grows in Christ so as to become God's holy temple, the place God lives on earth through the presence of his Spirit (2:20–22). The same Spirit now dwells in Jew and gentile alike. It serves both as a mark of their ownership by God and as a guarantee that they are jointly God's adopted children, and so also heirs of the one God who is the Father of both (1:13).

Because of its central importance in the display of God's purpose, this passage warrants even further scrutiny. When the passage is viewed against the backdrop of the collective representations of the period, a vision of the calling of the church appears that is even more encompassing than the brief exposition above suggests. The central phrases used to refer to the church track the effect of belief in Christ upon what might be called the "socio-logic" of the Hellenistic world. They track this logic in a way that draws the social constructions of ancient society into God's purposes for the church rather than in a way that categorizes the church as but an aspect of these very constructions.[2] If one looks at the relation between these phrases—fellow citizens, members of a household, and holy temple in the Lord—the meaning of the above statement immediately becomes clear.

---

2. The analysis that follows relies heavily upon that of Reinhard Hütter. See, e.g., Reinhard Hütter, *Suffering Divine Things: Theology as Church Practice* (Grand Rapids: Eerdmans, 1997), 160–64. See also John Milbank, *Theology and Social Theory: Beyond Secular Reason* (Oxford: Blackwell, 1990), 364–69.

Fellow citizens are citizens of a single city. Fellow members of a household belong to a family grouping under the authority of God who is Father of all (Eph. 4:5b). In antiquity, the city and the house constituted two solidarities. City and house defined on the one hand public and on the other private spheres of existence. They provided identity to their members, but these identities, as Greek drama so painfully shows, could conflict on occasion, with tragic results. The city was thought of as a circumscribed space (it had walls) within which a citizenry could act together for common purpose. The city was contrasted to an open space whose lack of definition rendered coactivity far more difficult and less extensive. Walls, however, were not the most basic determinant of the identity of a city. A city was defined primarily by the purpose for which it existed and by the laws that served its collective purpose. In accord with its purpose and under the constraint of its laws, the citizens of a city, among whom slaves, women, and children were not counted, freely acted upon a public stage. The household was a different kettle of fish altogether. Women, slaves, and children were members along with adult males. However, one's place within the household was not determined on the basis of free activity as was one's place in the city. Rather, one's place in the household was determined by a fixed system of relations governed by a head.

The passage cited above indicates that the writer of this letter, in his attempt to understand the purpose of the church within God's providence, found it useful to employ terms present also within Hellenistic social and political terminology. On the one hand, by calling the saints fellow citizens, he presented the church as a public, "political" body drawn together from all the peoples of the earth and ruled over by the one true God. On the other hand, he found it necessary to call members of the church a single household because, in Christ, he knew God to be an adopting Father who had made the saints, along with Christ, heirs to all that is his. The two characterizations (fellow citizens and members of a single household) display different aspects of God's relation to his people. To make the precise nature of the relationship clear, however, it was necessary to transform the meaning commonly attached to each categorization so that each displayed clearly the nature of the unity it is God's purpose to bring about. Thus in calling members of the church "fellow citizens," it had to be made clear that, in Christ, women, children, slaves, Jews, and gentiles were all to be included as free citizens within God's public gathering in a way that they were not included in the city. In terming the saints members of God's household, it had to be made clear that the fixed order of the particular households in which Christians lived was to be transformed by a form of "mutual subjection" that imitated Christ's subjection to God the Father, who is head of a larger household, the church, which includes all the little households in which Christians live and carry on their daily lives (Eph. 5:1; 5:21–6:9).

Christ's administration of the fullness of time as depicted in Ephesians 1:9 thus has a public, political, and social form. He calls together God's assembly both as a household and as a citizenry. He has been designated both head of the house and ruler of the city. It is not difficult to see why Christ's administration of the fullness of time is next said to have built this people together in such a way that they can be termed a holy temple in the Lord. The idea of the church as a temple flows naturally enough from the notion of the church as God's household. The earthly sanctuary in which God is present is often called "the house of God" in the Septuagint. Similar usage can be found throughout the New Testament.[3] Thus, if the church is God's household, it is reasonable to view it also as God's temple, the place of God's residence.

Depiction of the church as the place of God's residence on earth is yet another way to represent God's purpose for the creation—one rooted in Israel's piety and in the visions of the prophets. Psalm 47 pictures YHWH Elyon as king over all the earth who has subdued the nations. It goes on to portray the princes of the nations assembling along with God's people to worship YHWH in either Jerusalem or Samaria. The prophets Isaiah and Micah also have a vision of the nations flowing toward Zion to be instructed by YHWH (Isa. 2:2–4; Mic. 4:1–3). Ezekiel sees the rebuilt temple as the source once more of the rivers of paradise that bring abundance and healing to the land (Ezek. 47:1–12). The presence of God in Zion and in his temple thus both establishes his rule over the nations and renews the creation. In short, the vision of the church as the temple from which God establishes his rule and unites all things in his Son summarizes and fulfills the Old Testament's witness to God's purpose.

Unity occupies no minor place in the providential governance of God. The blessing with which the letter begins (Eph. 1:3–14) deploys God's name in its fully trinitarian form, and it does so in order to display forcefully the entire scope of God's purpose. It is thus God the Father who, before the foundation of the world, destines both the Jewish and gentile members of the church for adoption as "sons" and "heirs" and assigns them their calling within his providential purposes (1:4–6). It is through the Son that the Father reveals his purpose. It is through the Son also that the Father establishes the conditions by means of which his purpose can be fulfilled. That is, through his death, God's elect, both Jew and Greek, have redemption and forgiveness. Together these create conditions of peace and so also of unity (cf. 2:13–14). Finally,

---

3. See, e.g., Mark 2:26; 11:17; cf. Isa. 56:7; 60:7 LXX.

those who are "in Christ" have been "marked off" as the Father's own children by the Spirit, and by the same Spirit have been given a foretaste of or down payment on the inheritance that will be theirs when God's purposes are fully realized (1:13–14).

Given the deployment of God's full name, and given the emphasis upon the steadfast and majestic nature of God's purposes for his adopted children, it is not surprising that in Ephesians 4:3 the author uses a participial phrase that has the force of an imperative to appeal to his readers to make "every effort to preserve the unity of the Spirit in the bond of peace."[4] Behind this appeal lies the entire purpose of the Triune God in history. God's good name and God's eternal purpose are bound up with the sort of life lived by those whom he has called and adopted.

This life is one of unity, and as we have seen in Ephesians 2:19–22, the author employs a wide range of imagery—political, domestic, and religious (fellow citizens with the saints, members of the household of God, and a holy temple in the Lord)—to emphasize the extraordinary and complete unity for which Jew and gentile together (in the Lord) are to strive. To strengthen his appeal, he links these images with two others that are even more comprehensive and more pointed. Christ's reconciling act is done, he says, so that through it God might create (in Christ) a new humankind or, if you will, a new Adam. This new humankind is not divided as are the peoples of the earth, and so in Christ, Jew and gentile, as the new Adam, can be said to be "one body" (2:15–16). Here, the author pushes back behind the witness of the Psalms and the prophets and anchors God's unifying purpose in the primeval history of humankind. Echoes of the story of the scattering of humankind after the transgressions of Adam, Eve, and Cain, and the subsequent call of Abraham sound loudly.

A new humankind, one body, a commonwealth, fellow citizens, members of a single household, children of one God and Father, those who share one Spirit and one inheritance, the temple of the Lord—the images of unity cascade one after another! Standing back for but a moment, one can say without forcing the evidence that according Ephesians, from "before" the creation of the world God has had a clear purpose for his creation. That purpose is to unite all things created in Christ. This unity has its center in Christ and God's elected people who were chosen or picked out "before" the creation of the world (Eph. 1:4) to live in a way that redounds to God's glory, thus eliciting the praise of God from the remainder of humankind and indeed the entire created order (1:12; 3:9–11). The chief calling of the church is then to

---

4. For this translation see Lincoln, *Ephesians*, 237.

manifest the unity God intends in its common life. In this way, through the peace God has brought about by Christ's sacrifice (2:14–16), God's glory will be perceived and praised by the peoples of the earth. There will then be one God and Father of all. Through this divinely wrought unity, the entire creation will be caught up in the blessing God desires to bestow.

For a number of reasons, it is not uncommon to pass over the link Ephesians makes between the fulfillment of God's purpose, the perception of God's glory, and the common life of God's assembly. To do so, however, is to miss the central point the letter makes about the goal of the common life of the church. The members of God's assembly have been chosen "before the foundation of the world" to be "holy and blameless" before God "in love" (Eph. 1:4–5). The grace bestowed in Christ engenders love, and love in turn elicits praise. Indeed, the destiny of those who make up the assembly is to live for the praise of God's glory (1:12). The idea seems to be that the love manifest in the sacrifice of Christ and imitated in the common life of the saints (5:1–2) shows forth God's grace and glory and so manifests God's majesty to the entire creation. This manifestation in both the sacrifice of Christ and the life of the church draws all things to God and restores the unity of creation. Conversely, by implication, failure to walk in love brings not honor but shame upon God's name—and this leads God to take action that will clear his name.

This last remark calls for further comment. To this point, unity in Christ has been presented as the goal or purpose of the church. That goal must now be qualified by noting that an even deeper purpose for life together in Christ has appeared during the course of this investigation. The common life of the assembly is to be one that manifests God's glory and so calls forth the praise of the one true God on the part of the whole creation. It can be said that unity in Christ is a good ancillary to the recognition on the part of the peoples of the earth of God's glory "in, with, and under" his work of unification.

The point is not unimportant, for it serves as a check on making the purpose of Christian ethics subservient to some form of self-determined human flourishing. To say that the most basic goal of Christian ethics is the glorification of God is not to say that human good plays no part in its intentionality—only that such good is subservient to a greater good upon which it in fact depends and apart from which God becomes at best an adjunct to human purposes. It is also the case that promotion of God's glory as the basis of Christian ethics raises a negative and fearful possibility. Failure to live in a way that glorifies God opens the possibility that the church will fail to fulfill the purpose for which it has been called into being.

Given the divided state of the churches and, in the West, their increasingly marginal social place, what is one to make of such a vision and such a claim? It is tempting to look upon this account of the calling of the church as at best a pious hope. Indeed, one might even make a case for saying that, given the intractability of denominational divisions, it would be better to recognize the limits these divisions present and for the denominations to get on as best they can with their own particular forms of ecclesial life and ministry. In short, it might be best to view the possibilities of the church through a "postlapsarian" lens similar to the one used by Christian realists to view the state, and so settle for divisions, though amicable ones, as the best that can be achieved within the limits of a fallen world. Or it may seem wiser to adopt the point of view of postmodern "pluralism" and take a positive view of church division as adding to the richness of Christian belief and practice.

It would appear that precisely this latter strategy has been in fact adopted within in the modern ecumenical movement.[5] In 1967 the World Council of Churches issued the Bristol Report, which drew a parallel between the divisions among the churches and the variety of texts and meaning to be found in the Bible itself. In 1971 the same council issued a paper that openly tied the work of the Holy Spirit to granting authority to diverse interpretations of Holy Scripture within different churches. Here we have nothing less than a pneumatic approval of Christian division rooted in contemporary notions of pluralism.

Nevertheless, given the dominant place God's purpose of unity occupies not only in Ephesians but also in the biblical narrative as a whole, one must wonder at the probity of such a compromising settlement. It would, of course, most certainly be false to say that "unity" is the only way in which the purposes of God, as portrayed in Holy Scripture, can be described. But it is also certainly the case that "unity" provides an extraordinarily inclusive way of describing those purposes — one that receives ample support from a wide range of scriptural texts.

---

5. For documentation of this claim, see Ephraim Radner, *The End of the Church: A Pneumatology of Christian Division in the West* (Grand Rapids: Eerdmans, 1998), 22-25. Radner notes that, as early as 1950, Jean-Jacques von Allmen warned that the ecumenical movement would be confronted by three grave temptations. In Radner's words,

> The first temptation leads to the conclusion that ecclesial unity is a kind of "edenic" state imaged in the first apostolic community, but abandoned almost just as quickly as the church began to engage in the struggles and compromises of the real world. Such a vision of ecclesial "falling" from visible catholicity may lead to a second temptation, which is to view the fulfillment of Christian unity as something to be accomplished by God's grace at the end times.... Finally, and where both these two first temptations lead in terms of attitude, there is the sense of "fatalism that simply recognizes the intractability of our present Christian distinctions and differences, leaving their ultimate sense to God's inscrutable working." (4-5)

In a monograph written at the close of the Second World War, Stig Hanson notes that the theme of unity provides one of the strongest links between the way in which Christians view both the beginning and end of history. "That which is characteristic of the biblical conception of unity," he says, "is its *eschatological* character, i.e., that an original unity is thought of as having been broken, and only by the intervention of God in Christ shall be restored at the end of time."[6] In short, God's providential governance of the world with the purpose of restoring its unity provides a major, if not the major, thread that ties together the entire biblical narrative. Given the Bible's testimony to the importance of unity within the providence of God, it is difficult simply to settle for the divisions of the church as if they have in some way become "approved by God." Further, given that the goal of life in Christ is the unity of all things, it is difficult to escape the conclusion that the primary focus of Christian ethics, as presented by the author of Ephesians, is the common life of the church as it is lived to glorify God.

The Basis of Life Together in Christ

The same focus of attention appears if one inquires after the basis of life in Christ. It is well to note at the outset that the basis of the unity to which Ephesians testifies is certainly quite different from that most commonly imagined and sought in the classical and Hellenistic worlds. For the unity of the world according to the Old and New Testaments does not reside, as among the Ionian natural philosophers, in an original substance; nor, as with the Pythagoreans, in an underlying harmony of parts; nor, as with the Stoics, in a universal structure of reason. Neither does the Bible conceive of the unity of creation as organic. The world is not compared to a body. Rather, the idea of unity encountered in the Bible is properly "political" in that it is based in the rule of God. As Hanson contends, "It is a question of God and God's will. The world being a unity means, from a Jewish viewpoint, everything in the world conforming to the will of the Creator. The personal relationship between God and the world, especially mankind, is thus characteristic of the Jewish idea of unity."[7]

The unity (and so the peace and fruitfulness) of creation depends upon the rule of God. Unity is "politically" rather than "metaphysically" conceived.[8]

---

6. Stig Hanson, *The Unity of the Church in the New Testament: Colossians and Ephesians* (Stockholm: Almqvist & Wiksell, 1946), 3.

7. I owe this summary of the way in which the biblical notion of unity is distinguished from various others to Stig Hanson. See ibid., 7.

8. I am aware that some might object that I have given insufficient attention to the kingdom of God as the goal of Christian ethics. I note only that it would be a mistake to place unity and

The author of Ephesians was most certainly a Jew, and in respect to this matter he thought like a Jew. The basis of the unity of all things is the rule that God has established through the death and resurrection of Christ. The course of the argument by which the author makes his case is not sequential, but it does hang together. He locates God's unifying purpose first in a sovereign choice made by God before the foundation of the world. The choice is to adopt those who will become members of God's assembly as children and so heirs. As obedient children of God, those adopted are to live a holy and blameless life in the presence of their Father. The holy and blameless life for which the saints have been marked out beforehand is a life of love (Eph. 1:4–6, 11–12), and what might be called the final purpose of this life, as already noted, is to evoke the praise of God's grace, presumably on the part of the entire creation (1:9–10; 3:1–11). It seems adequate to say that God's eternal purpose is for the entire creation to find its unity in the praise of God's glory, and that election of Israel and so also of the church is the point at which the counsel of God's will for the creation begins to take effect (1:11–12).

The ultimate basis of the unity of all things in Christ is the eternal purpose of God who accomplishes all things "according the counsel of his will" (Eph. 1:11). The unity of all things has a penultimate basis, however, in Christ's sacrificial death. It is the death of Christ that actually procures for believers both redemption from their bondage to the powers that oppose God's rule and the forgiveness of their trespasses and sins (Eph. 1:7; 2:1, 13). The saving efficacy of Christ's death is made manifest in the power by which he is raised from the dead and seated at the right hand of God. The right hand clearly designates both the place of power within the commonwealth ruled by God and the place of honor reserved for the firstborn son who is to inherit from the head of the household (1:20). Christ, vindicated by God through the resurrection, has been given a position far above that of any ruler or patriarch within the created order. However, he exercises this authority in a most immediate way within God's assembly (1:22–23).[9] Indeed, in ascending to the right hand of

---

the kingdom of God in opposition. It seems clear that the kingdom of God is best depicted as that state in which the rule of God brings unity to the creation because in the kingdom God rules his creation fully.

9. There is some dispute about how to translate the dative form of *hē ekklēsia* that appears in Ephesians 1:22. It can mean "for the church," the dative here being used to indicate to or for whom something is done. For this view, see Lincoln, *Ephesians*, 66–72. M. Barth argues, on the contrary, that the dative here should here be taken to mean that Christ's rule over all things makes him also head of the church. See M. Barth, *Ephesians: Introduction, Translation, and Commentary on Chapters 1–3* (Garden City, NY: Doubleday, 1974), 156–57. In the first instance God's actions in putting all things under Christ are for the benefit of the church. In the second interpretation, God's subordination of all things sets the stage for stating that Christ is also

God the Father, Christ appears as a conqueror that, in triumphal procession, distributes the fruits of his conquest to the citizens of the commonwealth (4:8).

Mention of the gifts distributed by the triumphant Christ suggests a third basis for the unity God purposes. The quotation from Psalm 68 that appears in Ephesians 4:8 ("when he ascended on high he led a host of captives . . .") indicates that the saints now share in Christ's rule over all things, and that they are being showered with gifts that equip them to participate in God's work of unity. What is the nature of this participation? If Christ has died and has been raised and seated in the heavenly places, so also have those who, upon hearing the announcement of his victory, by grace believe (2:4–10). What does it mean to say that the saints are now seated with Christ in the heavenly places (2:6)? The author means two things. In the first instance, the saints are seated with Christ because Christ is fully representative of God's people. When he ascends, so do all those who are represented in him. As such, they now share the authority over all things that Christ exercises from God's right hand. In the second instance, they are seated with him because they have received the Holy Spirit. In the Spirit, believers are connected in an immediate and living way to the ascended and regnant Christ. The Spirit links them immediately with Christ as he sits upon his throne in the heavenly places. This connection marks them as Christ's adopted siblings (1:13). As such, they now enjoy an initial distribution of their share in Christ's inheritance—one that serves as a guarantee of a full share that will come when God's purpose is fully accomplished (1:14).

It is the real connection through the Spirit between Christ and the saints that gives meaning to the frequently repeated phrase "in Christ." As is often pointed out, "in Christ" on many occasions merely indicates the means of Christ's agency. However, in this particular passage, where the phrase appears no less than eleven times, it clearly refers as well to a sphere in which people exist. Consequently, the author can assert that "in Christ" the saints have been blessed "with every spiritual blessing in the heavenly places" (Eph. 1:3). The sphere in which Christ rules is the sphere in which they now participate. Chief among the blessings that come from participation in the sphere of Christ's rule is the seal or mark of the Holy Spirit, which guarantees that believers are indeed full members of God's household and so also heirs of all that God bestows upon his children.

---

head of the church. Lincoln's translation is less grammatically complex than that of Barth, but Barth's fits well with the significance assigned within the letter as a whole to the church in relation to God's purpose for the creation as a whole. It also coheres with the letter's presentation of the place of the church within Christ's administration of the last age. Barth's translation, "He has put everything under his feet and appointed him, the head over all, to be head of the church," is awkward but perhaps best captures the true sense of the verse.

The Spirit also strengthens and informs believers by attaching them more closely to Christ (Eph. 3:14–19). The connection the Spirit establishes between Christ and the saints makes it possible for them both to live their lives on a different basis and to take in the full dimensions of God's purpose and the extraordinary glory of his nature. So the author prays (3:16) for the members of Christ's body to be strengthened by the Spirit in the "inner man." The "inner man," as it appears here, is best understood as the "base of operation at the center of a person's being."[10] There the Spirit works to strengthen believers, as agents, by the gift of power. Such power is associated in Ephesians 3:18–19 with the saints' ability to comprehend or grasp both the full dimensions ("what is the breadth and length and height and depth") of God's intentions for the creation, the full dimensions of the salvation wrought in Christ, and the full dimensions of God's love.[11]

The gift of the Spirit is understandably linked also with Christ's residence (through faith) in the center of human agency—the heart—and with a new ground for their life—namely, love (Eph. 3:17). It is unclear whether the love here mentioned as the ground or foundation of the Christian life refers to the love of God in Christ or the love believers have for God and others.[12] There seems little reason, however, to exclude either meaning since both uses are found in the letter.[13] The sense of the passage would seem to be that, through the Spirit, Christ resides in the hearts of believers, and so their lives are based both in God's love for them and in the love that is engendered within their lives.

The basis of the life of God's assembly is a real link through the Spirit between the saints and the risen and ascended Lord who now reigns at the right hand of God. Through this link the saints sit with the ascended Christ

---

10. See Lincoln, *Ephesians*, 204–6. M. Barth (*Ephesians 1–3*, 369) has suggested that "the inner man" should here be understood to refer to Christ whom the author in the next verse prays will live in the hearts of believers through faith. If this translation were right, the verse would contain a prayer that the Spirit draw believers closer to Christ. The petition that Christ dwell in the hearts of believers that is found in verse 17 surely asks that this be the case, but, as Lincoln points out, this verse also indicates that Christ is *to dwell in the heart*. It is, consequently, more likely that "the inner man" is to be equated with "the heart" and so with the center of human agency as understood in both Hellenistic and Jewish thought.

11. There is, as might be expected, little agreement among the experts about the exact reference of the height, depth, length, and width the saints are to comprehend. Do the four dimensions have a cosmological reference? Do they refer to the fullness of salvation given in Christ? Do they refer to God's wisdom or the depth of the divine love? My own view is that the dimensions are here used to sum up all that the author of Ephesians desires his readers to grasp about the mystery made known in Christ—namely, the full dimensions of the salvation wrought in Christ, or the manifold wisdom of God and the extent of God's love. See Eph. 1:9–10, 18–20; 2:6–7; 3:9–10.

12. For a summary of the case for each position, see Lincoln, *Ephesians*, 207.

13. See, e.g., Eph. 1:4, 15; 2:4; 4:2, 16; 5:2, 25; 6:24.

in the heavenly place, and through this link Christ resides in the heart of each believer. Through this link also, both Jew and gentile have access to a single Father. Thus "in the heavenly places" Jew and gentile are one, and together they enjoy the blessings just enumerated. Furthermore, the blessing that comes from participation in Christ and the Spirit "in the heavenly places" also includes the gifts that the victorious Christ bestows upon those who are fellow citizens here below.

It is too infrequently noted that the gifts spoken of in this passage do not refer to a range of abilities but to a range of people. "And his gifts were that some should be apostles, some prophets, some evangelists, some pastors and teachers" (Eph. 4:11). The gifts spoken of in Ephesians must, therefore, be distinguished from the lists Paul provides in Romans 12:3–8 and in 1 Corinthians 12:4–11, 27–31. In these passages the gifts mentioned refer not only to people but also to abilities and/or functions. They include the abilities and/or functions of exhortation, liberality, the utterance of wisdom and knowledge, and faith. They include also certain sorts of people—namely, those who work miracles, administer, heal, help, speak in tongues, and interpret tongues, and those with the ability to distinguish spirits. The gifts of Christ and the gifts of the Spirit mentioned in these passages are graces of the soul, and they are people. They spring from the foundation of the church's life in the Father's sovereign action of election and in Christ's redeeming and reconciling sacrifice, and they serve the goal of unity that springs from the counsel of the Father's will.

The author of Ephesians correctly interprets both Romans and 1 Corinthians—the gifts of Christ are also the gifts of the Spirit and they are given, as 1 Corinthians says, "for the common good" (1 Cor. 12:7). Nevertheless, the emphasis in Ephesians falls on the fact that persons are given as gifts to the church and that these persons are to be received with respect. Thus Ephesians links the gifts given the church to a series of purpose clauses that indicate the importance of these people for the health and unity of God's assembly. The clauses remind the reader of the purpose for which these people have been given—namely, "for bringing the saints to completion [πρὸς τὸν καταρτισμόν] for the work of ministry, for the edification of the body of Christ" (Eph. 4:12).[14] The gifts that have their basis in Christ and the Spirit have a goal—namely, a form of edification that will produce a particular sort of unity, one in which the knowledge of Christ and love of Christ are united.

This process of edification suggests that Christians should consider themselves *in via*—on a road that will take them from a childish state to one in which they are fully grown and have reached a stature that takes its measure

---

14. I owe this translation to Andrew Lincoln. See Lincoln, *Ephesians*, 253.

from or reflects the fullness of Christ's nature (Eph. 4:13–16). On the way to maturity, they are to be obedient to the teaching that stems from the apostles and prophets and has been passed on by evangelists, teachers, and pastors. It is the destiny of the church, through a process of maturation aided by those given as gifts by the ascended Christ, for its members to become "the one new man" mentioned in Ephesians 2:15 or the "fully mature person"[15] referred to in Ephesians 4:13.

It seems fair to say that the basis of the unity God intends, as presented in Ephesians, is the economy or outworking of God the Father, whose purpose is the unity of all things in Christ; of God the Son, who establishes the conditions for this unity through his sacrificial death and his administration of God's plan; and of God the Holy Spirit, who incorporates believers into Christ and so makes available to them an understanding of God's purposes and the reconciling benefits of his death and resurrection. Though it is anachronistic to say so, it nonetheless seems reasonable to say that the author of Ephesians bases his focus on unity in the life of the Holy Trinity. The entire economy of God is placed at the foundation of what the author presents as the goal of God's people and the providential purpose of God himself. Given the place of the unity of the church within the providence of God, one must conclude that willingness to accept the division of the churches as a necessary and acceptable adjustment to human weakness and sin or as a positive step toward a rich pluralism of religious expression constitutes either a serious misunderstanding of what God is up to or a form of self-justification that at best indicates an unwillingness to face the true status of the divided churches before God.

There is yet another conclusion to be drawn from the discussion of the purpose and basis of the life of the church. Neither can rightly be discussed apart from the doctrines of the Trinity and of the person and work of Christ. By implication, therefore, if things are in their proper order, "ecclesiology" and the ethics that necessarily form part of an adequate account of the life of the church should not be treated as distinct theological topics that (in all probability) take on a life of their own. Rather, ecclesiology and ethics are rightly seen as necessary aspects of an adequate exposition of the central Christian mysteries concerning God and his saving purpose. In his study *The Gospel and the Catholic Church*, Arthur Michael Ramsey noted that Greek theology gave its fullest exposition of the church while expositing Christ's work as redeemer. He went on to say that in the thought of the Eastern fathers, "the Church is dealt with not as a subject in itself, but as an inevitable

---

15. I owe this translation to Andrew Lincoln. See ibid., 223.

part of teaching about Christ as the Second Adam and the head of a new humanity."[16] Ramsey quotes Irenaeus to illustrate his point—an illustration, incidentally, that clearly has its roots in Ephesians. In the process of refuting the gnostic claim that the gods of creation and redemption are separate, Irenaeus says,

> There is one God the Father, and one Jesus Christ our Lord, who cometh by a universal dispensation and sums up all things unto Himself. Man is in every respect the formation of God, and, therefore, He recapitulates man into Himself, the invisible becoming visible, the incomprehensible becoming comprehensible, the one superior to suffering becoming subject to suffering, and the Word becoming man. Thus He summeth up all things in Himself, that, as the Word of God is supreme in heavenly and spiritual and invisible matters, He may also have the dominion in things visible and material; and that, by taking to Himself the pre-eminence and constituting Himself Head of the Church, He may draw all things in due course unto Himself. (*Adv. Haer.* 3.16.6)[17]

Ramsey may be faulted for not linking the person and work of the Son more closely with that of the Father and the Spirit. Nevertheless, we have in both Irenaeus and Ramsey clear examples of an understanding of the church that, as it were, folds that understanding into a discussion of the universal dispensation or the providential and salvific purposes of God. My reading of Ephesians suggests that the Eastern fathers were right to take this course in their discussions of the church, and that the proclivity of the Western church to focus attention on the order of the church as in some degree separate from the saving mysteries of the faith represents a false step. To anticipate the future direction of this discussion, one can see the difference between East and West in the way in which each treats the place of truth and tradition within the life of the church. As Ramsey says,

> The ideas of truth and authority in the East have been free from the legalistic and scholastic tendencies apparent in the West. Truth, tradition reside in the Body as a whole; they are not something clerically imposed upon the Body. Hence truth is very close to life and worship. Both in Russian and Slavonic the phrase *hē orthodoxia* is translated so as to mean not right "opinion" but right "glory" or "worship." . . . The singing of the Creed in the Liturgy is introduced by the words, "let us love one another, that with one accord we may confess."[18]

---

16. Arthur Michael Ramsey, *The Gospel and the Catholic Church* (London: Longmans, Green, 1956), 142.
17. Quoted by ibid.
18. Ibid., 148.

The close connection Ramsey sees between truth, authority, worship, love, and the common life of the church echoes what we have found to be the goal and basis of life in Christ as presented in Ephesians. These in turn clearly reveal what I hold to be the primary focus of Christian living—namely, the common life of the church. The goal of this life is the glorification of God through the unity of all things in Christ Jesus, and the basis of glory and unity is the economy of God the Father, God the Son, and God the Holy Spirit. If these claims are to escape vacuity, however, an answer to an additional question becomes essential. What is the character of life in Christ?

5

The Character of Life Together in Christ

A Reading of the Epistle to the Ephesians (Part Two)

Introduction

What is the character of life in Christ? With this question, one comes to the heart of my argument. If ecclesiology is properly an aspect of the twin mysteries of the Trinity and the person and work of Christ, so also are Christian ethics an aspect of these realities. As such, their primary focus is neither the sanctification of the individual nor the reform and renewal of the social order. It is rather the common life of God's assembly. As displayed in Ephesians, the Christian life requires participation in and imitation of the life of God as present in the life of Christ. Participation in this life is indistinguishable from life in Christ's body, the church. The *ekklēsia* is the place on earth where the life to which God calls its peoples is to be found. The character, stamp, or public face of this form of life both defines and manifests the unity that it is God's purpose to bring about. God accomplishes this purpose not only through the sacrificial death of Jesus but also through the constant struggle of the church in the power of the Spirit to imitate that sacrifice within its own life.

Once more, the argument of the letter, though not sequential, does hang together. The best place to begin is with the double reminder that appears in the letter's second chapter. First, after praying that his (gentile) readers will have "the eyes of their hearts enlightened" (Eph. 1:18) to understand their calling, their hope, the richness of the inheritance that is theirs, and the power that is at work toward them, he reminds them that though they were once subject to the rule of rebellious spiritual forces and so dead through their trespasses and sins, they have been made alive with Christ. Like Christ they also have been raised from the dead and now live with him in the heavenly places (2:1–6). Next he urges them to remember that at one time they were separated from Christ and so cut off from the benefits they, along with Jewish believers, now enjoy "in Christ" (2:11–13). Accordingly, the author prays to the Father that his readers will have power to comprehend the fullness of God's purpose and receive power to do their part in bringing that purpose about through the good works that God has prepared beforehand for them to "walk in" (2:10; 3:14–19).

The double reminder and the prayer suggest the possibility that believers may fail to grasp the nature of their calling and so fail to carry it out. To put the matter another way, the double reminder coupled with the prayer suggests that life in Christ may well involve a struggle to remember (and so be obedient to) the basis and purpose of the common life of the assembly. It is this possibility that leads the author of the epistle to "beg" his readers to live a life that is "worthy" of their calling (Eph. 4:1). It is in describing this worthy life that the letter displays the character of the common life of the church. As will become plain, this life is one of struggles in which believers in their life together seek to imitate God in Christ and so make manifest the unity it is God's purpose, through the sacrifice of Christ and the common life of the church, to bestow upon the entire creation.

A Worthy Life

The key question therefore is, what is the shape or form of this worthy life—these works prepared beforehand to be walked in? The simple answer to this question is love. We have already seen that the saints have been chosen to be holy and blameless before Christ "in love" (Eph. 1:4–5). In a summary imperative, the Ephesians are commanded to become imitators of God in the way adopted children of a gracious father should, and they are instructed that this imitation requires that they give themselves up in love for one another as Christ did (5:1–2). A life of love imitates the sacrifice of Christ. Only such a life is "worthy." Furthermore, according to the author, this worthy life of love has an identifiable form and content. The love of Christ as reflected in the life of the church has a face that makes its presence recognizable. Love involves more than an inner attitude. It expresses itself in recognizable behaviors that indicate the presence of what might be called "graces" that make these behaviors possible.

What are these behaviors, and what is the nature of the "graces" that make their enactment possible? The first mentioned (Eph. 4:2) are lowliness (ταπεινοφροσύνη) and meekness (πραΰτης). Both words offer severe challenges to any would-be translator. By derivation ταπεινοφροσύνη (humility) comes from two words, the first of which means "of humble condition" and the second "mind" or "intellect." The humility enjoined by Ephesians is thus of a certain kind. Both its derivation and the context in which it appears in the letter suggest that it refers to a particular form of humility—namely, humility of mind. It is consequently a form of humility that opens one to instruction in ways that imitate Christ's attitude to his Father.

In like manner, it is difficult to find the right English word for πραΰτης, which is generally translated as "meekness." The word can mean either "gentleness" or a form of "lowliness" that is accompanied by reliance upon God to vindicate one's cause. The latter meaning seems to predominate in Matthew where the adjectival form πραΰς is used to refer to those of low estate who wait faithfully upon God (Matt. 5:5; 21:5). However, in the Pauline Epistles the word is often best translated "gentleness." It is difficult to tell in the case of Ephesians which of the two is the better translation. However, the dominant usage in the genuine letters of Paul is "gentleness." This use, along with the context of the use of πραΰτης in Ephesians 4:1, suggests that "gentleness" more accurately captures the meaning than humble openness to God. The context is of particular importance. In this passage, πραΰτης appears between "humility of mind" and "long-suffering patience" (μακροθυμία) and precedes two participial phrases with an imperative sense. In the Pauline Letters, long-suffering patience is connected in particular with the long-suffering of God, who provides space for repentance.[1] In like manner, Christians are to show forbearance to others. Consequently, in the participial phrases they are urged to be "forbearing" (ἀνεχόμενοι) with one another in love (4:2) and to be "eager" to maintain unity in the bond of peace (4:3). The close connection between humility of mind, patience, a demand to be forbearing in love, and a demand to have a desire to maintain peace all suggest that πραΰτης here denotes gentleness in the treatment of an erring brother or sister so that the unity and peace of the church can be maintained.

According to Ephesians, a life worthy of one's calling is one that accords with or is proportionate to God's election of the church to be "holy and blameless before him . . . in love" (Eph. 1:4–5). Further, the sort of love that characterizes a holy and blameless life has a definite purpose and character. It is directed to maintaining unity and peace within the common life of the

---

1. 1 Thess. 5:14; Gal. 5:22.

church so that God will be glorified and so that the secret of God's will becomes manifest both on earth and in the heavens. The graces that serve to bring about glory, unity, and peace are humility of mind, gentleness in correcting others, and patience in respect to their trespasses and sins. These graces are put to good effect through the constant practice of forbearance and by watchfulness in respect to those attitudes and behaviors that might disrupt the peace and unity of Christ's body.

This account of the character of the common life of the assembly is spelled out in further detail in the admonition that appears at the end of the fourth chapter and at the beginning of the fifth. There believers are urged, because they are "members one of another" (Eph. 4:25), to be "kind" and "tenderhearted" toward one another (4:32). These graces require that they forgive one another because they themselves have been forgiven (4:31). This admonition is capped off with a command—namely, that in their common life members of the church be imitators of God (as beloved children should be) and so walk in a way that imitates that of the Firstborn who loved them and gave himself to death for them as a sacrifice to God (5:1–2).

Ephesians 4:2–3 and 4:32–5:2 contain a list of moral qualities that I have called "graces" but which are normally called "virtues." It is often pointed out that lists of "virtues" and "vices" like those that appear here in the Pauline Letters and in other New Testament writings are common in ethical writings of the period. The implication is drawn that in taking over these lists, New Testament authors simply incorporated generally held moral ideals into Christian moral instruction. The argument I have presented above clearly runs counter to this common opinion. It may well be the case that in many instances these lists were incorporated in just this way, that is to say, without much modification and without much regard for particular context. However, in the case of Ephesians, one must conclude that the list of what I have called "graces" that the author deploys, though certainly parallel to that found in the Letter to the Colossians, has been adapted in a way that gives them a particular focus and content. The way in which the author of Ephesians selects and deploys the list both highlights the significance of unity for believers and gives content to what might be called an encompassing moral notion—namely, love. Close reading of the text of Ephesians brings to light not an unmodified catalog of morally admirable traits that would have been approved by the average person in the street but a coherent presentation of qualities that define the basic moral notion of love that itself underpins the life of unity that God intends for his assembly.

In a similar manner, commentators often miss the significance of the repeated use of "one another" in this section of the letter. The term appears no less than five times (Eph. 4:2, 25, 32 [2x]; 5:21). It is found equally frequently in the ethical portions of the genuine letters of Paul.² The dominance of duties owed "one to another" within Pauline circles surely points to the common life of the church as the primary setting for Christian living and the primary focus for Christian ethics. The central importance of the common life of the church as the primary focus of Christian ethics is confirmed by the discussion of the gifts of Christ that appears immediately after the description of a worthy life found in Ephesians 4:1–6.

The gifts bestowed upon the church stem from the generosity of Christ, who in his death and resurrection has proven victorious over all the enemies of God in heaven, on earth, and under the earth. This victorious Christ, like a triumphant general, has lavishly distributed the fruits of his victory among the citizenry who acknowledge his victory and rule (Eph. 4:7–10). The chief gift is that of grace (4:7), which is a gift to each member of the commonwealth. However, this single gift takes specific form in respect to certain persons who, by grace, become particular gifts to the church. As noted above, the gifts are people, and the purpose of their being given is to build up the church until its members find themselves both unified and mature in faith (4:11–16).

The point is one of extraordinary importance. Though there is no reason to speak of anything like "ordination" as being implied in this passage, there is nonetheless recognition of the authority of certain specific classes of persons to pass on and guard the faith and practice of the church. These groups are listed as apostles, prophets, evangelists, pastors, and teachers (Eph. 4:11). In contrast to the lists of ministries found in Paul's genuine letters, this list does not refer to functions or abilities. Rather, it refers to people who have a special authority and responsibility for teaching and ordering the church.³ Thus the apostles are the source of the original witness to Christ. The prophets are those who were recognized as being able to mediate divine revelation. Both the apostles and the prophets in Ephesians 2:20 are said to stand at the foundation of the church because of their proximity to Jesus. It may well be that by the time Ephesians was written, both the apostles and the prophets were a thing of the past. But they were looked to as the source of "truth," and their work was to be carried on by the groups that are next mentioned. The evangelists, the pastors, and the teachers are clearly still active. In the postapostolic period, evangelists continued to carry out the work of apostles. They planted churches and were involved primarily in the proclamation of the

---

2. See, e.g., Rom. 12:5, 10, 16; 13:8; 14:8, 13; 15:5, 7, 14, 16; 1 Cor. 11:23; 12:25; 16:20; 2 Cor. 13:12; Gal. 5:13, 15, 26; 6:2.

3. For a more complete discussion of this account of the gifts of Christ to the church, see Lincoln, *Ephesians*, 249–53. For a slightly different account, see M. Barth, *Ephesians 4–6*, 477–84.

gospel. By referring to evangelists immediately after his reference to apostles and prophets, the writer calls his readers' minds to the message they originally received and to the authority of the one who brought that message. Mention of evangelists is followed immediately by reference to pastors and teachers. The noun "pastor" or "shepherd" suggests a form of leadership that centers on care and guidance. These people are linked closely with teachers. In the subapostolic period, their particular job was to preserve, transmit, interpret, and apply the apostolic teaching.

Clearly, these people have authority within the assembly and their particular responsibility is to build up or edify the church in faithfulness to the witness of the apostles and prophets. They are to do so until the saints are fully mature. Growth to "mature manhood" or "to the measure of the stature of the fullness of Christ" (Eph. 4:13) is threatened, however, by anyone who remains a child who, because of immaturity, is subject to the influence of false and deceitful teachers. These children are easily led astray and are prone to be attracted by fashionable but false teaching. In the words of the epistle, they are "carried about with every wind of doctrine" (4:14). The only way in which these "children" can reach "mature manhood" is for those who are mature to maintain the truth and correct those who are still children. These are the evangelists, pastors, and teachers who have particular responsibility for the edification and unity of the body. If, however, their effort at formation is in fact to result in those who are children growing up in every way into Christ, the correction provided must be offered "in love" (4:15).

To understand all this, one must realize that at this point the letter doubles back on itself. Recall that the saints have been chosen in Christ from before the foundation of the world "to be holy and blameless before [God] . . . in love" (Eph. 1:4–5). If the saints are to be worthy of this calling, they must forbear with one another in love (4:2). As established at the outset of the chapter, forbearance in love calls for humility of mind, gentleness in admonishing others, patience, kindness, tenderheartedness, and a willingness to forgive. These graces and practices are to define the common life of the church and looked for in the life of each of its members. However, they are of particular importance for those with a primary responsibility for the maturation of the "children" who are part of the body, and for its unity in truth, love, and peace. At this point it does not seem unfair to say that the maintenance of "one faith" is unbreakably linked to a life of love by means of which those who are children in Christ are both protected from false and crafty teachers and brought to a mature understanding of Christ. Within God's assembly, therefore, authority, truth, love, and unity are not competitive, perhaps even opposed, notions. Rather, they are different sides of the same reality. That reality is the growth of Christ's body to the point at which it manifests the full stature of Christ—that is to say, the fullness of his knowledge of the Father and the fullness of his love for both the Father and the Father's adopted children.

At this juncture, it will prove useful to note a point of singular importance. Contrary to a currently popular opinion, authority within the assembly (as represented in the apostles, prophets, evangelists, pastors, and teachers) does not stand opposed to what in modern parlance is often called community. Authority is, in fact, necessary for the peace and unity of the assembly both because of the immaturity of some of its members and because of the craftiness and deceit of others. Authority, as pictured in this passage, does not stand outside of the assembly as an alien and coercive force but within it as an instrument for (1) passing on common beliefs and practices that have their origin in the life and teaching of Christ, (2) guarding those beliefs and practices from false representation, and (3) helping those who are immature to reach a state of greater maturity.

Authority then must be joined with truth, love, and unity if God's assembly is in fact to be worthy of its calling. Within God's assembly, truth, love, authority, and unity are, to stretch a metaphor, Siamese quadruplets. To sever the links between them is to kill all four. The point at issue now, however, is the primary locus of Christian living. The discussion of Christ's gifts to the church and their significance is yet another instance of the Christian life being located first of all within the common life of the church. It is only within an ethical circle of love—a circle circumscribed by the graces of humility of mind, gentleness in correcting others, patience, forbearance, eagerness to maintain unity, sympathy, tenderheartedness, and forgiveness—that the truth of Christ and so the purposes of God can be grasped. It is, furthermore, only within this circle that one can grow in this knowledge and receive these graces. Finally, it is only within this circle that authority can be exercised in a way that supports growth, unity of belief, and the love that serves as the foundation of both.

Life Together as "Walking Carefully" or as Appropriate Wisdom for Members of Households

The fourth chapter of Ephesians contains a thick description of what it means to be "holy and blameless" before God "in love," or "to lead a life worthy of the calling to which you have been called." The fifth chapter adds another dimension to the holy and blameless life. It admonishes the saints, because they live in evil days, to be aware that such a life requires careful attention. They are in fact ordered to "look carefully" how they walk and in so doing make certain that they live their lives as "wise" rather than "unwise" people (Eph. 5:15–17). Wise as opposed to foolish living requires that one thoroughly understand (συνίημι) the will of God (5:17). Further, thoroughly understanding the will of God is closely associated with being filled with the Spirit. Being filled with the Spirit, in turn, is connected with reverence for Christ that expresses itself as thanksgiving and mutual subjection (5:18–21).

It is clear from the text that giving thanks and being mutually subject are practices incumbent upon all Christians. They are conducive both to unity and to the glorification of God. They are, in consequence, imperatives directed to all the saints without regard to gender or social status. Thus thanksgiving and mutual subjection join the ranks of the graces set forth in chapter 4. A life of thanksgiving expressed by mutual address in hymns and spiritual songs might prove an embarrassment to modern sensibilities, but such practices are not problematic to the modern interpreter in the way the examples of mutual subjection that follow are. These examples all have to do with relations within the household—wives and husbands, parents and children, masters and slaves—and they all require forms of sub- and superordination. At this point the writer's views appear to collide with some of the most fundamental moral convictions of modern democratic society. The hierarchical depictions of domestic relationships found in chapters 5 and 6 raise fundamental questions about the consistency, coherence, and acceptability of the author's picture of a worthy life. Does the "household code" found in Ephesians 5:21–6:9 actually subvert the more "egalitarian description" of Christ's administration of the last age found in Ephesians 2:3–18? These are questions that cannot be ignored. To a contemporary reader they suggest the possibility that what have been called the graces of the common life may in fact compose an ethic of demeaning sub- and superordination.

How are these perplexing verses to be interpreted? At the outset, it is important to make some determination about the significance of the very size of this section of the letter. It has been argued that its length suggests that it contains the letter's central point—namely, that both the peace of the household and the peace of the church depend upon respect for hierarchical order.[4] A more likely explanation of the length of the passage, however, can be found elsewhere. There are sociological reasons located in Greco-Roman accounts of the life of a polity. These require, in addition to proposals about the public life of the polis, a discussion of the ethics of household relations. To the Hellenistic

---

4. See, e.g. Cynthia Kettredge, *Community and Authority: The Rhetoric of Obedience in the Paul Tradition*, Harvard Theological Studies 45 (Harrisburg, PA: Trinity, 1988).

mind, the household constituted the basic building block of society. Thus if the author of Ephesians were to give an account of the larger social unit (the commonwealth of the church) that made sense to the people to whom he wrote, he also had to give an account of its constitutive units (households).[5] These were the rules of social, moral, and political thought laid down by both Plato and Aristotle, and these rules continued to hold sway in the Hellenistic period.

For sociological reasons, an account of the common life of the church required a discussion of domestic relations. There were also theological reasons that made such a discussion necessary. As Francis Watson has written, "If within the one body, the relationship between a husband and wife is impaired, this is a threat to the 'unity of Spirit' and the 'bond of peace' that binds together the body as whole. Within the body there are no purely private concerns; 'for we are members one of another' (Eph. 4:25)."[6] If God's chief business is indeed the unity of all things in Christ, the way in which that unity is to be expressed and worked out in the household becomes a matter of primary importance. If the church is to fulfill its calling, it can do so only if its basic units manifest the peace and unity in Christ that God's assembly has been set aside to manifest.

That being said, it nonetheless comes as a shock, immediately after reading that all Christians are to be subject one to another, to find that the command for wives to be subject to their husbands is not accompanied by a similar one for husbands. Given what has been said in the previous chapter about the character of love, mutual subjection seems the only possible form of relation for those who are reconciled to God and one another in Christ. Nevertheless, the woman rather than the man is singled out for subjection. Clearly the writer holds an understanding of relations within the household wherein the male head of the house exercises authority over the other members.

However, the reason given for the subjection of the wife is not, as well it might have been, good order, custom, or male superiority. Rather, the headship of the husband is based on an analogy with Christ being head of the church. The sense in which the husband is head of the wife thus depends upon the way in which Christ is head of the church. Christ's headship in respect to the church is associated early in the letter with his death (Eph. 1:20). Further, in 4:10 his death is connected with a descent into the lower parts of the earth. If we take the meaning of headship from its christological characterization in the early parts of the letter, it does not seem unreasonable to say, as has

---

5. For this point, see Lincoln, *Ephesians*, 357–58.
6. Francis Watson, *Agape, Eros, Gender: Towards a Pauline Sexual Ethic* (Cambridge: Cambridge University Press, 2000), 226. The interpretation of Ephesians 5:21–6:9 that follows owes much to the treatment of this passage by Watson.

Francis Watson, "If the husband is to be head of the wife as Christ is head of the church, he must, like Christ, be familiar with the depths as well as the heights."[7] Further, it seems reasonable to conclude that in subjecting herself to her husband "in all things" the wife subjects herself to one who has first subjected himself to her.

This interpretation receives strong support from the admonition to husbands that immediately follows the call to wives to be subject. Husbands are commanded to love their wives "as Christ loved the church and gave himself up for her" (Eph. 5:25). The headship of the husband here does not depend upon his gender but upon an analogy between Christ's love for the church and a husband's love for his wife. That analogy is defined by giving oneself up. Further, the analogy is expanded by linking Christ's care for his body the church with the account of marriage given in Genesis 2:24. Because members of the church are members of Christ's body, his care for the church may be likened to the prudential care any person gives to their own body (Eph. 5:29–30). In a similar manner, because a man and woman in marriage become one flesh, in caring for his wife the husband shows care for his own body (5:28a, 31). More important still for our present purposes, in caring for their wives in this way, husbands fulfill the second of the two great commandments. In loving their wives as Christ loved the church, they learn to fulfill in a particular and defining instance the second part of Christ's summary of the law. Thus the writer concludes, "He who loves his wife loves himself" (5:28b).

Indeed, because the notion of self-giving after the manner of Christ plays such a central role in defining the love husbands are to show wives, marriage between a man and a woman who are "in Christ" is termed a "mystery" that leads one into a more profound one—the mystery of the relation between Christ and the church (Eph. 5:32). This mystery in turn draws one into what might be called God's big secret—namely, his intention to unite all things in his Son. One must conclude, therefore, that domestic relations "in the Lord," according to this writer, are to provide an expression in miniature of the unity to which all people are called and a particular expression of the imitation of God that constitutes wise as opposed to foolish living in an evil time.

If one pays attention to the most obvious sense of the text, certain conclusions seem to follow that render this text far less subversive of "mutual subjection" than is often claimed. To be sure, the text maintains a form of what today is termed "patriarchal marriage." Wives are to respect their husbands and submit to them "in all things." However, the exercise of authority as normally understood is being subverted and transformed. Christ's giving

---

7. Ibid., 234.

of himself becomes the pattern of domestic life that transforms domestic relations in a way that bridges the gulf between "above" and "below" and so begins a radical deconstruction of "patriarchal marriage." Indeed, it can fairly be said that the notion of "mutual subjection" begins to deconstruct any social form of marital relations including the modern one of equal partners in an economic enterprise.

In fact, after a careful reading of this passage, one is reminded of the account of the effects of Christian belief on all forms of social relation given by Søren Kierkegaard in *Works of Love*.[8] There he compares social relations to an enormous net in which all people are caught. Love demands that all persons, be they high or low, rise above the net and meet in a different way even though the net and their place within it remain as they were. For those reconciled to God and one another in Christ, everything is different though everything remains the same. Kierkegaard notes, anticipating his contemporary and future critics, that such a demand will be counted both as asking too much and too little—too much in that it is too much to expect people to discount their station in life and too little in that the structures of society are left as they have been. One may grant the critics' point that hierarchical structures carry always the potential for doing harm (both to the high and the low) and yet hold to Kierkegaard's point that in Christ they are to be regarded in ways that render their harmful potential impotent.

Obviously, the issue here is whether there is a Christian warrant for leveling social relations. This particular issue now dominates Christian moral argument, but, whether the present concern for social equality is adequately grounded and conceived or not, the point remains that Ephesians 5:21–6:9, though admittedly not egalitarian, is best understood as subversive of patriarchy as it was understood in the ancient world rather than as a covert argument in its defense.

The letter's account of mutual subjection subverts any and all patterns of domestic relations, but it does not serve as a charter for the sort of leveling that now occupies center stage in many normative accounts of social and ecclesial relations. As in the genuine letters of Paul, equality in respect to having received the grace of Christ means neither the elimination of social distinctions within the assembly nor the absence of hierarchy. For the author of Ephesians, the apostles, the prophets, and particularly the apostle Paul are not only distinguished from the other members of the body; in a real sense, they stand above the assembly as the source of the truth that is to be maintained within the assembly in all places and through subsequent generations (Eph.

---

8. Søren Kierkegaard, *Works of Love: Some Christian Reflections in the Form of Discourses*, trans. Howard and Edna Long (New York: Harper, 1962), 79–98.

2:20; 3:4; 4:11). Furthermore, in the present time, God has given the church evangelists, pastors, and teachers to maintain the truth in love and so protect those who are children in the Lord and guide them to full maturity. Clearly, as God's gift to the church, these people are to be accorded authority within the assembly. It is not an unreasonable extrapolation to say that those who are children in the Lord are to display humility of mind toward those whom the Lord has made responsible for the truth and good order of the common life of the church. In like manner, it is incumbent upon those who have been given by God and have risen to prominence within the church as evangelists, pastors, and teachers to manifest the graces that define love's face so that their maintenance of the truth in fact builds it up.[9]

What one finds in the discussion both of domestic and ecclesial relations contained in Ephesians is not a defense of patriarchy but a subversion of its normal basis and conceptualization. One also finds subversion of the virtues commonly associated with that social institution. St. Augustine, in his criticism of pagan notions of public life and virtue, noted that pagans were resigned to the presence of unruly elements both in the body politic and the life of individuals. Hierarchy was necessary, therefore, to discipline unruly elements in the populace, and private virtue was necessary to reign in unruly elements in the psyche. Public virtue, accordingly, was essentially military in nature. As John Milbank points out, it was designed to secure "inner dominance of one class over another, and outer security against enemies."[10] Social dominance in turn was designed to secure the interests of the whole over the parts. Conversely, and ironically, public virtue in fact became private in that, through achieving inward control of the vices and passions, one was able to conquer rivals in the agonistic process of furthering both the interests of the city and personal honor.

The presentation of hierarchical relations within assembly and household along with the account of the graces given by Christ to each member of God's commonwealth are radically different from such a heroic ideal. We have already indicated the significance of the frequent use of "one another" in chapter 4. Such usage is most unusual, perhaps even unique, in the literature of the time. Thus instead of the top-down flow of command and obedience that levels

---

9. John Koenig has argued persuasively that it is inaccurate to speak of the valorization of equality over hierarchy in the New Testament writings. He shows that authority is accorded leaders within the assembly and that this authority is based upon recognition of a call on the basis of having risen to prominence within the assembly. The authority accorded these people was, however, linked necessarily to the service provided by them to the assembly. See John Koenig, "Perspectives on Leadership in the New Testament," *Word and World* 13, no. 1 (Winter 1993): 26–33.

10. Milbank, *Theology and Social Theory*, 410.

social distinction into the two categories of "above" and "below," one finds a reciprocal set of relations (some of which are hierarchical) that are governed by love and truth. Within this sequence, each "member" has his or her own place, liberty, and worth, and each is subject to the other. As Kierkegaard noted and Ephesians clearly affirms, each member of the assembly is to rise above his or her place within the body. This does not mean that there are no longer distinctions to be made between the parts of the body, nor does it mean that some do not have authority over others within it. It does mean, however, that these relations are shaped by what might be called "agapic practice," or the exercise of the graces that give love its face. That is, in living and maintaining the truth in love, no matter what their place and authority might be, each is to be truthful and demonstrate humility of mind, gentleness, and patience. In manifesting these graces, they are to be forbearing toward one another, and they are to be eager "to maintain the unity of the Spirit in the bond of peace" (Eph. 4:2–3). Further, they are to seek not to grieve the Holy Spirit by being kind, tenderhearted, and forgiving one of another (4:32). In all these relations they are to live a life of thanksgiving and practice mutual subjection in the Lord.

Through the manifestation of the graces, all members of the body become imitators of God not by declaring an end to all distinctions and all hierarchy but by giving themselves up one for another as Christ gave himself up for the church; the body as a whole, by means of the exemplary lives of its members, shows itself worthy of its calling to manifest the unity God purposes for all things (Eph. 4:32–5:2). Though it eliminates neither hierarchy nor distinction, agapic practice of this sort does produce at least four results of (one might say) revolutionary importance. In the first place, by eschewing what the writer calls "the unfruitful works of darkness" and by providing a counterexample to life as normally lived, the graces expose those ways of life that oppose the will and purpose of God (5:11). Manifestation of the graces thus provides an exemplary rather than compulsory form of discipline that serves to maintain the truth in love against the forces that might subvert both.

In the second place, manifestation of the graces introduces into all expressions of distinction and hierarchy respect for the liberty and value of each and every member of the assembly. As such, all cultural forms (including egalitarian ones) come under pressure from the graces that shape and enable agapic practice. Kierkegaard is thus wrong (save in a superficial sense) to say that everything remains the same. Over time, the agapic social ethic of the assembly both collides with and serves to transform from within all social configurations.

In the third place, within the assembly, the exercise of authority and the significance of difference are circumscribed and authenticated by being embedded in the web of social practice outlined above. In this way, difference and hierarchy are yoked to communal peace and a common good. Apart from the web of agapic practice, difference and hierarchy in fact lose their character as divine gifts and become instead imposters, instruments of power that undermine the very ends for which they are given.

In the fourth place, because it serves as a justification for no particular social form, agapic practice easily migrates across cultural boundaries. The beliefs that form its foundation do not serve as a sacred canopy for any given social order. Rather, by their power to attract, the graces may be taken in by the denizens of any order. Maintaining the truth in love then leaves them with the task of "thoroughly comprehending" (translation mine) the will of the Lord within the order in which they happen to find themselves (Eph. 5:17). Such comprehension allows each person to walk as a wise person in his or her own place, but, in walking as wise rather than as unwise imitators of God, no pattern of life, even an egalitarian one, is left just as it was (5:15).

Ephesians 5:21 through 6:9 are then far indeed from a panegyric on behalf of patriarchy. The patriarchal form of domestic relations is certainly upheld. Wives are to submit to their husbands "in all things," and in doing so they are to respect them. But submission and respect are contained within the husband's subjection to his wife—a form of subjection that imitates Christ's self-offering on behalf of the church. One might say that the agapic practice of mutual subjection is something like a mutant gene that produces a different species over time. Thus the account of domestic relations found in Ephesians 5:21–6:9 may in fact be taken as an ideal picture of the way in which Christian belief and practice are to migrate from one culture to another. They simply take up residence in the social forms of the day. Consequently, to become stuck on the household codes, as now seems to be the case, either as legitimate or illegitimate defenses of patriarchy is to miss the revolutionary character of this particular example of what it is to walk as wise rather than unwise. To be wise is to comprehend thoroughly the will of God and by so doing to imitate his self-offering in Christ. Such wisdom requires no particular social form for its expression, and yet, one suspects, no social form can long remain impervious to its influence.

Life Together as Combat or as "Putting on the Armor of God"

No account of the character of the common life of the assembly as presented in Ephesians would be complete apart from a depiction of the sort of conflict that life inevitably calls forth. The letter ends with a peroration urging its recipients to "be strong in the Lord" and to "put on the whole armor of

God" (Eph. 6:10–11). They are to arm themselves as if preparing for a battle. In the course of this struggle, they will find themselves contending against "the spiritual hosts of wickedness" that inhabit the heavens and preside over a form of life best characterized as "dark" (5:11; 6:12). The gentile readers of this letter once lived under the sway of these forces, but they are admonished to do so no longer (2:2; 5:8). Indeed, they are urged to take no part in this way of life and to refuse to associate with those who do (5:6–7). They are further reminded that the power to which they have access has already shown itself to be mightier than the forces that confront them.

If one links Ephesians 5:6–13 to Ephesians 6:10–18, a picture emerges in which the assembly of the saints who are now "children of light" stand in stark contrast to the "sons of disobedience" who are "darkness." The "children of light" are commanded to "walk as children of the light." The fruits of this way of walking are found in "all that is good and right and true" (Eph. 5:9). To manifest these fruits, however, the saints must discern or thoroughly comprehend "what is pleasing to the Lord." Conversely, they must take no part in the unfruitful works of darkness. In short, the worthy life to which the saints are called is to serve as a counterexample (of light) that by contrast exposes the character of ordinary life (darkness). As pointed out above, this counterexample makes the purposes of God visible in such a way that the spiritual powers that rule over the antipathetic world of the "sons of disobedience" become aware of their own doom.

The saints are thus admonished to "look carefully then how you walk" (Eph. 5:15). As has become apparent in the previous discussion, careful walking requires wisdom and a life of both thanksgiving and mutual subjection. It requires also a life of constant watchfulness and combat because the spiritual forces that oppose God's rule of the creation, though defeated, continue to rule what the letter calls "this present darkness" (6:12). The idea would seem to be that, though they know they are defeated, they nonetheless fight on. Even in their weakened condition, they are too powerful for the saints themselves to defeat. The saints can "withstand" this onslaught and "remain standing" only by taking weapons that belong not to them but to God. These are the weapons that compose the grace by which they have been saved through faith—namely, "truth," "righteousness," "the gospel of peace," "the shield of faith," "the helmet of salvation," "and the sword of the Spirit, which is the word of God." These are the weapons that become available to the saints in the context of vigilance, perseverance, and constant prayer "in the Spirit" (6:14–18).

The reader encounters another thick description of the character of life together in God's assembly—one that places the account given in chapter 4 in a wider context. Here the saints are given a more complete account of their circumstances. They live in what the author terms "the time remaining"[11] (τοῦ λοιποῦ) (Eph. 6:10)—a period that is later characterized as "the evil day" (6:13). These instructions, along with the description of the worthy life and wise walking found in chapters 4 and 5, compose a full account of what it means to live together "in Christ," or in the sphere of his victory; for this reason they require the same sort of close attention that was given to worthy living and wise walking. Indeed, they compose something like a book of instructions about how life is to be conducted in the time between the present and the return of Christ.

In the time remaining the assembly is to "be strong in the Lord" (Eph. 6:10) by availing itself of God's own might. The purpose of this resort to the might of God is to find strength to stand against the wily schemes of the devil (6:11). The reader has been warned previously about the wily schemes of crafty teachers (4:14). Presumably these crafty purveyors of false teaching have fallen under the influence of the evil one and are to be numbered among his minions, but they are nowhere near as fearful as other forces the saints will face during the remainder of Christ's administration of the fullness of time. In the time remaining, though Christ administers this period on behalf of the Father, the saints nonetheless face an onslaught of spiritual forces whose power far exceeds that of false teachers or for that matter any person of flesh and blood. These forces are variously termed "principalities," "powers," "world rulers of this present darkness," and "spiritual hosts of wickedness in the heavenly places" (6:12). They clearly are to be identified with "the principalities and powers in the heavenly places" to whom God's assembly is to make known God's purpose for all things (3:10).

To strengthen themselves and at the same time remain standing in the midst of this onslaught, the saints are admonished to "put on" the armor that God provides for the contest. This vesting for battle clearly involves the same things as "putting on the new nature" that was commanded in Ephesians 4:24. So in addition to humility of mind, gentleness, patience, truthful speech, kindness, tenderheartedness, and forgiveness, the saints are to "take up" certain additional graces. With these graces, they are to "stand" like soldiers at their post and in doing so "withstand" the perpetual onslaught they face both in the present and the days to come. These graces together can fairly be called the "awesome" or "splendid" armor [ἡ πανοπλία] of God—glorious armor that serves at one and the same time to give the saints confidence in the battle and to intimidate their enemies during their attack.[12]

---

11. I owe this translation to Markus Barth. See M. Barth, *Ephesians 4–6* (Garden City, NY: Doubleday, 1974), 759–60.

12. See ibid., 793–95, for this interpretation.

Of what exactly does the awesome armor of God consist? In the context of this peroration delivered, as it were, on the morn of battle, what meaning is to be attached to the various items that compose the armor God provides to the saints—namely, "truth," "righteousness," "the gospel of peace," "faith," "salvation," and the "word of God"? There is little agreement among commentators as to the metaphorical sense of these weapons. Some take them to refer almost univocally to graces bestowed by God. Thus they understand "truth" and "righteousness" as the truth of the gospel and the righteousness that is bestowed by God and appropriated through faith. The passage as a whole is taken to mean that the saints, in the midst of battle, are to cling to these graces as their only true sources of strength. Other commentators, though they recognize that many of these graces (salvation and the word of God, for example) can only be received, nonetheless assign a more active meaning to the instructions given for the conduct of the battle. "Truth" is taken, as in chapter 4, to refer to the truth of the message delivered by the apostles and prophets and so to truth that is to be actively maintained. "Righteousness" is understood to refer not to the alien righteousness bestowed by God as an act of grace but as a way of life that is "worthy" of the calling of the saints.

I know of no way to decide with any degree of certainty between these interpretive strategies. Both, however, fail to treat with sufficient seriousness the rhetorical nature of this particular passage. A peroration delivered on the field of battle must gather up a host of meanings and concentrate them within a limited field of symbolic representation. Each symbol becomes polysemous. The symbolic field must focus all the beliefs, values, and goals of the people and their army upon a relatively small screen. The rhetorical character of this passage calls out, therefore, for a broad rather than narrow interpretation of its content.

How, then, should one understand the first two bits of equipment—"truth" and "righteousness" (Eph. 6:14)? The Septuagint translation of Isaiah 11:5 provides the background of the verse. There the prophet uses "truth" to refer to the Messiah being faithful or true to his calling. Thus "the girdle of truth" may suggest similar faithfulness on the part of the saints. But it must be taken to suggest more. If one looks back over the letter as a whole, truth also is composed of the secret of God's providential purposes that is manifest in Christ and contained in the message of the apostles and prophets. This truth is to be not only received but also actively maintained. Thus "truth" suggests not only the truth about God and his purposes that is to be received but also a way of life that imitates, defends, and promotes those purposes.

In like manner, "righteousness" may well carry several meanings. The Greek text of Isaiah 11:5 regards "righteousness" as a quality that leads the Messiah to treat others "rightly." In one sense, therefore, "righteousness" may be taken as a reiteration of previous exhortations to the faithful for behavior that leads to truthful speech, humility of mind, gentleness, patience, and so on. However, it is not out of the question that "the breastplate of righteousness" might be taken to refer also to the justifying righteousness referred to in Romans 3:21–26. The readers of Ephesians have, after all, been reminded previously of the fact that they have been saved "by grace . . . through faith" (Eph. 2:8). They have been reminded as well that by grace they have been brought into the sphere of Christ's administration for the purpose of "good works" that have been "prepared beforehand." "The breastplate of righteousness" may well be taken, therefore, as an image that calls to mind both the righteousness bestowed upon the saints by grace and a way of life worthy of their calling.

"Truth" and "righteousness" in the broadest sense are thus to be both claimed and deployed in the battle with "the spiritual hosts of wickedness." Ability to claim and deploy these weapons depends, however, upon a certain sort of preparedness, and it is to adequate preparation for battle that the author next turns his attention. First, believers are to have shod their feet "with the readiness" (ἐν ἑτοιμασίᾳ) of the gospel of peace (Eph. 6:15).[13] Once more, one need not choose between what commentators depict as contrary possible meanings—namely, readiness in the midst of battle to rely upon or take refuge in the gospel of peace or readiness actively to proclaim the gospel of peace in the face of the enemy. It is, in short, both the reception and instantiation of the gospel of peace that makes one ready for battle with the spiritual forces that oppose the saints. Reception and instantiation of this gospel refer both to living "in Christ," whose reconciling death brings peace, and to living in peace with one's neighbors. Preparedness thus requires both remaining in the sphere of Christ's victory over the powers and living in a way that imitates the manner of his victory.

Preparedness also requires, naturally enough, that the saints take up "the shield of faith" (Eph. 6:16). Faith here refers to belief that Christ has defeated the powers and trust that the same power that raised Christ from the dead is at work in the assembly. It is this faith that will allow the saints to persevere in the battle and so repulse all forms of enemy attack, neatly summarized here in the phrase "the flaming darts of the evil one." This faith allows the saints to stand and not shrink back out of fear or despondency. Faith provides their purchase on God's victory and also their ability to continue in a battle against forces stronger than their own.

Preparedness to this point has required the saints not only to receive but also to deploy an array of weapons. It also requires, in respect to certain matters,

---

13. For this translation see Lincoln, *Ephesians*, 448–49.

a more passive stance. If they are to be prepared, the saints are required not to take up but to receive both "the helmet of salvation" and "the sword of the Spirit, which is the word of God" (Eph. 6:17). The graces mentioned to this point as characteristic of life within God's assembly, despite the fact that they are given, require deployment on the part of their recipients. Salvation, however, can only be received. This pure gift constitutes the greatest source of strength for the battle in which the saints are engaged. "Salvation" refers to God's deliverance, and in Ephesians this deliverance is said to be present. The saints do not await their rescue. It will be given and is to be received in the very midst of their present conflict.

The short sword (ἡ μάχαιρα)—that is, the word of God made effective by the presence of the Spirit—must also be received. Though the short sword was an offensive weapon, as the word of God it can neither be honed nor effectively deployed by the efforts of the saints alone. In the battle, the saints must receive this weapon, but they also must use it. That is, they must speak the word openly in the face of any attack. There is a positive injunction to proclaim suggested by mention of the short sword, but the author makes plain that only the Spirit can make this offensive weapon effective. The word the saints are both to receive and employ (and which the Spirit makes effective) is clearly the gospel itself—the good news of Christ's death, resurrection, and session at the right hand of the Father. Thus in the midst of the battle they may be assured both that they will be delivered from their enemies and that their enemies (wherever found) will be vanquished.

Though they are certainly called upon to employ the weaponry with which they have been provided, it is of the utmost importance to note that in this battle the saints do not overcome "the world rulers of this present darkness." God alone can win such a victory. By taking the armor of God, the saints do no more than remain standing in a battle that God alone can win. The armor of God allows the saints to stand, and only to stand. As they remain standing in the battle, no shouts of triumph are to emerge from their mouths. Such a shout would constitute blasphemy, for the victory belongs to God and not the saints. Prayers of thanksgiving for God's grace and supplication to God on behalf of one another (rather than shouts of victory) constitute the only appropriate response of the assembly (Eph. 6:18–20). Indeed, praying for all the saints and keeping alert in the Spirit may be taken as prerequisite practices that, as it were, mark the space for "standing" and "withstanding" through reception and deployment of the awesome armor God provides his assembly.

After reading this peroration, one might conclude that the author had what Ernst Troeltsch might have called "a sectarian mentality"; a mind that makes an absolute distinction between church and world. It is not inaccurate to say that his admonition not to associate with "the sons of disobedience" draws a sharper line between believers and their surrounding society than Paul does (see 1 Cor. 5:9–10). However, it is also the case that the author of Ephesians does not picture the battle between light and darkness as one that takes place univocally between church and world. There are a number of indications that the battle the saints carry on with "the spiritual hosts of wickedness" rages as well both within the assembly and within the spirit of each of its members.

Because of his desire to present in bold relief the way of life that is worthy of the calling of the saints, it is easy to believe that the contrast the author draws between "once" and "now" (before and after baptism?) is absolute in a way that in fact it is not (see, e.g., Eph. 5:8). However, close reading of the text gives the reader every reason to believe that its author was fully aware of the foibles and failures of "the children of light." Thus, as previously noted, he pictures some members of the assembly as children who are so immature that they follow after fashionable teaching put forward by teachers who are both cunning and deceitful (Eph. 4:14). This reference to false teaching is the most obvious indication of the author's awareness of sin and disunity within the church, but there are others less obvious and more serious. There are indications that a lack of maturity in the Lord is connected with the continuing presence among the saints of a former way of life that is contrary to the will of God. This contrary form of life is rooted first of all in a way of understanding the world that is both dark and futile.

Thus the writer prays that those to whom he writes will receive a spirit of wisdom and revelation in the knowledge of God and that they will accordingly have the eyes of their hearts enlightened so that they will know the hope to which they have been called, the riches of God's inheritance that is theirs, and the greatness of God's power at work among them (Eph. 1:16–20). Later in the letter, when speaking of Paul's stewardship of the mystery of God revealed in Christ, the writer prays that those to whom he writes will be strengthened through the Spirit and given power to "grasp" the love of Christ that surpasses in greatness the dimensions of the universe (3:14–19). These prayers hardly indicate a church in which all the members have reached "mature manhood" or "the full stature of Christ." Consequently, the writer must "affirm and testify in the Lord" that his readers are no longer to walk as the gentiles do "in the futility of their minds." In contrast to the way of life of those who have had "the eyes of their hearts enlightened," there is a way of life that stems from a darkened understanding and is characterized by ignorance and "insensibility of heart" (4:17–18).[14] It would appear then that darkened understanding,

---

14. For this interpretation see M. Barth, *Ephesians 4–6*, 500–501.

ignorance, and insensibility are not unknown among the saints. The saints are consequently open to foolish as opposed to wise behavior and so can be commanded "to comprehend thoroughly" (translation mine) what the will of God actually is (5:17).

It is not surprising that, in picturing this conflict between two ways of life, the writer places at the basis of each a form of understanding that is closely tied to one's disposition to do the right thing and to one's propensity to order the affections properly. As Julia Annas has pointed out, in ancient ethics "the virtuous person is not just the person who does in fact do the morally right thing, or even does it stably and reliably. She is the person who *understands* the principles on which she acts, and thus can explain and defend her actions."[15] Accordingly, she goes on to note, "All ancient ethical theories agree that fully to have the virtues, or even one particular virtue, the agent has to have practical wisdom"—the ability to reason well about the conduct of one's life.[16] In setting up a conflict between a form of understanding that is enlightened and one that is darkened, and in placing them at the base of two forms of life, the writer conceives of a wise as opposed to foolish life in a way that accords with the collective representations of his age. One's way of life is rooted in a way of understanding. Not surprisingly, therefore, in urging his readers to leave a former manner of life, he reminds them that this change involves first of all a renewal of the spirit of their minds (4:22–24). Such a renewal is the basic step that must be taken if one is to "put off" an "old man" and "put on" a "new man."

In this respect, the author of Ephesians is a person of his times, but in another way he is not. A renewed spirit of the mind is not a human achievement but one of the graces that come to the saints in the context of prayer (Eph. 1:16–23; 3:14–19). It is a gift of the Spirit rather than a permanent and self-garnered possession that results from habitual patterns of behavior. Indeed, in a way that runs counter to the mind of his times, the author suggests that "hardness of heart" (some form of implacable opposition to God) stands behind futility of mind and darkened understanding (4:18). Lack of right knowledge is rooted in a deeper place than mind. It lies instead in what we might call the center of personality and stems from an inexplicable resistance to God. It is grace that overcomes this opposition and so opens the way for the eyes of the heart to be enlightened (1:18). One must assume then that this most basic characteristic of the worthy life, like all the rest, is a gift given in the midst of a conflict in which believers stand only because of the armor

---

15. Annas, *Morality of Happiness*, 67.
16. Ibid., 73.

provided by God. Christian wisdom is, therefore, not a form of self-mastery that allows one to achieve a harmonious life. It is a gift given in the midst of a battle with superior forces that softens one's heart, enlightens one's understanding, and allows one to comprehend the will of God fully, walk as wise rather than unwise, and remain standing in a contest that is, from a human point of view, grossly unequal.

It would not be inaccurate to say that conflict is the chief characteristic of life together in Christ. The nature of the conflict becomes doubly plain when one views the way in which the writer portrays the battle believers have with what might be called the disruptive affections that divide humankind and frustrate the realization of God's purposes for the creation. After praying that his readers will have the eyes of their hearts enlightened, he reminds them that they once lived according to the pattern of a world ruled over by the spiritual forces that oppose God. As such, they were dominated by "the passions" of the flesh and acted according to the desires both of their bodies and of their (darkened) way of thinking (Eph. 2:3). Darkened understanding is linked with unruly desires. It is also linked with forms of ignorance that lead to a type of insensitivity that expresses itself in patterns of gross intemperance (4:19).

Again, the stark contrast between the way of life that characterizes the peoples of the earth and the life that ought to characterize the children of light may be taken to indicate a division between the two that makes them utterly distinct. Nevertheless, as was the case with *understanding*, so also with unruly *affections*: there are indications that the distinction is not as clear as one might be led to expect by the writer's rhetoric. Thus he not only reminds his readers of the state in which they once existed (Eph. 2:1–2); he also admonishes them to "put off" the form of life that has been corrupted by desires that deceive those whom they master (4:22). In its most obvious sense, "putting off" or "putting away" a form of life dominated by darkened understanding and craving requires that thieves give up taking what does not belong to them and that each person make sure that their speech is not foul, slanderous, or of the sort (ἡ κραυγή) that will brook no opposition (4:28–29, 31). In a less obvious and more interior sense, "putting away" requires ridding oneself of "bitterness," "rage," "anger," and "malice" (4:31). The hortatory form of these admonitions strongly suggests that these unruly emotions and divisive behaviors are still present among the saints. Thus in appealing to his readers to lead a life worthy of their calling, the author appeals also for them to put away a contrary form of life. It would appear that the contrast between a life "once" lived in the passions of the flesh (2:2–3) and that which is "now" to be lived does not define a clear "before" and "after" in respect to time. Rather, the "once/now" distinction refers to two modes of life that are in conflict with each other. The conflict, to be sure, is in one sense between the saints and "the rest of mankind" (2:3), yet in another sense it is a conflict that one can find within the life of the assembly and within each of its members. Thus, as it appears in Ephesians, life together in Christ is a life of conflict in which the saints contend on all fronts against a form of life that is antipathetic to God's purpose. This conflict requires that, by availing themselves of the grace given in Christ, they contend with forces hostile to God within themselves, within the body of the church, and among those the letter at one point terms "the rest" (2:3).

It is now possible to address one of the most perplexing aspects of Ephesians. How does one account for the stark contrast the writer makes between the lives his readers "once" lived and the lives they "now" live? This same question was posed in a different way some years ago by Nils Dahl when he asked a group of Protestant and Roman Catholic theologians who had reached considerable agreement on the nature of the church on the basis of a reading of Ephesians the following question: "This is a beautiful church! Where do I find her?"[17] Indeed, the ideal picture of the church and of the lives of its members that emerges from the letter's pages has proved to be a major challenge for interpreters from the time of the early church. How does one square this extraordinary account of the calling of the church and of relations between its members with the frequently squalid realities of the actual life of congregations?[18] Some, like the gnostics, have taken the account in Ephesians to refer to a spiritual, heavenly church made up entirely of "pneumatics." Ignatius, in his letters, locates the ideal unity of the church in its one Eucharist under the presidency of one bishop. Irenaeus locates unity in the public tradition of the apostolic *kerygma* and in the succession of bishops and presbyters from the apostles. Origen softens the contrast by interpreting the distinction between "once" and "now" as referring to a divine form of pedagogy that leads believers from one stage of growth to another. Chrysostom takes the "once/ now" contrast as descriptive of the faithful state of the apostolic church in comparison to the decay of the church in his own day. Theodore of Mopsuestia gave a sacramental interpretation of the contrast. In the Christian mysteries, believers "now" participate in the age to come, which stands in vivid contrast to the age in which "once" we lived. In the Western church, "once" came to refer to the time before baptism and then to the time before the availability

---

17. Nils Dahl, "Interpreting Ephesians: Then and Now," in *Studies in Ephesians: Introductory Questions, Text- and Edition-Critical Issues, Interpretation of Texts and Themes*, ed. David Hellholm, Vemund Blomkvist, and Tord Fornberg (Tübingen: Mohr Siebeck, 2000), 467.

18. For a concise summary of various ways in which the contrast between "once/now" has been interpreted, see ibid., 470–71.

of sacramental grace. At the Reformation, Luther took the contrast to refer to the dialectic between sin and justification.

This overly brief summary of the history of interpretation allows one to see that it would be possible, indeed desirable, to write a book about the way in which the contrast between "once" and "now" has been addressed over the ages. Enough has been said, however, to indicate that the issue remains. It is perhaps foolish to step into the midst of such a long and unsettled debate, but the reading of Ephesians presented here suggests a plausible way to view the contrast. The rhetorical form of Ephesians is that of a congratulatory letter in which the readers are asked not only to remember but also to be mindful of the grace they have received in Christ. This call to remember is followed by an appeal to live a life worthy of the grace they have received, and the appeal is not without suggestions that there is much room for growth on the part of those to whom the author writes. The ideal description of "now" thus does not constitute a form of triumphalism that disregards the spots and wrinkles of the church. Rather, it is an appeal to remember and pay close attention to the grace and purposes of God. Close attention to the knowledge of God's purposes that have been made known in Christ to the saints places their own immaturity and the continuing presence of a former manner of life in bold relief. In this context, the writer makes an appeal for his readers to eschew arrogance and to adopt more humble and loving attitudes that allow them to grow up *together* in the Lord and so remain faithful to their calling. He appeals also for his readers to pay close attention to how they live and to struggle (with the support of divine grace) to "put off" one form of life and "put on" another.

Conclusion

This reading of the contrast between "once" and "now" suggests furthermore a way to understand the nature of the unity to which the author calls his readers and the part ethics plays in that definition. It would not be inaccurate to say that in a "final" or "basic" sense, the unity of the church is rooted in the purposes of God and, in particular, in the reconciling sacrifice of Christ and the work of the Holy Spirit, who awakens faith and unites believers with Christ and his sacrifice. This final or basic unity is expressed most succinctly in the formula "one Lord, one faith, one baptism, one God and Father of us all, who is above all and through all and in all" (Eph. 4:5–6). The unity of the church, like the life of each believer, is constituted and maintained by the sovereign will of God, which is exercised through Christ's administration, in and through the Spirit, of the fullness of time. One can say without distortion that for the writer of Ephesians, the unity of the church is "hidden in God" (Eph. 3:9).[19] It rests in God's election of a people, in Christ's administration of God's purposes (1:19–23), and in the presence of the Spirit, who links believers to Christ and so guarantees that the promises of God will be fulfilled (1:13–14; 4:30).

It is not too much to say that according to the writer of Ephesians the unity of the church is first of all a matter of divine rule—a fact of existence under God. In a penultimate sense, however, this unity becomes manifest only in the midst of struggle. The "world rulers of this present darkness," though defeated, still exercise power both within the assembly and among the rest of humankind (Eph. 2:3). Consequently, those who belong to God's assembly must be "diligent to maintain" peace and unity (4:3). Put another way, they must "look carefully" to the way they live for, despite the victory of God in Christ, the times continue to be evil (5:15–16). Looking carefully, or paying close attention, requires both an attempt to "learn what is pleasing to the Lord" (5:10) and a struggle described as "putting off" an old form of life and "putting on" a new one (4:22–24). In this struggle, members of the assembly cannot rely on their own strength but must again and again avail themselves of weapons provided by God (6:11–18).

How then does the unity that is "hid with God" become manifest? How is it to be recognized? Given that the unity of the church constitutes the way in which God's glory is to become manifest to the peoples of the earth and to the spiritual forces that oppose God, the question is one upon which the case made by the writer stands or falls. As has become apparent, on one level the unity God intends is manifest by the assembly following one Lord, professing one faith, sharing a common baptism, and worshiping one God. All these manifestations of unity are compromised, however, by immaturity on the part of many believers, by their acceptance of false doctrine, and by trust in deceitful teachers. They are also compromised by continuing presence among believers of a certain hardness of heart that produces futility of mind and darkened understanding. These in turn express themselves in disorderly desires of body and mind (Eph. 2:3); insensitivity; licentiousness; greed (4:19); robbery (4:28); silly, foul, ribald talk (4:29; 5:4); bitterness, rage, and anger; argumentation that will brook no objection; slander; and, finally, malice (4:31).

The point is that at all levels—that is, in respect to truth, inner disposition, and behavior—the unity of the church is under constant threat from forces inimical to it. It is not the case that false doctrine, deceitful teachers, hardness of heart, disorderly desire, callousness, slander, rage, and malice appear in this

---

19. For this translation see M. Barth, *Ephesians 1–3*, 342–44.

letter simply as a standard list of gentile vices—markers that distinguish the children of light from the children of darkness. They exist as well within the assembly itself and so compromise its common life. Indeed, their continued presence among the saints occludes the saints' claim to have one Lord, one faith, one baptism, and even one God.

Consequently, it cannot truthfully be said that the unity that Christ's administration of the last age is to bring exists in what might be called a "pure" or "steady" state. Rather, its existence must be discerned in the midst of conflict—a conflict that does not rage simply between the church and the rest of humankind. Hardness of heart, darkened understanding, disorderly desire, callousness, and so on pop up everywhere, sadly even among the saints. The unity of all things in Christ must show itself, therefore, in a manner that imitates the way in which Christ confronted the "rulers of this present darkness." It must in fact imitate the sacrifice of Christ. This way of walking can be summed up by the word "love," but among the saints, imitation of the love of Christ has a definite profile. It can be recognized by eagerness "to maintain the unity of the Spirit in the bond of peace" (Eph. 4:3). Such eagerness shows itself in a willingness to "maintain" or struggle for the truth and so for the maturation of those who are still children in the Lord (4:15). Struggle for truth grows also out of an eagerness to watch over the unity of the church. Whether it springs from love of children in the Lord who may be led astray or from a desire to maintain the unity of the church, the struggle to maintain the truth is to be carried out in love. As has been pointed out, love that is eager to maintain unity and peace and that seeks the maturation of those who are still children in the Lord expresses itself in recognizable ways—as "humility of mind," "gentleness," "patience," and "forbearance."

In Christ's administration of God's assembly, unity, truth, love, and authority are inseparable. Each defines the other. The way in which one walks is part of the content of what one believes, and both belief and one's manner of life serve to give definition to the unity God intends. Accordingly, as presented in Ephesians, the primary focus of Christian ethics is the common life of the church. Life in Christ is tied to the truth with which the church has been entrusted and the calling it has been given. Both truth and calling testify to God's unifying purpose. In this respect, it is important to note that the way the saints walk serves as a particular way of confronting division and, at the same time, manifesting the character of the unity God intends. This way is to be followed when division is caused either by false teaching or by disordered desire and destructive social practice. Thus the saints are not only to put away those desires and behaviors that breed disunity. They are also to meet these threats to unity with truthfulness, kindness, sympathy, and forgiveness (Eph. 4:25–31).

In a memorable phrase, the writer of Ephesians suggests that Christ's "administration of the fullness of time" (1:10)[20] can be "rescued from misuse"[21] by careful attention to the way in which the saints live (5:15–16). In the course of his letter he gives a thick description of this way. It is a way modeled on Christ who "gave himself up for us" as a sacrifice to God (5:2). As this sacrifice reconciled people to God and one another, so its imitation manifests and effects (in the midst of continued conflict) the unity God intends for the entire creation. The focus of Christian living is thus first upon the common life of the church; its goal is the glory of God seen in the unity of the body; its basis is the redemptive economy of the Father, Son, and Holy Spirit; and its character is that of struggle carried out in imitation of Christ's sacrificial love. This love manifests itself in the first instance through the graces given the church through the Holy Spirit.

---

20. For this translation see Lincoln, *Ephesians*, 31–32.
21. Ibid., 342.

PART THREE

Possible Exceptions

6

Possible Exceptions

The Self

Introduction

The ecclesial focus of life in Christ present in the Epistle to the Ephesians is found throughout the New Testament writings. I believe it beyond dispute that the moral teaching of the Pastoral and Catholic Epistles has this focus. It is certainly present in Paul's authentic letters. As James Dunn has pointed out, Paul's moral instruction is intended to mark the present boundaries of the people of God and in so doing give them a visible identity.[1] It is not a stretch to say that, as in the case of the Letter to the Ephesians, these visible marks define for Paul a life that is worthy of the calling and destiny of God's people. For example, the calling and identity of the Christians in Rome is to become part of a people composed of both Jew and gentile (Rom. 11:25–27). Paul's instructions set forth those graces and practices that lead to the sort of peace he wishes for a body whose life together anticipates the future toward which God moves the peoples of the earth. In Paul's words, they are a reasonable form of worship (12:1) given in response to divine mercy.[2] This reasonable worship requires a renewal of the mind that produces a transformation in the way in which Christians relate one to another (12:3–21; 13:8–14; 14:1–15:6) and to their social and political environment (13:1–7).

---

1. James D. G. Dunn, *Romans 9–16*, Word Biblical Commentary 38b (Dallas: Word, 1988), 716.
2. For this interpretation, see ibid., 711–12.

An ecclesial focus is also given to the moral instruction found in the Gospels of Mark and John. Faced with the actuality or possibility of persecution, Mark's concern is to encourage his community. Faithful discipleship, he says, involves willing acceptance of persecution, suffering, and martyrdom. These traits reflect the necessity of the "Son of Man" to suffer and die. A disciple is called to follow this way and in so doing give a faithful witness to the life Christ has given as a "ransom for many" (Mark 10:45). Ethics, according to Mark, is a form of witness, not only on the part of individuals but also on the part of his disciples as a community of followers (14:27–28).[3]

Disciples in their communal practice are called to be like their master in a number of ways. They must consider themselves the least of all and the servant of all (Mark 9:35). As servants of all they must be willing to take up their cross and follow their Lord (8:38). They must even be willing to give up their lives rather than attempting to save them (8:35). Jesus instructs his disciples that, after his death, they are to follow him to Galilee where they will be his witnesses in the gentile world (14:28; 16:7). Accordingly, because they do not know when Christ will return, in their journey they must keep watch and be ready to confess Christ and follow wherever he might lead (13:35–37).

Though in a different way, John also focuses his account of life in Christ on faithful imitation of the Lord as a means of witness to the truth. For example, in Jesus's high priestly prayer in chapter 17, he prays that the disciples will be one even as he and his Father are one so that the world will know God has sent him (John 17:21). The unity of the disciples is thus a witness to the fact that Jesus has been sent by his Father. Further, the truthfulness and power of that witness depend upon the presence of the moral gift of love among the disciples. A true disciple is one who both believes in Jesus and obeys his command—namely, that the disciples love one another (13:34–35). The love disciples are to have one for another reflects the love Jesus has for them and in turn the love God has for Jesus. The love disciples have one for another and for Jesus is part of a great cycle of love (empowered by the Spirit) that moves from the mutual love of Father and Son, to the love God has for the world (3:16), to the love the disciples have for Jesus and one another, and then back again through Jesus to the Father (17:26). This cycle allows the world to know that God has sent Jesus. John's ethic is an ecclesial ethic of love in the service of witness (17:20–23).

At this point I must mention a previously noted gap in my argument. I have provided no study that establishes the pervasive nature of the focus on the common life of God's people that is to be found within the pages of the

---

3. Ernest Best has made this point forcefully. See Ernest Best, *Disciples and Discipleship: Studies in the Gospel according to Mark* (Edinburgh: T&T Clark, 1986), 12.

Hebrew Scriptures. As I pointed out in the introduction, a study of the ethical focus of the Law and the Prophets would prove too long and diffuse for present purposes. Nonetheless, I am convinced that it can easily be established that the clear focus of both God's covenant with Israel and the interpretation of that covenant by the prophets is the common life of the people as a response to God's grace and as a witness to the nations of God's call to them through Israel's worship and way of life. The witness of the New Testament locates the common life of the church within the same providential history.

The ethical teaching of the New Testament, like that of the Old, is weighted overwhelmingly in the direction of the common life of God's people. Nevertheless, one must ask if there are exceptions—exceptions that might shift the focus from the common life of the church to the life of the soul and/or to justice in the social order. One of the most likely is the Gospel according to Matthew. Matthew's account of Christ's command "You, therefore, must be perfect, as your heavenly Father is perfect" (Matt. 5:48) has been understood through the centuries as a guide to personal holiness. The Sermon on the Mount, which provides content both to the summary of the law (22:37–40) and to the perfection Christ demands, has been understood by some of the greatest figures in Christian history as a prescription for the cure of souls.

To be sure, along with St. Augustine, John Cassian, Leo Tolstoy, and many others, it is possible to read the Sermon on the Mount as a spiritual primer for the hungry soul, and in part it surely is. Nevertheless, the guidance it provides an individual for life in the Spirit is enclosed within a wider set of concerns—namely, the divine calling of the church. Before it is a guidebook for what we now refer to as "my spiritual journey," it is a charge to God's people for the way they, as a people, are to live together and the way in which they, as a people, are to relate to the world around them.

If we ask how Matthew portrays the basis, goal, and character of life in Christ, the ecclesial focus of his ethical concern stands out in bold relief. He makes all three (basis, goal, and character) plain in the prologue to his Gospel (Matt. 1–4) and in the summary of Jesus's teaching contained in the Sermon on the Mount (5–7). Careful examination of these texts clearly reveals that the Gospel of Matthew does not comprise an exception to the communal focus of the New Testament.

The Prologue (Matthew 1–4)

Matthew begins his Gospel with a book of origins that provides Jesus with a family tree—one that links him to two of the central figures in Israel's history (Matt. 1:1–17). Jesus is, through the titular fatherhood of Joseph, the descendent of both Abraham and David. His conception, however, is "of the Holy Spirit" (1:18). Through Abraham, Jesus is linked to God's promise that, by Abraham, "all the families of the earth shall bless themselves" (Gen. 12:3c). Through David, he is linked to the line of kings from whom Israel's savior will come. Through the Holy Spirit, he is "God with us" (Matt. 1:23).

Quite a lot has been said here. In Jesus, God has fulfilled his promise to open his blessing to the nations, his promise to Israel to provide a lasting kingdom, and his promise to his people, both Jew and gentile, to be with them until his purposes for creation are fulfilled (Matt. 1:23; 28:20). The promise to the gentiles that they will find blessing through Abraham is given particular emphasis in the prologue. Four gentile women are included in Jesus's genealogy—Tamar, Rahab, Ruth, and Bathsheba, the wife of Uriah the Hittite. Among the first people to worship Jesus are gentile astrologers (2:1–12). Jesus's association with Nazareth in all likelihood links him with a place that has a gentile name (2:23).[4] Finally, Jesus begins his public ministry in "Galilee of the Gentiles" (4:15).

Jesus's partial descent from gentile women, his recognition by astrologers representing the wisdom of the East, and the location of his ministry all point to the mission that the risen Christ will give his followers. They are to make disciples of all nations (Matt. 28:19–20). What might be called Jesus's trajectory toward the gentile world is partially explained by his reception at the hands of his own people. Herod along with "all Jerusalem" and its leaders are troubled by news of Jesus's birth (2:3–4). Herod seeks to kill the child and in a rage murders all males under two years of age. Joseph is forced to flee with his family to Egypt until Herod is dead. He then returns to Nazareth, a place with a gentile name.

The narrative of Jesus's birth tracks in miniature the course of his public ministry. Jesus is sent "only to the lost sheep of the house of Israel" (Matt. 15:24; see also 10:6), and his disciples are to go "nowhere among the Gentiles" (Matt. 10:5). However, Matthew goes on, through the course of his Gospel, to show increasing resistance to Jesus on the part of Israel's leaders and, in the end, the people of Israel themselves (27:1, 20). The resistance leads to Jesus's crucifixion. The Gospel concludes with the risen Christ, who claims "all authority in heaven and on earth," commanding his disciples to "make disciples of all nations" (28:18–19).

The mission to the gentiles, only hinted at in the prologue, is now the command of the risen Lord. The disciples, who were to go to the lost sheep of

---

4. For this interpretation, see Ulrich Luz, *Matthew 1–7*, Continental Commentaries (Minneapolis: Augsburg, 1992), 148–50.

Israel, are now to go to the nations, baptizing them in the name of the Trinity and teaching them to observe all that Jesus commanded both his disciples and the people (Matt. 28:18–20). The Gospel ends with Jesus, whose name is "God with us," promising his disciples that he will indeed be with them until the completion or consummation of the age (28:20b).

What the disciples are to teach the nations is contained in the Sermon on the Mount, wherein the content of Jesus's summary of the law is set forth. The character of the life Jesus's disciples are to live is displayed and taught not only by one that will be with them on their journey to the gentile world but also by one to whom they are to listen. They are to listen because his Father has delivered all things to him (Matt. 11:25–27). Thus the character of life in Christ is displayed within a comprehensive narrative that provides not only the model but also both the goal and basis of such a life.

The disciples are told that shaping their lives in the way Jesus taught is an "easy yoke" and a "light burden" (Matt. 11:30). However, Jesus also tells them that shaping their lives in this way means entering by a "narrow gate" and taking a "hard way" (7:14). Why then is the yoke easy, and why might it be good to take the hard way? What is the goal of a life with this character, and on what is it based?

In one sense, the goal is a form of eudaemonism. Jesus promises that by following this way, the disciples "will find rest for [their] souls" (Matt. 11:29c). Or again, he promises that it is a way that "leads to life" rather than destruction (7:13–14). As in the case of philosophical accounts of the moral life through the ages, so also in theological accounts: duty and beauty must, in the end, find a home together. Matthew's stern warning about the dire consequences of rejecting Christ and his teaching make it amply clear that both the evangelist and Jesus understood this necessary linkage (5:3–11; 7:21–27). Indeed, Matthew stresses that judgment for one's deeds provides an opposing possibility for the life and rest that follow from taking the hard way (5:20; 7:21; 25:31–46).

That said, the goal—or better, goals—that shape Matthew's account of the character of life in Christ lie on higher ground than the pain of harm and the satisfactions of blessing. The goals of entering by the narrow gate are on the one hand missiological and on the other doxological. Both are captured in Jesus's charge to his disciples, "Let your [plural] light so shine before [people], that they may see your good works and give glory to your Father who is in heaven" (Matt. 5:16). The works of Christ's followers are a testimony to the Son of God who listens to his Father. For this reason they are of the sort that cause God to be glorified. One might say that here divine will and human fulfillment come together. The human desire for rest and life finds its fulfillment in glorifying God. Glorifying the one true God who is the Father of Jesus is made possible by the testimony of action (before words) plainly visible in Christ's life and in the lives of his disciples. Mission thus provides the link between the human desire for life and rest and the satisfaction of that desire in finding something worthy of worship.

On what foundation do these goals rest? What is the basis of Matthew's account of life in Christ? His depiction of the life to which Jesus's disciples are called is rooted first in the will and pleasure of God—God, who guides the course of history. In a derivative sense it is rooted in the authority of the Son. He has made the Father's nature and will known, and he accompanies the Father's people until God's purposes for history have been fully realized.

The basis of the narrow way in Christ's life and teaching is clear enough. He delivers his teaching and presents his life to the disciples not as a new Moses but as God's beloved Son whom the disciples are to follow and to whom they are to listen (Matt. 3:17; 17:5c). The basis of Christian ethics in God the Father is presented in a less direct manner. Throughout the Gospel, Matthew takes great pains to show that what Jesus does is in fulfillment of the promises of Scripture.[5] In this way, Matthew depicts God's fidelity to his promises both to Israel and to the nations.

The character of life in Christ is based in a final sense in the providential will of a faithful God. It is also based in the fact that the faithful will of Jesus's Father is merciful. Israel's long history, a history that culminates in God sending his Son, above all else manifests the mercy of God. It is the mercy of God that lies at the heart of the prayer Jesus teaches his disciples (Matt. 6:12, 14). It is the mercy of God that most clearly defines the sort of love Jesus, in the Sermon on the Mount, marks out as the way to perfection (5:38–48). It is love expressed as mercy that most clearly defines the way in which members of the church are to live one with another (18:21–35).

Finally, entry through the narrow gate is possible because the one whose life is that gate accompanies the church until its mission is carried out and God's will for the nations is accomplished (Matt. 28:20b). For Matthew, Jesus is God with us—Immanuel. Faithful following on the part of the church is based on the providence of God expressed through the continuing presence of Christ in its common life. Unlike Luke, in Matthew's Gospel it is less the Holy Spirit that provides the church with strength to carry out its mission than the continuing presence of Christ with the church. As Christ rescues

---

5. Fulfillment sayings figure prominently in the prologue. See, e.g., 1:22; 2:6, 15, 17, 23; 3:3; 4:14. Fulfillment sayings are also found scattered throughout the remainder of the Gospel. See, e.g., 8:17; 12:17–21; 13:14–16, 35; 21:4–5, 15; 24:15; 27:9–10.

Peter (the representative disciple), whose weak faith causes him to sink in the storm-tossed waters, so also he accompanies and holds up the church through the storms it faces (Matt. 14:28–32).

The Sermon on the Mount (Matthew 5:1–7:28)

The Beatitudes

As presented by Matthew, God's will is not in the first place to save individual souls from their distress. It is rather for the nations of the earth to know his will and be obedient to it. The calling of the church is to make disciples of all nations and teach them to observe all that Christ has commanded them. This calling is accomplished through the faithful witness of the church, whose members are "salt of the earth" and "the light of the world." The ecclesial focus of Matthew's account of life in Christ becomes apparent in Matthew 5:13–20. These verses provide the (ecclesial) context for understanding the import of both the Beatitudes (5:3–11) and the following antitheses (5:21–48) that contain Jesus's interpretation of the law.

The explanatory beatitude about persecution found in Matthew 5:11–12 is clearly addressed to a church that is being reviled and spoken ill of by its opponents. Like the other beatitudes, it is addressed to "you" in the plural. In the context of persecution for his sake, Jesus addresses the disciples as a group and tells them that they (corporately) are salt and light to the world. He also makes it clear that the flavor they provide and the light they give stems from their "good works." The common life of the church is once again a form of witness.

He goes on to tell them that he has not come to do away with the law but to fulfill it. Thus the works enjoined upon the disciples include obedience to the full compass of the law, and indeed compose a righteousness that exceeds in both magnitude and quality that of the scribes and Pharisees. The Beatitudes (Matt. 5:3–11) and the antitheses (5:21–48) give content to this greater righteousness. The idea seems to be that when people see these works, they will understand that their source is God. The result is the glorification of the God and Father of Jesus and so also the fulfillment of God's purpose to give light to those who live in darkness (4:16; 28:19–20).

Matthew's account of life in Christ is set in the context of the common life of the church and its mission to the nations. Showing the nations a form of life taught and lived out fully by God's Son who hears and obeys every word spoken by God his Father carries out this mission. In this form of life, duty and beauty are conjoined. Those who, among other things, are poor in spirit, who mourn, who are meek, and who hunger and thirst for righteousness are "blessed" or "happy."

In keeping with his focus on deeds before words, Matthew, in contrast to Luke (Luke 6:20–26), makes their focus an internal rather than an external condition, giving them an ethical tone. The first four beatitudes point to a series of interior states that suggest certain virtues or, as I prefer to say, graces. In contrast to Luke, Matthew says the happy ones are not those who are in fact poor but those who know they are beggars before God. The happy ones don't weep. Rather, they mourn for the state of Israel or even the conditions of life prior to the establishment of God's kingdom.[6] To emphasize the interior and moral character he assigns the beatitudes, Matthew adds that the blessed include those who are "meek," or humble, before God. Further, they are not those who are simply hungry and thirsty. They are those who hunger and thirst to do right or to see right done.[7]

It is not surprising that these beatitudes have so frequently been understood as a road map for personal holiness—as the royal way that leads a person into the presence of God. Given the communal context in which they are presented, it is more reasonable, however, to take them as descriptive of the graces that give identity to the community that follows Jesus and does as Jesus did. No doubt they can and do map out a series of goals for those on a "spiritual journey," but before that they mark the common graces of what Matthew in 18:17 calls the church. If one is indeed to strive and/or pray for these graces, one is to do so primarily as a member of a community whose common life is distinguished by their presence. It is within a communal rather than a private context that one (rightly) pursues personal holiness.

The next four beatitudes rest upon these graces and are overtly communal in nature. They define forms of action in relation both to members of the church and to those outside its fellowship. Not surprisingly, the beatitudes meant to shape communal relations begin with the form of action Matthew regards as the primary expression of love. "Blessed are the merciful" (Matt. 5:7). Indeed, mercy is the essence of the law and lies between judgment and faith in the list of what Matthew calls "the weightier matters of the law" (Matt. 23:23; 18:21–35).

---

6. The meaning of πεντέω (mourn) as used here is notoriously difficult to determine. Its source is Isaiah 61:2–3 where "mourn" could refer to personal loss, to the state of Zion, or even to the state of the world. Here it might mean any or all of the possible uses mentioned above. See Luz, *Matthew 1–7*, 235. Or it might simply refer to human loss in general. See Eduard Schweizer, *The Good News according to Matthew*, trans. David E. Green (Atlanta: Westminster John Knox, 1975), 88f.

7. Given Matthew's emphasis on good works, this seems to me a more likely interpretation than one that focuses on righteousness that comes as a gift of God's power, or the righteousness that will come with the vindication of the just at the last judgment. See, e.g., Matt. 5:20–48. For a defense of the latter opinion, see Daniel J. Harrington, SJ, *The Gospel of Matthew*, Sacra Pagina (Collegeville, MN: Liturgical, 1991), 79.

Matthew's point would seem to be that one who does not show mercy should not expect to receive it (Matt. 6:14–15). In a more positive vein, in a community in which mercy is a standard way of relating to offenders or opponents, vengeance ceases to be a primary mode of social relation. Absence of revenge, in turn, paves the way for restored relationships, social harmony, or peace.

Mercy is both a grace and a practice that characterizes common life, and it sheds light in a manner that leads people to glorify God, the source of mercy. So also does purity of heart, the undivided center of moral agents that makes possible obedience to God (Matt. 5:8).[8] Mercy and undivided obedience (along with poverty of spirit, mourning, humility, and desire for right to be done) issue in forms of action aimed at peace. Thus those who make peace are among the blessed of God's kingdom (5:9). Nevertheless, these communal practices, which so clearly promote peace, provoke persecution. "Blessed are you [plural] who are persecuted for righteousness sake" (5:10, translation mine). Matthew's use here of the perfect passive participle of the verb "persecute" indicates that the persecution he has in mind is general. It refers to those "having been persecuted." Persecution is not an occasional misfortune. It is the mark of being a Christian (5:10).

Matthew concludes his version of the beatitudes with an explanatory note. The persecution that Christians can expect comes on Jesus's account—on account of seeking the righteousness that exceeds that of the scribes and Pharisees. Persecution places his followers in the company of the prophets and so at the heart of Israel's common life (Matt. 5:12). Like the prophets before them, the disciples of Jesus manifest what life in God's kingdom is like. In this way they are salt and light to the world. They also provoke attempts to extinguish that light. What is true of Christ is true also of the community that forms around him.

The Antitheses

The community Jesus draws to himself is called to obey the law and prophets. Jesus has both fulfilled what the prophets saw and rightly interpreted the law.

---

8. Understanding purity of heart to mean undivided obedience to God's will is suggested by Psalm 71:1 and by the ethical bent of Matthew's rendition of the beatitudes. In the history of interpretation purity of heart has been understood on occasion as freedom from desire or simplicity and integrity of motive. These may indeed be necessary companions of obedience, but Ulrich Luz has rightly warned of the following danger if these more spiritual meanings are separated from concrete forms of obedience. He says, "On the basis of the original meaning of the text one must constantly be on guard that purity of heart and seeing God will not lead to removal from the world or to private piety of one of the religiously gifted but will manifest itself as obedience toward God in the world and as hope for a future seeing of God which is more than private, individual experience." Luz, *Matthew 1–7*, 240–41.

The law, as lived and interpreted by Jesus and set forth in the antitheses (Matt. 5:21–48), defines the higher righteousness or the perfection the disciples are to seek. As such, the antitheses along with the beatitudes are exemplary of a form of life. For Matthew, the law in all its fullness, from which neither an iota or small pen stroke is to be removed, is in no way the opposite of grace. Rather, the form of life set forth in the law belongs to grace. The repeated phrase "but I say to you" indicates that Jesus, the definitive interpreter of the law, speaks the words of his Father, and these words are words of grace (11:15–27). Because he speaks his Father's word, it is now Jesus who provides access to Israel's Scriptures, and these Scriptures provide the form of life God wills to be a light to the nations.

What is the character or shape of that form of life? Its initial demand is a prohibition of murder, but the prohibition is extended to include anger and insult (Matt. 5:21–23). Jesus, the authoritative interpreter of the law, thus says that in its old formulation the law did not go far enough. With the inbreak of the kingdom, inner attitude (anger) and outward expression (violence and insult) are conjoined in a single prohibition. The most immediate application of this prohibition is then expressed positively and addressed in the first instance to members of the church. Thus if one remembers that a member of the church, a "brother," has been offended, one must immediately seek reconciliation (5:23–24). It does not stretch the imagination to see that a communal practice of reconciliation requires the support of the graces contained in the Beatitudes—humility, mercy, and the desire to see right done. These graces shape the lives of peacemakers, and peacemakers make a habit of seeking reconciliation.

Matthew next turns to three forms of action that compromise God's will for his people—adultery, purposeful seduction, and divorce (Matt. 5:27–32). Because of the stringency of these verses' demands, it is not surprising that the literature on them is enormous. I take the view that the Matthean exception in respect to divorce (5:32) refers to adultery. I take the view also that the focus of Jesus's (and Matthew's) concern here is the protection of marriage and so also, with the dawn of the kingdom of heaven, the restoration of God's original will for marriage. Among the good works of Jesus's disciples that are to shine before people are the sanctity and permanence of the marriage bond.

The fact that the prohibitions of adultery and divorce are conjoined indicates that the concern here is the sanctity of marriage rather than a generalized condemnation of unruly desire. Jesus not only affirms the prohibition of adultery in the Decalogue (Exod. 2:14) but also condemns an intentional expression of lust through the eyes that has adultery as its goal. Thus he makes the hyperbolic statement that the eye and hand, the instruments of adultery, are to be "cut off" (Matt. 5:29–30). In modern terms, in the kingdom of heaven, one simply is not to "go there." In like manner, divorce, save for adultery, is strictly prohibited. The exception provided by Moses that allows a man to divorce his wife was made only to accommodate "hardness of heart" (19:7–8). In the kingdom of heaven, God's original will for marriage, that "the two become one flesh" and so indivisible, is to be the practice of the church. Within the church, the only exception to the prohibition is adultery, an action thought by the Jews to desecrate the land and destroy marriage.[9]

The sermon turns next to two of the most fundamental mechanisms of social interaction—truth telling and promise making (Matt. 5:33–37). Jesus forbids his disciples to swear oaths. In these days only a few take this prohibition seriously, but it has not always been so. Anabaptists were once burned at the stake for adherence to it, while Anglican priests had to subscribe to an Article of Religion allowing oaths when required by a magistrate.[10] The disputed issue had to do with the extent of government's authority over its citizens. Refusal to take an oath was considered treasonous.

Despite the easy way in which it now is dismissed, this prohibition remains of fundamental importance. Two issues are involved in its interpretation. First, taking an oath, since normally it is sworn in God's name, might involve using the Lord's name in vain and so dishonoring it. Second, oaths are occasioned by the existence of falsehood. Oaths are made necessary by lies and are meant to invoke divine retribution in cases where false statements and/or promises are made. Despite the allowances made for oaths in the Old Testament, and despite their prominent (many would say necessary) role in public life, it does appear that Jesus forbade them. As in the case of the prohibition of divorce, it is likely he did so because, with the dawn of God's kingdom, lies and false promises, like fractured marriages, have no place.

If the marriage bond is sacrosanct, so also are what people assert or promise. Oaths are not to be part of the common life of God's people because lies and false promises are occasions for disharmony. They come from the evil one (Matt. 5:37b). In the kingdom of heaven, yes is to be yes and no is to be no. In the kingdom of heaven, a practice built upon falsehood has no place. Truth is simply to be spoken and promises kept. Piling up words and oaths only confirms the continuing presence of lies, and lies undermine the basic forms of

---

9. See, e.g., Lev. 18:25, 28; 19:29; Deut. 24:4; Hosea 4:2–3; Jer. 3:1–3, 9.

10. Article 39 of the 39 Articles of Religion reads: "We confess that vain and rash Swearing is forbidden Christian men by our Lord Jesus Christ, and James his Apostle, so we judge, that Christian Religion doth not prohibit, but that a man may swear when a Magistrate requireth, in a cause of faith and charity, so it be done according to the Prophet's teaching in justice, judgment, and truth."

interaction that make social life possible. Peaceful social relations require truth to be spoken and promises to be kept. Those who speak the truth and keep their promises are also those who make peace (5:9). These are the ones God will recognize as "sons" when he fully establishes his kingdom, but even now their truthfulness shines in a way that allows people to see the work of God (5:16).

To summarize, to this point the communal ethic presented by Matthew displays a form of life in which humility, mercy, and a desire to see right done (justice) are honored and coupled with a desire for peace and a communal practice of seeking reconciliation.[11] These graces and practices banish from common life those forms of action that most undermine social peace. Chief among these are anger, violence, and insult. These threats to harmony are closely followed by others. First come violations of the marital bond through infidelity and/or divorce. Next comes the prohibition of oaths—an injunction that indicates that within the community Jesus forms truthful speech is simply to be assumed in all forms of social relation.

In this community, justice, mercy, and truth are to shine forth to the world in exemplary fashion and, in doing so, reflect the glory of God. It is not surprising, therefore, that the fifth antithesis addresses the question of retribution (Matt. 5:38-42). How should the community and its individual members react when evil is done to them? Is an eye to be taken for an eye or a tooth for a tooth? Jesus's comment on the *lex talionis* (Exod. 21:24) precludes resistance and even proportional vengeance. Rather, be it the evil personal insult, the hostile and prohibited legal action against a poor debtor (22:26), or the unjust demand of forced labor by the colonial power Rome, it is not to be resisted (Matt. 5:38-41).[12] The key to understanding these prohibitions lies in verse 39a. Each is an example of a blanket command to refrain from resisting evil, and as Ulrich Luz has pointed out, the command applies to both the community and its individual members.[13]

No one commenting on these verses can escape addressing the extent of their application. Early Christians certainly took them to apply extensively, thus prohibiting not only private actions of self-defense but also public actions such as military service and public office. Others through the ages have sought to limit the areas of their application. This dispute remains and continues to divide Christian opinion.[14] It is my view that the interpretation Jesus and

---

11. These graces and practices clearly undergird the discussion of church discipline in Matthew 18. The verses that address the discipline of a wayward member of the congregation stress both honest speech and patience; and they are surrounded by verses that valorize mercy.

12. Luz, *Matthew 1-7*, 325-26.

13. Ibid., 330-31.

14. See, e.g., Paul Ramsey, *Speak Up for Just War or Pacifism* (University Park: Pennsylvania State University Press, 1988).

Matthew give to the weightier matters of the law (judgment, mercy, and faith) lessens the stringency of their teaching about resistance of evil and divorce. This is not to say that one is here dealing only with broad principles that never become rooted in concrete prohibitions. It is to say, however, that Christians have not been wrong to see possible tensions, for example, between a complete renunciation of resistance to evil on the one hand and the demand of love and mercy to protect a threatened neighbor on the other.

It is perhaps the weightier matters of the law that lead Matthew to couple his prohibition of resistance to evil with a positive command to give to those who beg and to lend to those in need (Matt. 5:42). Christ's disciples are to turn away from vengeance and practice nonresistance, but they are also to turn with generosity toward those in need. In this antithesis, renunciations are coupled with a positive injunction that directs attention to the needs of one's neighbors.

A more sweeping movement toward the neighbor follows the positive thrust that concludes the fifth antithesis. Jesus's disciples are to love their enemies and pray for their persecutors (Matt. 5:33–34). Mention of "the ones persecuting you [plural]" (translation mine) clearly indicates that Matthew here addresses the church, and he does so in a way meant to distinguish the behavior of Jesus's followers from not only that of the Jews but the gentiles (5:6–7). There is no command in the law for one to hate one's enemy, but by adding this phrase to the command to love one's neighbor (Lev. 19:18), Matthew suggests the love command, contrary to the popular (but wrong) understanding, does not apply only to those often called "near neighbors"—to those who love you or are your "brothers." These are standards even tax collectors and gentiles affirm. With members of the church, things are to be different. They are to seek perfection in both attitude and action that reflects the perfection of God (5:48). This perfection, love from the heart expressed toward one's enemies, imitates the perfection of God and exceeds the righteousness of both the scribes and Pharisees.

Needless to say, the stringency of this particular demand has led to all manner of attempts to either narrow its import or question both its wisdom and its applicability to actual human life. Chief among these efforts are ones that seek to present love of one's enemy in an instrumental light—as, for example, an engine for establishing justice. It is highly unlikely, however, that either Jesus or Matthew viewed the command to love one's enemy as instrumental. Even when seen as a light that shines, works of love for one's enemy are understood rightly only if one sees in them the glory of God. For Jesus and Matthew, they are not to be prized as instruments that serve as means for human purposes. As Ulrich Luz has written, "It was not the intention of Jesus to improve the situation of the world. Acts of love toward enemies are, in Jesus's view, an expression of the unconditional yes of God for human beings for their own sake. They are necessary in a fundamental sense and stand alongside of and *before* all realistic strategies of 'intelligent' love."[15]

Piety and Prayer

Analysis of the Beatitudes and the antitheses reveals an ecclesial focus to Matthew's account of life in Christ. However, the following discussion of Jewish piety—almsgiving, prayer, and fasting—gives instruction about what we might in this day call "spirituality" or "personal religion." If, however, we were to ask Jesus for "spiritual direction," he most certainly would mistake our meaning. If we were to rephrase our question and ask about the disciplines or practices incumbent upon a faithful Jew, he would answer almsgiving, prayer, and fasting (Matt. 6:1–18). These are assumed to provide the content of Jewish piety. They provide the practices that form a faithful people. Almsgiving binds Israel to the poor for whom God has a particular concern. Prayer refers all of life to God. Fasting is the human mechanism for admission of guilt and placement of that guilt before God in the hope of mercy.

Concern about the practice of piety expressed here is not that the disciples will fail in their religious duty. It is that they will "do their righteousness" so as to be seen and so attract glory to themselves rather than God. The point here is that, if wrongly used, the piety upon which the practices of the community rest will subvert the purpose of those very practices. Thus Jesus's disciples are to perform these actions in private so as to be seen and rewarded by God rather than others. Matthew provides no special Christian "spirituality." He assumes the continuation of Jewish practice on the part of his disciples. His concern is that the practice of piety might subvert the entire purpose of the way in which Christian life is to be lived, namely, that at the sight of the way Christians live, God will be seen at work and so glorified.

Prayer is central to the practice of piety, and Matthew places Jesus's instructions on how to pray right in the middle of his discussion of almsgiving and fasting (Matt. 6:7–13). Prayer is the engine that drives both. It is not surprising, therefore, that the prayers of the church are not to take the form of flowery requests for personal assistance. God knows what we need before we ask and will not be moved by ingratiating petitions. The prayers of the church are to focus on God's will for the world and for the church. Thus the disciples are to pray "Our Father"—a term of address that indicates

---

15. Luz, *Matthew 1–7*, 351, emphasis original.

the confidence of the community that the God to whom they pray answers prayer. With this confidence, they pray that they will hallow the name of God through the sort of righteousness that comprises the perfect obedience they seek. So also they pray that God will establish his kingdom over the earth and that in that kingdom he will enable his will to be done. It is within the frame of lives trustful of God's power to establish his will for the world that the disciples are then instructed to ask for "bread for the morrow" (translation mine). In modern terms, this petition means that insofar as nourishment is concerned, the disciples are to trust in God's provision and, as it were, "take it one day at a time."

The next petition is of particular importance for defining the nature of the community that Jesus teaches to pray. Assuming that God has forgiven them, they are to ask that their debts be forgiven as they forgive their debtors. The central importance of this petition is signaled by the fact that it is the only one that is given further explanation (Matt. 6:14–15). God shows mercy, but if those who have received mercy do not show it in turn, they will not be forgiven. The community Jesus draws to himself is one in which reconciliation is of primary importance. The Beatitudes and the antitheses certainly focus on the centrality of peace and reconciliation. So also does the discussion of church discipline in chapter 18 wherein the provision for "excommunication" is surrounded and indeed muted by discussions of forgiveness and mercy.

It is safe to say that the ecclesial focus of Christian ethics found in the Sermon on the Mount itself focuses on reconciliation. It is safe to say also that the Beatitudes simply state that those who are part of such a community must expect to be persecuted both for their righteous practices and for the sake of Jesus in whose name they act. Thus, the final petition of the Lord's Prayer is that the community will not be led into temptation, that is, that it will not be confronted with forms of persecution that are simply overwhelming.

The Beatitudes, the antitheses, and Jesus's instructions about the practice of piety all seek to form a community whose good works are visible and, as in the case of Ephesians, serve to draw from people the praise of God's glory. Jesus's sermon concludes with three additional discussions—one concerning wealth, one concerning trust in God's care, and one concerning judgment upon the behavior of a brother or sister.[16]

---

16. There is an additional command about giving dogs what is holy and throwing one's pearls before pigs (7:6). The meaning of this saying is extraordinarily obscure, and I am quite unsure of its meaning. I am inclined to believe that it is directed to the radical missionaries that clearly play a part in Matthew's instruction to the church. If these are those the evangelist addresses, the saying is likely to mean that when they meet resistance in their itinerant ministry, they are simply to move on. I am far from certain, however, that this is Matthew's meaning.

The question of wealth receives extensive treatment, beginning with the command that forbids heaping up treasure (Matt. 6:19–21). This warning should not be spiritualized so as to include all manner of earthly pleasures. Neither should it be internalized by means of the statement that follows about the eye being the lamp of the body (6:22–23). It should not, in other words, be understood to mean that wealth is okay as long as one is not attached to it; that is to say, wealth is fine as long as the "eye is sound" or the heart pure. The statement about heaping up treasure is a direct warning about the corrupting power of wealth. Like the Lord's Prayer, the sayings about wealth found in this section of the sermon lie at the center of Jesus's instructions because one cannot in fact serve God and money. Money turns out to be an attractive and powerful master that compromises the higher righteousness to which disciples are called. It tends to capture the heart and become the focus of life (6:21). If one's eye is not sound, if it does not reflect honest and obedient behavior, then one's life is dark.[17] One's treasure is located not only in a place where it can be lost but also in a place that turns disciples from undivided obedience to their Lord.

It is not surprising that the saying about single-minded obedience is followed by a parable that focuses on trust in God's willingness and ability to provide for the daily needs of the disciples (Matt. 6:25–34). The parable about the birds and the lilies links to the petition in the Lord's Prayer about "bread for the morrow" (translation mine). The credibility of both the petition and the parable depend upon God's knowledge of the disciples' needs and his willingness and ability to provide for those needs. A demand not to heap up treasure but to live for the day must produce anxiety. Anxiety about food and clothing can be addressed only by trust in the Father of Jesus to whom the disciples pray. Only this sort of trust will permit them to seek first the kingdom and its righteousness (6:33). As they wait, however, they may be certain that if they ask, they will receive. The Father of Jesus knows what they need and will provide it (7:7–11).

The discussions of wealth and trust in Matthew 6:19–34 and 7:7–11 set a remarkably high standard. High standards have a dark side. They lead to negative judgments about the people who do not meet them. Perhaps it is not an accident, therefore, that a cautionary statement about negative judgments within the fellowship of the church follows Matthew's treatment of piety and money. The example provided is a negative judgment on a "brother," suggesting perhaps a failure to live up to the sort of righteousness that exceeds that of the scribes and Pharisees. Life together as Christ wills it, however, is not one taken

---

17. Luz, *Matthew 1–7*, 397.

up with the failures of others. It precludes judgment on one's fellow disciple by someone who has a log in his or her own eye—by one who in fact can't see! Rather, life together as Christ wills it is one in which each looks first to his or her own struggle to follow. To focus attention first on one's own behavior allows one to make a true assessment of the behavior of one's brother or sister.

The sayings about judgment are meant to instruct the church about how its members are to live one with another and how they are to order their common life when the failure of a brother or sister threatens its integrity. The Lord's Prayer, in which the disciples are instructed to forgive as they have been forgiven, and the instruction given in these verses about the need to examine one's own life, bracket any judgment passed upon a brother or sister. As in chapter 18, so here forgiveness and repentance make possible mutual correction within the church. Apart from this prior ascesis, true judgment and appropriate mutual correction are impossible. If offered prior to this ascesis, correction will neither reflect the higher righteousness nor appropriately address the failure of a brother or sister.

Matthew ends his account of Jesus's instruction to the church with a promise and a threat (Matt. 7:13–14). The higher righteousness to which he calls his disciples is a "narrow gate," but it leads to life. There is another gate, which is wide. It leads to destruction. As in the Beatitudes, duty and beauty are conjoined in the kingdom of heaven. Naturally enough, because there is a wide gate that does not require a higher righteousness, there are many "false prophets" who insist the wide gate is the one to take (7:15). The disciples, however, are to judge these false teachers by the works of their followers. They will not be ones that lead people to give glory to God. What is more, the wide gate leads to destruction.

Matthew's account of Jesus's ecclesial ethic ends with an unresolved tension. Only those who do the will of Jesus's Father will enter the kingdom of heaven (Matt. 7:21). Matthew is quite clear that in the end each person will be judged on the basis of his or her works. Yet he does not end with a counsel of despair because of the one who in the end will judge our days and ways. He is the Father whose chief characteristic is to have mercy, and whose Son has taught us to forgive as we have been forgiven.

Concluding Comment

Matthew's presentation of Jesus's moral teaching is quite rigorous. It defines the character of a community by valorizing a set of graces and practices that have their center in mercy and reconciliation. These graces and practices issue in a form of luminous communal tranquility that shines before the world and provides a striking counterexample to the way in which most communities order common life. That said, the saints of the church have been right to see in Matthew's presentation of Jesus's teaching a form of ascesis that leads individuals on a path to holiness of life. Jesus's teaching does in fact mark out a royal way that leads to God. However, Matthew locates that royal way within the life of a people that has a particular calling under God. For Matthew, the practice of piety does not in the first place find its direction and meaning within a personal quest. Rather, it finds its direction and meaning within the grand purpose of God—that is, through a chosen people to bring the nations of the earth under divine rule.

7

Possible Exceptions

Society

The Gospel according to Luke

Introduction

Are their exceptions to the ecclesial focus in Scripture that direct attention first not to the common life of the church but to reform of the social order or liberation from oppression? There are two obvious contenders. One is the Gospel according to Luke, and the other is the Revelation to John. The first has been a primary source for the socio-political focus of liberation theology, and the second for Christian resistance to totalitarian forms of government. It would appear that in both places there is a focus on the power of governance and its capacity for evil, but is appearance reality?

Given the prominent place Luke's Gospel plays in the writings of the Latin American school of political theology and the present influence of that school on the churches in North America, it makes sense to begin there. The case that advocates of this school make for a social and political focus in Luke is more than plausible. In his opening sermon at Nazareth, Jesus claims that God has anointed him "to preach good news to the poor." He has been sent "to proclaim release to the captives" and "to set at liberty those who are oppressed" (Luke 4:18). In his Sermon on the Plain he pronounces blessings on the poor and promises that the kingdom of God belongs to them. Conversely, he pronounces woe upon the rich (6:20, 24). Throughout his public ministry he calls to himself the excluded members of Jewish society—women (some apparently prostitutes), children, lepers, tax collectors, the lame, and the blind. They are lifted up while those with money and status are disqualified from life in the kingdom of God.

It is plausible to think that Luke's Jesus is a messianic political figure, a son of David who has come to restore justice by elevating the low and putting down the mighty from their seats (Luke 1:52). Luke's primary moral (and religious) concern, however, is the establishment of a renewed Israel whose communal identity reflects life in the kingdom of God. His view of both the disadvantaged poor and the power of Rome is entirely shaped by a prior concern for the formation of a faithful community of people, both Jew and gentile, who follow "the way" marked out by Jesus as faithful to God's "plan" for the salvation of the world (see, e.g., Luke 7:30; Acts 2:22–23; 4:28; 5:38–39; 20:27). That way is defined by the life of Jesus, and Jesus's disciples are called to imitate this life so that they become "a light for revelation to the Gentiles, and for Glory to thy people Israel" (Luke 2:32).

The Character of a Renewed Israel

The primary actor in Luke's Gospel, however, is not Jesus but the God of Israel (Luke 1:35). The God whom Jesus calls Father has a redemptive purpose—namely, to restore his people as a faithful people so that through them all peoples will be brought under God's rule. History takes its meaning from this purpose. So also does the life of Jesus and the people whom God has elected to be his special possession. The question once more is, what is the basis and goal of a people so called and so designated, and what are the characteristics or identifying marks that distinguish them from the peoples of the earth?

In the case of Luke, the most clarifying place to begin is with the character of the people Jesus calls to follow him. Those who follow are understood by Luke to be the restored people of Israel. Their character is displayed, on the one hand, against the backdrop of God's plan to bring salvation to the peoples of the earth (e.g., Luke 2:29–31; Acts 2:23; 20:27) and, on the other, by resistance to that plan on the part of an evil force, Satan (Luke 4:1–13; 22:3, 53; Acts 26:18). Jesus initiates the final conflict between these adversaries, and he does so by placing his life fully in the service of God's purpose. Through his obedience, Jesus defeats the devil and in so doing marks out a "way" that is to be followed by the people whom God has chosen (Luke 13:10–17; Acts 18:25–26; 19:23; 22:4; 24:14).

The character of the life of the people is thus formed by the imitation of a particular life—in this case, that of God's own Son (Luke 1:35). In Luke's account, Jesus's life has clearly defined markers. These markers are displayed in an "orderly account" (ἀκριβῶς καθεξῆς) of the events that make up the fabric of his life and ministry (1:3). The account Luke presents is "orderly" in the sense that it is designed to bring out the significance of the things "that have been [fulfilled]" among his readers (1:1). Through this "orderly account," Luke hopes first to give his readers confidence in God and his plan and, second, to show what faithful adherence to that plan requires.

Luke's Prologue

The marks of Jesus's life are the marks disciples are to emulate, and Luke wastes no time in bringing them to his reader's attention. The prologue to his Gospel sets them out in a short but concentrated space (Luke 1:5–4:13). The account of the boy Jesus in the temple confronts the reader with the first mark. Jesus's parents have lost track of him but find him in the temple "listening" and "asking questions." When his parents scold him for wandering off and treating them badly, he responds by asking them why they did not know that "I must be in my Father's house" (2:49). The primacy of God's claim on Jesus is seen from the beginning and is without exception, even the exception of family obligation.

That the first mark of Jesus's life is absolute submission to God's plan for him, and it is made even more explicit in the temptation narrative (Luke 4:1–13). In the desert, the great adversary of that plan, Satan, confronts Jesus with the same temptations Israel faced in the wilderness. Each temptation in its own way calls Israel and then Jesus away from obedience to God's purpose for them. Each temptation leads Jesus beyond the boundary God has set for him. In a negative way, the temptations mark the borders within which Jesus (and the church) must find "the way." That way leads to the cross rather than to the blandishments placed by the devil along the path that it is God's will that he follow. Thus the temptation brought on by hunger teaches Jesus (and God's people) that they do not live by bread alone but by sustenance provided by God (Deut. 6:4–15; Luke 4:4). The temptation brought on by the possibility of power becomes the temptation to worship other gods (Deut. 6:4–15; Luke 4:7). The temptation to put God to the test exposes a lack of the trust, which compromises obedience to the call of God (Deut. 6:16; Luke 4:9–12).

The temptations exemplify Jesus's absolute devotion to his Father's business, and they place that devotion in relation to a struggle with a force of evil whose intent is to frustrate God's intention for his people and his Son. Jesus's fidelity to his Father reveals that obedience to God's plan leads to a life of conflict. What is true for Jesus is true also for his disciples (Luke 9:57–62). The chief mark of their lives is a fidelity to God that brings about conflict with the authorities of gentile and Jewish society (3:1–2, 19–20), the Jewish people as a whole (3:7–9), and finally Satan himself (4:1–13).

The life of the disciples is portrayed in exactly the same way. They must remain obedient to the heavenly vision in the midst of conflict brought on by that very vision (Acts 26:19–23). Thus Luke presents Mary the mother of Jesus as an icon of faithful obedience. Mary speaks the defining word, "Behold, I am the handmaid of the Lord; let it be to me according to your word" (Luke 1:38). The inevitability of conflict is linked in Luke's succeeding volume, the Acts of the Apostles, with two gifts of the Spirit that accompany and sustain followers of the way in the midst of their trials—wisdom (σοφία) and bold speech (παρρησία). Thus, faced with opposition, Stephen speaks with "wisdom and the Spirit" (Acts 6:8–10), and Peter and Paul speak with "boldness" (4:13, 29, 31; 9:27–29; 14:3; 28:31).

At this point a parenthetical remark is entirely in order. It is common (though less than once was the case) for those who write about religion and the moral life to make a distinction between religious ideals and moral duties. Religious ideals fall within a realm of personal choice and as such are not universally binding. Moral duties, however, are common to humankind and so are (all things being equal) universally obligatory. In Luke's account of life in Christ, however, this distinction is misleading in that it distorts all that he is trying to communicate to his readers. Disciples are called to follow "the way" of Jesus. That way is rooted first of all in faithful obedience accompanied by conflict with the orders of society and evil forces of superhuman strength. These circumstances in turn demand bold speech. These marks of the life of a disciple are of a piece with others that will appear—for example, care for the poor and inclusion within the circle of social life of those denied its benefits. Each in its own way is an aspect of "the way" and so marks out a path all peoples are called to take. That path has been blazed by Christ and charts the way in which one places one's life in the service of God's purpose for his creation.

Faithful obedience, willingness to face conflict, bold speech, care for the poor, and inclusion of the outcast are all part of "the way." Looked at from within Luke's perspective, distinctions between religious ideals and moral duties make no sense. To make a distinction between a religious duty (e.g., obedience to God's plan) and a moral duty (e.g., sharing wealth with the poor) is to impose categories that function within the confines of societies characterized by various forms of democratic pluralism. They come from another social space, and their imposition distorts Luke's meaning. He is not proposing a religious ideal for some that is accompanied by more universal moral obligations. He is proposing a way meant for all people, and he is asking Christ's followers to take that way so as to be, like Christ, a light to the gentiles and the glory of God's people Israel.

The Beginning of Jesus's Public Ministry

In addition to faithful obedience, willingness to enter into conflict with evil, and bold speech, other markers lie along the path. Joel Green helpfully points out that Luke 4:14–9:50 demonstrates "how Jesus, empowered by the Spirit, understood the nature of his vocation and engaged in its performance by means of an itinerant ministry."[1] Luke's account of Jesus's sermon in the synagogue at Nazareth provides an epitome of that ministry. In so doing, the sermon sets out the marks of a faithful community as well as those of a faithful Son. Jesus has been anointed by the Spirit "to preach good news to the poor" and to "proclaim the acceptable year of the Lord." The poor, the passage suggests, include more than those who suffer from economic privation. They include those who are captive, those who are blind, and those who are oppressed.

As I have said, this passage is understood by many to provide a charter for giving Christian ethics a social focus. So also is Jesus's teaching in the Sermon on the Plain, which is intended to instruct the people he has just called on the way of a disciple (Luke 6:29–49). His instruction begins with a description of the way things are when God's rule dawns. That rule begins with a great reversal. The poor are blessed, and the rich suffer woes (6:20, 24). The hungry are fed, while those who are full go hungry (6:21, 25a). Those who now weep will laugh, but those who now laugh will both mourn and weep (6:21b, 25b). Those who are excluded because of their loyalty to Jesus will leap for joy because of the reward that will be theirs. However, those who now enjoy social acceptance and honor will suffer woe because they exchanged God's way for a course set out by false prophets (6:22–23, 29).

Certainly the Sermon on the Plain expresses the great reversal Mary prophesies: "He has scattered the proud in the imagination of their hearts, he has put down the mighty from their thrones, and exalted those of low degree; he has filled the hungry with good things, and the rich he has sent away empty" (Luke 1:51b–53). Why then not take the sermons at Nazareth and on the plain as a charter for a "social gospel," even a "theology of liberation" that focuses on reform (even revolutionary change) of the social order?

The answer is that Jesus's instruction in both places focuses on a particular social order—that of Israel and the church. Both texts describe life in the

---

1. Joel B. Green, *The Gospel of Luke*, NICNT (Grand Rapids: Eerdmans, 1997), 197.

faithful Israel it is Jesus's mission to call forth. Mary's song of praise is quite specific. The great reversal she has just described is a sign that through Jesus God "has helped his servant Israel, in remembrance of his mercy, as he spoke to . . . Abraham and to his posterity forever" (Luke 1:54–55). The promise to Abraham is that both he and his posterity will be blessed, and that through this blessed people all the peoples of the earth will come to share in the blessing it is God's will to bestow. Jesus's mission is to establish a people through whom this promise will be fulfilled. It is not to place before the world a program for the political and social reform of the Roman Empire.

It is within the context of this mission to Israel that good news to the poor and the blessings and woes Jesus pronounces are to be understood. The poor constitute a category of persons that includes more than those who do not have enough to live a decent life. In Luke's account, the poor are all those who have a disadvantaged position within the life of Israel because of their material or physical deprivation, their gender, their vocation, or their moral and religious purity. The poor are Israel's dwellers on the margins who are denied the benefits of participation in the life of the people.[2] In the kingdom of God, these people will be drawn into the blessings God bestows on his people, and it is to these people that Jesus and his disciples are sent (Luke 15:1–32).

According to Luke, Jesus is a prophet sent to Israel (and particularly to its lost sheep) by God to both announce and bring these blessings into effect.[3] Thus, as the narrative that follows makes clear, the "release" (ἄφεσιν) that is such a central aspect of the good news Jesus preaches to the poor refers not only to release from material deprivation but also release from sin and the power of evil (Luke 4:33–35; 5:12–14, 17–25). Indeed, Luke makes the expansive and salvific sense he assigns "release" clear in his account of Jesus's rejection and death upon the cross. It is this event more than any other that procures "release" and salvation for Israel and the peoples of the earth.[4] This event signals God's forgiveness and his will to draw the excluded members of Israel into the circle of its blessed life. The news preached to the poor is good not only because their material, social, or spiritual condition has been altered for the better. The news is also good because by their "release" God establishes a faithful people destined to include all the peoples of the earth.

---

2. See, e.g., Robert C. Tannehill, *The Narrative Unity of Luke-Acts: A Literary Interpretation* (Philadelphia: Fortress, 1991), 1:103.

3. See, e.g., Green, *Gospel of Luke*, 210–14, and Luke Timothy Johnson, *The Gospel of Luke*, Sacra Pagina 3 (Collegeville, MN: Liturgical, 1991), 80–81.

4. See David P. Moessner, "Reading Luke's Gospel as Ancient Hellenistic Narrative," in *Reading Luke*, ed. Craig G. Bartholomew, Joel B. Green, and Anthony Thiselton (Grand Rapids: Zondervan, 2005), 135, 140.

The news is good because it proclaims the success of God's plan to save the world he has created and redeemed.

However, it still must be asked if the release procured is gained by a military victory over Israel's enemies, particularly Rome. The language of Luke 1 and 2 places great emphasis on Jesus's decent from David, and in keeping with royal imagery it is certainly both political and military. Are the references in Luke's prologue to military victory and the establishment of David's line to be taken literally or metaphorically?

If they are taken literally, one can only conclude that the prophecies Luke recounts proved false. As Luke's narrative unfolds, no acts of political deliverance are recorded. As I. Howard Marshall has written, "Instead we have a wandering prophet going around the country areas of Galilee and Judea, certainly with healing powers that he exercises, but equally certainly with no indication of starting a political revolution."[5] What we do see, however, in the healing powers and in other manifestations of Jesus's authority, is a battle with Satan and with those whom he controls. The battle begins in the wilderness and reaches its climax on the cross—an event Luke interprets as the "hour and the power of darkness" (Luke 22:53b). Jesus's submission to the devil's designs and his subsequent vindication in the resurrection and ascension manifest his victory and portend the successful completion of God's plan. In short, there is every reason to interpret the military language and royal imagery not as a political prediction about the nation of Israel but as a depiction of "a military campaign in which the ultimate forces are the supernatural powers of God and Satan."[6] Luke's purpose is to show the way in which God's purpose will be accomplished, and he does so by means of military language and royal imagery. Jesus's ministry fills the Davidic hope of Israel with new content.

The chief mark of "the way" is obedience (accompanied by bold speech) in the midst of conflict. Faithful obedience is, however, bracketed by faith on the one hand and repentance on the other. Both John and Jesus call Israel to turn to God in faith that he is about to restore the fortunes of his people. Faith expresses itself in trust that God will fulfill his promises; repentance expresses itself in turning from a way of life that runs contrary to those promises. In calling for a return to faithful obedience, Jesus has more in mind than the redemption and reform of individual lives. Luke gives a large portion of his two works over to showing that in calling disciples Jesus also sets about to resocialize his followers and shape among them a "way" that manifests the form

---

5. I. Howard Marshall, "Political and Eschatological Language in Luke," in Bartholomew, Green, and Thiselton, *Reading Luke*, 159.

6. Ibid., 161.

of life to which Israel is called. Faithful obedience to God's plan gives birth to a faithful people, and the life of that people has an identifiable character.

The Sermon on the Plain provides a condensed summary of that character. Jesus both calls his disciples and instructs them in the context of prayer—an act that shows divine authorization of new leadership for Israel (hence twelve disciples for the twelve tribes) and of new conditions that are to shape the behavior of God's people. The new conditions are the mercy of God (Luke 15:11–32), which breaks down the boundaries that exclude people from Israel's common life.

Thus, in this sermon, Jesus sets out the behavior appropriate for those who submit their lives to God's plan, and he gives an account of the foundation of this behavior. God's mercy provides the wellspring from which his plan flows. Accordingly, the grace that lies at the base of the disciples' common life is love of one's enemy (Luke 6:27). In the first instance, this grace expresses itself in refusal to return evil for evil done (Luke 6:28–29, 30b). In a more positive vein, love is manifest in willingness to lend to "everyone" who begs and to do so without expecting gain for oneself (6:30a, 34, 35a). Willingness to forgive offense produces peace. Willingness to lend without hope of gain erases the boundaries that divide people from one another and places them no longer in the outer circle of strangers but in the inner circle of family and friends. Kin do not need to beg. They are cared for. So in the book of Acts one expression of this form of common life is that within "the company of those who believed . . . there was not a needy person among them" (Acts 4:32a, 34).

In a few words, Jesus gives shape to a new form of society—one that is not based upon the quid pro quo of retaliation or debt incursion (as in Roman society) but upon a form of reciprocity that resembles the close relations within a family. Within this form of life, the "golden rule" defines all of one's relations. One is to act toward others in the way one wants them to act towards oneself (Luke 6:31). This rule, however, is not given content by self-determined wants and needs. Rather, it is determined by the way in which God acts toward his people—in kindness and mercy even to "the ungrateful and the selfish" (6:35c–36). Imitation of God in this form carries with it a reward that is different from that which results from the quid pro quo of retaliation and debt incursion. Another reward, one that cannot be taken away, replaces the unstable reward that comes from besting others. Because one acts in a way that reflects the way in which God acts, one is numbered among the "sons of the Most High" (6:35b).

A society founded upon kindness, mercy, and love of one's enemy and a new form of reciprocity has yet another characteristic. Its members, in forgiving one another as God has forgiven them, do not condemn (Luke 6:37). It is not that they fail to see the foibles and sins of others. It is that they are first aware of their own shortcomings and so do not place themselves in a moral and religious category above others. In this sense they "judge not." Rather, they judge themselves and so see their own faults. Only in this way can they see faults of others. Having removed the log from their own eyes, they can see the specks in the eyes of others (Luke 6:41–42). They see, however, not to condemn but to show mercy.

Jesus's message of "release" and his focus on forgiveness suggest, as do his sayings about mercy, a desire to break down the barriers that exclude those considered sinful and unclean from participation in the life of God's people. Three of the stories that follow the Sermon on the Plain further clarify this aspect of Jesus's ministry and so also the character of the people he calls to follow him. Chapter 7 contains an account of Jesus healing the servant of a gentile soldier (Luke 7:1–10), an episode in which he raises the dead son of a widow (7:11–17), and a story about Jesus forgiving the sins of a prostitute (7:36–50). Each of these stories suggests that a person excluded from the life of Israel has been taken into the circle of its blessing. The centurion is an unclean gentile. The widow has lost both her husband and her son and so has no share in Israel's common life. The prostitute is a sinner excluded because of her immoral behavior. Yet Jesus shows mercy upon them and so, with a call to repentance and amendment of life, makes porous the boundaries that once excluded them from the benefits of Israel's common life.

The Journey to Jerusalem

Luke 9:51–19:48 contains an extended account of Jesus's journey to Jerusalem—a journey he knows will end in his death. Jesus's teaching and actions along the way carry forward the themes presented in Luke's prologue and his "orderly account" of the beginning of Jesus's ministry. They are intended to impress upon the reader the universal character of the salvation God intends to bring about. Thus Jesus's words and deeds again and again focus on breaking down the barriers that exclude "the poor" from the life of God's people (13:10–17; 14:13; 17:11–19; 18:15–17). Indeed, this section of the Gospel ends with a summary. Jesus has come to seek and save the lost (19:10).

As in the prologue, Jesus's words and deeds are bracketed by faithful obedience and conflict with Satan and with the authorities that now govern God's people. He sets his face to go to Jerusalem (Luke 9:51) because, as the Son sent to establish the word of the prophets, Jesus, like the prophets, cannot perish in any place other than Jerusalem (13:33–34). On this journey Jesus makes clear his identity, authority, and power through the deeds and words that procure "release." He is the sign that the kingdom of God is dawning

(17:20–21). Some see and give glory to God, and others reject him. Those who see form an unlikely company. There is a leper (17:11–19), a widow (18:1–8), a couple of tax collectors (18:9–14; 19:1–9), and a blind man (18:35–43). Those who do not see and give glory to God are the Pharisees (16:14–18), a rich man (16:19–30), and a rich ruler (18:18–30).

Luke's orderly account clearly is intended to bring out the truth of Mary's statement about what happens when God visits his people: "His mercy is on those who fear him from generation to generation" (1:50). He shows strength, and in doing so he scatters the proud in the imagination of their hearts, puts down the mighty from their thrones, and exalts those of low degree (1:50–52). The account is also intended to make clear that in showing mercy as he does, Jesus, in accord with God's plan, breaks down the barriers that have excluded these people of "low degree" from the life of Israel. The boundaries so jealously guarded by the Pharisees are to be torn down by the tender mercy of God, and those who repent are invited to share the blessing God bestows upon those who are faithful.

Those who see are called to follow this way. They are both warned about what might divert them and given positive instruction about the attitude they are to maintain and the way in which they are to behave. The warnings and the guidance focus on three possible stumbling blocks—family, possessions, and status. These three are the most likely temptations that lead one to subordinate devotion to God's plan to another, lesser good. As is by now clear, similar themes appear in Matthew's account of Jesus's teaching.

The issue of family loyalty appears immediately after Jesus sets his face toward Jerusalem (Luke 9:57–61). As he and the disciples go along the road, a man says he will follow Jesus wherever he goes. In response, Jesus says he has no home. Others then chime in and say that they will follow, but first they must bury the dead or bid farewell to their loved ones. These qualifications, Jesus says, make them unfit for the kingdom. They are not even allowed, like Elijah in following Elisha, to return home to bid farewell to their parents (Luke 9:61; 1 Kings 19:19–21). In the parable of the great banquet (Luke 14:15–24), not even the obligations of a recently consummated marriage can stand in the way of God's invitation to enter his kingdom. If the disciples are not willing to subordinate familial obligations, they are not fit for the kingdom (9:62).

Jesus made clear to his parents that he must be in his Father's house, and he now makes the same point to his disciples. To follow the way requires that disciples be wrenched away from the social relations that most define them and forced to recalibrate the importance of their most basic loyalties. Conformity of one's life to God's plan now trumps the demands of even the closest human relationships. The same demand holds for ties of wealth. Luke positively dwells on the danger possessions pose. Early in the account of Jesus's journey to Jerusalem, in the story of the rich man and his ever-larger barns, Luke warns his readers that wealth's value does not extend beyond death and urges them to seek their wealth with God (Luke 12:13–21). The parable is a gnomic tale that calls the attention of readers to true wisdom.

As the narrative progresses, however, wealth becomes more than a delusion. It becomes an actual threat—a barrier to entering God's kingdom. One of the first reasons given for unwillingness to follow Jesus appears in the previously mentioned parable of the great banquet. Possessions are here mentioned before familial obligations as reasons given for not following Jesus on his way. There is also the fact that the Pharisees who reject Jesus are said to be "lovers of money" (Luke 16:14). Further, at the end of his account of the journey to Jerusalem, Luke contrasts the rich ruler (18:18–30) who turns his back on eternal life because he will not give up his wealth with the tax collector who does, finds salvation, and in so doing, makes the wise choice (19:1–9).

The way marked out by Jesus reverses the way of the man who builds barns. Trust in God's love and care (faith) frees Jesus's followers from the sort of anxious mind that, like that of the nations, devotes its energies to seeking first of all food and drink. Devotion to the kingdom teaches the disciples that "life is more than food, and the body more than clothing." They also learn that God provides for the daily needs of his people (Luke 12:23, 30). Indeed, God gives his people more than daily necessities. In seeking the kingdom first, the disciples find that daily necessities are theirs also (12:31–32).

What is more, in conforming their lives to God's plan, disciples find freedom to divest themselves of their possessions, and in so doing provide themselves with money to give alms. Joel Green has provided an excellent summary of what happens to disciples when they are freed from an anxious mind. He writes,

> Divestment and almsgiving grounded in a thoroughgoing commitment to the kingdom are to be practiced in recognition that God is the Supreme Benefactor who provides both for the giver and the recipient. Such giving has the effect not of placing one person in debt, but rather of embracing the needy as members of one's own inner circle. In the economy intrinsic to the kingdom, those who give without exacting reciprocation . . . are actually repaid by God. Such giving, then, is translated into solidarity with the needy on earth and into heavenly treasure (see 6:35).[7]

If family and wealth can stand in the way of obedience, so can social status. The critics of Jesus, as portrayed by Luke, are the rulers, the lawyers and, most

---

7. Green, *Gospel of Luke*, 495–96.

of all, the Pharisees. These are all people whom Luke calls eminent men in his account of the meal at the home of a "ruler who belonged to the Pharisees" (Luke 14:1–11), and they are the ones who most oppose Jesus. Jesus offers this group a bit of wisdom that runs counter to their entire strategy of life. He offers this advice because if the Pharisees are lovers of money, they are lovers of status as well (11:43). He advises them that, when invited to a meal of this sort, they not seek the seat of honor but take the lowest place. In that way, a more important person will not displace them. Indeed, they might even be asked to take a more honorable seat.

This might be a simple bit of wisdom, but it is far more. It is counsel about entry into the kingdom. Within the logic of the kingdom, those who exalt themselves will be humbled. Those who humble themselves will be exalted. Thus Jesus counsels his disciples to think of themselves as servants who, having done all that is asked of them, think that they have only done their duty and no more (Luke 17:7–10). They are in fact "unworthy."

Within the logic of the kingdom, the search for status is countered by humility—willingness to take the low rather than the high place. Mary the sister of Martha, like Mary the mother of Jesus, becomes an icon of the attitude that should form the lives of Jesus's disciples. They are to be like the two Marys. Mary the mother of Jesus says, "Let it be to me according to your word," and Mary the sister of Martha sits at Jesus's feet listening to what he has to say. The humble person is open to instruction and willing to do what is asked, no matter how humble that task might be.

Thus on the other side of family obligations stands the requirement that disciples be willing to forsake the closest family ties if they prevent proclaiming the kingdom of God. On the other side of the power of possessions stand three God-given abilities—trust that God will provide for his faithful children, the ability to let go of one's wealth, and generous giving that breaks down the barriers that exclude the poor from the blessings God bestows upon his people.

The Basis and Goal of the Way of the Disciples

THE BASIS

The chief characteristics of the life of those who follow the way are trust in God's power to bring his plan to fulfillment and belief that Jesus is God's chosen servant, through whom he will triumph over all opposition. Trust that God has fulfilled his promise in Christ's life, death, resurrection, and ascension demands lives that conform to that promise; it demands a recalibration of one's most basic loyalties, along with willingness both to suffer and to speak boldly when confronted with opposition. The recalibration of loyalties comprises a radical form of repentance. Family ties are made subordinate to the demands of the kingdom. Disciples are released from the power of wealth so that they can sell their possessions and give alms. Within the church the poor are cared for. In like manner, the pride that comes with status is renounced for humility and a life in service to Christ.

The recalibration of loyalties produces a distinguishing form of common life—one that, along with bold speech and acts of power, serves as a light to the nations and the renown of God's people. The marks of that common life derive from the overarching grace of the merciful love of God. These marks, as in the case of Ephesians, give love a face—a recognizable form. Love first of all shows mercy to those who for one reason or another have been excluded from Israel—those who are poor, unclean, or even immoral. The extreme example is, of course, the inclusion of the gentiles into God's elect. Christ is a light to the nations, and Paul, in Acts, becomes an iconic embodiment of Christ's charge to preach repentance and forgiveness to the nations (Luke 24:47).

Jew and gentile are both, by mercy, drawn into God's people, and they are, as a faithful people, to live in a way that witnesses to what life is like when ruled by God. Within a faithful church, disciples imitate the love of God. Thus they forgive their enemies, refuse to return evil for evil, and forswear judgments on their neighbors that elevate themselves and preclude kindness and mercy. Furthermore, they are to lend to their brothers and sisters in the same way they would to members of their own family. In all these ways, they are to live at peace one with another and so inhabit God's kingdom—the reward for the relocation of the center of their lives.

What is the basis of such a radical relocation of life's center? It is, first of all, the plan and promise of God, which he pursues out of love for and mercy toward his people. Throughout Luke and Acts, God is the primary actor in the ordered account Luke provides. The primacy of God is made utterly clear in the Gospel's prologue. Neither Elizabeth nor Mary is in a position to have a child, but in both cases God acts, as with Abraham and Sarah, to bring about the conception of children through whom his plan will be fulfilled. Luke makes it clear that these events occur because "with God nothing will be impossible" (Luke 1:37). So, in a way similar to Elijah, John comes to prepare the way for God's decisive intervention in the affairs of his people. He does so in the person of Jesus, who is both Son of David and Son of God.

The primacy of God is once more displayed in the prophecy of Zechariah. In the births of John and Jesus, none other than the God of Israel has fulfilled his promise to Abraham. In Jesus, as promised through the prophets, God has visited and redeemed his people (Luke 1:67–79). John prepares the way for this decisive event. The theme of divine sovereignty is also present in the words of Simeon who, referring to various prophesies of Isaiah, announces that in seeing Jesus he has seen the salvation of God. Anna, who arrives at the same time as does Simeon, responds to the action of God as is appropriate for a faithful Jew. She gives thanks and speaks "of him to whom all were looking for the redemption of Jerusalem" (2:38).

Anna makes only a brief appearance, but like Mary she provides an image of what might be called the ur-disciple—the one who sees what God has done in Christ, conforms her will to the will of God, gives thanks, and speaks well of him. Before anything else, disciples conform their will to the will of God. Because God has the power and authority to bring his plan to completion, Luke, when displaying both the life of Jesus and the Acts of the Apostles, makes constant use of the terms "it is necessary" or "it was necessary" (Luke 4:43; 9:22; 13:33; 17:25; 22:37; 24:7, 26, 44; Acts 13:46). What transpires in the life of Jesus and the ongoing life of the church is the result of the will of God to bring his plan to completion. The foundation of all that transpires in Luke and Acts is the overruling providence of God. The question is whether this providence is recognized.

Jesus is the one who does recognize the purpose of his Father and conforms his life perfectly to that purpose. Jesus's two direct confrontations with Satan—one in the desert and one on the Mount of Olives—display his absolute submission to God's plan and his part in that plan. His predictions of the passion make clear that he understands and accepts the necessity of the path he must follow. His last words, "Into thy hands I commit my spirit" (Luke 23:46), indicate obedience to and trust in God even at life's most extreme margin.

Jesus's life, death, resurrection, and ascension are God's way of accomplishing his will for his people and the peoples of the earth. That life thus sets the pattern that is to shape the life of the people God has chosen to bring his plan to completion. The marks of Christ's life imprint themselves upon the life of his people. They now share in the mission set forth in the sermon at Nazareth. They share in the blessings promised and the form of common life enjoined in the Sermon on the Plain.

The basis of life in Christ as understood by Luke is the providential activity of God brought to a point in his Son, Jesus. The foundation lies also in the Holy Spirit, through whom both the Father and the Son work. The Holy Spirit speaks through the Scriptures about the Christ and what would befall him (Luke 1:16). Jesus's conception is the work of the Spirit (1:31–35). John is filled with the Spirit even in his mother's womb (1:15). Elizabeth and Zechariah, through the Spirit, recognize who Jesus is (1:41, 67). So also does Simeon (2:26–27). Jesus himself, though the Spirit, knows that he is God's beloved Son (3:22). Through the Spirit he withstands the temptations of Satan (4:1).

So also Jesus's teaching and his works of power are done through the Spirit (4:14, 18). Finally, Jesus gives the Spirit to the disciples (Acts 2:33), a gift that fulfills God's promise (Acts 2:17–18) and both guides and empowers them to be faithful to God's purpose (Acts 26:19).

The basis of the ecclesial focus of Luke's account of life in Christ is thoroughly trinitarian. The will of God the Father for the peoples of the earth is, through the Spirit, fulfilled in Christ and brought to completion by the power of the same Spirit. The character of the life of the church and that of each disciple is to be understood in the context of God's plan, patterned after the Spirit-filled life of Christ, and both guided and effected by the presence of the Holy Spirit in the church.

The Goal

What is the goal of a life lived in accord with the foundation laid by the work of the Father, Son, and Holy Spirit? Luke understands the goal (or perhaps better, goals) of the life of the church first of all within the context of the plan of God to bring knowledge of God to nations of the earth through the restoration of his chosen people. Thus a primary goal of life in Christ, as found in Acts, is to render the boundaries of God's people porous, as Jesus did. The crucial cases of this opening out of boundaries are found in Acts, where Luke records the movement of Philip, Peter, and most of all Paul toward the gentiles. The entire movement of Acts is designed to show how this opening out occurs.

Knowledge of God comes to the nations through a restored people who carry news of God's plan to the ends of the earth. It is therefore also a goal of life in Christ to live faithfully in a manner that manifests to the world what God's rule is like. Jesus's purpose in the Sermon on the Plain is to give his disciples the requisite knowledge to fulfill this task. He seeks to resocialize them so that, like his life, their lives serve as a light to the nations. The previous readings of the New Testament show that Karl Barth was right to insist that Christian ethics is first of all a witness to what God is like and what God is up to.

The church is to be like a good tree that bears good fruit (Luke 6:43–44). It is to do what it has been told to do (6:46–49). In this way the common life of the church not only bears witness to the nature of life in the kingdom but it also enjoys the blessings of that life (6:20–23). There is, as previously noted, a hedonic element in the goals of Christian living. A wise way of living brings with it a reward no earthly good can provide (6:23). However, the blessing promised to those who do as they have been taught is accompanied by a warning. Those who continue in the normal way the world works will suffer woe (6:24–26, 49).

The way of life that Christ commands has its rewards, and these rewards are clearly presented as a goal of living what Christ calls a good life (Luke 6:35). Odd though these rewards may appear at first, they are, nonetheless, a reason for living life in a way that does not produce the sort of rewards most people seek. The Christian way, according to Luke, is a way of wisdom, but it is a wisdom that reverses the wisdom of life as normally lived.

As in all accounts of the way life ought to be lived, there is a hedonic element in Luke's presentation of the Christian way. However, there is a more encompassing, higher goal—that is, to give glory to God and to God's people. Luke nowhere makes a statement like Matthew's—namely, that disciples are to let their light shine so that people will see their good works and give glory to their Father in heaven. Nonetheless, he places life in Christ within the defining context of glorifying God. The shepherds glorify God when they receive news of the birth of the Messiah (Luke 2:20). The people glorify God when they see Jesus heal the sick, forgive sins, and raise the dead (5:25–26; 7:19; 13:13; 17:15; 18:43). The first person to glorify God because of what he saw in Jesus's death is a gentile centurion (23:47). In Acts one finds a similar glorification of God when people hear what the disciples have to say and witness what they do (Acts 4:21; 11:18; 13:48; 21:20).

For Luke, God is glorious in his power and righteousness. Throughout the Gospel, when God appears, he appears in glory. God is glorious and deserves to be glorified. Jesus's words and actions do precisely this. He turns down the glory of the nations and in so doing takes the role of a servant (Luke 4:8–11). The disciples are called to follow a similar path. A blessing is attached to following, but it is an attendant hope rather than a primary goal of Christian living. Blessing accompanies a more basic set of goals—glorifying God by showing what life in the kingdom is like, breaking down the barriers that prevent people from entering that life, and drawing the nations into the blessings promised to God's people.

Revelation

Introduction

Another possible exception to the ecclesial focus that directs attention first not to the common life of the church but to reform of the social order or liberation from oppression is the Revelation to John. In its pages there are to be found no lengthy lists of the graces that sustain the unity and peace of the congregations to which he writes. The passage that comes closest to this concern is John's warning to the church in Ephesus, "You have abandoned the love you had at first" (Rev. 2:4). This is not to say that, for John, the presence of the graces in the common life of the church is an unimportant matter. He commends the Ephesians for their "works" and "toil" (2:2). It is to say, however, that the graces receive only slight attention. John's primary concern is not the character of relations within each of the seven churches. Neither is he concerned to reform the Roman government—a political force he regards as idolatrous. That force is to be defeated rather than transformed.

John's primary concern is neither the particular graces present in the seven churches to which he writes nor the redemption of the social order. Rather, his concern is similar to that of St. Mark. It is that the members of the seven churches, in the face of great tribulation, witness to God's victory over the forces of evil by holding fast to Christ's name and remaining faithful even unto death (Rev. 2:10c, 13a).

John's concern for fidelity in the face of tribulation explains the two additional characteristics or markers of Christian living that he highlights—true witness and patient endurance. The question is whether these identifying marks of Christian living reveal an ecclesial focus, or whether their significance lies either with the moral and religious perfection of individual believers or with their impact upon the Roman Empire and the various societies of which that empire was composed.

The Character of Christian Living

If one places these characteristics and others within the context of John's account of the goal and basis of life in Christ, the ecclesial focus of his ethic becomes apparent. Indeed, the character, goal, and basis of Christian living—all three—are displayed in a cosmic drama in which God enters into battle with the forces of evil that now distort creation and control the political and economic powers that rule the peoples of the earth. These forces are controlled by and expressed in the Roman Empire (Rev. 17–18). That empire, trusting in its power and wealth, has taken upon itself divine pretensions. However, for the Jewish author of Revelation, there is but one God, and this God will allow no pretenders. The true God is "the Almighty" and as such must both contend with and prevail over the false gods personified and worshiped in and through the imperial cult (1:8). The war between God and the pretender who would take his place begins in heaven, where Michael and his angels fight with the dragon (the devil) and his forces (12:7). The devil and his allies are thrown down to earth where they now fight a last, desperate series of battles against Christ and his followers, who are God's agents in this earthly battle.

John sees clearly that tribulation will necessarily come to the churches because of Rome's pretentious claim to divinity and God's necessary opposition to this claim. It is in the Roman Empire that the devil has concentrated his earthly forces. John writes to prepare the churches for an inevitable struggle and to make them aware of the central role they play in the providence of God. He does so by presenting a series of heavenly visions that display the certain defeat of the devil and all the heavenly and earthly powers he controls.

John wants his readers to understand that the victory won in heaven will be repeated on earth through three forms of divine action, in one of which they will play a key role. The first is the judgment of God manifest in the visions of the seven seals (Rev. 6:1–17; 8:1, 3–5), the seven trumpets (8:2, 6–21; 11:14–19), and the seven bowls (15:1, 5–21). The second is through the death of the Lamb, Christ (chap. 5). The third is through the faithful witness of the church (chaps. 1–3; 12:11). The goal of this divine work is the universal rule of God, the creation of a new heaven and a new earth, and the worship of the one true God by the entire creation (15:4; 19:5–7; 21:1).

It is within this drama that the ecclesial focus of Christian ethics becomes apparent. It is within this drama that the character of Christian living becomes intelligible. Truthful witness and patient endurance are the means by which the saints contribute to the victory of God and the fulfillment of his purposes for his creation.

How so? The saints are called to imitate Christ not by following from afar but by direct participation in the same sort of suffering, even death, he endured. Thus in Revelation 2:10 John warns the members of the church in Smyrna that they are about to suffer, and in undergoing this ordeal they will be put to the test. This warning, though anticipating certain specific events, alerts the churches to what lies ahead for all of them. The question is how they are to meet the tribulation they soon will face. Chapters 1–3 may be taken as a sort of primer about how the saints are to pass through the tribulation so that, in the end, they "conquer."

In a negative sense, they are not to fear, and certainly they are not to deny or disown Christ's name (Rev. 2:10; 3:8). In a positive sense, they are to "be faithful unto death" (2:10). How then are they to persevere in the face of such tribulation? Because a faithful witness on their part is so crucial, John wishes to instruct the churches in just this matter. Pursuant to that end, he dots a number of bits of sage advice throughout his text about what might be called the habits of mind the saints are to have and sustain. They are, first of all, to "remember" what they have "received and heard," and they are to "hold fast" to it (3:3, 8, 10, 11). That is, they are to "hold fast" to what they have (3:11). They must be steadfast, which is to say have a settled mind. In a more active sense they must also be "zealous" (3:19). Finally, if they fall away—if they do not show fidelity, do not remember and hold fast what they have received and heard, do not show a steady mind and are not zealous—they are to "repent" (3:19). If they maintain these habits of mind and act in a way that is faithful to what they have received and heard, they will "conquer" the demonic forces against which they contend and contribute to the victory of God over the forces that oppose him.

Here we have a basic moral vocabulary—a primer for faithful witnesses. The saints are to remember, hold fast, maintain a settled mind, be zealous, and repent. The vocabulary is repeated, expanded, and explicated in the succeeding chapters. These latter chapters enumerate in greater detail the characteristics that flow from these habits of mind and communal practices. Of particular importance is "wisdom," a game that allows the saints to recognize the true significance of Rome's pretensions. Rome is a false savior (Rev. 13:18)! Indeed, it is difficult to avoid the author's concern that the churches be wise and that they recognize the true nature of their circumstances. It is just this concern that lies behind many of the author's admonitions to the seven churches. So the church in Sardis is chided for not recognizing that its reputation for liveliness is in fact false (3:1). The church in Laodicea is scolded for having a false idea of its own strength (3:17). By way of contrast, the church in Ephesus is commended for recognizing false prophets and for rejecting the teaching of the Nicolaitans, a group that apparently advocated accommodations to the culture of the empire that compromised what the church is "to hold fast" (2:2, 6). The church in Pergamum is similarly commended (2:14–15).

The point would seem to be that Christ, the true witness, is present with the churches and sees the true nature of their common life. The members of these churches are called upon to see their lives as Christ sees them. This task calls for wisdom that comes from remembering, keeping, holding fast, and so on. So also does the prized quality of patient endurance (Rev. 3:10). The importance of patient endurance appears at crucial points as the drama of God's conflict with the lies and deceit of the devil unfolds. In chapter 13, where it is noted that for a time the beast (the Roman Empire) will rule and receive worship from the peoples of the earth, the importance of endurance is highlighted. In these circumstances the saints are called upon to show "endurance and faith" (13:10). Again in chapter 14, the saints are urged to show "endurance" by keeping "the commandments of God and the faith of Jesus" (14:12).

If remembering, keeping, and holding fast produce patient endurance, they also issue in "truthful witness." Indeed, the entire Apocalypse can be read as depicting a titanic struggle between truth and falsehood, and in this struggle the truthful witness of the churches plays a necessary and crucial role. The pretensions of the Roman Empire to divinity constitute a huge lie. As Richard Bauckham has written, "The special significance of Christian martyrdom is that it makes the issue clear. Those who bear witness to the one true God, the only true absolute, to whom all political power is subject, expose Rome's idolatrous self-deification for what it is."[8] The witness of the saints is convincing because their faith in Christ's victory over death is so clearly present in the way they face death (Rev. 12:11).

Throughout, the Apocalypse traces this conflict between the false claims of Rome and the true claims of Christ and the church. The dragon deceives the world (Rev. 12:9; cf. 20:2–3, 7–8). The second beast deceives the peoples of the earth with propaganda supporting the cult of the emperor (13:14; cf. 19:21). Babylon (Rome) deceives the nations with sorcery (18:23). In contrast, the followers of the Lamb are, like the Lamb, entirely without deceit. "In their mouth no lie was found" (14:5; cf. 3:14).

Martyrdom is, in short, an unimpeachable witness to God's sovereignty that exposes the lie of Rome's pretense. Again, as Richard Bauckham has written, "When the martyrs testify to the true God against the spurious divine claims of the beast and refuse to admit the lies of the beast even when they could evade death by doing so, they win the victory of truth over deceit."[9]

By way of summary, it can be said that truth and truthfulness are central both to the witness of the churches to the nations and to the integrity of their common life. They are not only to expose, by the integrity of their lives, Rome's false claim to divinity, but they are also to maintain a true account of their own state before God by remembering and holding fast. This double account of the importance of truth and truthfulness for the faithfulness of the saints is underscored by the importance of both for Christ and his prophet John. John bears witness (as in a court of law) "to the word of God and to the testimony of Jesus Christ" (Rev. 1:2). Jesus, who gives the testimony, is "the faithful and true witness" (3:14). By being a witness to the faithful and true witness of Jesus, the prophet claims the truth of what he has to say to the churches, and on that basis he declares false the prophecy of the Thyatiran prophetess Jezebel, who advocates practices that do not hold fast but rather encourage idolatry and immorality (2:19–23; 22:6–7).

---

8. Richard Bauckham, *The Theology of the Book of Revelation* (Cambridge: Cambridge University Press, 1993), 39. To all those who know Professor Bauckham's book, it will be clear that the exposition of the Apocalypse found here owes an enormous debt to his work. I have also been helped by the magisterial three-volume commentary by David Aune. See David Aune, *Revelation 1–5; 6–16; 17–22*, Word Biblical Commentary 52 (Nashville: Thomas Nelson, 1997, 1998, 1998). I have also profited from Elisabeth Schüssler Fiorenza, *The Book of Revelation: Justice and Judgment* (Philadelphia: Fortress, 1985).

9. Bauckham, *Theology of the Book of Revelation*, 91.

The Goal of Christian Living

The victory of God is achieved by the true witness of Christ to the will of God, the true witness of the prophet to the churches about their state and calling, and the true witness of the churches to the nations about the sovereignty of the one true God. Clearly we have here an ethic whose focus is the fidelity of the church to its calling under God. What, however, is the goal of living such a demanding and perhaps very short life?

If one were to stop reading the words of the prophet at the end of chapter 3, the most obvious conclusion would be that the goal is the reward of paradise. The goal of Christian living would appear to be a form of eudaemonism. Christian living apparently amounts to a quest for reward on the other side of life. Those who conquer are told that they will "eat of the tree of life," escape a final death, and be given protection and victory during the great tribulation. They will be counted "worthy." Because they are worthy, Christ will confess their name before God; he will establish them as key people in the heavenly worship of God. Christ himself will come to them and share with them in the heavenly banquet. He will also allow them to share with him in the governance of the earth (Rev. 2:6, 10, 17, 28; 3:4–5, 12, 20–21).[10]

If indeed the goal of Christian living as presented in the Apocalypse is heavenly reward for a sacrificed life, then it would be reasonable to conclude that John presents an argument that can be used for deliberately seeking martyrdom. The headlines emanating from the Middle East, Europe, and North America ought to elicit justifiable caution in respect to arguments such as this one. A close reading of the text, however, shows that heavenly reward is properly understood as a consolation given for faithful witness rather than as its goal. This is made clear by the important place conquering plays in John's account of Christian living. The Apocalypse is in part structured around a conflict between two sovereignties and two forms of worship—one false and the other true. The true goal of life in Christ is not a personal reward but the destruction of a pretender to God's rule and the establishment of true rather than false worship.

So the first goal of perseverance and true witness is the conquest of evil. As Christ conquered through his death, so do the saints (Rev. 12:11; 15:2). The witness, even the death of the saints, does not have value in itself. Its value resides in the fact that the witness of the saints is a continuation of the

---

10. A reward for those who conquer is promised at the end of John's word to each of the churches. The symbolic terms in which the reward is couched are often obscure, and I have here given an interpretation of the meaning of the symbols. For further details, see the comments on the verses by David Aune in *Revelation 1–5*.

witness of Christ. They conquer because Christ did. The conquest of evil is, however, tied closely to another outcome of endurance and true witness—the conversion of the nations.

The role of Christ's followers in bringing the nations to worship the one true God is made known in Revelation 10:1–11:13, wherein the contents of the scroll are presented. God raises the witnesses (who are also martyrs) from the dead and calls them to heaven to be with him. This vindication of the saints is accompanied by fearful judgment but also by the glorification of God. Thus some were terrified, but others "gave glory to the God of heaven" (11:13). It is not only that the martyrdom of the saints effects a victory over evil. It is also the case that the witnesses will be a means by which the nations are converted. Because of patient endurance and faithful witness on the part of the saints, the sacrificial death of Christ, which ransomed "men for God from every tribe and tongue and people," is brought to completion (5:9).

Similar themes are contained in chapter 15, wherein the sacrifice of the martyrs is likened to the passage through the Red Sea. In Exodus 15 God's act of judgment simply inspires terror. In Revelation 15, however, God's judgments and the "exodus" of the saints lead the peoples of the earth to worship the one true God and to "fear and glorify" God's name. John's account of the goal of Christian living is consistent with that of Ephesians, Paul, John, Matthew, and Luke. The goal of Christian living is witness, and witness serves both to establish God's rule and to convert the peoples of the earth to the worship of the one true God.

The Basis of Christian Living

What, however, is the foundation upon which this stringent ethic rests and gives such a goal credibility? The foundation is first of all the rule of God over both nature and history. Chapters 19 through 22 attest to the fact that God will bring his work as both creator and redeemer to completion. It is God's purpose both to destroy the evil forces that distort creation and enslave the peoples of the earth, and to create a new heaven and earth wherein all things are made new. The titles employed by John to refer to the one true God are all designed to assure the saints of God's victory in the battle in which they are engaged. Thus in Revelation 1:8 three terms for God appear. He is the Alpha and Omega, the Lord God Almighty, and the one who is and who was and who is to come. All three of these phrases mean the same thing. Alpha and Omega comes from Isaiah 44:6 and 44:1 and clearly refers to God as both Creator of the world and the Lord of history. The one who is and who was and who is to come is a favored term by John because it calls to mind both the divine name and God's coming to his people as savior. It does not refer to God's eternity but to his faithfulness. Finally, Lord God Almighty is also connected to God's name and is intended to call to mind God's rule of history and his certain victory over his opponents.

All these titles emphasize the sovereignty of God. As is the case with Luke, divine sovereignty provides a necessary foundation for the communal ethic of patient endurance and faithful witness to which the churches are called. It provides the basis for John's assurance that the saints will conquer. In this respect, chapter 4 is of crucial importance. Here the reader is transported into the divine throne room where God's power is clearly on display. It is from the throne that all the judgments upon earth issue—those portrayed through the seven seals, the seven trumpets, and the seven bowls. The saints know that their victory is assured because the victory of God has already been won in heaven and on earth, and it will be brought to completion in a new heaven and a new earth.

This victory is won on earth as in heaven because of the death of the Lamb who, having conquered sin and death, now sits upon the throne with God his Father. The second basis for the way of life John commends is the Son's victory through suffering. The victory is underscored by John's vigorous claim that what can be said of the Father can also be said of the Son. If God is the Alpha and Omega, so also is the Son (Rev. 1:8, 17–18; 21:6; 22:13). If God is the one who is to come, so also is Christ (1:7; 2:5, 16; 3:11; 16:15; 22:7, 12, 20). If God is to receive the worship of the peoples of the earth, so also is Christ (5:13).

Christ's particular role in the drama of God's victory is, however, to establish God's rule upon earth. His work is set forth in the elaboration of three symbolic themes. One has already been mentioned. Christ is the faithful and true witness both because he speaks God's word and because he dies for having spoken it (Rev. 1:2, 9; 2:13; 6:9; 11:7; 12:17; 20:4). A second theme is that of Christ, the Davidic Messiah, the Lion of Judah, and the Root of David (5:5) who conquers the forces of evil with a mighty army, the church (14:1). Again, as in Luke, the motif of battle is closely connected with the theme of the Davidic Messiah (11:7; 12:7, 8, 17; 13:7; 16:14; 17:14; 19:11, 19). In these struggles the Davidic Messiah defeats the devil by means of his own death and resurrection. His followers do likewise through their witness, and Christ completes these victories when he comes again (3:21; 5:5; 12:11; 15:2; 17:14). A third theme is that of the eschatological exodus. The central image in this theme is Christ the Passover Lamb (5:6, 9–10). Christ's blood ransoms a people and makes of them a kingdom of priests who, through their witness, share in his suffering and help complete his victory. So in Revelation 15:2–4 the martyrs are pictured in heaven as the people of a new exodus who have passed through a heavenly Red Sea and now sing a version of Miriam's victory song. The vision of the martyrs in heaven points to the final victory of the Lamb and his followers, after which the followers will share with him in ruling a new heaven and a new earth (20:4–6; 22:3–5).

The victories of God Almighty and of the Lamb who was slain assure the saints that they too will prevail and play their part in accomplishing the purposes of God. Further confidence is given by the role of the Holy Spirit in this struggle between truth and falsehood. References to the Spirit fall into two categories—those that refer to the "seven spirits" and those that refer simply to "the Spirit." Reference to the seven spirits comes from Zechariah 4:6, which states that the victory of God comes "not by might, nor by power, but by my Spirit." In Revelation 5:6, the seven spirits are associated with the victory of the Lamb. So the victory of the Lamb does not come by power but by the seven spirits. As Bauckham has astutely observed, the seven spirits are sent out into the world to make the victory of the Lamb effective. God now sits on his heavenly throne along with the victorious Lamb. The seven spirits, however, are active throughout the earth implementing the victory of the Lamb. The seven spirits are in fact the way in which the exalted Christ is present throughout the world furthering the purposes of God through the witness of the churches to the truth. The close relation of the seven spirits to the churches is particularly obvious in their connection to the two witnesses (the church) mentioned in Revelation 11:3–13. The power of the seven spirits makes the witness of the churches throughout the world effective.

There are, however, a number of references that do not refer to the seven spirits but only to the Spirit. What is the meaning of this reference to the Spirit rather than the seven spirits (Rev. 1:10; 4:2; 14:13; 17:3; 19:7–8; 21:2, 10; 22:12, 17, 20)? The seven spirits speak to the whole world through the churches. The Spirit, however, speaks specifically to the church. It is through the Spirit that prophecy is directed to the churches and so equips them for their witness and their role in establishing God's kingdom. As chapters 1–3 make abundantly clear, the Spirit not only equips the saints with truth and power but also makes them aware of their faults and corrects them. It is through the Spirit that Christ speaks to the churches. It is through the Spirit that the churches speak truth to the world. It is through the Spirit that the churches patiently endure the great tribulation through which they conquer with the Lamb.

Again, to speak in an anachronistic manner, the basis of Christian living is the Holy Trinity. God, who is almighty, conquers the forces of evil in the heavenly realm and sets in motion the forces that will bring his purpose for nature and history to fulfillment. Christ the Lamb, with the saints, conquers these forces on earth and establishes the conditions for God's rule. The Holy Spirit equips the saints for the tribulation through which they must pass and makes their witness effective throughout the earth. It is upon this triune base that the saints speak the truth, suffer its consequences, and patiently endure its cost. The focus of Christian living as presented in the Apocalypse is, as in the case of Luke, ecclesial through and through. Its character, goal, and basis make no sense whatsoever apart from their setting under the providence of God and within the common life of the saints.

PART FOUR

The Shape of an Ecclesial Ethic

8

The Goal, Basis, and Character of an Ecclesial Ethic

The Goal and Basis of Life in Christ

The Goal

Of the three examples with which this study began, John Howard Yoder's account of the focus of Christian ethics more nearly resembles those found in the New Testament texts I have considered. In that review, I noted that despite its many strengths, Yoder's account of life in Christ has several weaknesses. These include an overly moralized account of the person and work of Christ; a failure to base the common life of the church sufficiently in the work of the Holy Spirit; an incomplete and sometimes distorted account of the character of Christian ethics; and, finally, a highly debatable depiction of the relation between living within the perfection of Christ and living as a member of a social body whose purpose under God is to provide order and establish "right" during the time prior to God's final victory.

In the following attempt to sketch the goal, basis, and character of the common life of the church, I do not intend to return to the points where there is agreement or disagreement with Yoder's account. The points of agreement and difference should be clear enough after considering my reading of the exemplary New Testament texts. My hope is that they will stand out in even bolder relief as the sketch that follows unfolds. It is clear, however, that whatever its weaknesses may be, Yoder's account is far more faithful to the biblical sources than the other two are. The synthesis of the biblical witness at which he arrives, despite its differences from my own, is still quite close to it.

Yoder and I both aim at a synthesis, and this is as it should be. All attempts to root a theological tradition within the various books of the Bible require a work of synthesis, and all attempts at synthesis are bound to suffer from omissions and distortions. The present project is no exception to this rule. Yoder and I both base life in Christ within an ecclesiology that we believe accords with the witness of Scripture. In consequence, both of us must assume that the witness of Scripture, despite significant differences between its various books, is nonetheless coherent. Given this assumption, what then is the synthesis that can reasonably be abstracted from the books considered here as exemplary?

It is important to begin such a project by noting that all the authors so far considered subscribe to a form of what today is called ethical realism. They hold that when we make moral claims, we refer to a moral order external to ourselves. Moral speech is about the way things are rather than the way in which people desire them to be. Thus all these writings present life in Christ first as a form of witness to the truth as comprised by the nature and purposes of God. Chief among God's purposes is the unification of the peoples of the earth in a communion of faith, hope, love, and worship. God has this purpose because it is his nature to show love and mercy toward his creation. Christian living is a way of life that is proportionate to or worthy of who God is and what God wills. It is, in short, the calling of the church to live in a way that bears witness to God's nature and his will for the world he has both created and redeemed.

To put the matter another way, the manner in which Christians live together and in relation to the societies in which they find themselves is a sign that points to Christ, through whom the peoples of the earth have access to a moral order that accords with what God wills and what God is like. God desires the nations to see a people who, though drawn from all races and tongues, are nonetheless joined together in a unified response to the way things are—a response of faith, hope, love, and praise. This manner of life, because it is born of God's power, love, and mercy, reflects the glory of God revealed in Christ. Once God's glory is glimpsed, it has power, through the work of the Spirit, to draw forth the appropriate human response. An appropriate human response is first of all a life that glorifies God not only in worship but also in a worthy life. It is this goal that encompasses any and all moral purposes that compose a life that is "worthy." It is this goal that gathers all God's purposes for his creation.

A way of life that elicits love and praise is not only a witness to God's nature and purposes. Because it fits with reality, it is also a way of life that leads to human fulfillment. It is a way of life that does not run across the grain of things. It is, therefore, a goal of Christian ethics to provide a manner of life that unites what is right to do with what is good to do. Human life always involves a quest for a worthy object of worship and a worthy way to inhabit the world. What we seek is an object that can both fill the soul and render us at home in the world. Christian ethics, as a form of witness, points the peoples of the earth to the true object of their search and so also to the true source of their blessing.

Because right worship and a worthy form of life are chief among the purposes of life in Christ, Christian ethics also has as a primary goal a form of common life into which all peoples are welcomed through conversion and formed into a new pattern of common life that coheres with the purposes of God. For this reason, the author of Ephesians speaks of the church as a commonwealth in which all, both Jew and gentile, are fellow citizens, and he urges his readers to live a life worthy of the purposes of the commonwealth into which they have been gathered.

St. Matthew, St. Luke, and the author of the Apocalypse also track the creation and calling of a people through the person and work of Christ and the witness of his church. Each stresses the fact that the church, because of its calling, is to be a society that includes all the peoples of the earth. As such, its members are to be resocialized into a community that has porous borders. The way into this community is not through the sorting gate of nationality, gender, age, status, occupation, moral rectitude, or any other distinguishing and excluding feature. The way in is open to all. Nonetheless, it can be entered only through the narrow gate of conversion, repentance, and amendment of life. The way into this people passes through a narrow door that requires what those of us who live in an electronic age might call a "recalibration" of all our attachments and commitments and a reformatting of our most common habits and practices. Another way to say the same thing is that a goal of Christian ethics is not in the first instance to transform a culture but to form one. One goal of Christian ethics is to form a culture that does not reflect what comes from the world—that is, "the lust of the flesh and the lust of the eyes and the pride of life" (1 John 2:16). It is to form a culture that springs from the love and mercy of God—a culture that bears the stamp of Christ's own life.

Because the calling of the church is to gather the peoples of the earth in a communion of love and worship, it follows also that Christians have a duty to ensure that each person in this polyglot nation, regardless of status or ability, has an honorable place. If all are not honored, some are in fact excluded. It also follows that each member of the church, in all their differences, is to live in peace with all the others. Without peace there can be no unity, and without unity the witness of the church is compromised. An ecclesial focus to Christian ethics thus requires a form of community life that fosters those graces and practices that make for peace and unity. These goals are accomplished within the common life of the church through worship, reading Holy Scripture, the practice of prayer, exemplary living, mutual subjection, and an incessant call for reconciliation. Mutual subjection is a form of life that serves not as a mechanism of status and control but as a work of love that sets people free, each in their own place, to make a distinctive contribution that is equal in value to all other contributions. Reconciliation is a practice that changes enemies into friends and provides a bulwark against the forces that lead to conflict rather than peace.

Perhaps all these ways of stating the goal of Christian living can be summarized in the words of Matthew's gospel: "Let your light so shine before [others], that they may see your good works and give glory to your Father who is in heaven" (Matt. 5:16). St. John, however, insists that the light shines in darkness (John 1:4–5). Matthew, Luke, and Revelation are clear that Christ's arrival calls forth a terrible conflict with the forces of evil. What is true of the light of Christ is true also of the light reflected by the common life of the church. The author of the Apocalypse never tires of reminding his readers that the statement of truth by the saints confronts the world with its lies, and the world reacts by attempting to stamp out the truth and those who speak it. In a similar manner, Ephesians concludes with an address suitable for soldiers on the eve of battle—an address that encourages the saints to enter the battle and stand deploying what the author calls the "awesome armor of God." The texts imply that one goal of Christian ethics must be to live a form of life that, by its contrast with the way life is normally carried on, both exposes evil and provides the resources to remain standing in an ensuing battle that God will win through the faithful witness of his saints.

The Basis

What is the basis of life lived as a witness to the truth—a witness that exposes the lies that issue from the mouths of those who rule the world? The short answer is the full economy of God—the way in which God the Father, God the Son, and God the Holy Spirit act to reconcile and redeem the creation. Stated negatively, the basis of Christian ethics is not simply a command issued from on high by an omnipotent ruler. Neither is it imitation of the life of an exemplary man like Jesus. Nor is it special illumination by the Holy

Spirit, who delivers inspired messages directly to the human heart. The basis of Christian ethics, according to the exemplary texts I have chosen, is the will of the Father carried out in obedience by the Son and brought to fulfillment by the Holy Spirit.

As Ephesians puts it, a worthy life is one that is proportionate to the plan of God the Father to unify all things through the sacrificial death and subsequent resurrection and ascension of his Son. Through the presence of the Holy Spirit in the church, those who have been chosen to live this life are made both fully to understand God's purposes for the world and the church, and to have power to live in a way worthy of those purposes. In like manner, Luke speaks of the plan of God that is fulfilled through the obedience of his Son and testified to by the Holy Spirit at work in the life of the church. Luke speaks in a similar vein of the "necessity" of certain events both in the life of Christ and in the ensuing work of Peter and Paul. These things are necessary because, in the language of Ephesians, they accord with the "counsel" of God's will and they come to be through the presence of the Holy Spirit in the life of the church.

Matthew makes a similar point by his insistence that what Jesus says and does occurs in fulfillment of God's revelation in Holy Scripture. These things occur because they are of God's will and because Christ, who is born of the Spirit and filled with the Spirit, is, by the Spirit, obedient to the will of his Father. Likewise, the author of the Apocalypse roots his account of Christian living in the work of God the Father, God the Son, and God the Holy Spirit. God the Father conquers the forces of evil in the heavenly realm. In this way he sets in motion a conflict that establishes his rule over nature and history. Christ the Lamb, with the saints, conquers the forces of evil on earth and so establishes the conditions for God's rule. The Holy Spirit equips the saints for the suffering through which they must pass and makes their witness effective. It is on the basis of the work of Father, Son, and Spirit that the saints speak the truth, suffer its consequences, and patiently endure its cost.

Christian living has its foundation in the nature and purposes of God the Father. This nature is revealed and these purposes brought to fulfillment through the work of the Son and the Spirit. The Spirit's witness to Christ within the church engenders a form of life that reflects this nature and furthers these purposes. The entire economy of God stands at the base of the way in which Christians are called to live with one another and in relation to the various societies of which they happen to be a part. In, with, and under this economy and pervading its every expression stands the love, mercy, and truthful judgment of God.

In summary, we may say that in an objective sense the basis of the common life of the church is the economy of God the Father, God the Son, and God the

Holy Spirit working out a plan for the salvation of the world in history. In a subjective sense, however, the basis of that life is faith, hope, and love evoked in the life of the church by the manifestation in Christ of God's love and mercy. The character of the life Christians are called to live is rooted in faith that God has acted decisively to reconcile and redeem the world he created, in hope born out of this faith, and in love for God, who has condescended to do such a thing. It is this foundation and these goals that provide a focus for the way in which Christians are called to live. It is this foundation and these goals that shape the character of the common life of the church.

The Character of Life in Christ

Reordered Love Expressed in Changed Practices That Honor the First Commandment and Enable the Second

The Greek word *charactēr* means first of all an "engraved mark." Character is above all else a visible mark that distinguishes one thing or person from another. In everyday speech, it can be used to refer either to individuals or to communities. I have used the term with both references. In a normative sense the chief characteristic of the common life of the church and of the lives of its individual members is love of God and love of neighbor. The love command summarizes the law of God for the life of his people. Love gives form to the practices and graces that provide the church with a visible identity. It is reasonable, therefore, to begin this summary of the character of Christian living with a discussion of the first and second commandments and the definition of love to be found therein. However, I believe that the nature of love is more easily discerned if we begin not with a definition but with the graces and practices that render love recognizable.[1] How best might one summarize the graces and practices that give love a face?

The first commandment requires that one love God with *all* one's heart, soul, mind, and strength rather than with a portion of each (Matt. 27:22, 37–39; Mark 12:30; Luke 10:27–28). The total and encompassing nature of this demand requires what I have called a "recalibration" of life's attachments.

---

1. This is not to say that attempts to define *agapē* in a summary phrase like equal regard, self-sacrifice, or mutuality are not necessary. It is to say that one cannot arrive at an adequate summary or definition without first looking, as Paul says in 1 Corinthians 13:4–13, at what love is. That is, before we can give a summary definition we must understand, for example, that "love is patient and kind"; and we must understand why, if love is to be love, these graces must be present. For the most adequate attempt I know of to arrive at a summary definition of the moral content of love, see Gene Outka, *Agape: An Ethical Analysis* (New Haven: Yale University Press, 1972).

Matthew and Luke identify three forms of attachment that love of God renders subordinate to one's devotion to "the kingdom of heaven." They are family, status, and possessions. If one is to enter through the "narrow" rather than the "wide" gate, the importance of these goods must be subordinated to the love of God. Christian living is rooted in the love God has for the world and the faith, hope, and love God's mercy engenders. The first visible fruit of the new orientation of life that love brings about is the reordering of life's priorities. If status is understood to include power, surely family, status, and wealth summarize primary goods to which we generally devote our lives.

In a normative sense then, the character of the life Christians share is one in which these goods no longer define life's chief goals. They are, after all, the primary sources of competitive and hostile social division. Thus the character of the life Christians share is one in which family, status, and possessions are no longer the organizing centers of life. Rather, they become aspects of life provided by God because God knows them to be necessary. In the case of status, Christians are called upon to form a society in which status is a good accorded not on the basis of present relations of sub- and superordination but on the basis of service to God. In this society, the greatest become the least and the least became the greatest. Status is ascribed on the basis of the extent to which people have become the servants of God and others rather than on the basis of the extent to which others have become servants to them.

The recalibration of life's attachments requires, as St. Augustine well knew, a reordering of love.[2] It requires placing one's attachments within and under that love that demands all one's heart, soul, mind, and strength. This shift in the foundation of life is traditionally referred to as conversion. Because over time conversion works profound changes in the shape of life, it is often linked with two other terms—repentance and sanctification. However, no matter which term one may choose to employ, all three point to a lifelong process that works itself out not only in the life of each believer but also, necessarily, within the common life of the church. Within this fellowship, the loves of one's life are challenged, redirected, and reordered.

It is not surprising that interior changes of this magnitude express themselves in changed attitudes and altered forms of common practice. These changed practices, along with the attitudes they support and to which they give expression, are aspects of the character that is normative for the common life of the church. They give identity to a culture in which Christ is taking form. Thus,

---

2. See, e.g., John Burnaby, *Amor Dei: A Study of the Religion of St. Augustine* (London: Hodder & Stoughton, 1938), and Oliver O'Donovan, *The Problem of Self-Love in St. Augustine* (New Haven: Yale University Press, 1980).

in respect to family, marriage practice is altered. Within the church, marriage is no longer to be viewed as a social necessity. Rather, the single life is to be considered as honorable an estate as marriage. Marriage is no longer to be considered a necessary entry point for a full social life, and the single state is no longer to be viewed as a tragic form of social failure. Marriage is to be regarded as a vocation rather than a social necessity. Marriage is to become a relationship wherein, through mutual subjection, the bond between Christ and his church is signified and the love of neighbor learned. Marriage and the single state, each in its own way, become honorable modes of life. Each becomes a vocation rather than a social necessity because each in its own way provides a means to serve and love God and one's neighbor.

Despite notable and all-too-common exceptions, it is difficult to overestimate the effects this change in social opinion and practice has had both within the common life of the church and within the societies in which the church has taken root. Something similar can be said about the view of status given such a prominent place in the Synoptic Gospels. I mentioned earlier Kierkegaard's metaphor that portrays society as a large net in which everyone is caught and given a particular place. He noted in his comments on the "works of love" that everyone, both those of low status and those of high status, is required by love to rise above their place in the net and meet there as equals before God. What Kierkegaard missed was that, though on one level each is of equal value before God, within the fellowship of the church and so within that particular part of the net's webbing, some are given particular honor—namely, those who measure their lives not by their social status but by the service they render both to God and to their neighbor. They become examples of the life to which all are called, and accordingly they are given the sort of moral authority due to a person whose life is exemplary. Within the net of the church, locations do change, even if each retains equal value before God.

As Jesus's response to the request to be given the seats of honor in the kingdom by the disciples James and John makes abundantly clear (Mark 10:35–45), too often the reordering of love that produces a change in the way in which status is viewed is, within the church, in practice either incomplete or absent. Nevertheless, in its prayers the church accords honor to those whose status is measured by service rather than by social power and position. In this way the church makes a life rooted in service rather than status a normative practice for Christian people. Mother Theresa is the most well-known contemporary example of this fact, and St. Francis perhaps the best known from history.

These figures exemplify the sort of recalibration of the nature and importance of status made necessary by the totality of God's claim on human attachments. These figures exemplify also a practice that ensures dethronement of the human quest for status. That practice is mutual subjection in the body of Christ. The author of Ephesians, as a preface to his discussion of relations within Christian households, issues a generalized command. He then gives instructions for households as an example of a more encompassing practice. "Be subject to one another out of reverence for Christ" (Eph. 5:21).

The command to be mutually subject addresses one of the most fundamental aspects of social life—namely, the ubiquity of hierarchy and alliance. Hierarchy and alliance are necessary ways of structuring social relations within any group, the church included. However, the pernicious possibilities of hierarchy (and so status) are counteracted within the church not only by the valorization of service but also by forms of mutual subjection that make both those of higher status and those of lower status subject one to another in a way that allows each to be of service to the other.

The effects of these exemplary lives and this practice indicate clearly that the Christian insistence that status should be granted on the basis of service rather than social position and that social differentiation should be a vehicle for mutual benefit rather than domination has had profound effects on all societies in which Christianity has taken root. This form of life and this practice has extended the notion of service beyond the boundaries of the Christian fellowship and given birth to the powerful and now common (but severely threatened) idea that it is more important to find a vocation than it is to achieve a status.

The way in which mutual subjection is to work "on the ground" is exemplified not only by the nature of the marital bond but also by the way in which authority is to be exercised within the church. Like hierarchy and alliance, the exercise of authority is a practice found in all social groups, but within the church the purposes of God are to guide both its purpose and the manner of its application. Authority's purpose is protection of the integrity of the life and witness of the church and guidance of those whose Christian lives are not yet "mature." Even a cursory reading of the Corinthian correspondence indicates that authority is to be used within the church to guard its peace and protect the integrity of its witness. Authority serves a similar function as presented in the eighteenth chapter of Matthew. In Ephesians, authority assumes an allied function. It serves a pedagogical role.

Within the church, many are still children. They have yet to "learn Christ" (Eph. 4:20) and easily fall prey to false teaching. There are, however, within the community "evangelists, pastors, and teachers." These people stand closer than others to the original message and way of life passed on by the apostles and prophets, and so they have a particular responsibility for the health of the church's common life. They are to carry out this responsibility, however, in imitation of Christ—in truth and love. Accordingly, in exercising authority, they are to do so with humility of mind, gentleness, patience, forbearance, kindness, tenderheartedness, forgiveness, and a controlling desire for unity of the Spirit in the bond of peace. In short, when it comes to the exercise of authority within the church, the medium and the message are one.

Thus if those with authority are to be accorded the authority due to people with a more adequate grasp of the truth as revealed in Christ, they are called upon to exercise their authority in the way in which Christ exercises his. This means also that if those under authority are to mature in their knowledge of Christ, they are to respond to the authority of their teachers in a way that is not identical but analogous to the way in which Christ responded to the authority of his Father. Thus they are urged to be open to instruction. Each in an appropriate and particular way is subject to the other, and as a result hierarchy and alliance no longer provide a way for the few to dominate the many. Rather, they provide a way for those with and those under authority to benefit from the gift each has to offer. If each is open to instruction by the other, all are strengthened. If each is gentle toward the other, all more effectively "learn Christ."

The exercise of authority is necessarily connected with the practice of mutual subjection. Both, however, are practices often ignored in discussions of Christian ethics. I believe this is the case because in these days accounts of life in Christ so often center on the broad issues of justice or the moral life of individuals. If, however, Christian living is given an ecclesial focus, the character of common life takes center stage, and with this change of focus relations of sub- and superordination along with the nature and function of authority become unavoidable questions. If the chief goal of the Christian way of life is witness to the truth about God and his will for the world, then the witness must be protected from distortion, and provision must be made for what is now called "Christian formation." Neither goal can be reached apart from the practice of mutual subjection and the right exercise of authority.

The recalibration of life's attachments and goals within an ecclesially focused way of life works changes not only in the way status and authority are understood but also in the attitudes and practices related to wealth. Luke has a particular concern for this matter. According to Luke, the attitudinal change begins with the birth of a form of wisdom. Wealth doesn't last and in the end will be taken by death. Its claim upon and promises for life are illusory. At an even more basic level, however, a recalibration of life's priorities reveals that wealth powerfully threatens the new form of life Christ calls for. Matthew has a similar concern. In his account of Jesus's moral teaching it is important to recognize "mammon" for what in truth it is—a powerful attachment that claims the sort of allegiance that is properly given only to God. The place of wealth and the place of God in one's life pose a clear choice. One cannot serve both.

Attitudinal changes of this magnitude inevitably call for practices that express them. Both Luke and Paul pay considerable attention to this matter. Luke notes that, upon conversion, people began to sell their possessions so as to have money to share with fellow believers who were in want. Indeed, he notes that all things were held in common and that, as a result, there were no needy persons to be found within the church at Jerusalem. The letters of Paul, with their several references to the collection for the saints in Jerusalem, provide a less striking but nonetheless similar example of the way in which a change in life's priorities finds expression in the practice of giving alms to fellow believers in need.

There are several things to note about the way in which New Testament texts present the practice of giving alms. First and foremost, it was a practice whose primary beneficiaries were fellow believers. In our day we attach the name "philanthropy" to the practice of "charitable giving." Our idea is that wealth should be shared without reference to the particular identities of those who might be its recipients. Philanthropy, in fact, means love of humankind as such. The qualification for aid in our minds is thus threefold—one, the recipient is a fellow human being; two, the recipient is a fellow human being in need; and three, the need is one about which the donor has a particular interest. It is the extent and seriousness of the privation in question rather than the particular identities of the people involved that, for philanthropists, properly determine the appropriateness and extent of aid. In the texts of the New Testament, however, aid is not given simply on the basis of need or interest. Rather, those with whom one's wealth is shared are, in the first instance, those who share one's beliefs and way of life and for whom one has a particular responsibility. Indeed, in both Paul and Luke, giving is a means to express and solidify common faith and practice and so also the purposes of God.[3]

---

3. I have given attention previously to the ecclesial focus and significance of giving in the New Testament. See, e.g., Philip Turner, "The Burning of Churches and the Communion of Churches," in *Out of the Ashes: Burned Churches and the Community of Faith*, ed. Norman A. Hjelm (Nashville: Thomas Nelson, 1997), 48–57, and "Philanthropy's Inconstant Friend, Religion," in *Good Intentions: Moral Obstacles and Opportunities*, ed. David Smith (Bloomington: Indiana University Press, 2005), 127–45. In these two articles I point out that many religions stress the importance of giving to fellow believers. A focus on duties to co-religionists is not at all unusual. Perhaps the key question in respect to giving is not the focus on one's own religious community but the resources within a religion that lead to forms of generosity that extend love's expression beyond these borders.

Take, for example, Paul's collection for the church in Jerusalem (Rom. 15:26–29; 2 Cor. 8–9). At first glance, his concern might seem to a contemporary Western reader to be a simple appeal for philanthropic generosity—a straightforward plea for those who have to come to the aid of those who have not. Nevertheless, an analysis of the vocabulary used to describe both the money collected and the collection itself shows that Paul uses specifically religious terms to refer to both. He terms the money collected "grace," "ministry," "church service," and "blessing." The collection as a whole is referred to as "this grace." By using this particular vocabulary, Paul makes clear that the generous gift of the gentiles to the Jews concretely expresses the grace both have received. The gift of the Macedonian Christians thus imitates the gift Christ has given to both Jew and gentile. In this case, sacrificial giving, particularly to those fellow believers who were formerly estranged, imitates the gift of Christ intended by God to reconcile Jew and gentile and include both within his people. The gift of the Macedonians to the poor of Jerusalem thus serves as a witness to the deep purposes of God in human history. As Lionel Thornton wrote many years ago, "St. Paul, by his choice of words, was sometimes suggesting deliberately the connection of commonplace things . . . with the highest mysteries of the Gospel."[4]

Luke adds a twist to the normative account he gives of the practice of giving. He makes it clear that, as a practice, giving alms requires that, among God's people, givers require no recompense from recipients. Giving alms was, as mentioned previously, one of the pillars of Jewish piety, and Jesus upheld the practice. His concern was that almsgiving not be used as a means of self-glorification. He was also concerned that giving alms not become a means of exercising power in a way that creates dependence and submission in others. As Marcel Mauss made clear in his classic essay on gift giving, gifts create relations of sub- and superordination.[5] They pretend to be free but are not. Nevertheless, the reordering of life's priorities among those who follow "the way" is to be manifest in willingness to lend to "everyone" who begs and to do so without expecting gain for oneself (Luke 6:30a, 34, 35a). Willingness to lend without hope of gain does two things. First, it renders gifts true gifts rather than means of besting others. Second, it reaches out across social divisions and makes clear to those who are needy that they have been included within the category of near rather than distant neighbors. A "no strings attached" gift places a needy person within the circle

---

4. L. S. Thornton, *Common Life in the Body of Christ* (Westminster: Dacre, 1941), 27. See also Turner, "Philanthropy's Inconstant Friend, Religion," 136–37.

5. Marcel Mauss, *The Gift: Forms and Functions of Exchange in Archaic Societies* (New York: Norton, 1967).

of kin, and kin do not need to beg. They are cared for. So in the book of Acts, one expression of this form of common life is that within "the company of those who believed . . . there was not a needy person among them" (Acts 4:32a, 34).

There can be no doubt that Jesus's teaching on giving and lending cannot be made the basis of an economic system. In various times and places it has been and still is being tried, but as an economic practice it will always prove to be an utter failure. It is not my purpose here to work out what might be called a "Christian economic ethic." The point at issue is not general economic policy but the use of financial assistance among Christians and in their relations with those who do not share their beliefs. These gifts and loans, both to believers and nonbelievers, are not to be means of establishing dominance. They are a means of coming to the aid of those in need and, by so doing, establishing them on equal terms as members of a community of people of which one is also a member.

Yet another example of the recalibration of life's attachments as presented in the New Testament is a change in the relation of believers to the state. St. Paul views the state as a providential means of ordering a disorderly world. He understands, however, that behind the state lie rebellious powers of cosmic proportion and that these powers can convert the state into a demonic force. To the mind of the author of the Apocalypse, these demonic powers are present and active in the Roman Empire. He calls the churches to faithful witness that will expose the idolatrous claims of the empire. Their witness will also display their love for God and their obedience to the truth. There can be no more strategic sphere than the realm of political power for displaying a recalibration of basic loyalties. It is fair to say that giving idolatrous authority to the state (or to one's people) is an even more powerful threat to the claims of God than are family, possessions, or status. Consequently, the most powerful expression of truth by the church is the martyrdom of the saints who refuse to bow down before the state's pretensions. To aid in this perilous calling, the author of Revelation provides his readers with a basic moral vocabulary—a sort of primer for faithful witnesses in the face of attack. The saints are to "remember," "hold fast," "maintain a settled mind," "be zealous," and "repent." These habits of mind will sustain them in the "tribulation" through which they must pass. These habits of mind create in the saints a form of "wisdom" that allows them to recognize the true significance of state pretensions. When the state exalts itself, believers will see by wisdom that the state has decked itself with the clothes of a false god and a false savior (Rev. 13:18). From a new center of loyalty, they will worship the true God and in so doing expose a false one.

A recalibration of life's priorities leads naturally enough to significant changes in practice in respect to family, status, wealth, and political authority. This reordering of loyalties also produces a change in the practice of piety. If the author of the Apocalypse exposes the false use of religion as a means of glorifying the state, St. Matthew exposes the false use of personal piety as a means of self-aggrandizement. Not only must divine honors be withheld from the state, but they must also be withheld from individuals in search of social prestige.

How so? Piety is composed of the practices that bind believers, both individually and corporately, to God. Christian piety, like Jewish piety, is shaped by three practices—almsgiving, prayer, and fasting. The key thing about church practice in respect to these matters is that it be carried out for the glory of God rather than that of its practitioners. The practice of piety is to be carried out without the sort of fanfare that calls attention to itself. It is, as it were, to be done "in secret." Further, its reward is in secret. In this way, it is God rather than the agent that is glorified, and it is from God rather than the public that approbation is sought.

Christ's admonitions in respect to the public display of piety have become so commonplace that it is easy to forget the extent to which piety is put on public display so as to lead to the glorification of the practitioner. One need only follow reports of charitable events to recognize the truth of this statement. Common though it may be, disingenuous religious practice is nonetheless the ultimate form of self-glorification and so also the ultimate form of blasphemy. However, a people whose common practice binds them to God through care of the poor, through prayer that the will of God rather than their own be done, and through repentance, amendment of life, and hope for forgiveness does not put on public display its own magnificence but God's.

Reordered Love Expressed in Changed Practices That Directly Honor the Second Commandment

To give primacy to the love of God involves not only a reordering of all other loves but also a change in the form of all one's social relationships in a way that serves God's purpose to unify all things in Christ. The second commandment, serving as it does as an aspect of the "higher righteousness" required of disciples, engenders among them a specific set of concerns that serve God's unifying purposes. These concerns express love of one's neighbor particularly through showing mercy and promoting reconciliation and peace. Jesus's account of the law provides an epitome of the practices that make these concerns concrete (Matt. 5:17–48). In the first instance, mercy and a desire for peace require renunciation of negative reactions to people considered enemies. Chief among these reactions are violence, insult, and disparagement (5:21–23). In a positive sense, mercy and a desire for peace require two quite specific ecclesial practices. In the first instance, those who believe a fellow member of the church has something against them are not to wait for the "injured" party to take the initiative but rather begin a process leading to reconciliation. Second, if the members of the church as a body believe the behavior of a fellow member is unacceptable, they are to enter into a process designed to bring about a change in behavior rather than one that leads immediately to exclusion from the fellowship of the church (18:15–20).

Another communal practice issuing from a desire to show mercy and establish peace is renunciation of vengeance and nonresistance to evil (Matt. 5:38–41). It is no doubt because this practice, as presented by Matthew, includes not only fellow believers but also those outside the church (including the occupying Roman power) that it has proven so controversial. I have already pointed out that the requirement to show mercy may conflict with love's demand to protect a neighbor under the threat of harm. I personally do not see any way of resolving this tension between what appear to be contrary practices and contrary understandings of the demands of love. That said, I would prefer, like St. Augustine, to regard defense of one's neighbor as a different matter than defense of oneself. In these cases neighbor love leads in different directions. It is love that requires renunciation of vengeance in response to an attack on one's own person, and it is love also that produces resistance when the attack is directed to persons other than oneself. In both cases, however, love expresses itself in a practice that takes into account enemies of all sorts. Each member of the church is to pray for enemies of any variety because, as in one's own case, God loves them (5:43–47).

Renunciation of violence, anger, insult, and vengeance, coupled with a positive demand to love one's enemy and seek reconciliation, lies at the heart of Christian practice in respect to one's neighbors and plays a central role in what is now often termed "the social mission of the churches." These are practices that provide the quintessential witness to what God has revealed about himself in the life of Christ. There are, however, two other practices that express God's relation to his people and support peace and reconciliation. They are care that the bond of marriage (now a vocation rather than a social and personal necessity) is not compromised, and care that truth telling is present in all forms of human exchange.

In Matthew's account of Jesus's teaching on marriage, adultery is the only admissible justification for breaking the marriage bond (Matt. 5:31–32). Mark and Luke do not allow even this exception (Mark 10:11–12; Luke 16:18). The

Matthean exception is striking in view of the stricter presentations by Mark and Luke. Indeed, indicative of the sanctity of the marital bond in Christian practice is the fact that in the history of the church, only three exceptions to Jesus's teaching have been allowed—adultery, desertion, and (in the Eastern Church) "moral death."[6]

Without entering into the stormy debates that rage among Christians about the meaning and authority of the practice Jesus insisted upon, one can safely say that Christian practice (until recently in the West) has sought to protect the sacrosanct character of the marital bond. It has been taken to reflect God's will in creation and his means of protecting society from the destructive effects of disordered sexual desire. It has also been taken as a school of charity and a sign of God's faithful relation to Israel and to his church. The point is that the practice, for Christians, reflects the will and nature of its author. It is not surprising, therefore, that to protect this practice and the bond it establishes and protects, Jesus prohibited not only adultery but also the motives and actions that lead to adultery. Thus Matthew records the hyperbolic statement that the offending eye that motivates adultery is to be plucked out and the offending hand that initiates it cut off (5:27-30).

The link between the marriage bond and God's nature and purposes is underscored in the Pauline, Pastoral, and Catholic Epistles.[7] The importance of truth telling receives similar stress. Matthew presents Jesus's prohibition of oaths as a means of underscoring the importance of speaking honestly. In Matthew's account of Jesus's life and teaching, Jesus speaks only what his Father gives him to say. He speaks the truth and only the truth. Truth telling is characteristic of God and his Son and so also is to be true in the church. In Christians' relations with one another and in their relations with the society in which they live, yes is to be yes and no is to be no. Only in this way will the witness of the church to the truth about God be a true witness.

Truthful speech, however, does more than give veracity to the church's witness. It also enables peace and reconciliation in both the internal and external relations of the church. Wherever there is a living tradition of social wisdom, wherever proverbs name life's recurrent situations, the tongue is recognized as the most terrible weapon for the promotion of social discord. It is certainly

---

6. For a discussion of the causes for divorce that have been recognized, though only by some of the churches, see Philip Turner, "The Marriage Canons of the Episcopal Church: (1) Scripture and Tradition," *The Anglican Theological Review* 65, no. 4 (October 1983): 371-93, and "The Marriage Canons of the Episcopal Church: (2) The Case from Reason," *The Anglican Theological Review* 66, no. 1 (January 1984): 1-22.

7. See, e.g., Rom. 7:1-3; 1 Cor. 7:8-40; Eph. 5:22-33; Col. 3:18-19; 1 Tim. 3:2, 12; 1 Pet. 3:1-7; Heb. 13:4.

so recognized in both the Old and New Testaments.[8] A guarded tongue, one given to speaking the truth, and one that does not sow discord or speak disparagingly of others is normative for life together in Christ (Eph. 4:25, 31).

Finally, the practice of speaking truthfully is intended to expose falsehood, and for this reason it is to be carried out with boldness. Within the churches and the societies of which they are a part, sin expresses itself as an all-encompassing lie. The way in which Christians live one with another and speak are intended, in part, to expose falsehood. For this reason Luke places great emphasis on the fact that Peter and Paul speak "boldly." In like manner, as portrayed in the Apocalypse when the saints are confronted with the beast, no lie can be found in their mouths.

The command to love God with all one's heart, soul, mind, and strength and one's neighbor as oneself is accompanied within the common life of the church by a set of characteristic practices. Among other things, these manifest faithfulness to God, concern for the truth, care for one's neighbors, and a desire for peace within the church and between disciples and those among whom they live. The reordering of love leads to the reordering of all forms of human relationship. As the brief survey above makes plain, the reordering of love and the consequent recalibration of life's attachments work changes in all forms of human relationship, be it one involving sex, money, power, speech, or religion.[9]

Reordered Love and Changes of Heart

No doubt it is because the reordering of life's attachments is so radical that Christians speak of conversion as "rebirth" or "dying and rising." The changes called for are so radical that they require what can only be called a change of heart. Conversion thus involves more than a recalibration of loyalty. It carries with it the gift of a number of enabling "graces" that together give expression to a change within the inner core of people's lives. These graces are skills and capacities that empower love in a way that supports the practices that lead to reconciliation, peace, and unity. The author of Ephesians lists them as truthfulness, humility, gentleness, patience, forbearance, a keen desire for unity and peace, kindness, tenderheartedness, and forgiveness. These graces stand opposed to a range of inner dispositions like deceitfulness, bitterness,

---

8. See, e.g., Pss. 10:3–4, 7; 15:2–5; 34:11–13; 50:19–21; Prov. 6:16–19; 18:20–21; Isa. 59:3–4; Jer. 9:3–9; Mic. 6:12; James 1:26; 3:6–11; 1 Pet. 3:10.

9. For an extended study of the way in which Christian belief shapes the basic forms of human exchange, see Philip Turner, *Sex, Money and Power: An Essay in Christian Social Ethics* (Cambridge, MA: Cowley, 1985).

wrath, anger, and malice. These "unruly affections" express and produce results opposite to the graces—namely, enmity and division.

Matthew and Luke provide a similar list both of the graces and of the attitudes and habits of being that compose their opposite numbers. Thus those who are pronounced blessed in the Sermon on the Mount are those who are undivided in the allegiances of their hearts. Standing before God with an undivided, "pure" heart provides self-knowledge. Self-knowledge allows no space for arrogance. Jesus's disciples know that before God they are beggars. They know their disobedient state and that of God's people, and they mourn because of that state. In their mourning, they long for a change of heart both for themselves and for the church. Humility allows them to be truthful about themselves, the state of the church, and that of the nations. They long also for a change in the character of all forms of human relationships. They long both to do what is right and to see that right is done. They are consequently eager to make peace with their enemies. In place of anger and enmity, they are to be motivated by love, mercy, and forgiveness. Their desire is not to be for vengeance but reconciliation.

There is yet another inner disposition that accompanies love, mercy, and forgiveness. Matthew in particular points out that life together in Christ requires of people that they not be taken up with the failures of others. He cautions against making judgments about one's fellow disciples prior to examining whether one has a log in one's own eye. Life together as Christ wills makes possible what might be called a habit of being—one that leads a person to look first to one's own struggle to follow Jesus before making judgments about another's success or failure in this matter. Only in this way can true judgments about oneself and others be made.

Matthew and Luke also stress that Jesus's followers are gifted with a remarkable degree of inner freedom from the normal blandishments of life. Their freedom stems from faith that God will provide for the needs of his children and care for them when they are in distress. They are people whose faith leads them to hope, and this confidence "releases" them from the attachments and concerns that normally direct the course of daily life. Release opens new possibilities for love's expression. Specifically, it makes possible inclusion within the circle of "near neighbors" those who, because of one form of difference or another, are normally excluded from this circle. In short, confidence in God's love casts out fear and in turn gives birth to a form of love that makes one ready to become a neighbor to the most unlikely candidates for that honor. Love born of confidence in God's love changes the exclusionary question "Who is my neighbor?" to the open question "To whom am I called to be a neighbor?"

The traditional list of virtues is composed of four cardinal virtues (wisdom, fortitude, temperance, and justice) and three theological virtues (faith, hope, and charity). The graces mentioned so far are much more numerous than either the cardinal or the theological virtues. This is so because they are the children of faith, hope, and love and the shapers of wisdom, fortitude, temperance, and justice. They fill out, as it were, the theological virtues and give direction to the cardinal ones. They show that these virtues are fruitful. They multiply! It is for this reason that they are far more extensive in number and far more specific in nature than their parents. Further, each is to be pondered. None can be ignored. They are the little helpers that empower and refract love's expression.

I once had a teacher who called the accounts of these graces given in the Pauline letters "St. Paul's to-do lists." Her meaning was that we demean their importance by treating them as items to be checked off as we might do with a list of tasks. Her plea was that we pause and take stock of the qualities of life Paul and others present as christlike. These, she was fond of saying, describe the inner qualities that make possible the form of life Christians are called to live. She was also fond of saying that these qualities are children of the defining features of a life lived in Christ—faith, hope, and love. For this reason alone, they are not to be skipped over as one hurries to get on to more important matters.

She urged us also to remember that, as depicted in the texts of the New Testament, what I have called the graces are deployed in the midst of conflict with forces whose strength is greater than any possessed by human beings either individually or collectively. In God's battle with evil, it is the power of God that prevails rather than human strength. In following Christ, his disciples are always waiting for God to show both his justice and his mercy. Thus the texts we have considered stress that Christ's followers always live "in troubled times," and in such times they are called not to rely on their own strength but to "wait upon the Lord."

Taken together, the texts stress five other graces that, because the Christian life is one of waiting on God in the midst of "tribulation," stand at the foundation of Christian practice. They are wisdom, attention, truthfulness, boldness, and patient endurance. For Christ's followers, trials and tribulations are daily companions rather than occasional visitors. Accordingly, in his mercy, God provides the capacities that preserve faithful obedience in the midst of struggle. Wisdom provides knowledge of God's purposes and the particular ways in which to remain faithful to those purposes. Attention (being careful about the way in which one walks) allows one to recognize the true nature of the circumstances in which one lives. Truthful and bold speech, along with love, exposes evil for what it is. Patient endurance makes one able, in the face of evil's attack, to wait patiently for God to show both his mercy and his righteous judgment.

The Challenge of the Present Hour

I am aware that I have not taken the advice of my teacher. I have hurried over the lists of practices and graces of love's face. My purpose, however, has been to stress the ecclesial focus of Christian ethics rather than to write a full account of the contents of that way of life, and I have said enough to make plain that if the churches were to shift their focus to the constitution of the church and its way of life, they would be confronted with a challenge of gigantic proportions.

That the churches now face formidable challenges is widely recognized, but there is considerable disagreement about the nature of these challenges and how they should be addressed. For some, the challenge is one of social relevance. For others it is a failure to speak to the deep spiritual needs of the age. Some see a way forward by focusing on "social ethics," and others focus on "spirituality." However, I hope I have shown that neither point of concern provides the right place to begin the process of rebuilding the churches. The place to begin is with the integrity of their common life. To repeat, the basic question is how Christ forms a culture rather than how Christ might transform one.

John Howard Yoder has shown himself closer to the nub of the problem than H. Richard Niebuhr, despite the latter's concern for the reform of the churches. Nevertheless, being closer to the nub of the problem does not solve it in and of itself. The issue is this. If indeed the proper focus for Christian moral thought is the common life of the church, how is that life to assume the shape outlined above? This question is pressing because the form of life characteristic of the nations of the West is becoming increasingly adverse to a form of life that, as presented in the New Testament, can rightly be called "worthy."

At this point I am willing to let this statement stand without spelling out the points (many of which are moral) at which there is conflict. That would take another book. Everyone knows, however, that things have changed. The signature theologian of my (Anglican) tradition, Richard Hooker, assumed in his *Laws of Ecclesiastical Polity* that there was and ought to be a permeable membrane between the life of the soul, the life of the family, the life of the village church, the life of the town, and the life of the English nation. In passing from one dimension of life to another, he assumed that one ought never to enter a culturally alien territory. All dimensions of life were to be shaped by

Christian belief and practice. The churches in North America made a similar assumption for many generations. However, no one now living in North American can possibly make such an assumption. For Christians who have to any degree been formed by immersion in the common life of the church, the disjunction is proving particularly painful. Everywhere they turn they cross cultural boundaries—one might even go so far as to say that at every turn they meet different forms of life.

The challenge presented by giving Christian ethics an ecclesial focus can be presented in a way that further clarifies the issues. George Lindbeck's thesis in *The Nature of Doctrine* is that religious doctrine is best understood as a grammar characteristic of a religious culture and its language.[10] Significant objections have been and can be made to Lindbeck's thesis, but certainly he is right in part to suggest that learning one's way about a religion is like learning to function in a culture and speak its language properly. The challenge is to draw each new generation and those who might be called "settlers in the land" into that culture. The challenge is to teach them its language and its ways of living so that they know how to behave and speak in a manner that other native speakers recognize as in accord with the way they live and speak.

In his monograph, Lindbeck speaks of doctrine, but the same thing must be said of moral values, judgments, and practices. As Sabina Lovibond has pointed out in her book *Ethical Formation*, moral reasons for the sorts of people we are to be and the sorts of actions we are to take do not exist simply within the hearts of individuals. Rather, they exist within cultures.[11] In a sense, the reasons we admire the people we do and the reasons we give for our actions and our judgments upon them are simply "there" in the cultural air we breathe. As Lovibond has said, "The ethical, let us say, pertains to what people learn to value through immersion in a community acquainted with ideas of right, duty, justice, solidarity, and common social or cultural interests extending beyond the lifetime of the present generation."[12]

If a way of life is to extend beyond the present generation, the transmission of what a culture holds to be virtuous, right, and good must occur, and if it is to occur, there must be both generally accepted means of moral formation and people who exemplify in their lives the values and behaviors that the culture prizes. There must be means of transmission, and there must be people who, though imperfectly, *are the truth*—people who exemplify the way of life into which newcomers and strangers are to be drawn and by which their lives are to

---

10. George Lindbeck, *The Nature of Doctrine: Religion and Theology in a Postliberal Age* (Philadelphia: Westminster, 1984).
11. Sabina Lovibond, *Ethical Formation* (Cambridge, MA: Harvard University Press, 2002).
12. Ibid., 33.

be shaped. As Lovibond has said, "To undergo (moral) formation is to come to have in one's soul the same structure—the same *logos* or system of *logoi* as anyone else who exemplifies correct judgment (or who is the truth)."[13] To the extent that this process of transmission is successful, a "second nature" is formed, and this "second nature" is characteristic of a culture. Behind this process of transmission stands what might be called "a social teleology." There must be present within a culture a commitment by one generation to initiate another into a body of common wisdom.[14]

Here one comes face to face with what I take to be the central problem the churches face. Assuming that the "social teleology" is present (and it may not be), how is the transmission of a culture to take place? Of course, in some ways, because passing on a way of life takes place in history, the process will always be contested. No tradition is seamless. Each has internal disputes, some of which are never resolved. Further, no culture is without its "outsiders"—people who occupy only a marginal place and consequently see things differently. Finally, there are other cultures that impinge upon us and whose ways are markedly different. These factors usually exist in combination and so make passing on a way of life an occasion for disagreement and conflict on the one hand and cultural enrichment on the other.

However, the challenge now faced by the churches is more difficult than those normally encountered within a culture as it forms a new generation or resocializes an immigrant population. The churches in the West have lived for centuries with the support of their surrounding cultures. This situation has changed markedly. The differences between the goals, values, and practices of the postindustrial societies of the West and those of a culture in which Christ is taking form are increasingly marked, and for this reason transmission within the churches of a form of life that issues in a shared and mutually recognizable "second nature" is increasingly difficult. To use a phrase I have borrowed from a colleague, it is now increasingly difficult to pass "the Christian thing" on.

Indeed, in this age, despite continuing efforts by the churches, for Christ to transform culture would be a most unusual event. It is far more likely that Christ (as presented by the churches) has already been transformed by culture and turned into its image. The results are churches whose way of life closely resembles that of postindustrial society and whose use of language has absorbed so many aspects of a foreign tongue that it sounds more like a form of pidgin than a way of speaking that Paul, Matthew, Mark, Luke, or John would recognize.

13. Ibid., 57.
14. Ibid., 63.

The first question before the churches, therefore, is not how they can become socially relevant or spiritually helpful. The first question is how they can form a life together that is worthy of the calling to which they have been called. I do not know the answer to this question and must leave it for people whose gifts are different from mine. There are, however, two remaining questions that do fall within the scope of this study: If one does focus an account of Christian living on the common life of the church, what then must be said about the relation between the common life of the church and what I have called "the life of the soul"? And what is the relation of an ecclesially focused ethic and the common life of society? It is beyond the scope of this book to respond in detail to these questions, but it does lie within its boundaries to indicate the directions in which the churches ought to look for answers.

9

The Ecclesial Setting of a Devout and Holy Life

Introduction

If the focus of Christian ethics is properly the common life of the church, what is to be said of the private lives of its individual members? What in particular is to be made of the call for each Christian to live a devout and holy life? The question is unavoidable. Jesus's command "Be ye perfect" echoes through Christian history. It is a command directed to both the church and its individual members. This command has been rightly heard and followed by countless individuals. Across the ages it has produced lives of admirable virtue and remarkable holiness. Unquestionably, however, the way in which this command has been understood and followed has on numerous occasions produced lives whose notable accomplishments have been compromised by self-absorption, moralism, pride, and even ruthlessness. Aspects of these vices are present in John Cassian's account of Christian perfection. They have appeared with troubling regularity within both the Eastern and Western churches.

I take it as a given that the Achilles's heel of those forms of Christian ethics that focus on the state of individual souls is the temptation to take an inward turn that produces forms of vice rather than virtue. I take it that the issue is whether one can give an account of a devout and holy life that protects against this unfortunate inward turn. The issue is a serious one. The appearance of these flaws among morally earnest persons has a peculiarly unattractive quality—one that is often captured more effectively in fiction than in straightforward reporting. One thinks, for example, of Father Péricand in Irène Némirovsky's novel *Suite Française*.[1] From a wealthy family, Father Péricand despises the orphan boys in his charge. He has a duty to love them, but he can't. This struggle reveals an impatient desire to be holy. Impatience with his shortcomings eats away at him. In his eyes, no effort to be holy is ever enough. His piety, says the author, has turned him into a greedy man who hoards his spiritual accomplishments as if they were gold. Father Péricand is an unattractive man.

Unattractive as spiritual greed may be, it is nonetheless the case that a similar form of the vice has been strongly supported in postindustrial societies by the more recent turn away from the cultivation of character and toward the more subjective enterprise of "spirituality." As present today in popular culture, spirituality manifests a frankly narcissistic character. A visit to any bookstore will demonstrate that popular accounts of the "spiritual life" more often than not are more concerned with personal identity, growth, meaning, and felicity than with moral seriousness. In these accounts the same unattractive self-absorption one finds in quests for moral perfection is easily detected. As if to underscore excessive concern for the "self" and its inner state that is now so common, the moral concerns that generally accompany a desire for rectitude or holiness are regularly portrayed in this literature as inhibitors of personal identity and growth rather than a necessary component of an admirable life.

It is not my purpose to document the above description of our moral and spiritual state, but I will provide further examples of the sort of things to which I refer—examples that suggest American society (and perhaps postindustrial societies in general) may be particularly prone to the sort of self-absorption that a focus on personal moral and/or spiritual advancement tends to spawn. Robert Bellah's account of a form of personal religion that he terms "Sheilaism" lies closest to hand. Bellah and his colleagues track the movement inward of religious belief and experience to its logical conclusion in an account of "spirituality" that is tailored to the needs and wants of a single individual—in his example, a woman named Sheila. Bellah's work *Habits of the Heart* displays a movement away from the sort of serious moral concern traditionally associated with the quest for a good or even holy life and toward an inner world of personal taste and meaning.

I believe it is fair to say that the authors of *Habits of the Heart* depict a demotion of moral concern and an increase of interest in individual experience.

---

1. Irène Némirovsky, *Suite Française* (New York: Vintage, 2007), 135–38.

Whatever questions may be raised about Bellah's rendition and interpretation of the social facts,[2] it seems true that the trajectory of much modern religion in the West is not toward what William Law termed "a devout and holy life" but toward a psychological state that is an antidote to the sort of "unhappy disquiet" that so troubled John Cassian centuries ago.

James Davison Hunter has traced a similar movement in *The Death of Character*, his study of moral education in America's homes, schools, and churches.[3] Hunter's basic point is that in response to the pluralism characteristic of America's consumer society, the emphasis of moral instruction has shifted from the development of character toward a form designed to "protect" and "mold" children "to responsible and rational living out of their *personal freedom*."[4] Under the influence of the quasi-scientific claims of psychologists, moral instruction has moved from a focus on the contents of a good character that require widespread social agreement to a concentration on psychological development that downplays specific moral content. The hope has been that by avoiding content-filled accounts of good character and steering a person through the stages of moral development, a culture will produce mature, responsible individuals—individuals free to espouse (largely on the basis of its emotional affectivity) a mature form of morality of their own choosing, one that honors the agent's freedom and respects that of others.

The developmental theories of Lawrence Kohlberg and Jean Piaget are thoroughly representative of this trend. Hunter summarizes the triumph of developmental psychology over content-filled moral instruction in this way:

> When it comes to the moral life of children, the vocabulary of the psychologist frames virtually all public discussion. For decades now, contributions from philosophers and theologians have been muted or nonexistent. Anthropologists and sociologists are likewise absent from the discussion. Historians have been busy documenting the major developments in this realm of social life, but their influence has been limited mainly to their guild. Further it is the psychologists, and in particular the developmental and educational psychologists, that have owned the field—in theory and in practice.[5]

The point is that the move from a social enterprise of character formation to a private enterprise in the service of individual psychological development

---

2. For Bellah's response to some of the main criticisms of his work, see Robert Bellah, "Reading and Misreading *Habits of the Heart*," *Sociology of Religion* 68, no. 2 (2007): 189–93.
3. James Davison Hunter, *The Death of Character: Moral Education in an Age without Good or Evil* (New York: Basic Books, 2000).
4. Ibid., 66, emphasis added.
5. Ibid., 81.

parallels the move from a desire for a socially recognized form of personal holiness to a quest for individual and personally appropriated spiritual experience. In both cases morality becomes an increasingly private affair with vastly diminished content. It is, furthermore, subject to the vices of self-absorption that often accompany a focus on the moral or spiritual state of individuals. In this sort of social world, to quote Hunter again, "Life and its ethical challenges are best approached through a kind of utilitarian calculus ordered by the imperatives of emotional well-being."[6]

The call of Christ to be perfect often goes awry when coupled with a project centered on the self. What happens, however, if the call to perfection is heard first as a call to participate in a form of common life in which each individual lives a life that exemplifies the goods and goals most prized within a social body? What happens if the plea of the author of Ephesians for the members of that congregation to live a life worthy of their calling is understood first as a plea to live life together in a way that is proportionate to or reflective of common purpose? What happens if our personal struggles are placed first in a corporate rather than a personal setting? What would happen if our first question were not how we are doing spiritually but how our lives are affecting those with whom we share a common social space? Would not a social focus such as this not only issue in a call for a devout and holy life but also guard against the sort of self-absorption that spawns narcissism, moralism, and pride?

I ask these questions to show that an ecclesial focus for Christian ethics does not eliminate a concern for living a holy life or lessen its demands. Rather, it places that concern and those demands in a context larger than that of the self and its spiritual and moral state. It is in a public place rather than in the privacy of its own room that the soul learns its notes, as it were, and begins to practice its scales.

The Necessity of a Communal Setting for the Moral Life

In support of this observation I note first a simple matter of fact. Traits of character are necessarily formed in a social setting. What is true for all forms of moral excellence or failure is certainly true for Christians as they seek to obey Christ's call to perfection. One need only note that the contents of a devout and holy life are not a matter of personal taste for Christians. The contents and the manner of acquisition of such a life are social facts composed of the socially defined features of those deemed by others to follow "the way"

---

6. Ibid., 104.

marked out by Jesus. It is within the body of the church that what I have called the graces are interpreted, modeled, and received. It is within the body of the church that individual lives that exemplify a right interpretation of the graces exert their influence and offer their assistance. It is within the social setting of the church that people acquire a second nature that reflects that of Christ. It is within the church that communal support and divine assistance become available to individuals.

To put the matter in another way—one that has no religious content—I will cite once more the work of Sabina Lovibond. She is right to argue that the moral reasons we give for the sorts of people we ought to be and the sorts of actions we ought to take do not exist simply within the hearts of individuals. They exist within cultures, and they are modeled and fostered within a culture by people who, in a sense, "are the truth." It is fair to say, I believe, that no moral or spiritual enterprise can in the first instance be "private." These enterprises are necessarily social in nature. They presuppose a moral and spiritual vocabulary and a set of moral practices that are socially transmitted. Indeed, the social nature of moral and spiritual virtue and practice confirms the argument of George Lindbeck in his *Nature of Doctrine*. "The way" Christians follow is part of culture and must be learned in the same way one leans a language—by participation and imitation.

As a prime example, I cite St. Benedict, who understood each monastic community as a "school for the service of the Lord." The school belonged to Christ, and in it monks received grace and instruction through which they learned a new form of life—one that manifests love of God and love of neighbor.[7] He believed these graces could be acquired only by living over a protracted period of time with others who adopt similar practices and have similar goals. Hence, central to his monastic discipline was the vow of stability. This vow requires each monk to remain in place for the remainder of his life. In this way, no monk can escape the demanding and often annoying presence of other monks. Here, in the give and take of a daily round of work, study, and prayer, one learns charity and a new way of life. As Benedict wrote,

> For as we advance in the religious life and in faith, our hearts expand and we run the way of God's commandments with unspeakable sweetness of love. Thus, never departing from His school, but persevering in the monastery according to His teacher until death, we may by patience share in the sufferings of Christ and deserve to have a share also in His kingdom.[8]

7. Leonard J. Doyle, trans., *St. Benedict's Rule for Monasteries* (Collegeville, MN: Liturgical, 1948), 5–6.
8. Ibid.

Unquestionably, Benedict emphasized growth in holiness by each monk in a way that did not, as in the case of Ephesians and St. Augustine, link this effort in an obvious way to communal witness.[9] Nevertheless, by placing the search for perfection in love within a communal setting, the monastic communities of his followers transformed the face of Europe by their example.[10] The great architect of my own Anglican tradition, Thomas Cranmer, understood the common life of a congregation in a similar manner. He produced the Book of Common Prayer designed to form each congregation within England as a "school for the service of the Lord." His plan for the parishes of England was thoroughly Benedictine. Cranmer sought to structure a set of practices that would, over the years, foster devout and holy lives within the settled life and common worship of a parish congregation.[11]

It is true that his goal, like that of Benedict, was what today we call "Christian nurture" or "Christian formation." He did not, as we have seen in the case of John Howard Yoder, envision the congregation as a gathered community whose common life is designed to render a common witness to God's purpose to unite all things in Christ. Cranmer lived in what used to be known as "Christendom," and within Christendom the primary calling of the church was not evangelical witness but pastoral care and Christian nurture. It is also true that Cranmer lived in a simpler era—one characterized both by less individualism and by far less mobility and social diversity.

It was easy for Cranmer to model the local parish church on the settled life of a monastic community, but not so for us. Particularly among Protestants, the congregation is less the focus for a common purpose and more the provider of religious goods and services. In search of more adequate provision of the goods and services we desire, individual seekers move from congregation to congregation in a way similar to our move from shop to shop in search for new or better merchandise. Sad though it may be, the ideal of "stability" and common purpose hardly enter our religious vocabulary.

The nature of social life in our time and the way in which the churches, particularly in America, have adapted to that life in many ways render nostalgic the notion of the congregation as a school for the service of the Lord, and so also as a place where God's final purposes in history are put on display. Yet schools for the service of the Lord are necessary if the Christian way of life

---

9. Markus, *The End of Ancient Christianity*, 63–83.
10. See, e.g., Dom David Knowles, *The Benedictines* (Eugene, OR: Wipf & Stock, 2009).
11. See, e.g., *The First and Second Prayer Books of Edward VI* (London: J. M. Dent & Sons, 1957). These, along with the translation of the Bible into English, clearly demonstrate Cranmer's purpose and its Benedictine character.

in both corporate and individual expression is to be passed on in a way that makes it an effective witness.

Matthew's admonition to let our communal light shine and the author of Ephesians's plea that we live a life together that is worthy of our calling are sayings that accord both with the social nature of moral education and with the communal reference of Christ's command to be perfect. As such, they invite the churches to reconsider the consumer-driven approach they have taken in the way they understand themselves and organize their activities.

The Congregation as a "School for the Service of the Lord"

I do not know how to change the commercialization of American religion. This way of thinking about and ordering its activities must change, however, if the churches are to pass on their beliefs and way of life. What is needed is a description of what it would be like if the churches were to understand Christ's demand first within the context of "life together." What would the life of a congregation and its individual members look like if that life were understood as a school for the service of the Lord—a school whose students' life together is a witness to God's purposes in history and a means of receiving the graces and passing on the practices that make that witness credible? How would this change in focus affect the moral component of what we now often call "personal religion"?

First of all, if ethics is given an ecclesial focus, a common effort to live life together in a way that manifests love of God and neighbor takes center stage, dislodging in the process self-concern and reducing one's own role to a bit part in a remarkable drama. A shift in perspective of this magnitude requires each member of the congregation to enter a painful process of recalibrating basic loyalties and reconfiguring basic forms of relationship. Throughout Christian history, the recalibration of loyalties has been expressed communally through making common worship the central act of the church. As with the Jews nothing trumps Sabbath observance, so with Christians nothing should trump celebration of the Lord's Day. Here the unity of God's people in love and praise is clearly manifest, people are gathered from every nation and language, and grace to live a worthy life is again and again made available. To excuse oneself from this primary expression of love for God because of other priorities is to show that one has missed or turned their back on the point of God's entire history with his people.

An ecclesial focus for Christian ethics springs from common worship.[12] In this context, God addresses his people. In this context, allegiances are questioned and must be assessed in relation to one's love of God. In this context, each individual stands as a member of a people, and in this context each individual is called upon to assess his or her priorities. In this context, as the church hears the first and great commandment, family, status, and possessions—the idols that bemuse us—are toppled over and over again.

It is also in the context of worship that the congregation and each person in it learns to "remember" the long account of God's relation with his people. It is no accident that the author of Revelation lists remembering as one of the ways in which the saints to whom he writes pass faithfully through the "tribulation" they face. Remembering is a grace that establishes identity, and identity allows both communities and individuals to maintain integrity in the course of time and in the face of adversity. In the words of Revelation, remembering helps one to "hold fast" and go through both change and trial with "patient endurance." It also calls forth "repentance" when the community and its individual members fail in these and other respects.

For Christian congregations and for their individual members, common worship tests basic loyalties, and it calls to mind the common history that, across time, provides identity, meaning, and perseverance. In the context of worship, what Matthew calls "purity of heart" (singular devotion to God) and what the author of Revelation calls "remembering," "holding fast," and "patiently enduring" become aspects of the "second nature" both individuals and congregations acquire and share.

Worship is the wellspring of the common life of the church. It is of fundamental importance to note, however, that Christians believe worship sustains common life in a way that does not dishonor or suffocate its individual participants. The primary metaphor Christians have used to describe the church and the place of each individual in it is a "body." Christ is designated the "head," and each person individually is a "member." To be sure, the metaphor that identifies society with the human body does not belong uniquely to a Christian vocabulary, and it has been put to quite totalitarian use. Nevertheless, Christians have emphasized the unique importance and honor to be attributed to each "member" in a way that guards against collectivist abuse (Rom. 12:3–8; 1 Cor. 12:12–26). Within the body, each member has a specific, necessary, and honorable part to play. Another way of putting the matter is to say that

---

12. For a thorough exposition of the way in which worship and ethics are related, see Bernd Wannenwetsch, *Political Worship: Ethics for Christian Citizens*, trans. Margaret Kohl (Oxford: Oxford University Press, 2004).

within the church, each member has, under God, a particular calling or vocation. As such, each person stands uniquely before God and has a particular gift to offer that is indispensable for the health of the body as a whole. In this way, members, as the author of Ephesians writes, are to be "subject one to another" (Eph. 5:21) so that no member or group of members can simply be subsumed in a collective.

As suggested above, any ethic that begins by positing the primary character of social life must address the charge that by so doing it submerges individuals in a mass and thereby make them merely instrumental to a good in which they may not share. Thomas Aquinas responded to this sort of charge in a way that coheres with the social vision in Ephesians. He pointed out that society and individuals are mutually dependent—the good of one cannot be achieved apart from the good of the other. Thus just as individuals are dependent upon society if they are to realize what is good for them, so society, because of the complexity of the common good, depends upon each individual having the opportunity to exercise his or her skills. This conclusion, so it seems to me, accords with what St. Paul writes in both Romans and Corinthians, and with the balance between corporate and individual interests that produces a healthy life for both societies and individuals.

Having a vocation within the church provides the context in which the graces characteristic of the life of a Christian are spawned, developed, and, through example, passed on. Exercising a vocation within the church (everybody has one) brings one into relationship both with people whose vocations are different and with people who, though they serve "in the new life of the Spirit" (Rom. 7:6), are nonetheless still capable of error and childlike, even sinful, behavior. Differing gifts make possible a rich and diverse common life but at the same time provide occasions for conflict, enmity, and division. The give and take of life together provides opportunity to manifest the sort of unity it is God's purpose to establish. Give and take within a social space also provides opportunity for the expression of bitterness, wrath, anger, clamor, and malice—the vices that breed conflict and destroy unity and peace (Eph. 4:31).

It is no doubt because of the negative possibilities presented by error, immaturity, and the continuing influence of "darkened understanding" and "hardness of heart" that the author of Ephesians "begs" (παρακαλῶ) rather than asks his readers to live a life worthy of their calling (Eph. 4:1, 18). It is within these negative possibilities that eagerness to maintain unity of the Sprit in the bond of peace is required, tested, and acquired. It is also within the stresses and strains of common life that people are given grace to acquire a second nature made up of what I have called love's little helpers—"humility of mind," "gentleness," "long-suffering patience," "forbearance," and "truthfulness" (4:2–3, 15) (translation mine). Here also they encounter other believers who in a derivative sense "are the truth"—living examples of the sort of life to which Christ calls his followers.

In short, it is within the attempt to live a life with others that people with various vocations and various degrees of maturity in living a worthy life learn to love God with all their heart and their neighbors as themselves. It is also within this struggle that they acquire the graces that make love recognizable and effective. Looked at from this perspective, the congregation becomes a school for the service of the Lord rather than a purveyor of religious goods and services. Jesus's call to holiness of life becomes first of all an undertaking for each congregation, but it is one in which each member has a vital part to play.

The point is of sufficient importance to warrant a fuller account of what I mean. If one gives ethics an ecclesial focus, the struggle to "be perfect" is not made less demanding than it would be in an ethic focused on the state of an individual's soul. It is simply placed in a different context. If ethics is given an ecclesial focus, gatherings of the congregation for worship, fellowship, and common business become occasions for the exercise of one's vocation in service of a common good. They also become occasions in the midst of conflict for reconciliation and the establishment of peace and unity. Important as church programs no doubt are, diligence in the pursuit of unity changes the very notion of why, under God, a congregation exists. In, with, and under any particular purpose (no matter how worthy or important) lies a more basic one—to be a school for the service of the Lord wherein each learns the ways of love, unity, and peace.

Concretely, a change of perspective of this sort and degree carries with it a change in the way the various activities of a congregation are understood and carried out. Meetings to discuss the business of the congregation do indeed have responsibility for its financial health and good order. Nevertheless, at a more fundamental level, the purpose of each meeting is to "learn Christ" by awakening an eagerness for unity in the bond of peace that is enabled by love's little helpers—namely, humility of mind, truthfulness, gentleness, long-suffering patience, and willingness to practice restraint in one's treatment of those with whom one may feel enmity or experience profound disagreement.

Suppose, for example, a serious disagreement arises about the amount of money to be spent within the congregation and the amount to be expended on, say, a program to aid returning veterans. In disputes such as this, there are all manner of impediments to unity in the bond of peace. One might well encounter, among other things, differing estimations of relative importance, vested interests, personality clashes, stubbornness, heated argument that will not stand for opposition, outright dislike, and even malice. How are such obstacles to be overcome?

Simple admonitions to be loving toward one's neighbor are generally ineffective because they float above the fray as no more than vague reminders of a rather general moral commitment. However, if those involved in the conflict share a second nature that renders them open both to instruction and truthful speech, a way into the resolution of the conflict opens. If these graces are accompanied by a gentle approach to one's adversary coupled with restraint in what is said and done, the possibility for reconciliation increases even more. If these graces are undergirded by patience over time, the possibilities for reconciliation again increase. Deployment of these graces in fact makes forbearance in love more than a vague moral ideal. Their deployment rightly interprets what the author of Ephesians means when he admonishes members of congregations in that city to "be subject one to another out of reverence for Christ" (Eph. 5:21). Their presence makes eagerness to maintain the unity of the Spirit in the bond of peace visible both to the congregation and to anyone privileged to catch a glimpse of its inner workings. In this way, private matters that lead to social conflict become the public business of God, and the personal struggles of individuals that underlie the conflict are displayed on a public stage.

The Practices of a School of Charity

Thus far I have placed Christ's command to follow the way of perfection within the common life of the church before locating it in the private life of individuals, and I have linked this call to the vocation each Christian receives through baptism. The call to holiness of life is, however, linked also to certain practices that give a public face to the common life of the church. These settled ways of doing things both express and foster the character or identity of the church, and they provide the setting in which individuals acquire the graces that mark this identity. As examples, two are of signal importance. One is marriage, and the other is almsgiving.

The choice of marriage might at first glance seem odd. Within American society, and increasingly within its churches, marriage is understood as a private contract of indefinite length based upon individual choice, mutual love, care, and fidelity. It is for the purpose of promoting the happiness and personal fulfillment of the parties involved. Since children are not considered one of the constitutive "goods" of marriage, the union may be between persons of different or identical sexes. In keeping with the contractual nature of contemporary marriage, the contract may be broken if either of the parties proves unfaithful or uncaring. Here a divorce may be granted on the basis of a "fault." The marriage covenant may also be broken if either or both of the parties determine that the union does not yield the happiness and/or personal fulfillment for which they contracted. In this case, voiding the contract involves "no fault."

Sadly, this view of marriage, despite the contrary beliefs contained in most of their liturgies, is now part of the operative practice of the churches. Current marriage practice among the churches provides a prime example of the culture of the churches being transformed by their host culture rather than the reverse. Changes in ecclesial practice may, however, be in accord with or contrary to Holy Scripture and church tradition. In this instance, a good case can be made for saying that the changes are in accord with neither.[13] Readings of Scripture inscribed in church practice and tradition have accorded marriage three and sometimes up to five goods (each of which in recent years has either diminished in importance or disappeared). One is the unity of the couple, which is a blessing to them and a sign to others of the union between Christ and his church. Another is the blessing of children. A third is marriage as a means of domesticating sexual desire and linking it to both unity and procreation. A fourth good (of particular importance to the Puritans) is that marriage serves as a school of charity. A fifth, common particularly among Anglicans, is that marriage is a little commonwealth that serves as the basic building block for social and political life.

It is the first and the fourth of these "goods" upon which I wish to focus attention. How, in the changes and chances of life, is unity capable of signifying the union between Christ and his church to be sustained until (as the vows usually state) the parties are parted by death? The answer to this question has already been presented. For Christians, marriage is not a social necessity but a vocation. As such, it is through the exercise of that vocation that one grows in the love of God and love of one's neighbor. If marriage is understood as a covenant that binds the parties until death as well as a vocation, it is analogous to the Benedictine vow of stability. It is within this relationship and in fulfillment of one's vocation that, through mutual subjection, husband and wife learn to live together out of "reverence for Christ." It is this venue that becomes the primary location in which two people learn love of God and neighbor and the graces that foster and express such love.

It is, therefore, upon this stage and within its limits that the question of reconciliation is most frequently (and often painfully) presented. The question is how reconciliation between husband and wife is to occur without

---

13. For the best discussion of the shifting view of marriage and the way in which it has been understood by the churches of the West, see John White Jr., *From Sacrament to Contract: Marriage, Religion and Law in the Western Tradition* (Louisville: Westminster John Knox, 1997).

reconciliation becoming a de facto surrender of one to the other. Whatever forms of hierarchy culture and circumstance may establish within the union of husband and wife (they are multiple), subjection must be mutual if marriage is to become a true union. True union of husband and wife cannot be established (as in many contemporary relationships) by simply according each partner a body of "rights." Rights protect from intrusion and allow for freedom of action, but they do not link people in a union that can fairly be termed "one flesh."

True union can be sustained and renewed if the conditions for reconciliation are present within a relationship. These conditions, once again, are provided by the presence of the previously mentioned graces in the lives of the parties in the marriage. Openness to instruction and truthfulness create the possibility for mutual understanding and the admission of wrong. Gentleness of approach as opposed to clamorous argumentation invites open minds and hearts, as do patience and forbearance in love. Within the permanence and fidelity of the marital relation, graces are acquired, and marriage functions as a school for charity—a place where one learns to love one's closest neighbor as oneself. The vows of fidelity and permanence act like the Benedictine vow of stability. Among many other things, they create a space in time where two people who become as one learn Christ, and in doing so become through their relationship an evangelical symbol of the relation of Christ and his church.

A second practice in which the graces are acquired and operate is that of giving alms. As previously noted, giving alms is one of the three pillars of Jewish and Christian piety. It is a practice that makes visible obedience to both the first and second commandment. In respect to the first, it is a mark of the primary nature of one's allegiance to God. In respect to the second commandment, it is a practice that turns attention away from one's own needs and wants and toward those of others.

Giving alms is a practice in which Christians most frequently engage. Yet, in present circumstances, many may well misunderstand its nature as a Christian practice. In the previous discussion of Matthew and Luke, I noted that giving alms (now commonly termed "making charitable contributions") is apt to be considered in the first instance as simply one of many examples of philanthropic activity. That is, giving is generally understood as sharing what one has with others who have less (regardless of status or proximity of social relation) and of giving aid to causes and institutions one supports. To the contemporary mind, there is no real difference between giving to the community chest drive, the local symphony, or one's church. All three are freely elected forms of "philanthropy" that, all things being equal, stand on all fours with all other forms.

If, however, giving is viewed first from within a moral commitment that has an ecclesial focus, it takes on a different character. In the first instance, giving becomes an expression of a basic loyalty to God, and in the second, it becomes an expression of love for one's neighbor. The question is which neighbor, and why this neighbor rather than another one. For the philanthropist, the answer is response to a need that is of sufficient gravity and coheres with the interests of the donor. However, from within an ecclesial setting, priorities for giving are not based in personal interest alone. Certain neighbors take precedence over others because of beliefs about the purposes of God and the teachings of Christ. Distasteful as it may be from the perspective of a philanthropist, one's fellow Christians, and in particular fellow Christians with whom there is or has been conflict, have a high priority as one makes judgments about to whom and for what to give. In these cases, gifts are most certainly meant to remedy need. However, they are also intended to signal reconciliation and the sort of unity Christ came to establish within his people. Small things, in this case money and possessions, convey the most basic beliefs of the Christian people.

The example of Paul's collection for the saints in Jerusalem has already been mentioned. A more contemporary example of what I mean arises from the understanding Christians in the West and Christians in the former colonial territories have of one another. There is a good bit of church aid that flows from North to South of the equator. Both parties understand this aid as an expression of fraternal relations. Both parties also understand it as a much-needed movement of resources from rich to poor. Increasingly within my own denomination, this flow of wealth is also considered by some as a form of foreign aid whose purpose is in part to buy influence with the numerically strong (but financially weak) churches in the southern hemisphere.

What, however, would things look like if the purpose of this aid were to be reenvisioned by both parties? What if giver and recipient alike considered aid as more than a flow of wealth from rich to poor? Suppose they considered it also as a no-strings-attached means of sharing in a common goal and a common form of life? What if donors in the North considered their gifts as a means of expressing regret for the insult and devastation brought through a history of exploitive colonial rule, and what if those in the South received gratefully this expression of regret? What if both parties took the gifts and their reception as expressions of peace, reconciliation, and common purpose?

If these conditions were to obtain, giving would be a communal practice that in fundamental ways forms the conscience of believers often separated by both distance and culture. In this case, communal practice challenges the basic loyalties of individuals and groups. It cultivates generosity as both a communal and individual habit. Sharing wealth also spawns eagerness for unity in the bond of peace, and in so doing provides fertile ground for the graces of sympathy, tenderness, and forbearance in love to spring up between alienated or potentially hostile co-religionists. People involved in a communal enterprise of sharing wealth with others grow in grace, but not as an enterprise in self-improvement. They grow as part of a community learning what it means to love one's neighbor, that neighbor being in the first instance those with whom they share in a "commonwealth" built upon a common faith and way of life. The citizens of this commonwealth are responsible one for another because they are all, no matter where they may live, not only fellow citizens but also brothers and sisters, part of one family.

Philanthropists will immediately say, "But what about people who are not Christians. Have they no place in your moral imagination?" The answer is yes, but for different reasons than those provided by modern forms of philanthropy. Philanthropists, often with good reason, are suspicious of common religion being the determining factor in making decisions about giving or making grants. From their perspective, these decisions are supposed to be made only on the basis of the type of need, its worthiness, and/or its intensity. It's not supposed to matter if the need belongs to Muslims, Christians, or Hindus.

It does, however, matter to many co-religionists, and not necessarily for nefarious reasons. As the history of the nineteenth and twentieth centuries well illustrates, it has certainly mattered to Jews, Christians, and Muslims.[14] Indeed, it would appear that the only way in which special care for co-religionists can be removed from the moral equation of sharing wealth is to remove from consideration special obligations to fellow believers. One cannot do this without changing the nature of these religions or imposing a moral or legal prohibition that would trample upon the free exercise of religious belief.

The issue from a religious perspective, therefore, is not paying special attention to the needs of one's fellow believers. That seems, as it were, "built in." The issue is what resources exist within a given set of religious beliefs and practices to extend care for one's fellow human being beyond the circle of special relationships—family, fellow countrymen, or co-religionists. In this respect, Christians have a positive answer to the philanthropist's question about the extent to which their moral imagination includes those who do not share their beliefs, family ties, or nationality. They answer yes because of the primary purpose they assign to giving. Giving is for Christians a sign of God's care for all people and his intention to unite the peoples of the earth

---

14. For an example, see Philip Turner, "Philanthropy's Inconstant Friend, Religion," in *Good Intentions: Moral Obstacles and Opportunities*, ed. David Smith (Bloomington: Indiana University Press, 2005), 129–35.

in a single family of which God is the Father, Christ is the firstborn Son, and all others are adopted children. The chief sacraments of the churches are baptism and the Holy Eucharist. Both symbolize and serve to effect this belief. These constitutive rituals imply giving, both to friend and stranger. If giving is directed as a matter of first importance to fellow believers as a sign of both unity and care, it is directed necessarily also to strangers for whom Christ died as a means of including all peoples within that unity and the sphere of his care.[15] It seems fair to say that the circumference that inscribes the range of giving for Christians is summed up by Paul in Galatians 6:10: "So then, as we have opportunity, let us do good to all [people], and especially to those of the household of faith."

Making Room for Christian Mediocrity

Mention of the primary part reconciliation plays in the common life of Christians by a strange twist links Christ's command to seek perfection with a realistic and compassionate acceptance of failure on the part of both the church and its individual members. In his battles with both the Donatists and the Pelagians, St. Augustine rejected any notion of two-tier Christianity—a form for a Christian elite that sought perfection and a form for the ordinary man or woman who is content to live in what W. H. Auden, in his *Christmas Oratorio*, nicely termed the everyday world of "darning and the 8:15."[16] All, be they "elite" or "ordinary," stood in need of grace, and none reached or even came close to the perfection held in store for the "end of the ages." So it was that Augustine made room for what Robert Markus has nicely termed "Christian mediocrity."[17]

A Christian ethic that focuses on the common life of the church must do just that. If it does not, it will place itself in service of a "pure" or "true" church and show contempt for the imperfect body that is ever and always an inescapable reality. If no place is left for Christian mediocrity, individual attempts to follow the way of Christ to perfection (incumbent upon all) will produce pride, self-righteousness, contempt for others, and spiritual ruthlessness. If the call to perfection is not linked to the constant need for repentance and forgiveness, things go wrong for both the churches and their individual members.

---

15. For an interpretation of Matthew's account of Jesus's saying about care for the poor, the sick, the stranger, and the prisoner being the basis upon which the church will be judged by God at the last day that supports this claim, see Ulrich Luz, *Matthew 21–28* (Minneapolis: Fortress, 2005), 282–84.

16. W. H. Auden, *Collected Poems*, ed. Edward Mendelson (New York: The Modern Library, 2007), 399.

17. Markus, *End of Ancient Christianity*, 45–62.

St. Augustine saw that the basic error of the Donatists and the Pelagians was identical. Both had fallen victim to what might be called a premature eschatology, characterized by "the impatient, peremptory anticipation here and now, before the time, of the Church's eschatological purity."[18] Augustine saw in a way his opponents did not that within history, the church remains a mixed body. Unlike his perfectionist opponents, Augustine believed that baptism did not cure the ills that beset everyone. Rather, it set one on "a lifelong process of convalescence."[19]

Augustine rightly saw that an ecclesial ethic must leave room for Christian mediocrity and also "merciful healing."[20] There are three church practices that create such a space, and these in turn provide the context in which love operates and the graces are acquired and exercised. The practices are repentance, reconciliation of the penitent, and, strangely enough, excommunication. Each of these practices has a foundation in the Gospels and the Epistles. Thus, for example, Jesus's admonition to take the initiative with a person who may have something against you suggests readiness to admit and address wrongdoing (Matt. 5:23). So also does his instruction that one should look to the log in one's own eye before fixating on the speck in the eye of another (7:3–4). Undergirding both these commands stands the demand that one love and forgive one's enemy (5:44; 18:21–22). Strangely enough, the love command also stands as a foundation even for the practice of excommunication. Matthew is quite clear that any action that excludes a brother or sister is to be preceded by an elaborate process designed to get the offending party to admit and remedy his or her fault. Only when all reasonable efforts have been expended is the "brother" to be considered a "Gentile and a tax collector" (18:15–17). Even when an offense is deemed serious enough for expulsion, Paul considers exclusion of the offender as an action taken for his benefit—so that in the end, no matter how serious the offense, he will be saved (1 Cor. 5:5).

Given the purpose of the church within the providence of God, the inexpungable presence of mediocrity within it creates a constant need for repentance, reconciliation, and, on occasion, even excommunication. It is impossible to imagine that any of these activities, including the administration of church discipline, can be expressions of both truth and love apart from the presence of the graces listed, for example, in Ephesians among the members of the church. Each set of practices provides an ever-present opportunity for their acquisition and exercise. So, for example, is reconciliation possible if the truth

---

18. Ibid., 52.
19. Ibid., 54.
20. Ibid.

is not spoken and received in love? Can the truth be either spoken effectively or received honestly if the parties to a dispute are not gentle toward one another and open to instruction? Can broken relationship be mended apart from a space in time provided by patience and long-suffering sustained by an eagerness to maintain unity in the bond of peace (Eph. 4:2–3, 15)? Finally, is the mutual understanding that leads to reconciliation likely apart from compassion, tenderheartedness, and forgiveness on the part of the disputants (4:32)?

In this respect, a specific comment on the imposition of discipline is necessary.[21] On the surface, love and discipline do not seem easily matched. Nevertheless, any parent knows that love that exercises no discipline is harmful. In like manner, if, as Ephesians indicates, many fellow believers still behave as children in Christ or have fallen victim to false teaching, love can ignore neither misconduct nor error. To do so is to harm both individual and community. Appropriate discipline is required. Nevertheless, it is also the case that appropriate discipline will not be correctly discerned or rightly administered if the offender is not adequately understood. It is hard to imagine either adequate understanding of the offender or appropriate discipline apart from the graces Ephesians lists.

Love of neighbor is characteristically expressed as forgiveness, and forgiveness is tied inextricably to a desire for reconciliation. If, as Matthew indicates, judgment begins with the household of God, so also does forgiveness. Here, within the common life of the church, there is wrath, anger, clamor, slander, and malice aplenty. It is necessary that these disruptive forces be addressed in a way that serves the unity of the church, the integrity of its common life, and the welfare of its individual members. To the extent that forgiveness and reconciliation do not obtain, Christ's body will be divided and the witness of the church compromised.

Walk in Wisdom

The continuing presence of immaturity, false teaching, darkened understanding, and just plain wickedness within the common life of the church presents

---

21. The most problematic of these, of course, is excommunication. This sanction, though frequently exercised for reasons of power rather than charity, has nonetheless always been considered properly as an action taken for the benefit of the offender and only as a last resort. Thus, it has been considered necessary for the benefit of the recipient or to protect the integrity of the church from being compromised by insistent advocacy of false belief or unacceptable conduct. Discussion of the practice properly belongs within a treatment of the polity of the church, but its proper exercise requires the presence of the graces that make it an expression of love as opposed to coercion.

an issue additional to the constant need for repentance, reconciliation, and discipline. The imperfections of both individual and corporate life call for what can rightly be called "wisdom in the Lord." By this phrase I mean two things: first, sufficient knowledge of Christian belief and practice to be able to see the various circumstances of life through that lens, and second, sufficient love for the people involved and knowledge of the facts to act in a way appropriate to the circumstances so discerned. Wisdom of this sort is required of each member of the church if they are to grow in the love of God and learn more about what it means to love one's neighbor. Nevertheless, the acquisition of such wisdom does not issue from espousal of a private project of self-improvement. It stems from participation in the life of the church through which the ability to walk in wisdom rather than foolishness is mediated and in which it is exercised.

There is a long-standing tradition among Christians that associates holiness of life with wisdom. Holy men and women convey wisdom to the perplexed, but the wisdom they convey, illumined though it may be by the Holy Spirit, is nonetheless of a social rather than private nature.[22] Holy and wise men and women are known by their ability to see clearly into life's circumstances, but the wisdom they bring to life's situations is not private. It is the wisdom of a people—wisdom passed on over the generations from the apostles through evangelists, teachers, and exemplary lives. Wisdom in the Lord is a common possession and a common project. In this sense it is similar to proverbial wisdom as found throughout the world. Proverbs allow people to identify the common situations that emerge within a culture and respond successfully to them. For example, in the ancient kingdom of Buganda there was a proverb that said, "The person who attends the king's court knows the reason for things." Within this hierarchical culture, wisdom requires that one pay attention to what goes on in the centers of power if one wants to succeed.

Wisdom in the Lord is similar in that it is a common project. It is, however, distinguished by the fact that it requires a thorough understanding of God's purposes and will accompanied by an ability to order one's desires and affections so as to see clearly the nature of one's circumstances and act in a worthy manner within them (Eph. 3:18; 5:17).

If the acquisition of wisdom is an essential aspect of a devout and holy life, and if such wisdom is the possession of a community before it is that of its individual members, what does that suggest about the ecclesial focus of

---

22. The tradition of the wise, holy man is particularly strong among Eastern Orthodox Christians. St. Seraphim of Sarov is among the most famous. Dostoyevsky's character Father Zosima in *The Brothers Karamazov* is the most well-known example in literature.

Christian ethics? It suggests that passing on and acquiring wisdom in the Lord is a function of both corporate and individual responsibility. It suggests that life together is rightly understood as a seedbed from which grows the ability for each believer to walk in wisdom rather than foolishness.

The question, of course, is how wisdom is acquired. This question pertains to all people and not to Christians alone. Thomas Aquinas thought of wisdom as first among virtues to which all peoples are ordered. Its acquisition, he said, requires the cultivation of a range of habits. He calls them *experimentum, memoria, docilitas, solertia,* and *providentia.* It is difficult to find the right words in English to translate these terms, but roughly they mean this: the wise person makes a patient effort to cultivate experience (*experimentum*), trains the memory so as not to distort reality (*memoria*), is open to instruction (*docilitas*), is able to respond calmly and swiftly to unexpected circumstances (*solertia*), and can estimate the future consequences of an action (*providentia*).[23]

The acquisition of wisdom is a moral task that Christians share with all peoples, and perhaps this common task is best summed up by the author of Ephesians when he writes, "Look carefully then how you walk" (Eph. 5:15). With this admonition he clearly has in mind avoiding certain destructive behaviors like heavy drinking and the dissolute form of life that is likely to accompany this vice (5:18). Nevertheless, he has the more positive concern of urging his readers to pay close attention or to "look carefully" (βλέπετε ἀκριβῶς) through the lens of their beliefs at the course of their daily lives. Close attention to daily life no doubt implies the presence of the habits to which Thomas points. Nevertheless, Ephesians urges careful attention for what might be called evangelical reasons. The author wants his readers to pay close attention both because the times are evil and because the time is short. He urges his readers, therefore, to "preserve from misuse" (ἐξαγοραζόμενοι) the time in which they live. They are to do this by walking as wise rather than foolish people. Wise walking can take place only if the people to whom he writes "comprehend thoroughly" (συνίετε) the will of the Lord (Eph. 5:17, translation mine). The will of the Lord, therefore, shapes wisdom and gives it a purpose beyond the successful management of life. The will of the Lord, as administered by Christ, is to unite the peoples of the earth in his Son. Wise walking, therefore, refers back to a life worthy of the calling to which they have been called. It provides a necessary component of that worth.

23. For an excellent presentation of Aquinas's account of wisdom and its auxiliary virtues, see Josef Pieper, *The Four Cardinal Virtues*, trans Richard Winston and Clara Winston (Notre Dame, IN: University of Notre Dame Press, 1967), 10–18.

Conclusion and Transition

Placing Christ's call to perfection first within the common life of the church rather than in the personal aspiration and life plans of individuals accomplishes a number of things. A focus on the common life of the church in no way lessens the demand to "be perfect." It remains as a call and challenge to each member of the church. In issuing such a challenge and call, however, an ecclesial focus acknowledges the social nature of all moral aspirations, locates the moral and spiritual struggles of individuals in a common enterprise, and guards against the dangers of self-absorption. Augustine believed that the human problem begins with self-isolation—isolation from God, one's neighbor, and oneself. Luther was fond of speaking of sinful life as life "curved in upon itself." An ecclesial focus for Christian ethics turns attention away from the self and toward the way in which one lives with others—be they near or distant neighbors. In this context, as one struggles with the sins and foibles of others, one must struggle as well with "darkened understanding," callous feelings, and disordered desire that dwell in the center of one's own being.

If ethics is given an ecclesial focus, each congregation becomes a school for the service of the Lord. Each congregation gathered for worship and life together becomes the place where the church and its individual members "put off" an old form of life and "put on" another. In this way, Christ forms a culture and people learn to take on this culture as a second nature.

How this is to happen remains a question I do not know how to answer. Indeed, how congregations become schools for the service of the Lord as opposed to providers of religious goods and services denominated on the basis of taste is a question few even ask. It is, however, a question that must be asked and answered if the churches are to find the way out of the ordeal they now face. That ordeal (at least in the West) is not, as it was for the author of the Apocalypse, persecution by a demonic force that found a home in a hostile political power. It is rather relegation by social opinion and political intention to the realm of private taste. The consequence of this social relocation is confinement of religious belief and practice to private spaces that take up less and less social room.

If and when the churches awake to their circumstances, they will have to rethink the way they understand themselves within the providence of God and within the larger social matrix in which they exist. This exercise of reconception will, however, not take place apart from the graces to which the author of the Apocalypse called attention when he addressed the ordeal through which the churches to which he wrote were passing. He wrote, "*Awake*, and strengthen what remains and is on the point of death, for I have not found your works perfect in the sight of my God. *Remember* then what you have received and heard; *keep* that, and *repent*" (Rev. 3:2–3a, emphasis added).

To wake up, remember, keep or hold fast, and repent are the graces, communal and individual, that are required if the churches are indeed to become schools for the service of the Lord. These graces will lead congregations to become places where people take on a second nature that is worthy of the life to which they have been called. When present, this second nature becomes an integral part of the witness congregations and their individual members make to God's purposes for the world. These graces necessarily lead those who are taking on a second nature into the common life of the various societies that helped, for good and ill, to form their first nature. Since God's purposes are indeed for the world (and not just for the church), the question of the relation of believers to that world must be addressed. Thus a rendering of Christian ethics that focuses on the common life of the church must do more than map the common life of the church and the life of the soul. It must also give an account of the relation of the church and its members to the social orders of which they may be a part.

10

An Ecclesial View of Life in Civil Society

Introduction

If the focus of Christian ethics ought indeed to be ecclesial, what is to be said about the relation between the common life of the churches and the social relations and political institutions of the larger societies in which Christians live? How, in short, ought a person whose moral focus is the common life of the church to view the relation between church, society, and the multitudinous forms of human governance? This question is both emotionally charged and fraught with complexity. It is also unavoidable. It is emotionally charged and complex because it puts on display marked disparities between present-day social agreements and the way in which Christians through the ages have thought both about their place in the social and political order and about their defining moral beliefs and practices. It is unavoidable because the changed social location of the churches in the minds of many has rendered obsolete (and to some even offensive) the account they give of their social place and importance.

What indeed is the place of the churches in the pluralistic societies of the West? How ought they to understand the basis, goal, and character of political authority within societies whose moral point of view is in many ways no longer one they share? How are they to relate to a political order that legitimates social and moral practices that in many instances are contrary to the defining beliefs and practices of Christians through the ages? More specifically, what, for example, are Christians to do when the legal definition of marriage appears in the minds of many no longer congruent with these defining beliefs and practices? What are they to say and do when social beliefs and practices associated with such basic matters as birth and death are no longer ones they may be able to accept? These questions are indeed emotionally charged and fearfully complex.

They nonetheless present the churches with an agenda that the churches ignore at their peril. To alter their identity so as to fit more comfortably into the changed social landscape is to lose integrity. Yet to grasp the nettle, to risk engagement with a rapidly changing society and ask again how Christians are to comport themselves in a fluid, indifferent, and sometimes even hostile social and political environment is to risk, among other things, loss of integrity, internal strife, social ridicule, and exclusion. On the other hand, failure to grasp the nettle is to risk closed-mindedness and in consequence fail to address a larger world in both its struggles and insights. It is no wonder that the churches, confronted with these alternatives, are so tempted to make ill-advised compromises, circle the wagons, or simply keep on as if the ground had not shifted under their feet. The ground has shifted, however. At each of the points that mark the course of human life, the churches are confronted with an understanding of life in society that is in important ways contrary to the one to be found in their Holy Scriptures and in their defining traditions. They now exist in a social world in which familiar landmarks have been moved. This chapter and the next two represent an attempt to chart a way forward in these changed, confusing, and in many ways unfriendly circumstances.

It is tempting to undertake this task by looking first at relations between church and political authority. This issue is, after all, the first that comes to mind. Nevertheless, there is good theological reason to begin the other way around—with church and society rather than church and state. Christian tradition depicts the role of political authority in human affairs as limited and temporary in a way that life in society is not. That tradition is not uniform as to whether political authority would have arisen as a natural expression of human nature, but it is uniform in its insistence that God has assigned the various forms of human governance no redemptive function. In a fallen world, human governance serves not as a means of salvation but as a means to preserve life and relative forms of justice until Christ comes again. Political authority plays no part in God's creation save to protect and order life in a fallen world. Its time is limited by the coming of God's kingdom. At Christ's final appearance, human governance will end. Christ will rule the nations and hand all authority over to his Father. By way of contrast, Christians hold that the final destiny of all people is to live with one another in society ruled by God. Life under human governance is not a permanent feature of human life, but life with one another is. Life in society will not pass away. It will endure forever. For the time being, however, forms of human governance preserve it as it waits for its redemption.

Even though the questions hovering about relations between church and society are extraordinarily difficult, it nonetheless makes both theological and practical sense to begin here. Indeed, it is urgent for churches to take up the challenge. Extensive changes in social practice and a more marginal place in society have left the churches in a state of confusion that for the sake of their own integrity must be addressed. Because assimilation to culture has gone so far, they now find themselves with limited ability to address effectively either their own members or the members of the larger societies of which they are a part. Even if, as is rarely the case, they have something important to say, it is difficult for them to get any "air time."

What is the change that has brought with it such uncertainty and weakness?

The most common answer is that American society and the societies of Europe have become secular. To be sure, many rightly question the view that a growth in secularism is as pervasive and inevitable as is often claimed.[1] Nevertheless, secularism, as understood by commentators like Charles Taylor and Jeffrey Stout, does in part describe the circumstances in which the churches and their members now seek to make a "social witness."[2] Taylor notes that secularism may be understood in no less than three ways. It can refer to (1) circumstances in which public spaces have allegedly been emptied of references to God; (2) circumstances in which religious belief and practice have declined in a significant manner; or (3) circumstances in which religious belief is no longer pervasive but rather has become no more than one option among many others. This third sense is close to the way in which Stout understands the phenomenon—namely, as a social condition in which people do not take for granted "a set of agreed upon assumptions about the nature and existence of God."[3] It is this frame of mind, along with internal incoherence,

---

1. See, e.g., Robert D. Putnam and David E. Campbell, *American Grace: How Religion Divides and Unites Us* (New York: Simon & Schuster, 2010), and John Atherton, *Marginalization* (London: SCM, 2003), 37-49. See also Luke Bretherton, *Christianity and Contemporary Politics* (Oxford: Wiley-Blackwell, 2010), 10-14.

2. See, e.g., Charles Taylor, *A Secular Age* (Cambridge, MA: Belknap Press of Harvard University Press, 2007), 1-22, and Jeffrey Stout, *Democracy and Tradition* (Princeton: Princeton University Press, 2004), 97-99.

3. Stout, *Democracy and Tradition*, 99.

that accounts in part for the difficulty the churches face as they seek to make an effective social witness.[4]

I do not wish to enter an argument about the sources of secularism, its inevitability, its extent, or its value, positive or negative. I wish to say only that it seems correct to say that the churches in North America, and even more so those in Europe, now inhabit a social and political space wherein they cannot assume that all people share their religious beliefs or their view of life in society. To put the matter another way, the churches of the West now inhabit societies that no longer accord them the role of moral and religious tutor. Even in nations with established Protestant churches, these circumstances obtain.[5] Further, long before the demise of the moral authority of Europe's established Protestant churches, the links between the Roman Catholic Church and the royal houses of Europe had come undone.[6] Viewing this scene, Dietrich Bonhoeffer was correct in his observation that the churches in Europe now exist in a time in which humankind has "come of age."[7] In respect to faith and morals, the citizenry of Europe, he argued, had thrown off the tutelage of the churches and claimed the autonomy of an adult.[8] I believe something similar can be said of American society.

In light of their own incoherence and the withdrawal of their social and political charter, the first task of social ethics for the churches is not, as is too frequently thought, to reclaim their former social position. Rather, their first task is to restore integrity to their common life. The present challenge before

---

4. Rowan Williams, the former archbishop of Canterbury, proposes another aspect of secularism that works against any effective witness on the part of the churches. His position is that secularism is inseparable from "functionalism." As a result, discussions of social practice and evaluation (in the public square) are dominated by instrumental or managerial considerations that rule out other points of view that might better display the complexity of social interaction. Thus, for example, in the secular public square it becomes impossible to speak of evil (or for that matter good) when we discuss social events and practices. One can only argue about means and ends. This sort of restriction on public speech does indeed preclude much that religious believers might have to say, but the churches have in large measure not chosen to speak publically in these terms. Rather, they have chosen to avoid their own vocabulary and use instead the same language of means and ends as have their "secular" fellow citizens. See Rowan Williams, *Faith in the Public Square* (London: Bloomsbury, 2012), 12–13.

5. See, for example, the account of the marginal place of the Church of England in Atherton, *Marginalization*, 33–37.

6. See Russell Hittinger, "Introduction to Modern Catholicism," in *The Teachings of Modern Christianity on Law, Politics, and Human Nature*, ed. John Witte Jr. and Frank S. Alexander (New York: Columbia University Press, 2006), 1:3–12.

7. Dietrich Bonhoeffer, *Letters and Papers from Prison* (New York: Macmillan, 1971), 341–42.

8. For a helpful discussion of what Bonhoeffer meant by the phrase "come of age," see Eberhard Bethge, "The New Theology: An Essay," in *Dietrich Bonhoeffer, Man of Vision, Man of Courage* (New York: Harper & Row, 1977), 757–95.

the churches is to develop what Bonhoeffer termed "arcane discipline" and thereby shape their common life in a way that is rooted in the biblical witness and, as such, provides a point from which to assess society and provide alternatives. As I have repeatedly argued, the first task before the churches is not the transformation of culture. Their challenge is to become a culture in which Christ is taking form.

Critics of this claim object that a focus on the common life of the church unduly limits the responsibility of Christians to make a social and political witness. An ecclesial focus, they charge in H. Richard Niebuhr's terms, pits Christ against culture and leads to a form of "sectarianism." The objection is initially attractive, but, upon reflection, is it valid? The answer is emphatically no, for reasons that are more than pragmatic. They lie deeper than H. Richard Niebuhr's observation in *Christ and Culture* that it is simply impossible to withdraw from a surrounding culture.[9] There are powerful theological reasons, as H. Richard Niebuhr also asserts, for saying that an ethical focus on the common life of the church does not exclude but leads to a profound concern for the common life of society. Indeed, an ecclesial focus includes a strong mandate to take full part in society.

As Oliver O'Donovan has said, there is an "evangelical mandate" for Christians to participate in God's ordering of the world.[10] Both life in society and the governance of rulers are aspects of God's providential ordering. Life in society is an aspect of the created nature and final destiny of humankind. As such, it provides the conditions for full and continuing life. Christians, along with all other people, are necessarily embedded in various forms of social order. The destiny of the denizens of these solidarities is to be gathered into the communion of saints. That destiny has now entered its penultimate state. Christ has been born, has died, has risen, and has ascended. Christ now rules the nations and through the witness of the church and the work of the Spirit draws all peoples to himself. The evangelical destiny of the social life of humankind and the overruling providence of God require participation on the part of the people who understand this destiny and this rule and bear witness to it.

O'Donovan's evangelical mandate for social participation is based in a belief in divine providence as presided over by the crucified, risen, and ascended Christ. Eric Gregory proposes a different but not antithetical theological foundation. It is based in an Augustinian dialectic that centers on the struggle between the transformative power of neighbor love on the one hand and the

---

9. H. Richard Niebuhr, *Christ and Culture* (New York: Harper & Row, 1975), 68-69.
10. Oliver O'Donovan, *Resurrection and Moral Order: An Outline for Evangelical Ethics*, 2nd ed. (Grand Rapids: Eerdmans, 1994), 72.

continuing power of sin on the other.[11] He suggests that modern Augustinianism might develop an account of neighbor love that analogically mediates ecclesial identity to the social role of citizenship without conflating the two. Following Paul Ricoeur, he suggests that neighbor love demands social involvement. Love has the power to pass beyond the borders of the church's common life and from there "pass through" our collective socio-political existence, even as it "rises up *against* it" at times.[12] It is false, he argues, to contrast direct charity to the neighbor and abstract charity on the part of the citizen. Love works in both ways, and it is the same love that works in both ways.

The Nature of Society

If indeed there is a divine mandate (be it rooted in divine providence or in neighbor love or in both) for Christians and the churches to which they belong to participate in the life of society and make a witness there, it makes sense to ask again how they ought to understand the nature of social life. This question must be asked before describing the sort of involvement into which Christians are called. In search of an answer, I begin with this observation. To the extent that their understanding has been formed within the common life of an obedient church, Christians carry into their social encounters a distinctive view of society's nature (and destiny) that is in many ways different from the one now regnant in the United States and to a lesser extent in Europe. At many points this contrary view sets them at odds with the cultures of which they are a part and within which they are required to make their witness.

As things now stand, when people in North America (and to a lesser extent Europe) think of social life, they tend to begin with a notion of themselves as individual social actors. From this base, they build an understanding of the rewards and challenges of living with others. To put the matter differently, in the West, and particularly in America, there is a pervasive tendency to begin social thought with individuals and then move on to the question of why and how individuals live together. The problem is not so much how "I," as a member of society, am an individual as it is how "I," as an individual, am a member of society. This way of thinking guided Thomas Jefferson and was central to the Declaration of Independence. One might even say it is a part of America's DNA. In this social environment, people tend to think of social relations as various dimensions of an enormous market wherein exchanges of

---

11. See, e.g., Eric Gregory, *Politics and the Order of Love: An Augustinian Ethic of Democratic Citizenship* (Chicago: University of Chicago Press, 2010), 55.
12. Ibid.

many sorts take place. There are commercial exchanges, political exchanges, marital exchanges, and various sorts of purely social ones.

These are all mechanisms by which individuals make their way in the world. They are also vehicles of competition by which to establish a place in the social order. As Marcel Mauss points out, though exchanges such as these are supposedly equal and freely given, they in fact rarely are.[13] To be sure, the various exchanges that make up social life create social bonds, but at the same time, they are occasions for self-assertion, conflict, and the creation of dependency and inequality.

Christians, to the extent that their minds have been shaped by the common life of a faithful church, will be led to an alternative view of social life. It is a view that bears down upon the dominant mindset of our time—a view that offers both a criticism of it and an alternative to it. Christian thought and practice offer a view of the world that begins in a different place—one in which there is always a "we" before there is an "I." To be sure, each person is called by grace as an individual, but all are called as individuals into communion with God and with his people. They are never called simply as individuals who stand alone before God. In being called as the particular individual they are, they learn to say "we" before "I." It is in the midst of this "we" that each "I" finds his or her identity and calling.[14] The common life of the church, rooted in Christ's reconciling life and the gift of the Holy Spirit, models (imperfectly) for believers the common life for which humankind was created and for which it is destined. *Koinōnia*, or communion, is one way in which Christians speak of this form of life.

Viewed in this way, society appears not as a body of people who have contracted with one another for private benefit but as a body bound together by what its members share. Society so defined is also understood as a system of unifying communication that takes place in various dimensions—language, the provision of goods and services, and the bonds of friendship and marriage. The point is that within a communion, understood also as a unifying system of communication, what individuals claim as their own, though it remains theirs, is in fact taken up into a larger and common possession from which what is "mine" derives its primary meaning. Thus what I "own" is indeed mine, but its meaning remains hidden until what I "own" becomes for me and for others the means by which I participate in and contribute to the larger life of society. Separated from a nexus of social meaning, what I "own" is no more than stuff. In short, rightly understood, what I claim for myself is indeed "mine" but only

---

13. Mauss, *The Gift*.
14. Oliver O'Donovan, *The Ways of Judgment* (Grand Rapids: Eerdmans, 2005), 242–60.

as located within a sphere of communication and shared goods. As O'Donovan nicely puts it, "To communicate is to hold some thing as common, to make it a common possession, to treat it as 'ours,' rather than 'yours' or 'mine.'"[15] Expanding on this idea, he observes, "Society exists simply as the coherence in which the spheres of communication flourish in relation to each other."[16]

Here is a view of social life markedly different from the more prevalent one noted above. Human communication, which is to say life in society, is not the product of a sovereign choice made by individuals. Life together stands prior to the choices we make about how we are to live. As O'Donovan has written, "Human communication is not a product of human foundation; it is a condition of being human, a gift of God."[17] As a condition of being human, social life is made up of complex forms of social interchange, and it is from that interchange that what is generally called the common good arises. A good that is genuinely common does not come about by adding together a lot of individual goods obtained in a competitive marketplace. It arises from the given quality of social life and the various forms of interchange that make up that life and make it worth living.

The Exemplary Power of Lives Well Lived: Truth and Reconciliation

For a mind shaped within the common life of an obedient church, to engage in the life of society is to take one's place with others who share a common good within a complex system of communication. It is also to enter a fallen world marked by a system of relations wherein the exchanges that make up the fabric of society manifest conflict and create inequality. What then do Christians and the churches to which they belong bring to this complex enterprise? As I have suggested above, they bring a critical judgment and a constructive vision of what it is to live in society. However, this vision does not carry with it, as current Christian opinion on both the left and right often has it, a body of social principles or resolutions to be used as templates to mold the world around them according to their likes. In the first instance, what they bring is not the model of an ideal world. What they bring is themselves as a certain kind of social presence.

To explain what I mean, I cite an essay by Amélie Rorty that has not received the attention it deserves.[18] Rorty notes that contemporary literature

15. Ibid., 242.
16. Ibid., 253.
17. Ibid., 249.
18. Amélie Oksenberg Rorty, "A Literary Postscript: Characters, Persons, Selves, Individuals," in *The Identities of Persons*, ed. Amélie Oksenberg Rorty (Berkeley: University of California Press, 1976), 301–23.

provides a number of ways of describing ourselves as social and moral agents. In present-day society, moral agents are thought of primarily as *persons, selves,* or *individuals. Persons* possess legal standing. *Selves* have acquired a personal history. *Individuals* are persons and selves perceived by themselves and others as unique. Persons who have become selves and individuals are primary categories in contemporary social and political thought. Rorty notes, however, that there is another model of agency to be found particularly in the Russian novel.[19] In this literature, one encounters an actor like Alyosha in *The Brothers Karamazov*. Alyosha is not presented as a person, self, or individual. He is rather a "presence"—a human being who gives attention and is present to those around him. He is not an example of willfulness. One cannot make up one's mind to be a presence. As Rorty says, becoming a presence "cannot be achieved by imitation, willing, practice, or a good education. It is a mode of identity invented precisely to go beyond achievement and willfulness."[20] She concludes that the figure of the presence is "the Christian," whose power stems from "endowments of grace received beyond striving."[21]

What Christians can bring to the life of society (be it friendly to them or not) are "endowments of grace received beyond striving" that render them a presence. These graces are precisely those set forth in Ephesians and elsewhere in the New Testament—that is, truthfulness, humility of mind, gentleness, long-suffering, loving forbearance, eagerness for unity, kindness, sympathy, and forgiveness. Once again, I hope that provision of well-chosen examples will make this point clear.

The presence of men and women formed in a school for the service of the Lord has the potential for generating a society capable of critical judgment and creative social initiative. They can even provide society with alternative ways of living. The view that society is created and destined for a form of communion in which communication is genuine and exchange is tied to a common good provides an alternative social vision to societies rooted in forms of "possessive individualism." It also brings to the fore two issues that are both endemic to all forms of social life and deeply embedded in the graces and practices that give Christians capacities and ways of behaving that are central to their identity—truthfulness and reconciliation.

Why are truthfulness and reconciliation so important to life in society? Without the assumption of honesty in the basic forms of social exchange, the bonds that hold society together come undone. Without the ability to resolve

19. Ibid., 318.
20. Ibid., 319.
21. Ibid.

conflict, social life stands always in danger of collapse. Let us first take truthfulness. All the biblical texts examined thus far clearly indicate that truth is a matter of first-order importance within the common life of the church. This being the case, it would be odd if these concerns did not spill over into and pass though the forms of generalized social exchange in which Christians, along with their fellow citizens, are involved. It is, after all, within these various forms of exchange that the importance of truth and reconciliation becomes obvious. All forms of exchange, from the most intimate to the most public, break down if not undergirded by basic truthfulness. If marital relations are built around lies, they fail. If political speech is nothing but a great lie, political life devolves into an Orwellian dystopia in which words mean what people in power say they mean. Similar examples can be provided from the spheres of economics, education, and friendship. No form of social exchange can survive apart from a basic assumption of honesty. To put the matter another way, exchange that is not sustained by honest communication can only end in coercion, dominance, subservience, and/or social fragmentation.

Yet truth and truthfulness, fundamental as they are to social health, are precisely the things that seem at present in notoriously short supply. A recent edition of the *New Yorker* contained a remarkable article by Jill Lepore entitled "The Lie Factory."[22] In her article, she traces the history of the present manner of waging political campaigns. What she says about political speech applies to a disturbing degree to all contemporary forms of public communication, particularly advertising. In 1934 the team of Leone Baxter and Clem Whitaker were hired to defeat Upton Sinclair, the well-known author and popular Democratic candidate for governor of California. California at that time was a Republican state with not a single Democrat occupying a statewide office. Sinclair was nevertheless a popular candidate because of a very progressive plan to eliminate poverty within the state. Baxter and Whitaker nonetheless managed his defeat. In his postelection analysis Sinclair said he "got licked" because of what he called a "lie factory." He was referring in part to the fact that after his nomination Baxter and Whitaker had published each day in the state newspapers a quotation supposedly from Sinclair's own mouth and bound to place Sinclair in a negative light. In reality, the quotations were statements made not by Sinclair but by characters in the novels he wrote.

The defeat of Sinclair launched the first political consulting firm, Campaigns Inc. It is generally agreed that Baxter and Whitaker "wrote the book" on how to run a political campaign. Generally speaking, the strategy is always to bury or distort the truth. Some of the basic principles are: keep it simple,

---

22. Jill Lepore, "The Lie Factory," *New Yorker*, September 24, 2012, 50–59.

never explain anything, and never force people to work or think. If you can't find an enemy, invent one. If you can't fight, put on a show. One can see this strategy clearly in the successful effort of Campaigns Inc. on behalf of the American Medical Association to defeat Harry Truman's attempt to pass a national health plan. Addressing a meeting of the New England Medical Association, Whitaker said this:

> Hitler and Stalin and the socialist government of Great Britain all have used the opiate of socialized medicine to deaden the pain of lost liberty and lull people into non-resistance. Old World contagion of compulsory health insurance if allowed to spread to our New World, will mark the beginning of the end of free institutions in America. It will only be a question of time until the railroads, the steel mills, the power industry, the banks, and the farming industry are nationalized.[23]

The quotation provides a clear example of the principles of the "lie factory" at work. Bury the truth, keep it simple, find an enemy, and don't force people to think! The strategy is all too familiar. One can see it in operation across a range of public communication that lies outside the realm of politics. Ironically, one of the most egregious examples concerns a corporation whose business is communication. David Cay Johnston has shown how AT&T has misrepresented its business plans to the public by claiming it would lower costs while actually planning to raise them significantly. He also shows how AT&T disguised the nature of a rising set of charges by means of deliberately misleading itemized bills.[24]

I have chosen these examples from among many possible ones because they so clearly put on display the extent to which public speech, even in democratic societies, has become a "lie factory." The question is this. What do people formed in a school for the service of the Lord bring to a society whose public speech is so contaminated? They bring themselves as truth tellers. For them, devotion to truth is an aspect of grace received beyond striving. It is a primary aspect of who they are and the presence they are called to be.

The truth they bring, however, is of a certain sort. Following a line of thought that came to me through Tony Judt, I would argue that the truth they bring is in the first instance the "little truths" about the stuff of daily life rather than big truths that account for world historical events.[25] When speaking with

---

23. Ibid., 57.
24. David Cay Johnston, *The Fine Print: How Big Corporations Use "Plain English" to Rob You Blind* (New York: Penguin, 2012), 2–7.
25. Tony Judt with Timothy Snyder, *Thinking the Twentieth Century* (New York: Penguin, 2012), 284–90.

his friend Timothy Snyder, the dying Tony Judt made this comment on the failure of intellectuals in the twentieth century. His assessment applies equally well to intellectuals in the present century. Their reasoning, he said, was abstract and theoretical. They focused their attention on "big truths" like getting their national story right or the future of the Muslim world. These big truths may be important, but they tend to cover over smaller, more quotidian ones like how many people are apt to die in a "preemptive war" or how many people go to bed hungry each night as a result of such a war. These little truths are, as Judt's friend Timothy Snyder said, "ugly and complicated, whereas higher truth appears to be pure and beautiful."[26] America's democratic mission to downtrodden people is perhaps a noble ideal, but it covers over the realities of self-interest and war. Thus, he went on to say, "One thing that the Iraq War had in common with a number of other adventures is that it was portrayed in a kind of stylized, abstract way using general concepts such as liberation. Which allowed us to overlook things that we really ought to know: that war is awful, it kills people, individuals are now going to kill and die."[27]

I do not mean that people should show no interest in big truths. I mean only that they can easily get lost in them and so miss the mess of history that little truths reveal. I mean also that people whose lives are shaped in a school for the service of the Lord are formed so as to focus upon little truths, and they are formed to speak truthfully about what they see. The graces of which the author of Ephesians speaks do not float above the mess brought about in human affairs by bitterness, wrath, anger, clamor, slander, and malice. They are graces that compel truthful speech in the face of the incessant lies we tell about the human condition.

I do not mean to say that Christians automatically have these graces, nor that they always carry them into the life of society. Clearly they do not. I do not mean either that Christians are the only ones who have this moral equipment. Clearly they are not. I mean only that, by grace, some do and that, supported by a communion of shared purpose, they join others who have similar strengths and concerns in efforts to display the little truths most of the people most of the time choose to ignore. There is no area of human discourse where truth and truthfulness are not necessary to sustain healthy social relations. There is also no area of human discourse free from lies so easily told to cover the ugliness of the facts or to gain an unfair advantage.

There is no area of human discourse that does not need people capable of telling the little truths about the real character of our lives. Because more

26. Ibid., 288.
27. Ibid., 290.

often than not this truth is spoken in the face of falsehood, truth telling is frequently linked with an ordeal of some sort. Certainly this is the case in the New Testament texts we have examined. Because truth and ordeal are so closely linked, in the biblical narrative truthfulness often appears surrounded by a group of accompanying graces. In Ephesians, for example, the ones of particular importance are humility of mind, patience in the face of suffering, and forbearance (Eph. 4:2). In Revelation truthfulness leads to "tribulation." Tribulation is to be met with patient endurance and an ability not to grow weary (Rev. 2:3). Humility of mind allows one to confront what seems to be a lie with a mind open to be shown its own error. Patient endurance along with an ability to escape weariness allows one to persevere in what is often a long and painful struggle to establish the truth before an onslaught of falsehood. Forbearance allows for the possibility of keeping open a way for reconciliation with those who tell the lies that so distort social relations.

These graces that I have called love's little helpers thus predispose those who possess them to seek reconciliation between parties engaged in social conflict rather than the destruction of one by the other. Christians believe that Christ came to reconcile people to another one and to God. They believe also that reconciliation and peace are the final destiny of humankind. An eschatological vision of this sort presses down upon any and all involved in social conflict. It places before them a vision of peace that lies beyond conflict—a world in which enemies have become friends. It is, therefore, a vision that displays the fact that in human affairs truth is not enough. The vision of human destiny learned within a school for the service of the Lord teaches that truth is necessarily linked to reconciliation. Only in this way can the true end of life in society be realized.

Reconciliation as both a skill and a social goal requires certain forms of social capital that are abundantly present in the graces and skills stressed in New Testament texts. To repeat, what I have said about the link between truth and tribulation is true also of the link between truth and reconciliation. At the foundation of the strengths needed for both is humility of mind—a willingness to listen to and be instructed by others. Openness to instruction, if accompanied by a gentle approach and a willingness to bear with others, keeps lines of communication open even in the midst of bitter conflict. Conflict is rarely resolved quickly, and as a result there is little hope for reconciliation unless at least one party to a dispute is long-suffering and given to patient endurance. Kindness, tenderheartedness, and forgiveness support this sort of patience, as do a reluctance to fall victim to bitterness, wrath, closed-minded argumentation, slander, and malice. If these graces are driven, as in Ephesians, by an eagerness to maintain unity, reconciliation becomes a goal that cannot be relinquished rather than a pious hope that is easily abandoned in trying circumstances.

These graces that lie beyond striving are highly valued within the common life of a school for the service of the Lord, and to the extent they have become a way of being, they will be carried into all forms of social relation, be they with fellow believers, strangers, or enemies. As Rorty has said so well, they display the presence of "the Christian" whose power stems from "endowments of grace received beyond striving."[28]

The Power of Faithful Practice: A Note on the Estate of Marriage as a Form of Witness

The most immediate way in which Christians participate in and have influence on their society is through their presence as individuals in their various walks of life. It is also the case, however, that there is a social presence of the church as an institution and a corporate body. This institutional and corporate presence is most easily identifiable by the practices that give the church a public face. Among the most commonly recognized are marriage, birth, and death, along with various forms of outreach to people in need. In the early church, common life included a wider range of defining practices. Among these were a stringent sexual ethic, the prohibition of divorce, and refusal to kill unwanted children by exposing them to the elements.

Many of these practices have virtually passed out of existence, and many of those remaining are now subject to enormous social pressures pushing for change. As noted above, to the extent the moral vision of Christians has been formed within the common life of an obedient church, they carry into their social encounters a very different view of social life—one that can set them at odds with the cultures of which they are a part. The dominant view of social life that now obtains begins with autonomous individuals who contract with one another with a view to bringing to fruition their personal life plans.

This view of social life poses enormous problems for the churches—problems with which they have only begun to wrestle. A view of social life that begins with "I" and then tries to move to "we" stands in stark contrast to and places enormous pressure on the traditional Christian view that begins with "we" and provides a meaningful place for every individual. Nowhere is this pressure more obvious than the way in which marriage is now understood and lived out. In the previous chapter I discussed marriage and the place of that institution in the formation of a devout and holy life. It also serves, however,

28. Rorty, "A Literary Postscript," 319.

as a form of corporate witness through which Christian belief and practice are made socially visible. No social institution provides a better view of the basic assumptions of a society than that of marriage. When social relations are viewed through this prism, it becomes painfully obvious that the churches are now confronted with a pervasive view of marriage that stands in stark contrast to the understanding that has come down to them through the centuries.

In his account of marriage in the Western church, John Witte points out that there have been five models of marriage: the sacramental model of the Roman Catholic Church, the social model of the Lutheran churches, the covenantal model of Calvinist churches, the commonwealth model of the Anglican Communion, and finally the contractarian view set forth by various thinkers during the time of the Enlightenment.[29] Each of these models contains elements of the others, but each has a particular emphasis. In respect to the churches, the Roman Catholic sacramental model focuses upon the sanctifying grace made available to the couple through their union. The Lutheran model stresses the character of marriage as a social institution instituted by God in creation. The Calvinist model emphasizes marriage as a covenant to which God, the couple, and the community are parties, and the Anglican model holds that the marriage bond creates a small commonwealth that in turn provides a seedbed that produces citizens for the larger commonwealth of the nation.

The marriage tradition of the Western churches is far from uniform, but there are nonetheless certain common features that link all its strands. All agree that marriage is an institution or estate established not by humankind but by God in creation, and that it serves certain ordained purposes—the unity and mutual care of the couple, the procreation and nurture of children, and (after the fall) the domestication of sexual desire and activity. They agree also that marriage has the capacity to symbolize the relation between Christ and the church and, save for certain specified conditions and eventualities, it is held to be an exclusive and permanent relationship. This is not to say that there are no acceptable grounds for ending a marriage. For both Roman Catholics and Protestants, marriage might be defective in its origin, in which case the union could be annulled. For Protestants, a variety of offenses might justify divorce. The most common of these are adultery, desertion, and some form of cruelty. The point, however, is that in the Western tradition, the acceptable reasons for annulment and divorce are specified by the churches and (until recently) the legal system. In the Christian tradition, acceptable grounds for ending a marriage are not chosen by the parties involved.

---

29. John Witte Jr., *From Sacrament to Contract*, 2–3.

In broad outline, this is the tradition about marriage that the churches carried into the twentieth century. Witte observes, however, that for some time now the Enlightenment view that marriage is a contract between the particular wills of the marital partners has gained ground at the expense of the inherited tradition set out above. As we enter the twenty-first century, marriage is commonly seen as a private contract that can be undertaken and ended for reasons decided upon by the parties involved. Generally speaking, it is not seen as an estate with preset conditions. It is viewed as a voluntary relationship, the terms of which are determined by the likes and dislikes of the parties involved. These likes and dislikes, in a way that is striking, include the birth and nurture of children. Having and raising children is no longer considered a constitutive good of marriage but a personal desire that may or may not be present within the relationship. When it is present, the good of having children is linked first to goals of personal fulfillment rather than provision for future generations.

That marriage is viewed increasingly as simply a private, personal affair is plainly visible as well in a number of novel legal and social arrangements—prenuptial agreements, no-fault divorce, sexual autonomy, the disappearance of difference in gender as constitutive of marriage, and the loss of any distinction between the rights of married and unmarried people.[30] As Witte has written, the form and function of their marriage relationship is to be left to the "bargain" of the couple themselves.[31]

I have only anecdotal evidence for this statement, but nine times out of ten it seems to be the Enlightenment view of marriage that clergy meet when they seek to prepare couples for the sacramental establishment or the ecclesial blessing of their marriage. The rites of the churches still enshrine one or more of the traditional views sketched above. Nevertheless, acceptance by the churches of practices like prenuptial agreements and no-fault divorce, along with surrogacy contracts and same-sex marriage, undercuts at the level of practice the public statement of the nature of marriage contained in their rites and teachings. Marriage is indeed the point at which present-day social belief and practice are migrating into the culture of the churches and transforming them into something they have never been before. To be specific, prenuptial agreements suggest that the goods of marriage lie within the choices of the couple. No-fault divorce suggests that what constitutes an acceptable cause for ending a marriage is a matter to be personally determined. Surrogacy contracts and same-sex unions in principle decouple the good of having a

---

30. Ibid., 11, 195–97.
31. Ibid., 197.

child from the relationship between a man and woman who understand that good to be intrinsic to the married state.

Taking note of these changes, at the conclusion of his survey of the marriage traditions of the West, Witte makes the following observation:

> We seem to be living out the grim prophecy that Friedrich Nietzsche offered a century ago: that in the course of the twentieth century, "the family will be slowly ground into a random collection of individuals," haphazardly bound together "in the common pursuit of selfish ends"—and in the common rejection of the structures and strictures of family, church, state, and civil society.[32]

Witte may himself be guilty of a certain degree of Nietzschean hyperbole, but even so his observations are not far off the mark. Moral agents who understand themselves as persons with rights, selves with personal histories and life plans, and individuals who are utterly unique are often the victims of a heady freedom. They exist in a moral universe that limits their actions only by forbidding harm to others in the pursuit of self-appointed goals. When confronted with a moral universe such as this, one is indeed faced with a situation in which the family (along with other primary institutions of society) is "ground into a random collection of individuals."

To the extent that these views have infiltrated the common life of the churches, the integrity of that life has been compromised. I do not believe it is an overstatement to say that the degree to which that integrity has been compromised is profound. The possibility of a social witness on the part of the Western churches that expresses a faithful form of belief and practice in respect to marriage is tied to their ability to provide an alternative to the current beliefs and practices of the larger society of which they are a part. It is hard to escape the conclusion that at present their energies are directed to adapting to that culture rather than providing an alternative to it.

Concluding, Transitional Remarks

Something similar can be said about the practices that now cluster around two other defining points in human life—birth and death. Here also are displayed the fundamental beliefs and practices of both the churches and the cultures of which they are a part. I have noted that the understanding of marriage now regnant in Western culture is structured by the account we give of ourselves as moral agents. When we think of birth and death, we once again think of

---

32. Ibid., 215.

ourselves as *persons* with rights, *selves* with an identity conferring personal history, and *individuals* whose unique qualities distinguish us from all other human beings. As Kant famously argued, each individual has a dignity that is conferred by personal autonomy—that is to say, the freedom of each individual to legislate the moral law rather than receive it by divine command or the necessity of nature's law.

It is this understanding of moral agency that now controls not only the social debate about marriage but also a host of issues that cluster around two other points of human definition, particularly birth and death. Should persons decide when they die? Should children be conceived and brought to term on the basis of quality of life and their prospects for what we believe their prospects for a "good life" to be? Should we use all medical means available in cases where it proves difficult to conceive a child? What medical steps are we to take (or refrain from taking) when the end of life approaches?

These are but a few of the social issues now hotly debated in both the press and over the dinner table. In each case, however, the public debate is likely to be couched in terms of the autonomous individual. Further, in each case the very way in which the public debate is cast calls into question long-standing Christian beliefs and practices in respect both to birth and death. In each case both individual Christians and the churches to which they belong have been thrown into confusion by changes in social belief and practice that often do not sit well with their inherited traditions. How ought a community in which Christ is being formed respond to these challenges?

It seems fair to say that in seeking answers, the churches in the West have been torn apart by internal strife, and the churches in the global South have experienced a widening gulf between themselves and the churches whose missionaries first brought Christian faith and practice to them. It has become increasingly obvious that an account of Christian ethics that focuses on the common life of the church must, if it is to be adequate, address all these questions and a host of others as well. The social dislocation experienced by the historical churches of Europe and North America is forcing them to reexamine (though reluctantly) the very foundations upon which they were built.

The nature of this particular study precludes examination of such a wide range of issues. One can only provide what one hopes is a well-chosen example (marriage) and then go on to indicate the scope of the theological and moral work that lies ahead. The task is equal in scope to the challenge faced by St. Augustine and, later on, St. Thomas Aquinas. The model of the moral agent they inherited from classical and Hellenistic culture did not portray us as autonomous persons, selves, and individuals possessing dignity. Rather, their inherited tradition portrayed us as bodies, minds, and spirits whose desires and passions were to be controlled and directed by an intellect informed by truth. The great theological work carried out by these giants was to pry the accounts of moral agency they inherited out of their Platonic, Aristotelian, Stoic, and Epicurean frameworks and place them within the framework of Christian belief in God's creation, the fall of humankind, and the reconciling and redemptive work of Christ and the Holy Spirit. A similar task now lies before the theologians of the churches. If the churches are to retain or regain their identity and make an effective witness to society, the present account of moral agency in terms of persons, selves, and individuals possessing dignity must be pried out of its present setting within the bounds of human freedom and dignity and placed within the larger narrative of creation, fall, reconciliation, and redemption. In this way, the real moral gains (and they are significant) that have come from the discovery of persons, selves, and individuals can be preserved and strengthened because they have been formed and directed by common graces and practices, and by truth that lies beyond our own choosing. In this way the churches can also regain their own voice and learn once more to speak their own language rather than that of the market economy and the contractarian state.

In this way also the witness of the churches and their individual members to "the powers that be" has a far better chance of being taken seriously and having an effect. As Oliver O'Donovan has noted, the mission of the churches to proclaim and exemplify God's reconciling purpose has two frontiers, namely, "society and rulers." He notes correctly that success in addressing rulers in large measure depends first upon success in addressing society.[33] For this reason, I have taken a different route than O'Donovan who, for practical reasons, began not with a discussion of the relation between church and society but with considerations of the relation between church and political governance. I have begun the other way around because I am convinced that an effective political witness depends fundamentally upon an effective social witness. Having sketched the nature of that witness as a form of presence through graced lives and identifiable social practices, it is possible to sketch the relation of the churches and their members to political authority as a relation that is neither Erastian nor sectarian—that is, as one that is neither the servant of political power nor decisively separated from it.

I will say more in a later chapter about these possibilities, but they are well illustrated by another Christian practice—care of outsiders and the poor. This is a practice that if rightly understood revolutionizes social and political

---

33. Oliver O'Donovan, *The Desire of the Nations: Rediscovering the Roots of Political Theology* (Cambridge: Cambridge University Press, 1996), 193.

relations. Peter Brown has provided a powerful example of what I mean. He writes of the care the early Christians extended to outsiders—people who were not citizens of the Roman Empire and lived on the fringes of society. This witness, he writes, was socially transformative. Christian practice recognized strangers as children of God rather than participants in an alien form of life. Once this happened, charity could not be understood as a form of patronage that established social superiority. Rather, charity became a means of recognition, under God, of one human being by another. As Brown writes, "By giving to the destitute at the furthest edge of the community, the act of almsgiving made present on earth a touch of the boundless care of God for all mankind. The utter pointlessness of giving to those who, as beggars, could offer nothing in return highlighted the magnificent transcendence of God."[34] If understood in this way, few practices have power to transform social and political relations more than care of a stranger in need. However, if not understood in this way, charity takes on a dark face whose smile hides a will to dominate.

---

34. Peter Brown, *The Rise of Western Christendom*, 2nd ed. (Oxford: Blackwell, 2003), 69.

11

An Ecclesial View of Life within Political Society

Part One

Introduction

The purpose of this chapter and the next is to give a theological account of the basis, goal, and character of political authority, and of the relation of Christians to that authority. When I finished an outline of what I might say, I realized I had enough material for a book and that, given the constraints of space and time, I could do no more than say what seemed absolutely necessary. This thought forced me back to the purpose of this book—namely, to give an account of Christian ethics whose focus is the common life of the church. Having returned to my basic purpose, I found the task of giving a normative account of the evangelical and moral relation between individual believers and their churches to political authority became more manageable. It became clear that my task was not to render a moral judgment on the many issues that inhabit the realm of political perplexity, conviction, and action. My task was to give an account of those political beliefs, practices, and actions that fall to Christians simply by virtue of the fact that they are Christians.

The task is not to pronounce upon the myriad particular issues that daily present themselves within a political order. It is to identify those beliefs and forms of action that have clear Christian warrant. Thus, for example, there is clear Christian warrant to say that since all people are created as social beings in the image of God, no one should be excluded from full participation in society because of the color of their skin. It is quite another, however, to say that the way in which Christians must address such exclusion is by taking action *x* or supporting policy *y*. Or again, it is one thing to say God's concern for the weak and marginal members of society implies that Christians have particular duties to the poor. It is yet another to say that they are duty-bound by this belief to support a given policy of income distribution. Or yet again, it is one thing to say that because God holds all human life to be sacred, genocide is a hideous evil that Christians are duty-bound to point out, condemn, and resist. Nevertheless, it is quite another to insist that they must resist in this or that way, or that they must hold that their nation is duty-bound to intervene whenever and wherever a horror of this sort exists.

I am aware that I am stating a position that goes in a direction contrary to that taken by many Christians and their churches since the mid-1960s. During this era policy advocacy became the primary form of public speech and action on the part of individual Christians and their churches.[1] There are, however, many problems that a focus on policy advocacy presents when one or another policy is said to be one that Christians, as Christians, must support. Policy advocacy is in almost all cases based upon a prudential judgment that well may be mistaken. To say that because someone is a Christian, they are morally required to support policy *x* is in most cases to take the dubious and often harmful step of adding the engine of religion to a practical and fallible judgment. It is also a judgment that illegitimately faults the conscience of a fellow believer simply because their prudential judgment differs from one's own.

This cautionary note does not, however, remove concern for and involvement in the political order from the realm of Christian responsibility. I hope to show that concern for and involvement in the political order are responsibilities that flow directly from the church's understanding of its own identity and calling. The Epistle to the Ephesians testifies that Christians are to understand themselves as fellow citizens of a "commonwealth" brought into being by the actions of God in Christ and ruled over by Christ the King. Its basis is the saving action of God, its goal is set by its Governor, and its character is displayed by the graces and practices impressed upon it by the Holy Spirit.

Holy Scripture also testifies that, though ruled by Christ their King, Christians also live under other authorities. Thus, for example, in his Letter to the

---

1. See, e.g., Paul Ramsey, *Who Speaks for the Church: A Critique of the 1966 Conference on Church and Society* (Nashville: Abingdon, 1967).

Romans Paul writes, "The governing authorities . . . have been instituted by God" (Rom. 13:1). These authorities, he says, are to be regarded as "ministers of God." As such they are due "respect" and "honor" (13:6–7).

The witness of Holy Scripture is that the nature of the church as a "polity" is revealed when we identify its basis, goal, and character. The same thing holds for the various forms of political authority under whose rule Christians also live. The question, of course, is just what is the authority of God who governs his people and rules the nations, and what is that of "the powers that be," which rule over the peoples of the earth? This is a question that cannot be answered unless we know the basis, goal, and character of human governance. Just as we ask why it might be good for God to rule over human affairs, so also we ask why it might be good for some people to rule over others.

As is the case with the church, this other form of human association cries out for an account of its nature and origin. So also does the question of how this dual allegiance, to Christ and "the powers that be," is to be understood. Christians live under two authorities, and this fact poses the central issue of political theology. The witness of the Bible and the testimony of Christian tradition is that Christians live under the rule of earthly authorities, but they do so as "resident aliens" or "guest workers" whose "commonwealth is in heaven" (Phil. 3:20). A very early Christian letter, the *Epistle to Diognetus*, expresses this duality with unequaled clarity.

> For the distinction between Christians and other men is neither in country nor language nor customs. For they do not dwell in cities in some place of their own, nor do they use any strange variety of dialect, or practice an extraordinary kind of life. This teaching of theirs has not been discovered by the intellect or thought of busy men, nor are they advocates of any human doctrine as some men are. Yet while living in Greek and barbarian cities . . . and following the local customs . . . they show forth the wonderful and confessedly strange character of the constitution of their own citizenship. They dwell in their own fatherlands, but as if sojourners in them; they share all things as citizens, and suffer all things as strangers. Every foreign country is their fatherland, and every fatherland is a foreign country.[2]

Another way to state the purpose of this chapter is to say that it seeks to unravel the puzzle of this dual residence. This quest requires a description of how political authority appears to persons formed within "a school for

---

2. For this translation of the letter, see Oliver and Joan O'Donovan, *From Irenaeus to Grotius: A Sourcebook in Christian Political Thought, 100–1625* (Grand Rapids: Eerdmans, 1999), 12-13.

the service of the Lord." A quest of this sort reveals many things about both current social opinion and the traditions that for centuries have formed the consciences of Christians. At certain points, the differences are profound. One of the most fundamental is revealed in David Miller's very helpful study *Social Justice*. Miller begins his analysis with a profound (and to my mind troubling) remark. He writes, "A leading characteristic of contemporary political theory is its concern with a range of concepts and principles specifying the ends of government."[3] This interest in ends or political goals, rather than foundations, he goes on to say, has diverted attention from the more traditional concerns of political theory (and Christian theology)—namely, how political authority comes to be in the first place, and why it might place us under an obligation to abide by its judgments.

Miller implies (rightly) that this change in focus serves a very practical and immediately relevant purpose in the present era. It provides the normative ideas by which the policies of specific governments can be evaluated. Thus when confronted with political choices, we tend to ask, "Does policy x indeed further liberty, equality, welfare, or social justice (the four goals Miller identifies) or not?" In short, present-day interest in governance centers on what we want government to do rather than how it comes to be that we live under one or another form of political authority in the first place and why we might or might not be obligated to abide by the judgments and enactments of that authority.

There is something immensely attractive about beginning with normative political concepts like liberty, equality, justice, and welfare rather than the basis of political authority itself. It is a strategy that provides a way to plunge immediately into the nitty-gritty of political life. It is no doubt the practical advantage of this starting point that has, in recent years, led so many Christians to bypass the more traditional theological focus on the basis of political authority and, like their secular counterparts, go immediately to the question of political norms. In a time when political advocacy has, in the eyes of many, come to define both the mission of the churches and the primary duty of citizens, norms provide an immediately available launching pad for political involvement.

Christians have many good reasons for political advocacy. Indeed, they have a theologically grounded and overriding duty, when appropriate, to be so involved. The question is not so much *whether* they should be involved but *how*. Nevertheless, like their more secular fellow citizens, they render the foundations of that advocacy quite frail if they rush by the question of the

3. David Miller, *Social Justice* (Oxford: Clarendon, 1979), 1.

origin and moral basis of governance and our obligation to it. They place their advocacy on weak foundations for the simple reason that they offer no justification for the authority of the governments that stand behind the goals and policies they either support or oppose.

The proper goals of governance are in no way obvious, and a lack of serious attention to their foundation can lead to irresolvable conflicts on the one hand and some very serious errors on the other. Lack of attention to foundations also leads to the false belief that assumptions about moral foundations of governance have been established with a degree of adequacy that requires no further consideration. Thus it is often assumed that the authority of government rests upon a "social contract." This assumption is not surprising. It coheres with an account of moral agency that focuses on autonomous *persons* who are *individual selves* in pursuit of happiness. For people holding this view of moral agency, the authority of government along with the delineation of its duties and the obligations of its citizens is, generally speaking, thought to be rooted in the autonomy and prudential choices of those happiness-seeking agents.

These beliefs now have a very long and distinguished pedigree—one that gives them the appearance of well-established tradition. Some years ago, Ernst Cassirer noted that the Stoic idea of "the rights of man" stood behind Enlightenment ideas of political authority.[4] "The rights of man" were tied closely to the supremacy of reason as life's guide. Reason became the seat of human dignity and the basis of political authority. The dignity of persons as persons was thought to be the source not only of government but also of rights that protect the autonomy and dignity of each citizen. These rights, rooted in rationality and human dignity, were thought inalienable whether guaranteed by God or not. The authority of government was traced to the rational capacity of persons rather than divine provision. According to this view, political authority is *rightly* established by means of a freely entered but putative contract that stipulates the ends of government upon which reasonable agents would willingly agree.

It is important to note that advocates of the theory of social contract (both past and present) do not make claims about the historical origins of political authority. Their interest is in not the origin but the legitimacy of governance, and legitimacy comes only through the autonomous judgments of reason. The notion of a social contract is thus a way of saying that people are obligated to governance because governance, if it furthers or guards the "rights of man," is

---

4. For Cassirer's account of the Enlightenment view of moral agency and political authority, see Ernst Cassirer, *The Myth of the State* (New Haven: Yale University Press, 1946), 167–74.

what reasonable people possessing dignity would agree to regardless of time or place. Reasonable persons who are selves and individuals have interests in their well-being. Further, reasonable persons with interests will be led in the making of a contract to specify a list of freedoms they wish government to establish and guard because those freedoms are necessary for their well-being. According to John Locke, the necessary freedoms are life, liberty, and property. Thomas Jefferson had a slightly different list—life, liberty, and the pursuit of happiness. In recent years, a series of rights understood not as freedoms but as entitlements have been added to the rights of liberty. Among them are health, education, medical care, and a living wage, to mention but a few.

The inflation of rights language that has marked the development of political thought in recent decades has caused much dispute about those arrangements to which reasonable, free individuals will necessarily agree. No matter what doubts and disputes now cluster around what the appropriate goals of governance are, in the back of many minds resides the notion that the way to resolve these difficulties is to look again at the nature of the putative contract that lies at the base of social life and political obligation.

These developments in intellectual, moral, and political history mark what Cassirer calls "a great and decisive step." He writes, "If we adopt this view, if we reduce the legal and the social order to free individual acts, to a voluntary contractual submission, all mystery is gone." There is, he says "nothing less mysterious than a contract."[5] It is, however, the very mystery of the existence of political authority that, according to Christian tradition, requires explanation. According to Peter Brown, this view of political authority as a mystery, even in the midst of a rationalist tradition concerning the authority of government, may well be closer to the modern mindset than we think. He wonders about the extent to which "the myth of the state" still holds sway. He wonders whether this myth still provides a credible reason for obedience to political authority.

His question is whether the link between the individual and political authority can be adequately accounted for by rational obligation. He writes, "We are linked to political society by something that somehow escapes our immediate consciousness: by a whole tangled skein of pressures and motives, some rational, many more not so."[6] He notes that it is the nature of this skein that perplexes us. We simply find ourselves subject to authority, and we ask why. We ask, "Should this be so? Is it worth it? Is it right? May it be resisted? How is it to be controlled?"

5. Ibid., 173.
6. P. R. L. Brown, "Saint Augustine and Political Society," in *The City of God: A Collection of Critical Essays*, ed. Dorothy F. Donnelly (New York: Peter Lang, 1995), 18.

The Basis and Goal of Political Authority

The Basis of Political Authority

Christian tradition addresses itself to these perplexities. This tradition has been quite uniform. The existence of government is a mystery, and if an adequate account of the basis of governance cannot be found, the authority of governance cannot, from a moral point of view, be adequately established. The question is, how might a person formed within a school for the service of the Lord view the basis of political authority? And when looked at from this perspective, how might the still-common assumptions about the basis of governance in human autonomy and social contract appear? Christian tradition has been quite uniform in attributing the establishment and authority of government to the providence of God rather than to human wit and will. Nonetheless, there have been at least three interpretations of the way in which God's providential oversight works. One account locates providential action in God's selection of a particular person to rule. This view has been and remains a powerful influence in the Orthodox churches of the East. A second account locates the basis of political authority not in the choice of an individual to rule but in God's rule over the entire course of history and his ability, through the governance of the ascended Christ, to use the disordered state of human affairs to establish political authority and create spheres of order within a disordered world. This view has found its clearest and most powerful expression in the Augustinian tradition of the Western churches. A third account locates God's provision of political authority in the belief that human beings are created as social beings. Political order is thus considered an aspect of created order and as such is an aspect of God's providential ordering of his creation. This view has its origin in the Aristotelian thought of St. Thomas Aquinas and is characteristic of Roman Catholic social and political teaching to this day.

The central role that divine providence plays in Christian accounts of the basis of political authority necessitates further comment on each of these options. Gilbert Dagron, in his magisterial study of the imperial office in Byzantium, has provided an unequaled account of the view of the Eastern Church—namely, that divine providence, in establishing political authority, has appointed a particular person possessing both political and religious powers to exercise this authority.[7] This view arose in the early history of the Eastern Church. The church in these early days was confronted with the question of

---

7. Gilbert Dagron, *Emperor and Priest: The Imperial Office in Byzantium* (Cambridge: Cambridge University Press, 2007).

how it came to be that Constantine, a pagan, rose to power and both unified the empire and established Christianity as the religion of that empire. The why and how of this remarkable event was a mystery demanding a solution. Not surprisingly, Christians found a solution by reading Holy Scripture.

Their reading went like this. As God had appointed Saul and David, so he raised up Constantine to be not only a king like David but a king and priest after the order of Melchizedek. Like David, God directly chooses Constantine. Like David also, though he has been given absolute authority, God nonetheless holds the emperor responsible to divine law. Further, like Melchizedek, Constantine was seen to have religious powers. As Melchizedek, an uncircumcised pagan priest who came directly from paganism to the worship of the one true God, received tithes from God's people, so did Constantine. Like Melchizedek, Constantine was a king/priest who provided the *type* for politico-religious authority.

Dagron points out that from these ideas developed forms of caesaropapism that accorded the emperor both royal and quasi-religious significance. He points out also that, over the centuries, this form of dual sovereignty has compromised the independence and integrity of the churches. Citing F. Dvornik's work *Early Christian and Byzantine Political Philosophy*, Dagron notes that this way of viewing political authority became, for the church, a way of centralizing authority so that the church, though not identified with political authority, nonetheless participated directly in its exercise.[8] Following Dvornik, Dagron argues that the result of this close identification has proven less than ideal. The Orthodox churches, by his account, have too frequently become subject to the state and as a result have both become its tool and merged the interests of the church with those of a lay elite and a privileged class of clergy.

Ideas similar to these have appeared in the West—namely, in certain versions of the once popular theory of "the divine right of kings." This opinion, particularly favored by the Tudor and Stewart kings of England and Scotland, held that the king derived the right to rule directly from the will of God. As such, the king is not subject to the will of the people or to the aristocracy. By divine appointment, the king possesses both political and religious powers. This view came under fierce attack during the glorious revolution of 1688–89, and even more so during the American and French Revolutions. That attack received its most powerful expression in Locke's *Essay concerning the True Original Extent and End of Civil Government*, and for all practical purposes has been discredited within Western political thought.

8. Ibid., 291.

What might be called the politico-religious monism of the East, however, lives on and is easily contrasted with the West, where ecclesiastical and political authority, for various reasons, have been viewed as two distinct powers. In this arrangement, the church may receive the assistance of civil government and even accord those who govern certain powers, rights, and privileges within the organization of the church. Nevertheless, the church has always reacted against loss of sovereignty by asserting its independence from the authority of government, and on occasion its authority over it.

The effective source of this more independent stance is St. Augustine, who made a clear distinction between the basis of authority within the empire and the basis of authority within the church. From him comes the second view of the origin and basis of governance. God establishes political authority through his providential overruling of the conflicting forces that characterize life in a fallen world. Within history, Augustine argued, there are two cities. One is composed of God's elect, and its life is characterized by love of God and love of neighbor. The provenance of this city is the grace of God. It is in a quite literal sense "the city of God." As such it is eternal. The other city is characterized by love of self. Its provenance is human pride and rebellion against God. It is thus rightly called "the human city." As such, its governance is only a temporary measure established by divine providence in order to ensure the continuation of life on earth until God's restoration and transformation of his creation is complete.

In this account of the basis and goal of political rule, God uses human pride and the conflict that always accompanies it to create areas of what might be called "peace within the feud." That is, through providential overrule, by pitting force against force, God establishes institutions that check human greed and violence and prevent social life from becoming utterly chaotic. These institutions include private property, legal systems, and various forms of government. Nevertheless, necessary and effective as these arrangements may be, they are not a part of God's will in creation. They are made necessary by the incursion into the world of human rebellion and vainglory. For this reason these ordering institutions also carry with them the marks of their origin. They are the creatures of pride and violence. Consequently, though they are providential remedies for the harmful social effects stemming from human rebellion against God, they can never escape the conditions in which they originate. They must use coercion and repression, or they cannot maintain themselves. They are, in consequence, fragile and subject to destruction and replacement.

Herbert A. Deane has provided a summary of St. Augustine's account of the basis of political authority that is difficult to improve upon. He writes,

In view of the condition of sinful man, the peace, concord, and justice that are maintained by these economic, legal and political institutions are supremely important. Yet they are only imperfect images or reflections of the natural, uncoerced peace, order and justice that existed in Paradise or of the true and abiding concord, peace and order, and justice that will reign for all eternity in the heavenly city, the society built upon the love of all its members for God and for one another in God.[9]

St. Augustine's political theology continues to be influential to this day. So also does that of St. Thomas Aquinas, whose Aristotelian modifications of Augustine's Platonism introduced a distinctly humanistic note into the Western tradition of political theology. With this introduction came a third view of the providential basis of governance. Political authority has its basis not in an emergency action on the part of God but in the nature of humankind as created by God. Thomas holds that human beings are created as social beings. Their social nature is an aspect of a divinely ordered creation. Political authority grows out of this social nature. Communal life is natural, and Thomas holds that "the state" is a "perfect" or self-sufficient instance of human community. Its existence, therefore, allows in an ideal fashion for development of the division of labor and cooperation in the various intellectual activities that make life worth living. Thus political authority is necessary, even in ideal circumstances, as a means of coordinating these diverse forms of activity, talent, and interest. It is necessary also as a means of guiding the young and immature members of society as they progress toward maturity. Like Augustine, Thomas holds that political authority establishes order in a fallen world. Nevertheless, it has its foundation in creation rather than in the fallen state of the world. Governance is an aspect of God's ordering of the world at its very foundation, and though its coercive powers have been made necessary by sin, its administrative and pedagogical functions remain as created goods.

A survey of the history of Christian thought leaves us with three traditions concerning the basis of political authority. Each has its own strengths and weaknesses, and for this reason, it is reasonable to assume that the basis of political authority, like disputes over the relation between grace and free will, will remain a perennially contested issue within the life of the churches. Nonetheless, all three streams of this tradition are in agreement about one thing—political authority has its foundation in divine providence rather than in human intellect and will. As such, "the powers that be" are, in Paul's words, "instituted by God" (Rom. 13:1b).

---

9. Herbert A. Deane, *The Political and Social Ideas of St. Augustine* (New York: Columbia University Press, 1963), 96.

To say, however, that the authority of government is located in divine providence but that disagreement exists about the way in which providence works does not mean that it is a foolhardy venture to argue for the superiority of one view over the others. One can admit that each has its characteristic problems yet argue that one view has fewer than the others. I have noted that the Eastern view has a long history of caesaropapism resulting in the compromise of the church's independence. It is clear also that the Augustinian view suggests an unacceptable degree of passivity before the illicit encroachments of government. It is also true to say that the Thomistic view of the created nature of political authority is often accompanied by an undue optimism about the right and ability of government to administer the complex nature of social relations and to take charge of the moral formation of the citizenry.

Further exploration of the relative strengths and weaknesses of these three strands of Christian tradition lies beyond the scope of this book. I will say only that of the three, it seems to me that the Augustinian strand leaves the fewest difficulties. I don't know how to avoid the ills of caesaropapism if one locates God's providential activity in the choice and sanctification of a single person to rule. I also do not know how to avoid what appears to me to be an overly optimistic estimation of the ability of governing authority to administer the various activities that make up the common good of society, and I certainly don't know how to avoid the dangers of government undertaking the task of making us better people. I do believe, however, that there is a way to mitigate the unacceptable passivity that has so frequently accompanied Augustine's adaptation of Paul's belief that "there is no authority except from God" and that "he who resists the authorities resist what God has appointed" (Rom. 13:1a; 13:2).

It is one thing to hold that the mystery of the provenance of the various forms of political authority is best solved by attributing their existence to divine providence. It is quite another to say that there is no way to resist the powers that be without at the same time resisting God. First of all, within all forms of governance there are morally acceptable ways of resisting the judgments of those who hold authority. Second, even when resistance goes so far as to seek their overthrow, one can still lay the success or failure of those efforts within the realm of divine providence. That is to say, human governments and empires come and go; one can, in Oliver O'Donovan's nice phrase, "act into that history" in faith and hope that one's action accords with God's will.[10] To believe that there is no authority except from God does not mean that one cannot be part of bringing about a new political order.

10. O'Donovan, *Desire of the Nations*, 12.

All this being said, one still must give an account of *why* Christians have addressed the mystery that the existence of government presents by locating that existence in divine providence. The answer to this question is surely the clear witness of Holy Scripture. We have already seen how this belief shaped the thought of the writer of the Apocalypse. God is portrayed there as the almighty ruler of the creation and all peoples. He is the ruler of creation who will create a new heaven and a new earth. He is the ruler of the nations who, through the victory of Christ and the witness of the church, will bring all peoples to know, love, and worship him. In doing so, he shows his power by overcoming not only the might of the Roman Empire but also that of the spiritual forces that stand behind its blasphemous pretensions.

In writing as he does, the author of the Apocalypse clearly relies upon what he takes to be the witness of the Holy Scriptures as he knows them. From Genesis through Malachi God is presented as the ruler of creation, history, and his people. At no place in the Bible is this tripartite sovereignty more clearly presented than in the small collection of psalms beginning with Psalm 93 and ending with Psalm 99.[11] The reign of God is the theme of each of these psalms. Taken together they declare that reign to include the created order, the kingdoms of the earth, and the common life of God's people. Thus, for example, in Psalm 93 God ensures the stability of the physical world by controlling the chaotic energies of nature. In Psalm 97 the very force of the thunderstorm is taken as a demonstration of divine sovereignty that expresses itself in God's ability to shame the idolatrous nations. Psalm 99 focuses on God's rule over his people. So the psalm asserts that God is "great in Zion" and has "executed justice and righteousness in Jacob."

This same pattern provides the structure of the Exodus narrative. God is sovereign over the forces of nature and at the Red Sea uses them both to defeat Egypt's king and to free his people from the king's grip. At Mount Sinai, as Israel's king, God issues the law that is to form the common life of his people. This same pattern of God's reign over nature, the nations, and his people provides a template for the message of the prophets. Thus when the prophet known as Second Isaiah wishes to comfort God's exiled people, he begins by saying that God will show his glory by lifting up the valleys and leveling the hills so as to prepare a road for the people to return to their land (Isa. 42:4). He then goes on to say that God, who rules in might, will come to his people and care for them as a shepherd cares for his flock (42:10–11). Finally the prophet notes that before God's wisdom, justice, and might, the nations are "like a drop from a bucket" (40:14–15).

---

11. See O'Donovan's summary of the picture of the reign of God presented in a medley of these psalms, in ibid., 33–34.

For minds shaped by the view that governance has been brought into being and sustained by human will and wit, the thought that government owes its origin and continuance to divine power and the purposeful intervention of God in history no doubt appears at best fanciful and at worst more than a little frightening. After all, has it not been the case that when the power of God is linked to "the powers that be," too frequently a way has been opened for authoritarian rule? Those whose moral focus is the common life of the church should be fully alive to this possibility. Again and again in the history of the church, believers have been confronted by the dread power and divine pretentions of government. It is not without reason that martyrdom became a fundamental marker of Christian identity early on.

Aware as they may be of the demonic potential of all forms of governance, Christians nonetheless hold to a providential view of the basis of political authority not only because they rightly see that no government can guarantee its continued existence by the exercise of will alone but also because they believe the scriptural witness that God has power and authority to overcome all the forces (no matter how dreadful) that oppose his purposes. Because they believe that God's governance of the course of history is both dependable and good, they place the rise and fall of nations not within the orbit of human will and wit but within the providence of a good and faithful God. This belief, drawn forth by God's faithfulness, offers hope in the midst of history's most dire moments.

This belief also provides a way to address a question that remains unresolved by various contemporary attempts to root political authority and obligation in the dictates of human will and intelligence. The issue can be posed in this way. Contract theory roots political authority in a shared prudential judgment about what political arrangement best serves the interests of individual choosers. On this account we recognize political authority and accord obligation to it because, in doing so, we affirm our autonomy and so also our dignity as moral beings. One need not hold the beliefs in providence set out above to recognize three problems this view presents. First, speaking of an obligation to oneself hardly does justice to the standard meaning of the word (involving a debt to others). Second, if the authority of government rests finally upon our own will, in cases of serious conflict, if we find ourselves at odds with the judgments of authority, in a real sense we are forced to will against ourselves. As a result, we find ourselves in a state of alienation from the authority to which we once considered ourselves bound.[12] Third, it is notoriously difficult to give an adequate account of why people who, in theory, recognize their

---

12. I owe this point, as is the case with many others, to Oliver O'Donovan. See ibid., 31.

interest in a particular form of contract will in reality support this contract when they survey the less-than-ideal circumstances in which the putative agreement must be lived out.[13]

By way of contrast, the account of the basis of political authority given by those who root political order in divine providence does not begin with conflicts between contending human wills. For them the originating issue is not how to manage conflicting human wills. Rather, it is the profound conflict between divine and human will. As Oliver O'Donovan has written, the command of political authority "strikes us like a meteor from outside our world, cutting across our projects and ambitions, precisely because it is not the human will that has generated it, but the divine will mediated through human agents."[14] For those who root governing authority in divine providence, the first question is, therefore, not how conflicts between contending human wills can be resolved but whether God's providential ordering of our conflicted wills is in fact good.

The appropriate response to this question is not a political theory but a testimony to the faithfulness of a good and merciful God who will not desert his creation, who (again and again) will bring order out of the contending wills of the peoples of the earth, and who will preserve his people throughout the vicissitudes of history until his redemption of the world is complete. That said, the purpose or purposes of God's preservative providence remain unclear, as does the sort of order God wills to establish. In our hands, political order can serve any number of purposes. Indeed, some forms of order can prove more terrible than the worst forms of disorder. In response to this dread possibility, Christian tradition has stated with considerable boldness what the purpose of God's providential ordering of human affairs is. It has also insisted that not just any form of order will do.

The Goal of Political Authority

THE EVANGELICAL PURPOSE OF POLITICAL ORDER

Christian tradition holds that the basis of political authority is divine providence and that the first goal of divine governance is the establishment of political order. Order preserves life within a "war-torn" world, and as such is to be understood as an aspect of divine providence. Order is consequently a goal that Christians dare not pass by. The view of fallen human nature held by Christians through the ages (along with observation of what happens when public order breaks down) draws them to the conclusion that, in the absence

---

13. See, e.g., Amartya Sen, *The Idea of Justice* (Cambridge, MA: Belknap Press of Harvard University Press, 2009), 68–69, 90, 128, 138.
14. O'Donovan, *Desire of the Nations*, 32.

of political order, divine purpose cannot be realized and human goals cannot be reached. From an ecclesial perspective, however, the establishment of order does not exhaust God's providential purposes.

The Augustinian tradition holds that God's purpose in establishing political authority involves more than provision of a peaceful space in which life can continue. The deep purpose of that peaceful space is to provide opportunity for the church to carry out its mission. This tradition can and has been interpreted simply as a justification for governance that grants the churches special privileges. This interpretation entirely misses the point, however. The point is that the purpose of what we call "the state" cannot be properly understood until the fact of its existence is located within God's providential ordering of human history. Within the providence of God, the purpose of political authority is not to provide the church with political support. Rather, it is to provide space and time within a fallen world for God, through his people, to accomplish his purposes. In theological terms, all forms of governance (including church governance) can be rightly understood only as they are viewed through the lens of God's final purposes. From this perspective, all forms of governance are but temporary measures designed to facilitate God's eternal purpose—namely, in the words of John 4:23, to bring the peoples to the worship of God "in spirit and truth." It can be fairly said that Christians understand God's purpose for the establishment of political order to be evangelical. This is not to say that our various forms of governance serve as divinely appointed instruments of salvation. They emphatically do not! It is to say only that these temporary arrangements make it possible for the church (in the words of the Book of Common Prayer) to carry out its assigned task in "peace and tranquility." If, however, governance claims to be an instrument of salvation, or if it turns its face against the church and seeks its suppression or destruction, Christians may be certain that governance now stands in opposition to its assigned role within divine providence and, in consequence, has become demonic—the instrument of anti-godly power.

Political Order and the Establishment of "Right"

More will be said later about how Christians are called upon to react when faced with political authority that opposes its appointed role in human affairs. First, however, more must be said about the nature of the order God providentially seeks to establish. The order for which Christians pray is of a special kind. It is one that God approves. It is one in which justice prevails, and consequently one that is linked to a family of goods (like liberty, equality, and welfare) that in various combinations compose a "just" public space in which "right" prevails. That said, mention of a just or right political order (necessary though it is) does no more than present two further perplexing and frequently avoided questions. The first is, how are the various goods that might compose a just political order to be arranged? How, for example, is order to be balanced with equality, or liberty with welfare? These questions lie at the core of political argument, and the tensions between them cannot be resolved by mere repetition of a belief that each is a clear social and political good.

An even more difficult question concerns the manner in which social order and social justice are in fact to be brought together. The question arises because justice and order simply dangle in the air unless they are in some way united. How then is this connection to be established? For a variety of reasons we often pay no attention to the obvious answer. The link is forged by the actions of political authority. If justice is in fact to be justice, it must be part of a political order established by political authority. It is precisely here that the ecclesial focus of Christian ethics I have defended has something of crucial importance to say in an era in which the foundations of political authority have become notoriously weak.

As Oliver O'Donovan has cogently argued, Christians have something of supreme importance to offer an age in which discussion of this unpopular and frequently disparaged subject has become difficult if not impossible.[15] O'Donovan contends that a Christian account of political authority ought not to begin (as is now standard procedure) by extrapolating an account from observations of its operation. Rather, he argues that Christians ought to begin with an examination of the biblical witness to God's establishment of his authority over his people. Here is a depiction of the true nature of both political authority and the judgments it is called upon to render.

He points out that Old Testament texts testify that God establishes his rule over his people by saving acts of power, rendering judgment, and the gift of both land and a law to order their common life. This gracious activity in turn calls forth praise from a people who, through these gifts, recognize both their identity and its source.[16] In the New Testament, a similar pattern establishes the authority of the risen and ascended Christ over the church and the nations.

---

15. Those who are familiar with O'Donovan's writings will already be aware of the enormous influence they have had in the development of my treatment of the relation between the churches and the political orders in the midst of which they find themselves. I confess I feel no anxiety about the influence they have had on this work. From time to time a truly magisterial treatment of a subject appears, and O'Donovan's three works, *Resurrection and Moral Order*, *Desire of the Nations*, and *Ways of Judgment*, justly deserve that title. I see no need at this point to "reinvent the wheel" and so happily rely on his work. For his discussion of the nature of political authority, see especially *Desire of the Nations*, 30–81, and *Ways of Judgment*, 127–48.

16. O'Donovan, *Desire of the Nations*, 30–49.

O'Donovan notes that God accompanies his acts of power by acts of judgment. Acts of judgment define human political action. That is, they create a public space that is ordered by law, and law is meant to establish what is "right" within the public arena. Further, law generates a tradition. Tradition guides those with authority (and those under authority) as they make further judgments intended to sustain what is "right" in the midst of the changes and chances of history.

If we are adequately to understand the goals of governance, particular attention is due to O'Donovan's treatment of acts of judgment. Following his exegesis of the relevant biblical texts, he argues that political judgment "is an act of moral discrimination that pronounces upon a preceding act or existing state of affairs to establish a new public context."[17] Since judgment is before all else an act of "moral discrimination," it is also an act that establishes a public context in which "right" or "justice" prevails. Further, since it establishes a *public* order, it must also serve a recognized *public* interest. In doing so it deserves to receive the support of the public it serves.[18] An act of judgment does not qualify as a right judgment if it is unrecognizable as such by the people whose common interest and tradition it seeks to further and strengthen.

We may say then that if the first goal of governance is to provide order that allows the church to carry out its mission in peace and tranquility, it is also a goal of governance to render judgments that create a public space whose order accords with what is "right" and endures over time. It is easy to see that good order cannot be sustained if public space is in a constant state of disruption. It is less easy to see what a right order might look like. This question places Christian concerns about right order on equal footing with contemporary discussions of the nature of justice and the establishment of human rights. Within the academy, the question of justice and the rights it is to protect has become a center of attention and scholarly debate. Theories of justice and discussions of human rights abound. John Rawls's pioneering work, *A Theory of Justice*, has given new life to political philosophy and in turn has inspired a host of alternative accounts.[19] Some focus on equality, others on liberty, and others on provision of basic social welfare. In a similar manner, one finds among the churches discussions of the same subjects. Pilate famously asked, "What is truth?" It would seem that we now ask (with equal despair perhaps), a slightly different question: "What is justice?"

17. O'Donovan, *Ways of Judgment*, 7.
18. Ibid., 11.
19. See, e.g., John Rawls, *A Theory of Justice* (Cambridge, MA: Harvard University Press, 1971).

It is tempting to say that there is a *Christian* answer to this question, but despite the intensity of our partisan commitments, this is not the case. Is justice to be defined as equality? Or is justice to be understood in the first instance as the defense and promotion of human freedom? Or perhaps justice serves first of all to defend and promote the welfare of society's least advantaged members. Each of these candidates for the essential definition of justice has its advocates, and together these options make up the ever-changing landscape of political argument. I find it impossible to establish the supremacy of any one of them on the basis of clear Christian warrant. Neither do I find it possible to find a clear Christian warrant for the way in which each good is to be balanced with the others. Nevertheless, Oliver O'Donovan has made a response to this question that deserves the closest attention. It does not strike me as a theory that can be labeled "the Christian understanding of justice." I am not sure there is such a thing. Nevertheless, O'Donovan's account provides a way to think about the subject of right order and justice that coheres with concerns that flow directly from Christian belief.

Following the biblical account of life within the reign of God, O'Donovan places emphasis on community health and effective communication rather than the primacy of "rights." A focus on community health and effective communication coheres with the depiction of the social order to which humankind is called so clearly in Ephesians. Here right order is created and sustained not by the assertion of frequently conflicting "rights" but by "mutual subjection" within a form of common life. As Rowan Williams has insisted, "rights" are necessary aspects of social life, but if they do not flow from forms of mutual "recognition" that anchor them in "habits of empathy and identification" with "the other," they soon devolve into forms of competitive individualism that eat away at the heart of the communicative character of life together.[20]

O'Donovan's focus on the communicative character of social and political life locates the question of "rights" within a communal setting. In doing so, he provides a powerful response to the dispute over how conflicts between the various social and political goods are to be addressed. O'Donovan proposes that in discussing the establishment of a just order, we ought not to begin in the usual places—that is, with portrayals of justice as equality, liberty, or welfare, or with the establishment of a range of civil rights. He begins instead with an account of human society as a system of communication. If one begins here, right public order is based upon appropriate "personal recognition" rather than individual rights and the justice of various forms of giving and taking.[21]

20. Williams, "Reconnecting Human Rights," 162–63.
21. O'Donovan, *Ways of Judgment*, 36.

Borrowing from the work of Hugo Grotius, O'Donovan suggests that this shift in focus leads one to ask first not who has what "right" to what but what is a "fitting" form of action in a given set of social and political circumstances. For Grotius an action is "fitting" if moral discrimination leads to "the prudent allocation of resources" that add "to what individuals and collectives own."[22] We might say that a fitting judgment is one that protects or furthers a common good. Prudent allocation does not begin with measurements of who deserves what in a given social distribution. It begins with "moral discrimination" that leads to "recognition" rather than measurement of this claim against that claim.

Grotius termed this form of justice "attributive justice." Attributive justice is thus a form of judgment that is "forward looking." It seeks right order for a social whole. As such, it is "less than perfect" in the sense that it does not establish a "right" in the strict sense. That is, it does not allow one to claim something "as one's own."[23] What is given is given on the basis of a judgment not only about what is deserved but also about what serves the stake that individuals and groups have in common life.

In moving the discussion of justice in this direction, O'Donovan knowingly espouses a view that, as he says, "effectively sets justice free from equality."[24] Given the tenor of present discussions of justice as equality, this is, to say the least, an arresting statement, and it makes one wonder just where O'Donovan is going. Perhaps sensing this reaction, he hastens to say that he in no way means that equality plays no role in discussions of justice. Indeed, he holds that there is a fundamental human equality that impacts the various forms of relation that structure social life. Fundamental equality opens special relations like familial and national ones to a wider horizon. It also points to certain circumstances that require equal treatment. He gives as examples the way people are treated in the face of death, equality before the law, and requirements for equal treatment that arise when people lack the resources necessary to participate in the communicative life of society.

He does not wish to do away with standards of equality. His purpose is to limit the circumstances of their applicability. He worries that insistence on strict equality leads to the destruction of the variety of forms social life assumes. In his words, "The fate of all revolutionary equalization is to make human life unlivable."[25] What he means is that attributive justice, as presented by Grotius, "does not always have to make comparisons between one person and another (i.e., in respect to equality or inequality); it may simply be attending to what

22. Ibid., 38.
23. Ibid., 39.
24. Ibid.
25. Ibid., 42.

actions will be fitting to the salient features of a situation."[26] In respect to justice, his position stands in stark contrast to any position that assigns absolute priority to a single principle, be that equality, liberty, or welfare. Attributive justice, as he says, "elaborates differences." In making his point he says this:

> Attributive justice . . . strengthens relations of affinity and bonds of loyalty, it promotes talent and makes wise appointments to office, it gives opportunities to those who can use them. It represents the very opposite tendency to the demand for equal treatment, a demand that can only dissolve and degrade social structures, since differentiation is the law of every social organism.[27]

O'Donovan's account of political order, authority, and judgment is on first glance apt to appear strange. In this era, political authority is in large measure viewed negatively or simply ignored. An account of justice that does not focus almost exclusively on rights or equality or liberty may appear irrelevant or repugnant. Further, Grotius is not a name that comes immediately to mind. Therefore, to show that what O'Donovan is saying is neither strange nor repugnant, it may prove helpful to note that his account of justice is in important ways similar to two of the more recent accounts offered by political philosophers. First of all, Michael Walzer, in his book *Spheres of Justice*, notes that equality is not a good that is appropriate in identical ways and with equal force across the various spheres of social, political, and economic life.[28] Thus if we survey the various spheres of social life (say group membership, security, welfare, work, public office, or family life), equality will prove important in each sphere but in different ways and with different degrees of importance. Justice cannot be reduced to a simple matter of equality or liberty. Rather, the moral and political task is to locate their proper place and relative importance among a host of differing social locations and circumstances. This task, Walzer insists, is one that requires what O'Donovan calls "moral discrimination" within a community of shared meanings.[29] It is, in short, a task for attributive justice.

If one removes O'Donovan's theological foundations, the work of the Nobel Laureate Amartya Sen bears even closer similarities to his.[30] O'Donovan insists that attributive justice requires an act of moral discrimination by means of which one determines what, in a given set of circumstances, "a prudent

26. Ibid., 39.
27. Ibid., 42.
28. Michael Walzer, *Spheres of Justice: A Defense of Pluralism and Equality* (New York: Basic Books, 1983).
29. See, e.g., ibid., 312.
30. See, e.g., Sen, *Idea of Justice*.

allocation of resources" might require. His emphasis is not on perfect justice and the institutional arrangements that might bring such a about state. Rather, his focus is on "recognition," "moral discrimination," and the specific outcomes these moral abilities might enable. In a similar (though not identical) manner, Sen attacks what he calls contemporary accounts of justice that focus on ideal political institutions rather than on the actual societies that might emerge from these institutions. Sen's mentors are Condorcet and Adam Smith rather than Hobbes, Rousseau, and Kant. Unlike the latter three, the emphasis of the former two was not perfect justice and the institutional arrangements that might procure perfection. Their emphasis was on particulars—namely, the removal of manifest injustice. Their chief concern was actual circumstance and desired social outcomes. Their emphasis was more on recognition, moral discrimination, and remedy within actual circumstances than the sort of social construction that might produce a perfectly just society. Sen's view of justice, to use an image made famous by Isaiah Berlin and Ronald Dworkin, is more like that of a fox that knows many small things than of a hedgehog that knows one big thing.[31]

So is that of O'Donovan. So also is the view that comes first to mind among a people formed within a school for the service of the Lord. In a school of charity, one learns a form of moral discrimination that recognizes the equal status of each person before God and focuses on the persons who stand close at hand. The moral discrimination that is born of love for the neighbor demands recognition of the circumstances of individuals sharing a common life, seeks correction of any injustices that appear, and aims to further those activities that produce the goods that emerge from the communicative exchanges of social life. As Duncan Forrester has written, Christian thought about justice in society does not begin with a series of principles. Rather, following the example of the good Samaritan, Christian concern begins with the concrete case of a neighbor who is in a ditch. The demands of justice, he argues, are best disclosed in concrete situations.[32]

Right, Rights, and Justice in the Social Order

The goals of governance are to render an ordered space that endures over time and (1) provides opportunity for the church to carry out its mission and

---

31. See, e.g., Isaiah Berlin, "The Hedgehog and the Fox," in *The Proper Study of Mankind: An Anthology of Essays*, ed. Henry Hardy and Roger Hausheer (New York: Farrar, Straus, and Giroux, 1998), 436–98, and Ronald Dworkin, *Justice for Hedgehogs* (Cambridge, MA: Belknap Press of Harvard University Press, 2011).

32. See Duncan Forrester, *Christian Justice and Public Policy* (Cambridge: Cambridge University Press, 1997), 121.

(2) is structured according to what is "right" or "fitting" in relation to a common good. These are goals of governance that flow directly from beliefs about human nature and destiny that Christians share. However, if "right" defines a just social order, one must ask, what is the "right" that moral discrimination on the part of ruler and ruled is to discern? Christian tradition is uniform in its response. "Right" is determined by the will of God, and the will of God is to be found in the various "goods" of our created nature. These goods may be discerned by human reason and/or in the revealed law of God, to which Holy Scripture is a definitive witness. There is agreement that right is determined by God's will, but the interpretation of what that means is far from uniform. There is agreement neither about the power of reason nor the adequacy of revelation apart from reason.

When it comes to moral knowledge, sorting out the relation between reason and revelation is yet another task that lies beyond the scope of this book. Arguments about their competence and reach will not be laid to rest within the course of history. Given the uncertainties about the relation between the two and the fallible and limited nature of all human judgments, it is wise (when it comes to making judgments about what is fitting within a particular social order) to maintain a certain reserve about human judgment. Rather than certainty in these matters, Christian wisdom counsels prayer for the grace of practical wisdom—practical wisdom born of what I have called love's little helpers, namely, humility of mind, gentleness, long-suffering, forbearance, diligence for unity, kindness, tenderheartedness, and forgiveness.

These graces lead to the "recognition" of one's fellow citizens (all of them) as deserving of consideration and sympathy as one struggles to discern what is "right" or "fitting." That said, discernment of what is "right" or "fitting" cannot be adequate if the question of "rights" in the more modern sense is ignored. The question is whether Christian tradition has anything to say about "rights" that might be binding on Christians by virtue of the fact that they are Christian. The answer to this question is far from obvious. As Roger Ruston has pointed out, talk among Christians of universal rights is a relatively new phenomenon. Before World War II it was common to speak of "just judgment" and "the rights of man," but not "individual rights."[33] He then goes on to say, "Christianity and other biblical religions have traditionally expressed morality in terms of doing the will of God, which does not easily translate into the language of rights."[34]

Despite its novelty and the difficulties associated with it, the emergence of rights language into prominence cannot be avoided and in certain ways is to

---

33. Roger Ruston, *Human Rights and the Image of God* (London: SCM, 2004), 3.
34. Ibid., 4.

be welcomed. The language of "rights" now serves a very important moral purpose. In a pluralistic world, rights language speaks of the moral unity of humankind. As such, it has provided a language of international justice that can penetrate regional and national boundaries. Still, the language of rights poses questions that suggest careful consideration when it comes to its incorporation into Christian usage. Ruston points out that from its inception in the eighteenth century, political liberalism has tied rights to one form or another of individualism. In contrast to Christian tradition, liberalism begins with an abstract individual with interests rather than a notion of the common good. Christian social thought, however, has always located the good of an individual within a common good apart from which individual good cannot possibly be good.

No matter how attached one may be to the language of rights, there are obvious conflicts between its basic assumptions and those of Christian social thought. The point is of such importance that it bears repeating. To cite Ruston once again, what he calls the "Catholic view of rights" begins not with the free choices of individuals but with the social person made in God's image, endowed with reason and freedom, and able to tell the difference between good and evil.[35] According to this view of human nature, personality is not self-generated but grows out of relationships with God and with other people who have the same built-in goals and needs. These shared goals and needs set the conditions for human flourishing, and any justifiable account of what is "right" must be derived from them. Further, any claim to have "a right" must, among other things, be able to find a home within the circle that these goals and needs inscribe.

When it comes to the language of individual rights, there is due cause for caution, but there is also good reason to recognize the moral gains the notion of human rights has brought with it. The problem presented within an ecclesially focused ethic is how and to what extent this language is to be incorporated into the ways Christians speak when they are speaking not simply as interested citizens but also as Christians. The problem is difficult for a number of reasons, but one of the most basic arises because of the ambiguities connected with the phrase "to have a right." A right may refer to a freedom or entitlement one can claim as one's own by law. So one can say I have a legal or constitutional right to speak openly about a contested matter of public interest or religious belief. In this sense, legal rights serve within the social arena as "trump cards."[36] That is, in seeking what is right and fitting within a commonwealth (all things

---

35. Ibid., 11.
36. See, e.g., Dworkin, *Justice for Hedgehogs*, 329.

being equal), the right to free speech cannot be denied. More often than not, however, claims about rights do not refer to legally established freedoms and protections. They are not trump cards people actually hold. Rather, they are strong ethical statements about what they believe to be right rather than what actually is the law.[37]

These two senses of having a right are often run together in ways that cause enormous confusion, frustration, and bitterness. That is, having said that people *ought to have a right to x*, it is assumed that this statement leads necessarily to the conclusion that there *ought to be a law that guarantees x*. A prime example of this questionable elision is the way in which the Universal Declaration of Human Rights is commonly understood and used. The declaration is clearly a moral statement about the freedoms and entitlements human beings ought to enjoy simply on the basis of their common humanity. But does it imply the moral necessity of passing a law that guarantees this or that freedom or entitlement? In short, is the declaration a statement of aspiration about what we ought to work toward, or is it a moral demand for immediate legal action? For example, the declaration declares that since all people are born free and equal, they should enjoy freedoms such as equality before the law, a right to life, and protection from discrimination and slavery (articles 7, 3, 2, 4). It declares also on the basis of shared freedom and equality that all people ought to have a right to a number of entitlements such as affordable housing, medicine, education, child care, enough money to live on, and medical help when one is old (article 22). A similar list of rights, both of freedoms and entitlements, is contained in the recent social teaching of the Roman Catholic Church. So for example in 1963, in his encyclical *Pacem in Terris*, Pope John XXIII states,

> Man has a right to live. He has the right to bodily integrity and to the means necessary for the proper development of life, particularly food, clothing, shelter, medical care, rest and finally, the necessary social services. In consequence he has the right to be looked after in the event of ill health, disability stemming from his work, widowhood, old age, enforced unemployment, or whenever through no fault of his own he is deprived of the means of livelihood.[38]

This list is given particular force by Pope John's assertion that the very function of government is to procure certain rights. Indeed, he understands the function of public authority in terms of rights and duties. The authorities are to "recognize, respect, coordinate, safeguard, and promote citizens' rights and duties."

37. See, e.g., Sen, *Idea of Justice*, 357–58.
38. Pope John XXIII, *Pacem in Terris* 11, www.papalencyclicals.net/John23/23pacem.htm.

If this statement is taken as a description of those things toward which political authority ought to aspire, it can be understood as a restatement of the traditional view that the goal of government is to render just judgment. If, however, it is a statement to the effect that just government is under an obligation to see that laws are passed that guarantee not only the freedoms but also the entitlements that appear in the pope's list of "rights," it becomes more than problematic. For example, it is clear that political authority ought to prohibit any and all acts of murder. Everyone can agree on that. Murder robs the victim of freedom to continue existing. It is a right that obtains regardless of time and circumstance. The only morally acceptable argument in this case is whether a given act of taking life is in fact a case of murder. By way of contrast, assigning political authority an obligation to provide for public health, adequate housing, and education does not apply in all circumstances. To make legal arrangement for these entitlements makes government responsible for providing a range of services that for a variety of reasons may lie outside the realm of possibility or may be socially disruptive in unacceptable ways. These entitlements may be asserted as moral goals or ideals in ways that Christians, as Christians, certainly ought to support. Nevertheless, when the demand to pay attention to those rights that have justifiable claim on Christian moral belief and practice becomes also a claim that support of a law providing for, say, universal health care is a law that Christians, as Christians, must support, one moves into the realm of prudential judgment. In this realm, moral and practical decisions are matters of practical reason and as such are matters about which there can be reasonable disagreement. There is indeed a clear Christian warrant to care for the sick, but no matter how passionately we may support it, there is no such warrant for a particular public arrangement for the provision of care. This is a matter for public discourse and argumentation rather than religiously motivated judgment that speaks with dogmatic certainty.

Ruston is surely right to note that it is extremely difficult to translate a morality based in the will of God into the language of rights. Nevertheless, given that discussion of what constitutes a just society is now carried on in the language of rights, one cannot simply bypass this discussion and use the language of "right" without discussing the relation between "right" and "rights." It is at this point that the churches have a lot of work to do. In particular, they need to become far more conscious than they are now about the difference between using rights language to express a strong moral conviction and using that language to say that there ought to be a law that creates a particular right that individuals in a real sense "own."

Transition and Summary

As I have indicated, a good degree of caution is called for on the part of the churches as they seek to incorporate the language of rights into Christian moral vocabulary, for at least two reasons. First, as usually employed, the language of rights is tied to a view of social life that begins with autonomous individuals who claim "rights." These rights inevitably conflict, and so the work of political authority is to limit and order the struggle between the various claimants. By contrast, Christian social thought begins with a view of human nature that places each person first of all within a society that has a common good. The good of each individual is found by participation in that commonwealth. The work of political authority is to render just judgments that create a public space in which the goods of both society and its individual members are protected and enhanced. The second reason for caution is that failure to distinguish adequately between assertion of a right as a moral conviction and possession of a right as a matter of law leads Christians to fault the conscience of other Christians and other citizens simply because they have made different and fallible prudential judgments.

What then are the beliefs that Christians as Christians are to hold about the basis and goals of political authority? How does a person whose moral vision is formed within a school for the service of the Lord view the powers that be? To this point, our answers to these questions have proved modest in their extent, but as we will see, they are powerful in their implications. The basis of political authority does not lie in human wit and will but in divine providence—providence that provides ordered spaces within the conflicts that make the warp and woof of history. The goal of establishing these ordered spaces is to provide forms of civil order that allow the church to carry out its mission in "peace and tranquility" and to provide a public space that is ordered according to what is "right."

These are the things that Christians, as Christians, have to say about the basis and goals of political authority. They paint the origin and goals of political authority in broad perspective, and in doing so they place limits on the laws and policies that can claim support by clear Christian warrant. Most of what counts as political argument does not fall within the realm of clear Christian teaching. Rather, it falls within the realm of prudential judgment, which is best determined by public discourse rather than authoritative teaching. In the give and take of public argument, it is easier to claim clear Christian warrant for judgments about "rights" that protect the freedoms intrinsic to human nature than it is "rights" that (desirable as they may be) guarantee individual entitlements. It is also easier to find clear Christian warrant for condemnation of laws that violate the sacred character of each human life than it is to provide such warrant for particular policy decisions or legal arrangements meant to remedy those violations. These are things that Christians, as Christians, have to say about political authority. There remains, however, the question of the character of political authority and the relation of the churches and individual Christians to that order, and it is to these questions that we turn next.

12

An Ecclesial View
of Life within Political Society

Part Two

The Character of Political Authority

If a person's view of political authority has been formed within a school for the service of the Lord, how do they identify the marks that disclose the moral identity of the authority that rules over them? They begin with the general observation that political authority can serve both as an agent of God and an agent of evil. It is the former of these alternatives of which Paul speaks in the thirteenth chapter of his Letter to the Romans. It is the latter alternative of which John speaks in the Apocalypse. Because the former alternative describes the will of God for "the powers that be," it points the way to understanding the sort of character divine providence seeks to establish. It is appropriate, therefore, to begin with a positive account of the goal of political authority within the providence of God rather than its demonic potential. According to Christian tradition, the divinely appointed goal of political authority is to establish ordered spaces that (1) allow the church to carry out its mission in "peace and tranquility" and (2) provide an enduring public space that is ordered according to what is "right." These goals provide means to identify the moral character of political authority. Its character can be measured by the extent to which its judgments are rendered in accord with what is "right." In short, the moral character of political authority is to be identified by the extent to which it establishes justice.

That said, it is also the case that an account of life in Christ that focuses on the common life of the church will show awareness that political authority can rise up as a form of demonic opposition to these divinely appointed purposes. In establishing order, it can make blasphemous claims and, in the name of justice, establish grotesque forms of injustice. In short, political authority has a Janus face. One side is the face of justice, and the other is the face not simply of injustice but evil. One side is the face of a servant of God. Another is the face of a rebel who seeks to unseat a just ruler. When it comes to taking the measure of the character of political authority, the basic question to ask is, which face do I see? Do I see a face of authority that seeks justice, even if it is flawed and incomplete; or do I see a face that "speaks great things" that are in fact blasphemous—things that put political authority in the place of God?

The obvious question is how to recognize which face one is looking at. This question is not easy to answer. Because all forms of justice are incomplete and flawed, it's often difficult to determine which face one is looking at. Evil always cloaks itself as good and so can easily hide its true identity. When authority has become an instrument of evil there are, however, certain signs that indicate something more sinister than the presence of this or that form of injustice. The chief among these appears when political authority turns directly against the church because of its own claims to divinity. The first sign that political authority has gone rogue is a claim for loyalty that takes the place of loyalty to God. The chief mark of political authority that denies the limited ends for which it exists is its claim to be what Thomas Hobbes called "a mortal god."

A claim of this sort can take a variety of forms, but the subtlest and most dangerous is a failure by authority to recognize that it has only a "passing usefulness."[1] Within the providence of God, political authority is authorized to render judgment in respect to what is just and unjust, and that is all! It is not authorized to claim responsibility for procuring the higher goods of human nature and destiny.[2] When it makes such claims, political authority has certainly become an agent of evil.

It is of the utmost importance not to make an ill-considered judgment in this matter. Though the goal of political authority is to render judgment that

---

1. I owe this nice phrase to Oliver O'Donovan. See O'Donovan, *Ways of Judgment*, 4.
2. Ibid.

establishes a public space ordered according to what is right, that goal is never fully realized and may on many occasions be missed altogether. When it comes to justice, one is always dealing with imperfection and limits to what is possible. In the face of the uncertainty and imperfection of political judgment, it is tempting to identify differing political opinion or flawed political action as evil. However, the key to identifying authority as evil is not political disagreement but claims to absolute authority—claims that border on pretensions to divinity. Claims such as these do not recognize the temporary and partial character of political authority. When the claims of political authority burst the bounds of fallibility and imperfection, it always asserts itself by the use of power that replaces truth in public discourse with lies and replaces what is "right" for society with particular goals that serve only its own glory. When these things take place, one may be certain one is facing "the beast that speaks great things and blasphemies" (Rev. 13:5).[3]

Most of the time political authority does not go this far. In rendering judgment, it makes allowance for its own limits and fallibility. No matter what the form of government, there usually remains room for independent action and open criticism. Thus the more common question is not how to identify evil but how to identify and correct obvious injustice. This political task does not begin with a Platonic model of a just society that faults all other forms of governance. Rather, it begins with obvious cases of injustice that authority has brought about or failed to address. In the normal run of things, when one is not faced with the evil face of political authority, this is the place to begin measuring the character of government. To begin with the perfect state rather than particular cases of injustice is to step dangerously close to divine pretention.

As I have argued, when judging the character of political authority, the place to begin is with justice for foxes, who know many small things, rather than justice for hedgehogs, who know one big thing. In the Christian line of sight, the first thing to catch the eye is not the institutions of government or grand moral principles like human freedom, equality, and dignity. The first thing to catch the eye is people who are lying in ditches. Upon seeing them, the one big thing Christians recognize is that each sufferer is created in God's image. In this sense only are Christians hedgehogs. They believe that each human life has sanctity. Each is infused with and surrounded by God's holiness. Sanctity is not so much a principle that preoccupies Christians but rather the lens through which they view each person they meet. It is what they see

---

3. I owe this translation to Grant Osborne. See Grant Osborne, *Revelation*, BECNT (Grand Rapids: Baker Academic, 2002), 498.

that gives a moral location to whatever it is that they see. The focus of their lens is first of all that of a fox. It directs attention to particulars. The eye sees first the distress of those who suffer, and the measure of the moral character of government is taken by what is done or not done to remedy that distress.

This point calls out for further explanation. I have argued that something like Grotius's idea of attributive justice fits well with Christian beliefs about the call of government. Government is to render judgments that protect and preserve those public freedoms that allow for the various forms of communication that compose social life and produce a common good. These judgments require attention to particulars as well as to considerations of general welfare. If a government fails to pay such attention, then in protecting or furthering the good of the whole it may simply leave those who are in the ditch where they are. The late senator Hubert Humphrey once said that the moral character of a society is best judged by the way in which it treats "those at the beginning of life, those at the end of life, and those in the shadows of life." The character of political authority, like that of the people it serves, can be assessed by the same test, and there is particular Christian warrant for doing so.

Christians believe that people are created not only in God's image but also as social beings. The life of creatures formed in the image of God is both generated and fulfilled not as solitary and autonomous agents but as social beings in the company of God and other people. Participation in the communications that make up social life is, therefore, an expression of human nature. To deny participation in these social interchanges constitutes an attack, even if indirect, on their person. Defense of a person's right to be social thus becomes a fundamental obligation not only of individuals but also of society and its governing authorities. Thus it may not be the case (as John Rawls has argued) that justice requires any inequality in the distribution of social resources to benefit the least well off, but it is true that inequalities that result in the inability of some to participate in the social exchanges that make life worth living call out for address. The moral character of political authority *and those whom it serves* ought to be judged by the way in which they treat those whose privations prevent or severely limit their participation in the social exchanges upon which the goods of life in the society of others depend.

This point requires Christian moral thought to take account of "rights" as well as "right." I have already pointed out that contemporary use of rights language is too frequently tied to an unacceptable form of individualism. Nevertheless, justice can never establish a social space ordered according to "right" if it does not protect the members of society by granting them certain "rights." Despite the questionable link between language of rights and forms of autonomous individualism, without rights that individuals in a sense "own," one is left with a society whose members have no faces. They are merely part of a crowd ordered by a utilitarian calculus or by one designed to support the interests of the strong.

The question, therefore, is which "rights" both support the common good of society and at the same time guarantee the integrity of its individual members. For Christians, this question raises two additional ones. First, which rights enjoy clear Christian warrant? Second, among those that do, which are "natural" possessions because they accord with human nature, which lie within the realm of "moral aspiration," and which within the realm of legal establishment? Too frequently these three possibilities are simply run together. For example, recognition of the sanctity of people who suffer from some disadvantage or impairment might well lead to a legitimate aspiration to bring about a change in their circumstances, but it does not immediately follow that there ought to be a law that relieves their distress. When it comes to making laws, there is a profound difference between laws that protect basic aspects of human nature like freedom and equality and those that provide entitlements for this or that benefit. It is far easier to establish a clear Christian warrant for those rights that protect basic freedoms and fundamental equality than it is to find clear warrant for the particular entitlements that support equality and make those freedoms possible.

For example, it is easier by clear Christian warrant to establish freedom of speech and association as rights of nature, aspiration, and legality than it is to establish education as a legally guaranteed entitlement. Or again, it is easier by clear Christian warrant to establish equality before the law as a natural right, a legitimate aspiration, and a legal right than it is to establish an equal and legally sanctioned right to health care. Because of our basic equality before God, a system of education open to all and a health care system equally open are both aspirations that do indeed enjoy clear Christian warrant. Nevertheless, this is not the case for a particular law that changes these rights into entitlements. Why is it that in one or another of these cases rights enjoy a clear Christian warrant, and in others, though they may be rights that qualify as fully warranted aspirations, they do not qualify as clearly warranted legal "rights"?

The answer is that denial of a right (all things being equal) to speak freely or (again all things being equal) to associate with one's fellow human beings is a blow struck against our created nature as social beings. On the other hand, an equal right of access to publically financed education or health care is dependent upon available resources and public assessment of these social goods in relation to others. In short, rights of entitlement are relative to social resources and commitments in a way that freedoms that are aspects of what it means to be a human being are not. Social and/or legal restrictions on the those freedoms essential to human nature demand a level of justification that far exceeds restrictions on the entitlements that support those freedoms.

That said, recognition of both the sort of freedom and equality to which people have a right by virtue of the fact that they are human beings, along with aspirations that seek laws that establish them as rights, depends in large measure upon people recognizing their fellow citizens as human beings of equal value to themselves. Recognition of this sort is even more important when it comes to establishing rights to entitlements that enhance but are not directly attached to our created nature. Rowan Williams, the former archbishop of Canterbury, has made much of the importance of "recognition" when it comes to a society establishing the rights of its citizens.[4] He wants to connect thinking about human rights with "religious convictions," particularly about "human *dignity* and human *relatedness*—how we belong together."[5] He believes this connection is best established not by tying rights in the first instance to the claims of individuals but by asking "what is involved in mutual *recognition* between human beings."[6] He believes, in short, that rights are best understood as a way of people working out what it is for them "to belong together in a society." He then goes on to observe that the "world of rights" based in recognition is in fact "anchored in habits of empathy and sympathy."[7]

A. I. Melden, in his work *Rights and Persons*, has made a similar point but from a philosophical point of view. He says, for example, that central to the task of establishing a right "is the understanding of the normative status of persons not merely as the psychological subjects of good or bad experiences but as beings who as agents owe each other the treatment that they are to give each other during the course of their lives with one another."[8]

The graces of empathy and sympathy are ones that stand near the center of the common life of the church, and they are powers of spirit that for Christians translate readily into relations with their fellow citizens. Recognition, empathy, and sympathy therefore press down upon the view Christians hold of what is "right" within a social order. Recognition also presses toward establishing

---

4. Williams, *Faith in the Public Square*, 161.
5. Ibid. Emphasis added.
6. Ibid. Emphasis added.
7. Ibid.
8. A. I. Melden, *Rights and Persons* (Berkeley: University of California Press, 1980), 28.

those "rights" that establish and defend those who may be treated unfairly in the competitive push and pull of social life.

It is important to note that "recognition, empathy, and sympathy" press down upon rather than lead necessarily to the views Christians hold of what is "right" and what "rights" political authority ought to grant the citizens it governs. In most cases where rights are under discussion, these powers of spirit do not yield conclusions all Christians by virtue of their faith must reach. In the vast majority of cases, conclusions about the right ordering of society and the particular rights its members ought to enjoy are prudential decisions subject to inadequacy and/or error. This fact presents a thorny question to any rendition of Christian moral belief and practice whose focus is the common life of the church. To what extent can the churches provide authoritative moral teaching that serves both as a witness to society and as a norm for the political commitments and actions of their members?

The Moral Teaching and Social Witness of the Churches

The question is urgent. The churches rightly believe that they have a duty to provide moral guidance to their members and to make a witness about justice in society. It is becoming increasingly apparent, however, that the churches are severely limited in their ability to instruct either society or their own members in these matters. Over the past two centuries the Vatican has issued a large number of teaching documents (encyclicals), but as issues like sex outside the bond of marriage, divorce, and birth control make abundantly clear, these documents (though of a very high quality) have had a mixed reception among the faithful. As for the Protestant churches, they appear unable either to arrive at agreed upon social teachings or to instruct either their own members or society at large.

This last point demands amplification. Since Leo XIII's encyclical *Rerum Novarum*, the Roman Catholic Church has sought to give moral instruction on social, economic, and political matters to both faithful Catholics and all people of good will. The Roman Catholic Church has a procedural means of doing so through the teaching authority of the pope as expressed in papal encyclicals and canon law. It has a theoretical means of doing so by reference to the universally binding implications of natural law. What the Roman Catholic Church does not have is pervasive recognition of its moral authority.

Recognizing that the Roman church could no longer rely upon the legal and social backing of civil authority, the deference of the general population, or even the full loyalty of its own membership, Leo XIII insisted that moral instruction now had to begin "from below"—through winning the assent of both the faithful and the general populace. Leo told his cardinals that the temporal mission of the church would from then on center on the faith embodied in the conscience of people. His was a notion of indirect power or action from the bottom up. The church in its relation to society now had only indirect authority exercised through the adequacy of its teaching and the power of its example.[9]

It would appear that Leo, in respect to the political life of the nations, was calling the Roman Catholic Church to look first within the fellowship of faithful Catholics to find both adequate teaching on social and political issues and exemplary lives that provide a powerful witness to that teaching. No longer does the Roman Catholic Church share political authority with the state. The authority of its teaching office comes less from on high than from underneath—from lives instructed by the teaching office but formed by the common life of the church. Realizing this fact, for the better part of two centuries the Roman Catholic Church has sought to adjust in a creative and convincing way to the increasing secularity of Western society.

So also have the Protestant churches, but with far less coherence and far less success. After the Second World War, realizing their more marginal social position, the Protestant churches attempted to shore up the crumbling foundations of what was often called "a Christian society." Their search was for a means of instructing conscience that, on the one hand, did not take the form of vague generalities like "there is a Christian responsibility to care for the poor" or, on the other hand, specific policy advocacy like "Christians ought to support a rise of 15 percent in the minimum wage." In search of a middle ground between these extremes, men like John Oldham, William Temple, Willem Visser 't Hooft, John Bennett, and Ronald Preston started a debate about what constitutes a "responsible society." Their focus was on what they called the "principles" and "middle axioms" upon which a responsible society should be based.[10] "Principles" referred to broad moral commitments like dignity, freedom, and service. "Middle axioms" referred to action guides that stood between basic principles on the one hand and concrete political, economic, or social policies like public housing projects or a national health system on the other. What these thinkers sought was

---

9. For an excellent account of Leo's views, see Russell Hittinger, "Introduction to Modern Catholicism," in *The Teaching of Modern Christianity on Law, Politics, and Human Nature*, ed. John Witte Jr. and Frank S. Alexander (New York: Columbia University Press, 2006), 14.

10. See, e.g., W. A. Visser 't Hooft and J. H. Oldham, *The Church and Its Function in Society* (London: George Allen & Unwin), 1937.

a shared social vision for Christians that allowed for reasonable disagreement over specifics of policy. They hoped that their proposals might provide a social and political vision that would preserve and strengthen what they understood to be a "Christian society." A little later, the Protestant churches, under pressure from churches in newly independent nations, began to move from a discussion of the nature of a "responsible society" to what they called a "just, participatory, and sustainable society." This sort of discussion soon came to involve various forms of advocacy on behalf of the poor and marginalized members of society; and with advocacy came support of particular social, economic, and political policies.[11]

In hindsight, the recent history of Protestant political thought reveals a number of problems. To begin with, the whole idea of a responsible society guided by principles and middle axioms presupposes a morality that all share. By this account, the church stands as the guardian of this morality and society's expert guide. This account imagines a society in which people with higher moral knowledge impose their vision of the good upon an uninformed populace. Another problem that has emerged over time with rather stark clarity is that in their move from principle to policy the churches have shown a remarkable inability to pronounce on these matters in a responsible manner. What they have to say often appears simply foolish. An even more serious issue that has emerged in the move from principle to policy is this: by advocating in the name of Christ particular policy options over which there can be legitimate differences of opinion, the Protestant churches in particular fault in an illegitimate manner the consciences of those members who have good reasons not to agree with their pronouncements.

By way of summary, it is fair to say that, though the various encyclicals issued by the Holy Office are of a high quality, their authority in the eyes of a significant number of their own members is limited. Selective acceptance obtains to an even greater extent within the mind of the general public. In respect to the Protestant churches, it is fair to say that, on the whole, their pronouncements simply lack credibility. This lack stems in no small measure from the poor quality of what they have to say. Some years ago Professor James Gustafson noted in respect to the Protestant churches that "the situation ... with regard to moral teaching is only a little short of chaos."[12] In a later publication, he spoke even more forcefully. "What is reprehensible about a great deal of [Protestant] ecclesial moralizing is the intellectual and

---

11. For a helpful summary of this history, see Ronald Preston, *Church and Society in the Twentieth Century: The Economic and Political Task* (London: SCM, 1983), 83–88.

12. James Gustafson, *Protestant and Roman Catholic Ethics* (Chicago: University of Chicago Press, 1984), 130.

academic flabbiness of most of the pronouncements." He went on to say, "The single-minded moralism that Protestant churches engage in is morally irresponsible."[13]

Both the Roman Catholic and the Protestant churches rightly feel that they are called to instruct conscience and make a social witness, but both are confronted with formidable problems when doing so. How are they to bear a social witness in circumstances where they are but one voice among many, can claim no privileged place, and hold very limited authority even over the conscience of their own members? The question is both real and pressing for the reasons cited above. There are in addition social factors that make the problem even more difficult. James Davison Hunter has pointed out that, to a disturbing degree, groups within society now have validity only by rights conferred by the state. Problems affecting society are not viewed in the first instance as aspects of the interrelation of a complex of social practices and institutions or as matters concerning social relations between individuals. Rather, they are seen as aspects of the order provided by the state. As a result, social life in all its dimensions is increasingly interpreted through the filter of partisan political beliefs and attachments. It is commonly held that all conflicts must find a political solution. Thus, as Hunter writes, "Each and every faction in society seeks the patronage of state power as a means of imposing its particular understanding of the good on the whole of society."[14] He goes on to say, "This turn toward politics means that we find it difficult to think of a way to address public . . . problems or issues in any way that is not political."[15]

It is impossible not to notice that the same partisan conflict that so divides society now also divides the membership of the various churches. As I have noted, even though the Roman Catholic Church has more adequate tools to address these divisions, their effectiveness is in important respects limited. In the present age, all issues have in a sense become political, and the social divisions that follow have negatively affected the churches. No matter what the venue, whether the discussion concerns sex, marriage, the birth of children, or death, the issue is soon politicized. Politics runs all the way down, no matter what the issue might be, and the churches seem unable to handle these divisions any better than society as a whole.

The question is, what can be done to address this sad situation? Nothing can be done until the churches, particularly the Protestant ones, make clear

---

13. James Gustafson, *Ethics from a Theocentric Perspective* (Chicago: University of Chicago Press, 1991), 2:318.
14. James Davison Hunter, *To Change the World: The Irony, Tragedy and Possibility of Christianity in the Later Modern World* (Oxford: Oxford University Press, 2010), 102.
15. Ibid., 105.

who speaks for the church and what in particular the churches, as churches, are called upon to say. To arrive at a responsible answer to these questions, the churches must ask and answer some additional ones.[16]

1. Out of the many issues that arise in the realms of social, economic, and political life, which are the ones the churches are called upon to address, and why?
2. What purpose ought an ecclesial pronouncement or teaching on a given issue serve? Ought that purpose to be prophetic condemnation of a given practice or policy coupled with advocacy for alternatives? Or ought the purpose to be pedagogical—an attempt to instruct a given public in respect to the moral issues attendant upon a social or political controversy?
3. If the churches speak on a matter, what audience or audiences ought they to have in mind? Ought they to speak primarily to their own membership, or ought they seek to instruct or correct society as a whole as well?
4. If the churches decide they are called to speak on a given issue, what language ought they to use? Ought they to speak in terms that are generally negotiable in society, or ought they to speak using a specifically Christian vocabulary?
5. If the churches decide they are called upon to speak, what form of communication ought they to employ? For example, do the churches pass a resolution? Or do they seek to facilitate or moderate a dialogue in order to exchange views? Or do they favor a teaching document like those issued over the past couple of centuries by the popes?
6. Finally, what procedures ought to be followed and what tests employed so that, should the churches speak on a matter, one can be sure that those speaking indeed speak for the church rather than for a victorious party within the church?

In one way or another, Roman Catholic social teaching has taken questions like these into account, but their Protestant counterparts have not. Had they asked and sought to answer these questions in dialogue with the Roman Catholic Church, their moralizing would have had a better chance of escaping the "flabby," "reprehensible," and "irresponsible" character mentioned by Professor Gustafson. Had they thought things out with the same care as the Roman Catholic Church, they might be able, as churches, to take a constructive

---

16. For an extended discussion of these questions, see Philip Turner, "How the Church Might Teach," in *The Crisis in Moral Teaching in the Episcopal Church*, ed. Timothy Sedgwick and Philip Turner (Harrisburg, PA: Morehouse, 1992), 137–59. For background to the question of what might be called "the ethics of ecclesiastical pronouncements," see Paul Ramsey, *Who Speaks for the Church?* (Nashville: Abingdon, 1967), and *Speak Up for Just War or Pacifism*.

and credible part in the social and political struggles that now so divide the populations of North America and Europe. One thing that seems certain is that until the Protestant churches undertake the hard work of answering these questions in conversation with their Roman Catholic counterparts, they will continue to diminish rather than enhance their credibility in the eyes of the general population. In short, if the churches are to make the sort of social witness they are called upon to make, they will have to make clear who speaks for the church and what is proper for them to say.

The Social Witness of the Churches and the Defense of Their Integrity

These are the steps that, if taken, would clear the way for the churches to speak (as churches rather than as parties within churches) directly and with credibility to the issues that arise within political society. There are, however, things to be said and done by the churches that are tied more directly to specifically Christian beliefs about the calling of political authority under God and the integrity of the church as God's people. Chief among these is a witness to political authority and the people under its governance about the limited purpose and duration of political authority. To quote W. H. Auden, the existence and mandate of political authority is only "for the time being."[17] Even if one takes the more optimistic view of political authority contained in Roman Catholic social teaching, the authority of the various forms of governance lasts only as long as imperfection and sin have power to shape human affairs. When Christ returns to be our judge, God's rule will be fully established. Human authorities will pass away and God will be "all in all," the ruler of all things and all people who exercises his authority over the peoples of the earth directly.

The sway of political authority is for a limited time only. The extent of its jurisdiction is also limited. Political authority within the providence of God is established with the specific purpose of rendering judgment. That judgment is meant, within the providence of God, to establish "right" within the social order and so create a peaceful space in which the church can make its witness. The purposes of human governance are limited in both duration and extent; and they are linked to yet another specifically Christian belief. No matter what their nationality or tribe may be, Christians have a more fundamental citizenship and loyalty than to nation, tribe, family, or self. Their ruler and their citizenship is "in heaven." That is to say, their citizenship, the source of

---

17. W. H. Auden, "For the Time Being, A Christmas Oratorio," in *Collected Poems*, ed. Edward Mendelson (New York: Modern Library, 2007), 349–400.

their basic identity and their most fundamental loyalty, is rooted in God rather than in nation, tribe, family, or personal identity.

This is the basic political message the churches have been called to deliver, but sadly they rarely do. Family, tribe, nation, and personal identity are among the most common and powerful idols to which people turn to guarantee their fragile existence. To be sure, all provide a God-given place to stand (at least for the time being), but none provide either impregnable defenses or fulfilling identities. In relation to political authority, the chief calling of the church is, therefore, not to become a powerful player in the struggle to control public space and opinion. It is, rather, to remind its own members and all people both of the limited and temporary nature of the walls that they erect under providence to protect the fragility of their lives and of the strategies they devise to give them meaning. The identification of God's purpose with those of one's nation, tribe, family, or personal wants and needs is without question the most common form of idolatry. Chief among the responsibilities of the churches is to remind their members and all people of good will that these are limited goods that cannot provide the sort of fulfillment all people seek, and only God can provide them.

The chief political witness of the churches is therefore worship that declares the citizenship of their members, on the one hand, and witnesses to the limited good provided by the political order, on the other. It is also a responsibility of the churches to defend their own borders against incursions by political authority. If churches are not called to become the political architect of a society or the boosters of particular social policies, they are nevertheless called to defend their own borders against attempts by political authority to dictate either the terms of their common life or the nature of their engagement with the social and political order. In respect to relations between political authority and the churches, one can be certain that those in power will not want the churches interfering in their business. They will nonetheless want the blessing of the churches pronounced upon what they do. Pressures to provide such a blessing are relentless, and the history of the church is filled with examples of failure to resist them.

As long as history lasts, the churches will have to defend their borders against hostile incursion. As part of that defense, they will also be called upon to remind political authority that most of life rightly takes place beyond the reach of its controlling arm. It is the belief of Christians that people are created as social beings and that their destiny is to live as social beings. It is also part of their belief that the providential role of political authority is limited. People flourish as human beings by taking part in the various forms of communication and exchange that compose a common good. Within God's providence, political authority is charged with regulating these systems in a way that, as O'Donovan writes, preserves the public freedoms that create the space in which individuals can exercise their innate freedom to think and act.[18] Individual freedom is a part of the social air people breathe as they go about the business of living. It does not depend upon political authority for its existence. Indeed, when political authority extends its reach into the spheres that properly belong to individual freedoms, it exceeds its boundaries. It does so either by exerting authority to crush freedom or by using authority in a pretentious way to take charge of human betterment.

Political authority functions within its proper limits when it provides a framework in which people and social organizations can go about their daily business. Within this framework, the job of political authority is not to become the architect of public good. Its job is more reactive than constructive. Its work is to make right what injures public good. It exceeds its proper limits when it seeks to create an ideal social order or when it attempts on a smaller scale to make people better. O'Donovan terms this limitation on political authority as "the reactive principle."[19] As he says, it is a principle that "supposes that harmony is not a design conceived in a ruler's head, but a nexus of social communications that exist and flourish antecedently."[20]

He rightly points out that this view of political authority in no way implies minimal government. Defense against injury of one sort or another can in fact lead to extensive governmental responsibility. Further, overly restrictive limitation of these responsibilities and powers can in its own way prove just as harmful as overextension. In carrying out its appointed role, political authority is to be reactive rather than invasive or architectonic. This reactive view of political authority is rooted in Christian anthropology and in Christian views of the providential role of governance. Human beings are social, one wants to say, "all the way down." They rightly look to political authority not for the perfection of their lives but for an ordered space in which they can pursue their lives in ways that benefit both themselves and the societies of which they are a part.

Central to the witness of the churches to "the powers that be" is making clear the limits of political authority and protecting their own boundaries from illicit incursions. It is also a part of its witness to prepare its members for responsible citizenship. If Christians are to act politically, they must be capable of political action. The church, I have argued, should itself be understood

18. O'Donovan, *Ways of Judgment*, 55.
19. Ibid., 60–61.
20. Ibid., 61.

in part as a political entity that prepares its members for political action. In preparing to act politically, Christian wisdom does not begin with principles. Neither does it begin with support of specific political solutions to public issues. Rather, it flows from a community of men and women whose formation as Christians prepares them for political action within the political realm.

This experience, as previously noted, underlines the central importance of truth and reconciliation for political and social health. To these graces must be added a particular concern for the people whom the late senator Hubert Humphrey described as those "at the beginning of life, those at the end of life, and those in the shadows of life." The beginning, the end, and the shadows of life indicate the weakest and most vulnerable members of society. These are the people who have no power to help themselves. They are utterly dependent upon the care of others, and as such they exemplify the nature of the human condition and point to the depth of God's love. It is not possible by clear Christian warrant to demand support of any given policy that claims to be a solution to their plight, but it is possible to say that, in making public judgments, political authority is called upon to do what it can to protect them and see that they are included once more within the life of society.

There is yet another reason that this particular social concern and political interest receives direct support from Christian belief and practice. The Christian view of the social nature of human beings has a number of moral and political implications. Among the most important is the conviction that to reduce anyone to such a state of privation that they are unable to take part in the give and take of social life is a patent evil that demands address. Christian belief presses down upon conscience and calls out for people who are effectively excluded from participation in the give and take of social life to be *recognized*. Recognition of their plight seems to me a better way of expressing Christian concern than does the now popular call for giving a "preferential option for the poor." Baldly stated, "preferential option" calls to mind the writing of a blank check. Attributive justice, however, will not allow the writing of blank checks. It calls for making judgments that protect the particular forms of communication and exchange that compose the fabric of social life. This form of justice demands the exercise of practical wisdom—wisdom that can effectively order the various goods that compose one that is common.

In this judgment, the poor cannot be passed by. For Christian reasons they must be recognized and given special attention, but their needs are always held in a balance with others. Nevertheless, for a person whose moral vision and abilities have been formed within a school for the service of the Lord, the state of those at the beginning, those at the end, and those in the shadows of life is a matter of constant and pressing concern. These people provide a primary point for assessing the moral health not only of the church but also of society. It is an aspect of the social and political responsibility of the churches to form the moral sensibilities of their members so that "the needy are not forgotten nor the hope of the poor taken away."[21] For Christians, concern for the state of the poor is not a voluntary matter that can be attached to the calling of some people but not others. It is a clear implication of the most fundamental beliefs that Christians hold both about the nature of God and about the nature of human beings as created by God.

The Responsibilities of Christians as Citizens

Given what has been said about the calling of the churches in relation to political authority, what is to be said about the civic responsibilities of individual Christians? The first responsibility of Christians in their role as citizens is to participate in the political life of their society in the ways open to them. The most immediate means of participation is simply to pay one's taxes. Taxes make the exercise of political authority possible. St. Paul was quite right when he admonished Christians to "pay taxes to whom taxes are due, revenue to whom revenue is due, respect to whom respect is due, honor to whom honor is due" (Rom. 13:7). The authorities, he said, are "ministers of God" (13:6). Their responsibility under God is to establish forms of order that allow the church to carry out its mission. They are also there to establish a public space that provides people an opportunity to enter forms of common life that lie outside the circle of their private concerns. In these ways, Christians understand political authority to be divinely appointed. As such it deserves the willing support of God's people first of all with a share of their wealth.

The fact that political authority is, within Christian tradition, considered a divinely appointed provision implies as well that the public arena is one that requires their interest and appropriate involvement. The means and extent of involvement vary from political order to political order. The extent of involvement varies with the form of governance. The intensity of involvement varies with social location, particular circumstances, and particular responsibilities. No matter the degree of variation, however, some degree of participation is a moral requirement for Christians. Paying taxes is the first that comes to mind. Voting is the second. For one whose conscience is formed within a school for the service of the Lord, voting is more than a means of expressing one's political convictions, ensuring one's representation, or even pursuing one's self-interest. It is a means of public witness to and participation in God's

---

21. Book of Common Prayer, Suffrage A from Morning Prayer.

merciful provision for his creation. To withdraw from this public role into a purely private sphere of existence is, in a way, to turn one's back on God.

Within a democratic society, there are means available to the general public to participate in the political order that go beyond paying taxes and voting. One may become an advocate for or an opponent of one or another public policy, and one may express one's preference for or opposition to a given configuration of political judgment. At this point individuals are called upon to take account of their particular circumstances and, within that limit, exercise their own practical wisdom. I have insisted that it is not appropriate for churches to dictate the manner in which a person exercises such wisdom. This is a matter of conscience determined by the dictates of one's own practical reason.

The conclusions of that exercise are one's own, but insofar as they have been shaped by participation in the common life of the church, they will include "recognition" of those at the beginning of life, those at the end of life, and those in the shadows of life. This recognition will not lead to necessary conclusions about policy options, but it will necessarily include one concern—namely, the opportunity to work. To be sure, no society can provide full employment. Nevertheless, the limits of what can be done do not imply that opportunity for employment is a concern that can simply be shoved aside. For adults, if there is no opportunity to work, a primary door (there are others) that provides access to participation in social life is closed. To accept or even encourage unemployment as simply a necessary aspect of any economic system constitutes a direct attack on the social nature of humankind. Attributive justice requires prudential judgments that include the good of all, not just some. In this respect, conscience formed within a school for the service of the Lord is particularly sensitive to those who are weak or who have been excluded in the allocation of goods within a "commonwealth." Recognition of the importance of each member of the "body" is fundamental to an ethic focused on the common life of the church, and this form of recognition necessarily spills over into the public life of political society. It becomes a graceful habit of mind.

The fact that political order is divinely established and maintained requires various forms of participation on the part of Christians. There are, however, a few points at which conscience formed within the church has, for some, placed limits on this duty. The best known is war. For good reason, many Christians from the earliest time have thought Jesus's teaching and example prohibited participation in this particular form of political action. In respect to his teaching they ask, "In his Sermon on the Mount, did not Jesus forbid his disciples from taking revenge (Matt. 5:38–41)? Did he not teach them not to resist one who is evil (5:39)? Did he not insist that when the imperial power of Rome demanded forced labor of them, they were to do even more than asked?" Jesus's teaching is that, if struck on the right cheek, his disciples were to offer the left one as well, and that teaching applies to the question of killing an enemy in combat. In respect to his example, pacifist Christians point out that Jesus expressly forbade his disciples to use force to protect him and that he went voluntarily to his death trusting in the power of God rather than human might to save him.

Two of the men who have had the greatest influence on this book, John Howard Yoder and Stanley Hauerwas, are pacifists because they believe, on the basis of passages like this one, that to take up arms against one's enemy betrays central tenets of Christian belief and practice. They hold that Jesus forbade vengeance and violent attack not only because they are morally forbidden but even more because self-protection of this sort indicates a lack of faith in God's providential care. Thus John Howard Yoder draws a sharp distinction between life outside and life inside the perfection of Christ's victory. The specific calling of Christians is to be a witness to what life within that circle is like. It may be right for those who live outside the perfection of Christ to resort to force, but not for those who live within.

Some years ago, when I first began to think about war and peace and the relation of my faith to these two states, it was often said that pacifism was a matter of vocation to which not all were called. Pacifists, they said, had been specially appointed to bear witness to the depth of God's love for his enemies. On the other hand, those who did not have this call could with good conscience join in an armed struggle to defend their country. I note that I never heard this latter position supported by a pacifist, and with good reason. Their point is that nonresistance is not a special calling but of the essence of Christian belief and practice. For Yoder and Hauerwas, to fail to turn the other cheek, even be it in a "just war," is to manifest a lack of faith in God's providence. The job of Christians, they argue, is to make a witness from within "the perfection of Christ" and in this way show the world the way to God.

So the consciences of those formed within a school for the service of the Lord are confronted with a divided tradition on a grave matter of civic responsibility. On the one hand, Christians are called upon to protect, even by the use of force, their neighbors and the order providence has provided for their safety. This is one way to show both respect for God's provision and love for one's neighbors when they are under attack. On the other hand lies a view that the calling of Christians is to live within "the perfection of Christ." In this space, Christians (all of them) are called upon to give an uncompromised witness to God's providential care and love, even for their enemies.

In the earlier discussion of the Sermon on the Mount, I noted this division and said this argument will remain unresolved as long as time lasts. Now some pages later I continue to hold that belief. The difference between pacifists and those who are often called "just warriors" will continue as an unresolved dispute, even division, within God's people. For my part, I believe that God provides order within human affairs and that I have neighbors whose safety demands defense of that order and protection from their attackers. I believe also that my participation in efforts to defend my people against others can itself be understood as "acting into history" in a way that expresses trust in God's providence, even if those arrangements are fragile and obtain only "for the time being."

That said, there are good reasons, despite the divinely appointed ministry of political authority, for Christians in some instances to support outright disobedience to that authority. Political authority can exceed its limits or fail in the execution of its mandate in two ways. On the one hand, it can take on the trappings of divinity. On the other, it can fail to execute judgment according to what is right. Whenever the first occurs, Christians are required by their belief to withhold both their loyalty and obedience. Indeed, if political authority persists in its pretentions and demands for something like worship, Christians may be required by their faith to give up their life rather than "bow the knee." The demonic potential inherent in the very existence of political authority and the requirement of God that we worship only him implies that martyrdom is a possible calling for any and all Christians. The Greek word for martyr means "witness," and the giving of one's life for the truth of God is the quintessential expression of that witness. On the far side of citizenship lies the possibility of martyrdom. As Revelation makes plain, truth telling and the worship of one God are central marks of Christian identity. Either one or both of these can place one's life in the balance. Christians have always known that, and to the extent they have understood the depth of God's claim upon their lives, they always will.

When political authority makes divine claims for itself, Christians know that objection may cost their lives. In most cases, however, conflict between conscience and demands for obedience on the part of political authority do not go this far. The issue for conscience is usually not pretention to divinity but judgments that are manifestly unjust. What is to be done when political authority renders a judgment that, because of the egregious nature of its injustice, cannot in good conscience be obeyed? What is to be done if one is confronted not with a political disagreement (like the size of the national debt) but with a social policy (like segregation) that denies other human beings the right to adequate participation in the life of society? What is to be done if the normal political means of changing such a situation have proven to be ineffective?

If change through normal channels lies out of reach, rebellion against an unjust regime or revolution that seeks to change an entire political system is a possibility that lies at the extreme edge of what, for Christians, is a morally permissible means of protecting their neighbors. Far more frequently, the injustices of political authority are less extreme, and its persistence on an unjust path less adamant. In this sort of situation, concern to see justice done may lead properly to civil disobedience. Civil disobedience does not seek, as in a rebellion, to bring down a regime. It does not seek, as in a revolution, to change an entire political system. Its purpose, when normal political means are ineffective, is simply to be rid of a political judgment that is patently unjust, a gross offense to conscience, and in no way supportable. When this is the case, disobedience to the judgments of political authority is aimed only at being rid of a particular form of injustice. Civil disobedience does not call into question the authority of government. Indeed, from the time of Plato, acceptance of punishment has been required of those who are civilly disobedient as a sign that they do not dispute the authority of government, only one or more of its particular judgments.[22]

Politics as a Vocation

There is at least one more thing Christians, as Christians, have to say about their participation in a political order. Politics may and can for some people be a Christian vocation. Some people may be "called" in one way or another to make of politics what we now call a career. Politics may be for them the chief way in which they participate in the give and take of social life. It may be for them one of the chief ways in which they honor God, express love for their neighbors, and live out their social nature.

The questions are, on what basis might it rightly be said that politics may be a Christian vocation, and on what basis might one say that a person's gifts and graces qualify them for this particular calling? First, why might someone whose moral focus is the common life of the church say that politics is a calling for some citizens specifically because they are Christians? There are two reasons to say that politics, for Christians, is not a forbidden profession. The first is that political order comes to be as a providential arrangement that (1) provides space for the church to carry out its mission and (2) orders society rightly in the midst of a fallen world. Recognizing politics as a vocation is

---

22. For a helpful discussion from a Christian perspective of the ethics of civil disobedience, see James Childress, *Civil Disobedience and Political Obligation: A Study in Christian Social Ethics* (New Haven: Yale University Press, 1971).

first of all a way for Christians to honor God by honoring his provision for a fallen and imperfect world. It is also a way to show love for one's neighbor by providing order and establishing right within the conflicts that mark the course of human history. Politics as a vocation can, in short, be a way of living out the first and second commandments to love God with all one's heart, soul, mind, and strength and one's neighbor as oneself.

The next question is, on what basis might a Christian discern that politics is in fact a vocation for them? To begin with negative indicators, to the extent that entry into one form or another of politics is driven by the quest for notoriety or the quest for power for the sake of power, one can be certain that they are confronting temptation rather than a divine call. What, however, might be positive indications that in any particular case politics is a genuine calling under God? The first indicator is the presence of a certain form of wisdom. Politics is indeed "the art of the possible" rather than "the art of the ideal." No political solution is perfect. Every political act represents a compromise between what is best and what is possible within a given set of circumstances. It takes a certain kind of wisdom to discern where the point between the ideal and the possible lies. Few possess this sort of wisdom. Some do, and for them politics may well be a calling.

It will not prove to be a calling, however, if they lack or have minimal amounts of certain graces. Chief among these is a capacity for truthfulness. I do not mean that politicians must always tell the truth. In politics a certain amount of dissimulation and falsehood are necessary if disaster is to be avoided and anything of a positive nature accomplished. Winston Churchill is reputed once to have said, "I value the truth so highly because I get to tell it so infrequently." He knew as well as anyone that within politics, a devotion to truth does not require veracity in every case. He also knew that even when politicians are called upon to make compromises with the truth, they wish fervently that they did not have to. A person with a calling to politics should know that there are certain lies that they may not tell and certain actions that they may not perform. There are some lies and some acts that undermine the foundations of the society they are called upon to protect. As a friend once said, "What we want in our politicians are certain splendid incapacities." One of them is an inability to lie when a lie does not serve but betrays a political vocation. Recognition of this boundary by a politician is a primary aspect of the wisdom required for their profession.

There are other graces necessarily tied to politics as a vocation. Chief among them are courage, openness to instruction, a desire for reconciliation, sympathy, and mercy. Each of these is a grace that defines the character of life within the common life of the church. In addition, each has the capacity to spill over into the life of political society. Indeed, each is necessary for the health of political society. Without courage, politicians will never take the difficult path that must be followed if worthwhile results are to be achieved. Without openness to instruction, those with political authority become blind to the real state of the commonwealth they are called to serve. Without a desire for reconciliation, political struggle becomes a war in which only one party survives. Without sympathy, those in authority lose touch with the weak. Without mercy, the harsh rigors of the law are never tempered with the milk of human kindness.

Clearly something like a manual of the political virtues could be written to expand upon each of those just mentioned and others besides. Enough has been said, however, to indicate that discernment of a call to enter politics is a complex enterprise—one that itself requires both honesty and courage. Given the degree of mendacity and egoism now present in politics, it seems reasonable to say that a person whose conscience has been formed within the common life of the church will conclude that when it comes to a political vocation, many have chosen to follow that path, but under God, few actually have been called. This is an observation that among Christians ought to raise the question, "Am I called to a vocation in politics?"

These observations bring to mind a final one that is not moral but religious. Christians have a duty not only to participate in political society but also to pray for their governments. They also have a duty to pray for the full revelation of God's rule. In the second petition of the Lord's Prayer, Christians pray for God's kingdom to come. They pray this prayer because they have been commanded to do so and because they believe that the forms of governance under which they live have only temporary and limited authority. Christians do not wait for the perfection of the political arrangements under which they live. They wait for the full manifestation of God's rule over themselves and over the peoples of the earth. Christians know that God, not "the powers that be," rules their true homeland. As they await the full revelation of that rule, they see "the powers that be" as ministers of God. They are, however, ministers who are fallible, morally tainted, and sometimes evil. Because God rules their homeland, they wait with hope for its full establishment. They wait also with patient endurance because they have no lasting city here. They only have one whose justice is always mixed with injustice and whose provision is always inadequate.

Afterword

This project began with a question: What is and what ought to be the focus of Christian ethics? This question led me to identify three options in the history of Christian thought—self, society, or church. Each option has had powerful advocates within the Christian tradition. I was thus forced to ask which of these, if any, received the support of Holy Scripture. I concluded that a focus on the common life of God's people was pervasive in both the Old and New Testaments. I arrived at this conclusion by asking three questions: What is the basis, what is the goal, and what is the character of faithful living as presented in a representative sampling of New Testament writings? Having established that the unequivocal witness of these writings supports an ecclesial focus, I was able to sketch what an ecclesially focused ethics might look like.

That said, as I moved further and further into this project, I became increasingly aware that my findings suggest a need for extensive changes in the focus that the churches, particularly those in North America, now give to their moral teaching and practice. The extensive, indeed radical, nature of the changes required made me realize that I was presenting my readers with a problem I did not know how to solve.

Having now completed the project that began so many years ago, I remain unclear about how to return the ethical focus of the church to its proper object of attention—the common life of a faithful church. I do feel reasonably confident, however, that certain changes are necessary in the common life of the churches, especially those in North America. The first concerns how these churches typically address a problem. They construct a program. Thus if they identify a problem—say, inadequate teaching of the Bible—they put together a remedial program and try to get their members to sign on. They apply the same strategy to other aspects of church activity—worship, Christian education, spiritual formation, or social outreach. Thus, if at some future date the basis, goal, and character of the common life of congregations are seen to be misguided or given insufficient attention, programs designed to address the problem will come forth with the backing of committees, prestigious groups, or noted personalities. These programs will be carefully designed and well marketed by experts.

No matter what degree of support these programs receive, financially or otherwise, they will certainly fail to bring about the degree of change required. Change of the sort that the churches now need requires something more profound than more effective programs. It requires a change of heart. As I pointed out in my reading of Ephesians, the change to which God's people are called is best described as a new birth, or as dying and rising, or as taking off one suit of clothes and putting on another.

These metaphors all point to provision of a new foundation for life—one rooted in love for God. Some years ago, I preached a sermon in the chapel of the Yale Divinity School.[1] In it I said that the problem faced by the churches in North America is that many of their leaders and members have substituted the second commandment for the first. By that claim I meant that Christian belief had been turned into an ethical command to love one's neighbor. The second commandment had in fact become the first, with the result that love for God had been collapsed into a moral duty owed to one's neighbors. I would now add that for others the second commandment, to love one's neighbor as oneself, has become not an analogy but a positive command to make love of self along with love of neighbor a positive duty. In either case, love of God has become a secondary matter dependent upon a moral duty to society or to oneself. Throughout the execution of this project, a voice has spoken in the back of my mind saying that the key to establishing an ecclesial focus for Christian moral belief and practice lies not in programs but in reordering the commandments and once more establishing the first commandment as actually the first. The key to significant change lies in religion rather than morality.

Like this project as a whole, the question of placing the commandments in their proper order goes back to an event that occurred while I was in Uganda. On the day John Kennedy was assassinated, I was in a cattle camp on the banks of the Nile River. I had traveled there with the Anglican archbishop of Uganda at the time, Leslie Brown. He was to confirm a group of migrant herdsmen who had been gathered by a young catechist. The service was interminable and went on well after dark. The mosquitoes were fierce, and I remember thinking, *How am I going to get out of here?* Just then, a very old woman got up from

---

1. Philip Turner, "To Students of Divinity," *First Things*, no. 26 (October 1992): 25–28.

the edges of the circles around the fire that had been built. She walked up to the archbishop and handed him a gnarled and highly polished root, all curled round upon itself like a snake. She handed the object to the archbishop and in a firm and loud voice said, "Jesus lives! Burn it!"

What she had handed the archbishop was an object in which a powerful spirit was thought to live. She was thought to have the ability to call upon that spirit to do her bidding. She had paid what in local terms was a fortune to be initiated so as to gain this power. With it she could kill or give life. What she had done was hand over the center of her life in exchange for a new one. From that moment, I came to understand the first commandment as indeed the first.

It is as yet unclear to me what the churches in North America have to throw into the fire, but I am certain that the equivalents of this gnarled root are legion. I wonder how this tossing, this "taking off and putting on," can come about. My brain (but not yet my heart) tells me that only grace can accomplish such a miracle. But if not by a program, how then will things change? The conclusion I have reached through writing this book is that change will come about through men and women who are, in Rorty's terms, a "presence" who manifest in their lives "grace beyond striving."[2]

---

2. Rorty, "A Literary Postscript," 319.

Bibliography

Annas, Julia. *The Morality of Happiness*. Oxford: Oxford University Press, 1993.

Atherton, John. *Marginalization*. London: SCM, 2003.

Auden, W. H. *Collected Poems*. Edited by Edward Mendelson. New York: The Modern Library, 2007.

Aune, David. *Revelation*. Word Biblical Commentary. Nashville: Thomas Nelson, 1997, 1998, 1998.

Barth, Karl. *Church Dogmatics*. IV/2, *The Doctrine of Reconciliation*. London: T&T Clark, 1958.

Barth, Marcus. *Ephesians: Introduction, Translation and Commentary on Chapters 1–3*. Garden City, NY: Doubleday, 1974.

———. *Ephesians: Introduction, Translation and Commentary on Chapters 4–6*. Garden City, NY: Doubleday, 1974.

Bauckham, Richard. *Theology of the Book of Revelation*. Cambridge: Cambridge University Press, 1993.

Bellah, Robert, Richard Madsen, William Sullivan, Ann Swindler, and Steven M. Tipton. *Habits of the Heart: Individualism and Commitment in American Life*. Berkeley: University of California Press, 1996.

Bethge, Eberhard. *Dietrich Bonhoeffer: Man of Vision, Man of Courage*. New York: Harper & Row, 1977.

Bonhoeffer, Dietrich. *Letter and Papers from Prison*. New York: Macmillan, 1971.

Bretherton, Luke. *Christianity and Contemporary Politics*. Oxford: Wiley-Blackwell, 2010.

Brown. Peter. *The Body and Society: Men, Women, and Sexual Renunciation in Early Christianity.* New York: Columbia University Press, 1993.

———. *The Rise of Western Christendom.* 2nd ed. Oxford: Blackwell, 2003.

———. "Saint Augustine and Political Society." In *The City of God: A Collection of Critical Essays.* Edited by Dorothy F. Donnelly, 17–35. New York: Peter Lang, 1995.

Burnaby, John. *Amor Dei: A Study of the Religion of St. Augustine.* London: Hodder and Stoughton, 1938.

Carter, Craig. *The Politics of the Cross: Theology and Social Ethics of John Howard Yoder.* Grand Rapids: Brazos, 2001.

Cassirer, Ernst. *The Myth of the State.* New Haven: Yale University Press, 1946.

Chadwick, Owen. *John Cassian.* Cambridge: Cambridge University Press, 1968.

Dagron, Gilbert. *Emperor and Priest: The Imperial Office in Byzantium.* Cambridge: Cambridge University Press, 2007.

Dahl, Nils. "Interpreting Ephesians: Then and Now." In *Studies in Ephesians: Introductory Questions, Text- & Edition-Critical Issues, Interpretation of Texts and Themes,* edited by David Hellholm, Vermund Blomkvist, and Tord Fornberg. Tübingen: Mohr Siebeck, 2000.

Deane, Herbert A. *The Political and Social Ideas of St. Augustine.* New York: Columbia University Press, 1963.

Doyle, Leonard J., trans. *St. Benedict's Rule for Monasteries.* Collegeville, MN: Liturgical Press, 1948.

Dunn, James. *Romans 9–16.* Word Biblical Commentary. Dallas: Word, 1988.

Dworkin, Ronald. *Justice for Hedgehogs.* Cambridge, MA: The Belknap Press of Harvard University Press, 2011.

Fiorenza, Elizabeth Schüssler. *The Book of Revelation: Justice and Judgment.* Philadelphia: Fortress, 1983.

The First and Second Prayer Books of Edward VI. London: J. M. Dent & Sons, 1957.

Forrester, Duncan. *Christian Justice and Public Policy.* Cambridge: Cambridge University Press, 1997.

Green, Joel B. *The Gospel of Luke.* Grand Rapids: Eerdmans, 1997.

Gregory, Eric. *Politics and the Order of Love: An Augustinian Ethic of Democratic Citizenship.* Chicago: University of Chicago Press, 2010.

Gustafson, James. *Ethics from a Theocentric Perspective.* Vol. 2. Chicago: University of Chicago Press, 1991.

———. *Protestant and Roman Catholic Ethics*. Chicago: University of Chicago Press, 1984.

Hadot, Pierre. *Philosophy as a Way of Life*. Edited by Arnold I. Davidson. Oxford: Blackwell, 1995.

Hanson, Stig. *The Unity of the Church in the New Testament: Colossians and Ephesians*. Stockholm: Almqvist & Wiksell, 1946.

Harrington, Daniel J., SJ. *The Gospel of Matthew*. Sacra Pagina. Collegeville, MN: Liturgical Press, 1991.

Hauerwas, Stanley. *A Community of Character: Toward a Constructive Christian Social Ethic*. Notre Dame, IN: University of Notre Dame Press, 1988.

Hittinger, Russell. "Introduction to Modern Catholicism." In *The Teaching of Modern Christianity On Law, Politics and Human Nature*, vol. 1, edited by John Witte Jr. and Frank S. Alexander, 3–38. New York: Columbia University Press, 2006.

Hunter, James Davison. *The Death of Character: Moral Education in an Age without Good or Evil*. New York: Basic Books, 2000.

———. *To Change the World: The Irony, Tragedy and Possibility of Christianity in the Later Modern World*. Oxford: Oxford University Press, 2002.

Hutter, Reinhard. *Suffering Divine Things: Theology as Church Practice*. Grand Rapids: Eerdmans, 1997.

John Cassian. *The Conferences*. Translated by Boniface Ramsey, OP. New York: Paulist Press, 1997.

———. *The Institutes*. Translated by Boniface Ramsey, OP. New York: Newman Press, 2000.

Johnston, David Cay. *The Fine Print: How Big Corporations Use "Plain English" to Rob You Blind*. New York: Penguin, 2012.

John XXIII (pope), *Pacem in Terris*, #11. www.papalencycles.net/John23/23pacem.htm.

Judt, Tony, with Timothy Snyder. *Thinking the Twentieth Century*. New York: Penguin, 2012.

Kierkegaard, Søren. *Purity of Heart Is to Will One Thing*. New York: Harper, 2009.

———. *Works of Love: Some Christian Reflections in the Form of Discourses*. Translated by Howard and Edna Long. New York: Harper, 1962.

Kittredge, Cynthia. *Community and Authority: The Rhetoric of Obedience in the Paul Tradition*. Harvard Theological Studies 45. Harrisburg, PA: Trinity Press International, 1988.

Knowles, Dom David. *The Benedictines*. Eugene, OR: Wipf & Stock, 2009.

Koenig, John. "Perspectives on Leadership in the New Testament." *Word and World* 13, no. 1 (Winter 1993): 26–33.

Lepore, Jill. "The Lie Factory." *The New Yorker*, September 24, 2012.

Lincoln, Andrew. *Ephesians*. Word Biblical Commentary. Dallas: Word, 1990.

Lindbeck, George. *The Nature of Doctrine: Religion and Theology in a Postliberal Age*. Philadelphia: Westminster, 1984.

Lovibond, Sabina. *Ethical Formation*. Cambridge, MA: Harvard University Press, 2002.

Luz, Ulrich. *Matthew 1–7*. Continental Commentaries. Minneapolis: Augsburg, 1992.

———. *Matthew 21–28*. Hermeneia. Minneapolis: Fortress, 2005.

Markus, Robert. *The End of Ancient Christianity*. Cambridge: Cambridge University Press, 1997.

Marshall, I. Howard. "Political and Eschatological in Language in Luke." In *Reading Luke*, edited by Craig Bartholomew, Joel B. Green, and Anthony C. Thiselton, 157–77. Grand Rapids: Zondervan, 2005.

Mauss, Marcel. *The Gift: Forms and Functions of Exchange in Archaic Societies*. New York: W. W. Norton, 1967.

Melden, A. I. *Rights and Persons*. Berkeley: University of California Press, 1980.

Milbank, John. *Theology and Social Theory: Beyond Secular Reason*. Oxford: Blackwell, 1990.

Miller, David. *Social Justice*. Oxford: Clarendon, 1979.

Moessner, David P. "Reading Luke's Gospel as Ancient Hellenistic Narrative." In *Reading Luke*, edited by Craig Bartholomew, Joel B. Green, and Anthony C. Thiselton, 129–45. Grand Rapids: Zondervan, 2005.

Nemirovsky, Irene. *Suite Français*. New York: Vintage, 2007.

Niebuhr, Richard H. *Christ and Culture*. New York: Harper & Row, 1975.

O'Donovan, Oliver. *The Desire of the Nations: Rediscovering the Roots of Political Theology*. Cambridge: Cambridge University Press, 1996.

———. *The Problem of Self-Love in St. Augustine*. New Haven: Yale University Press, 1980.

———. *Resurrection and Moral Order: An Outline for Evangelical Ethics*. 2nd ed. Grand Rapids: Eerdmans, 1994.

———. *The Ways of Judgment*. Grand Rapids: Eerdmans, 2005.

O'Donovan, Oliver, and Joan O'Donovan. *From Irenaeus to Grotius: A Sourcebook in Christian Political Thought*. Grand Rapids: Eerdmans, 1999.

Osborne, Grant. *Revelation*. BECNT. Grand Rapids: Baker Academic, 2002.

Outka, Gene. *Agape: An Ethical Analysis.* New Haven: Yale University Press, 1972.

——. "Theocentric Love and the Augustinian Legacy: Honoring Differences and Likenesses between God and Ourselves." *Journal of the Society of Christian Ethics* 22 (2002).

Pieper, Joseph. *The Four Cardinal Virtues.* Notre Dame, IN: University of Notre Dame Press, 1967.

Preston, Ronald. *Church and Society in the Twentieth Century: The Economic and Political Task.* London: SCM, 1983.

Putnam, Robert D., and David E. Campbell. *American Grace: How Religion Divides and Unites Us.* New York: Simon & Schuster, 2010.

Radner, Ephraim. *The End of the Church: A Pneumatology of Christian Division in the West.* Grand Rapids: Eerdmans, 1998.

Ramsey, Arthur Michael. *The Gospel and the Catholic Church.* London: Longmans, Green and Co., 1956.

Ramsey, Paul. *Speak Up for Just War or Pacifism.* University Park: Pennsylvania State University Press, 1988.

Rauschenbusch, Walter. *Christianity and the Social Crisis.* New York: Macmillan, 1913.

——. *Christianizing the Social Order.* New York: Macmillan, 1913.

——. *A Theology for the Social Gospel.* Nashville: Abingdon, 1945.

Rawls, John. *A Theory of Justice.* Cambridge, MA: Harvard University Press, 1971.

Rorty, Amilie Oksenberg, ed. *The Identity of Persons.* Berkeley: University of California Press, 1976.

Ruston, Roger. *Human Rights and the Image of God.* London: SCM, 2004.

Schweizer, Eduard. *The Good News according to Matthew.* Atlanta: John Knox, 1975.

Sen, Amartya. *The Idea of Justice.* Cambridge, MA: The Belknap Press of Harvard University Press, 2009.

Smucker, Donovan E. *The Origins of Walter Rauschenbusch's Social Ethics.* Montreal and Kingston: McGill-Queens University Press, 1994.

Stout, Jeffrey. *Democracy and Tradition.* Princeton: Princeton University Press, 2004.

Tannehill, Robert C. *The Narrative Unity of Luke-Acts: A Literary Interpretation.* Vol. 1. Philadelphia: Fortress, 1991.

Taylor, Charles. *A Secular Age.* Cambridge, MA: The Belknap Press of Harvard University Press, 2007.

Taylor, Jeremy. *Holy Living and Dying.* 1651. Kindle edition.

Thornton, L. S. *Common Life in the Body of Christ*. Westminster: Dacre, 1941.

Turner, Philip. "The Burning of Churches and the Communion of the Churches." In *Out of the Ashes: Burned Churches and the Community of Faith*, edited by A. Hjelm, 48–57. Nashville: Thomas Nelson, 1997.

———. "How the Church Might Teach." In *The Crisis of Moral Teaching in the Episcopal Church*, edited by Timothy Sedgwick and Philip Turner, 137–59. Harrisburg, PA: Morehouse, 1992.

———."The Marriage Canons of the Episcopal Church: (1) Scripture and Tradition." *The Anglican Theological Review* 65, no. 4 (October 1983).

———. "The Marriage Canons of the Episcopal Church: (2) The Case from Reason." *The Anglican Theological Review* 66, no. 1 (January 1984).

———. "Philanthropy's Inconstant Friend, Religion." In *Good Intentions: Moral Obstacles and Opportunities*, edited by David Smith, 127–45. Bloomington: Indiana University Press, 2005.

———. *Sex, Money and Power: An Essay in Christian Social Ethics*. Cambridge, MA: Cowley, 1985.

———. "To Students of Divinity." *First Things* 26 (October 1992).

Visser 't Hooft, W. A., and J. H. Oldham. *The Church and Its Function in Society*. London: George Allen & Unwin, 1937.

Walzer, Michael. *Spheres of Justice: A Defense of Pluralism and Equality*. New York: Basic Books, 1983.

Wannenwetsch, Bernd. *Political Worship: Ethics for Christian Citizens*. Oxford: Oxford University Press, 2004.

Watson, Francis. *Agape, Eros, Gender: Towards a Pauline Social Ethic*. Cambridge: Cambridge University Press, 2000.

Werpehowski, William. *American Protestant Ethics and the Legacy of H. Richard Niebuhr*. Washington, DC: Georgetown University Press, 2002.

White, John, Jr. *From Sacrament to Contract: Marriage, Religion and Law in the Western Tradition*. Louisville: Westminster John Knox, 1997.

Wilken, Robert. "Amo, Amas, Amat: Christianity and Culture." *Reflections* 7 (2003).

Williams, Rowan. *Faith in the Public Square*. London: Bloomsbury, 2012.

Yoder, John Howard. *The Christian Witness to the State*. Institute of Mennonite Studies Series Number 3. Newton, KS: Faith and Life Press, 1964.

———. *For the Nations: Essays Evangelical and Public*. Grand Rapids: Eerdmans, 1997.

———. *The Original Revolution*. Scottdale, PA: Herald, 1971.

———. *The Politics of Jesus*. Grand Rapids: Eerdmans, 1992.

———. *Preface to Theology: Christology and Theological Method.* Grand Rapids: Brazos, 2002.

———. *The Priestly Kingdom: Social Ethics as Gospel.* Notre Dame, IN: University of Notre Dame Press, 1984.

———. *The Royal Priesthood: Essays Ecclesiological and Ecumenical.* Edited by Michael G. Cartwright. Scottdale, PA: Herald, 1998.

Scripture Index

Old Testament

Genesis
2:24 86
12:3 110

Exodus
2:14 116
21:24 118
22:26 118

Leviticus
18:25 117n9
18:28 117n9
19:18 119
19:29 117n9

Deuteronomy
6:4–15 127
6:16 127
24:4 117n9

1 Kings
19:19–21 134

Psalms
10:3–4 169n8
10:7 169n8
15:2–5 169n8
34:11–13 169n8
47 65
50:19–21 169n8
68 71
71:1 115n8
93 229
97 229
99 229

Proverbs
6:16–19 169n8
18:20–21 169n8

Isaiah
2:2–4 65
11:5 93
40:14–15 229
42:4 229
42:10–11 229
44:1 146
44:6 146
56:7 65n3
59:3–4 169n8
60:7 65n3
61:2–3 114n6

Jeremiah
3:1–3 117n9
3:9 117n9
9:3–9 169n8

Ezekiel
47:1–12 65

Hosea
4:2–3 117n9

Micah
4:1–3 65
6:12 169n8

New Testament

Matthew
1–4 109
1:1–17 110
1:18 110
1:22 112n5
1:23 110
2:1–12 110
2:3–4 110
2:6 112n5
2:15 112n5
2:17 112n5
2:23 110, 112n5
3:3 112n5
3:17 112
4:14 112n5
4:15 110
4:16 113
5–7 109
5:3–11 111, 113

277

5:5 79
5:6–7 119
5:7 114
5:8 115
5:9 115, 118
5:10 115
5:11–12 113
5:12 115
5:13–20 113
5:16 111, 118, 156
5:17–48 166
5:20 111
5:21–23 116, 167
5:21–48 113, 116
5:23 192
5:23–24 116
5:27–30 168
5:27–32 116
5:29–30 117
5:31–32 167
5:32 116
5:33–34 119
5:33–37 117
5:37 117
5:38–41 118, 167, 261
5:38–42 118
5:38–48 112
5:39 261
5:42 119
5:43–47 167
5:44 192
5:48 109, 119
6:1–18 120
6:7–13 120
6:12 112
6:14 112
6:14–15 115, 121
6:19–21 122
6:19–34 122
6:21 122
6:22–23 122
6:25–34 122
6:33 122
7:3–4 192
7:6 121n16
7:7–11 122
7:13–14 111, 123
7:14 111
7:15 123
7:21 111, 123
7:21–27 111
8:17 112n5

10:5 110
10:6 110
11:15–27 116
11:25–27 111
11:29 111
11:30 111
12:17–21 112n5
13:14–16 112n5
13:35 112n5
14:28–32 113
15:24 110
17:5 112
18 53
18:15–17 192
18:15–20 167
18:17 114
18:21–22 192
18:21–35 112, 114
19:7–8 117
21:4–5 112n5
21:5 79
21:15 112n5
22:37–40 109
23:23 114
24:15 112n5
25:31–46 111
27:1 110
27:9–10 112n5
27:20 110
27:22 158
27:37–39 158
28:18–19 110
28:18–20 111
28:19–20 110, 113
28:20 110, 111, 112

Mark

2:26 65n3
8:35 108
8:38 108
9:35 108
10:11–12 167
10:35–45 160
10:45 108
11:17 65n3
12:30 158
13:35–37 108
14:27–28 108
14:28 108
16:7 108

Luke

1:1 127
1:3 127
1:5–4:13 127
1:15 138
1:16 138
1:31–35 138
1:32–33 49
1:35 126, 127
1:37 137
1:38 128
1:41 138
1:50 134
1:50–52 134
1:51–53 129
1:52 126
1:54–55 130
1:67 138
1:67–79 137
1:68–75 49
2:20 140
2:26–27 138
2:29–31 126
2:32 126
2:38 138
2:49 127
3:1–2 128
3:7–9 128
3:19–20 128
3:22 138
4:1 138
4:1–12 49
4:1–13 126, 127, 128
4:4 127
4:7 127
4:8–11 140
4:9–12 127
4:14 139
4:14–9:50 129
4:18 139
4:18 125
4:18–19 49
4:33–35 130
4:43 138
5:12–14 130
5:17–25 130
5:25–26 140
6:12 49
6:20 126, 129
6:20–23 139
6:20–26 114

Scripture Index

6:21 129
6:22–23 129
6:23 139
6:24 126, 129
6:24–26 139
6:25 129
6:27 132
6:28–29 132
6:29 129
6:29–49 129
6:30 132, 164
6:31 132
6:34 132, 164
6:35 132, 140, 164
6:35–36 132
6:37 132
6:41–42 133
6:43–44 139
6:46–49 139
6:49 139
7:1–10 133
7:11–17 133
7:19 140
7:30 126
7:36–50 133
9:1–22 49
9:22 138
9:51 133
9:51–19:48 133
9:57–61 134
9:57–62 128
9:61 134
9:62 134
10:27–28 158
11:43 136
12:13–21 135
12:23 135
12:30 135
12:31–32 135
13:10–17 126, 133
13:13 140
13:33 138
13:33–34 133
14:1–11 136
14:13 133
14:15–24 134
15:1–32 130
15:11–32 132
16:14 135
16:14–18 134
16:18 167
16:19–30 134

17:7–10 136
17:11–19 133, 134
17:15 140
17:20–21 134
17:25 138
18:1–8 134
18:9–14 134
18:15–17 133
18:18–30 134, 135
18:35–43 134
18:43 140
19:1–9 134, 135
19:10 133
19:36–46 50
22:3 126
22:24–53 50
22:37 138
22:53 126, 131
23:46 138
23:47 140
24:7 138
24:26 138
24:44 138
24:47 137

John

1:4–5 156
3:16 108
4:23 232
13:34–35 108
17:20–23 108
17:21 108
17:26 108

Acts

2:17–18 139
2:22–23 126
2:33 139
4:13 128
4:21 140
4:28 126
4:29 128
4:31 128
4:32 132, 165
4:34 132, 165
5:38–39 126
6:8–10 128
9:27–29 128
11:18 140
13:46 138

13:48 140
14:3 128
18:25–26 126
19:23 126
20:27 126
21:20 140
22:4 126
24:14 126
26:18 126
26:19 139
26:19–23 128
28:31 128

Romans

3:21–26 94
7:1–3 168n7
7:6 184
11:25–27 107
12:1 107
12:3–8 73, 183
12:3–21 107
12:5 81n2
12:10 81n2
12:16 81n2
13:1 220, 227, 228
13:1–7 107
13:2 228
13:6 260
13:6 7 220
13:7 260
13:8 81n2
13:8–14 107
14:1–15:6 107
14:8 81n2
14:13 81n2
15:5 81n2
15:7 81n2
15:14 81n2
15:16 81n2
15:26–29 164

1 Corinthians

5:1–5 57
5:5 192
5:9–10 96
7:8–40 168n7
9–13 57
11:23 21n2
12:4–11 73
12:7 73

12:12–26 183
12:25 81n2
12:27–31 73
13:4–13 158n1
16:20 81n2

2 Corinthians

8–9 164
13:12 81n2

Galatians

5:13 81n2
5:15 81n2
5:26 81n2
6:2 81n2
6:10 191

Ephesians

1:3 71
1:3–14 65
1:4 66, 72n13
1:4–5 67, 78, 79, 82
1:4–6 65, 70
1:7 70
1:9 65
1:9–10 70, 72n11
1:9–11 62
1:10 103
1:11 70
1:11–12 70
1:12 66, 67
1:13 63, 71
1:13–14 66, 101
1:14 71
1:15 72n13
1:16–20 96
1:16–23 97
1:18 77, 97
1:18–20 72n11
1:19–23 101
1:20 70, 85
1:22–23 62, 70
2:1 70
2:1–2 98
2:1–6 78
2:2 91
2:2–3 98
2:3 63, 98, 99, 101
2:3–18 84

2:4 72n13
2:4–10 71
2:6 71
2:6–7 72n11
2:8 94
2:10 78
2:11–13 78
2:11–22 62
2:12 63
2:13 63, 70
2:13–14 65
2:14–16 67
2:15 74
2:15–16 66
2:16 63
2:18 63
2:19–22 66
2:20 81, 88
2:20–22 63
3:1–11 70
3:4 88
3:9 101
3:9–10 72n11
3:9–11 66
3:10 92
3:14–19 72, 78, 96, 97
3:16 72
3:17 72
3:18 194
3:18–19 72
4:1 61, 78, 79, 184
4:1–6 81
4:2 72n13, 79, 81, 82, 210
4:2–3 80, 89, 184, 193
4:3 66, 79, 101, 102
4:5–6 100
4:7 81
4:7–10 81
4:8 71
4:10 85
4:11 73, 88
4:11–16 81
4:12 73
4:13 74, 82
4:13–16 74
4:14 82, 92, 96
4:15 82, 102, 184, 193
4:16 72n13
4:17–18 96
4:18 97, 184
4:19 98, 101
4:20 161

4:22 98
4:22–24 97, 101
4:24 92
4:25 80, 81, 85, 169
4:25–31 102
4:28 101
4:28–29 98
4:29 101
4:30 101
4:31 80, 98, 101, 169, 184
4:32 80, 81, 89, 193
4:32–5:2 80, 89
5:1 65
5:1–2 67, 78, 80
5:2 72n13, 103
5:4 101
5:6–7 91
5:6–13 91
5:8 91, 96
5:9 91
5:10 101
5:11 89, 91
5:15 90, 91, 195
5:15–16 101, 103
5:15–17 84
5:17 84, 90, 97, 194, 195
5:18 195
5:18–21 84
5:21 81, 90, 161, 184, 186
5:21–6:9 65, 84, 87, 90
5:22–33 168n7
5:25 72n13, 86
5:28 86
5:29–30 86
5:31 86
5:32 86
6:9 90
6:10 92
6:10–11 91
6:10–18 91
6:11 92
6:11–18 101
6:12 91, 92
6:13 92
6:14 93
6:14–18 91
6:15 94
6:16 94
6:17 95
6:18–20 95
6:24 72n13

Scripture Index

Philippians
3:20 220

Colossians
3:18–19 168n7

1 Timothy
2 42
3:2 168n7
3:12 168n7

Hebrews
13:4 168n7

James
1:26 169n8
3:6–11 169n8

1 Peter
3:1–7 168n7
3:10 169n8

1 John
2:16 155

Revelation
1–3 142
1:2 144, 147
1:7 147
1:8 146, 147
1:9 147
1:10 148
1:17–18 147
1:18 141
2:2 141, 143
2:3 210
2:4 141
2:5 147
2:6 143, 145
2:10 141, 142, 145
2:13 141, 147
2:14–15 143
2:16 147
2:17 145
2:19–23 144
2:28 145
3:1 143
3:3 142
3:4–5 145
3:8 142
3:10 142, 143
3:11 142, 147
3:12 145
3:14 144
3:17 143
3:19 143
3:20–21 145
3:21 147
4:2 148
5 142
5:5 147
5:6 147, 148
5:9 146
5:9–10 147
5:13 147
6:1–17 142
6:9 147
8:1 142
8:2 142
8:3–5 142
8:6–21 142
10:1–11:13 146
11:3–13 148
11:7 147
11:13 146
11:14–19 142
12:7 141, 147
12:8 147
12:9 144
12:11 142, 144, 145, 147
12:17 147
13:5 247
13:7 147
13:10 143
13:14 144
13:18 143, 165
14:1 147
14:5 144
14:12 143
14:13 148
15:2 145, 147
15:2–4 147
15:4 142
16:14 147
16:15 147
17–18 141
17:3 148
17:14 147
19:5–7 142
19:7–8 148
19:11 147
19:19 147
19:21 144
20:2–3 144
20:4 147
20:4–6 148
20:7–8 144
21:1 142
21:2 148
21:6 147
21:10 148
22:3–5 148
22:6–7 144
22:7 147
22:12 147, 148
22:13 147
22:17 148
22:20 147, 148

Author Index

Annas, Julia, 6n8, 97
Atherton, John, 200n1
Auden, W. H., 191, 256
Aune, David, 144n8, 145n10

Barth, Karl, 40, 45, 139
Barth, Marcus, 70n9–71, 72, 81, 92n11, 96n14, 101n19
Bauckham, Richard, 144, 148
Bellah, Robert, 177–78
Berlin, Isaiah, 238
Bethge, Eberhard, 201n8
Bonhoeffer, Dietrich, 201–2
Bretherton, Luke, 200n1
Brown, Peter, 217, 223
Burnaby, John, 159n2

Carter, Craig, 41
Cassian, John, 3–19, 22, 36, 49, 56, 109, 176, 178
Cassirer, Ernst, 222–23
Chadwick, Owen, 9

Dagron, Gilbert, 224–25
Dahl, Nils, 99
Deane, Herbert A., 226–27
Dunn, James, 107
Dworkin, Ronald, 238, 240n36

Fiorenza, Elizabeth Schüssler, 144n8
Forrester, Duncan, 238

Green, Joel B., 129, 135
Gregory, Eric, 202, 203n11
Gustafson, James, 253, 254n13, 255

Hadot, Pierre, 4, 9n18
Hanson, Stig, 69
Harrington, Daniel J., 114n7
Hauerwas, Stanley, 31, 262
Hittinger, Russell, 201n6, 252n9
Hunter, James Davison, 178–79, 254
Hutter, Reinhard, 63n2

Johnston, David Cay, 208
John XXIII, Pope, 241
Judt, Tony, 208–9

Kierkegaard, Søren, 17, 87, 89, 160
Knowles, Dom David, 181n10
Koenig, John, 88n9

Lepore, Jill, 207
Lincoln, Andrew, 62n1, 66n4, 70–71n9, 72n10, 72n12, 73n14, 74n15, 81n3, 85n5, 94n13, 103n20
Lindbeck, George, 173, 180
Lovibond, Sabina, 173–74, 180
Luz, Ulrich, 110n4, 114n6, 115n8, 118–20, 122n17, 191n15

Markus, Robert, 13n29, 18, 181n9, 191
Marshall, I. Howard, 131
Mauss, Marcel, 164, 204
Melden, A. I., 250
Milbank, John, 63n2, 88
Miller, David, 221
Moessner, David P., 130n4

Niebuhr, Reinhold, 41
Niebuhr, Richard H., 172, 202

O'Donovan, Oliver, 159n2, 202, 204n14, 205, 216, 228, 229n11, 230n12, 231, 233–38, 246n1, 258
Osborne, Grant, 247n3
Outka, Gene, 14n31

Pieper, Joseph, 195n23
Preston, Ronald, 252, 253n11
Putnam, Robert D., 200n1

Radner, Ephraim, 68n5
Ramsey, Arthur Michael, 74–76
Ramsey, Paul, 118n14, 219n1, 255n16
Rauschenbusch, Walter, 19–37, 42–44, 48–49, 56
Rawls, John, 234, 248
Rorty, Amélie Oksenberg, 205–6, 211, 269
Ruston, Roger, 239–40, 242

Schweizer, Eduard, 114n6
Sen, Amartya, 231n13, 237–38, 241n37

Smucker, Donovan E., 20n3, 25, 30n51
Stout, Jefrey, 200

Tannehill, Robert C., 130n2
Taylor, Charles, 200
Taylor, Jeremy, 17
Thornton, L. S., 164
Turner, Philip, 163n3, 168n6, 169n9, 190n14, 255n16, 268

Visser 't Hooft, W. A., 252

Walzer, Michael, 237
Wannenwetsch, Bernd, 183n12
Watson, Francis, 85–86
White, John, Jr., 187n13
Williams, Rowan, 201n4, 235, 250

Yoder, John Howard, 31, 38–57, 153–54, 181, 262

Subject Index

Aquinas, Thomas
  on individuals and society, 184
  on moral agency, 215
  on political order, 224
  political theology of, 227
  on wisdom, 195
Aristotelianism, 216, 224, 227
atheism, 20
Augustine
  on communal witness, 181
  on Donatism and Pelagianism, 191–92
  on ecclesial ethics, 192
  on isolation, 196
  on love and desire, 159
  on moral agency, 215
  on the neighbor, 167
  on pagan virtue, 88
  on political authority, 227–28
  on the political state, 42
  political theology of, 226–27
  on the Sermon on the Mount, 109
  on sovereignty, 226
authority
  of Christ, 46, 50, 70, 110, 112, 133
    given to the church, 55, 71
    to forgive sins, 55
    over Satan, 131
  in the Christian East, 75
  in the church, 76, 81–83, 88–89, 161–62
  domestic, 85–86
  of God the Father, 64, 138, 200, 220, 256
  of the Holy Spirit, 68
    in biblical interpretation, 68
  moral, 160
  of churches in Europe, 201
  papal, 251–53
  political, 42, 44, 117, 165, 198–99, 220–23
    basis of, 224–231
    character of, 245–51
    and the church, 199, 216, 218, 220, 257
    demonic potential of, 245, 263
    disobedience to, 263–64
    Enlightenment forms of, 222
    goal of, 231
    and idolatry, 165
    limits of, 46, 256, 266
    within the providence of God, 245, 256, 260
    and social contracts, 222
autonomy
  of citizens, 222, 224, 230
  personal, 201, 215, 222
  sexual, 213

baptism, 96, 99, 101–2, 186, 191
  of Christ, 50
Beatitudes, 113–23
body of Christ
  edification of, 73
  mutual subjection within, 161
boundaries
  cultural, 90, 132, 173
  of the people of God, 107, 132–34, 139, 161
  political, 240, 258
    and the church, 37

capitalism, 30
Cassian, John
  on discretion, 16
  on grace and freedom, 10
  and monasticism, 3

and perfection, 6, 9
on *philosophia*, 4–5, 8
on prayer, 16
on renunciation, 8, 13
on vices, 10, 12, 14
on virtues, 11, 14
Christ
  life in
    Cassian on, 4–17
    ecclesial focus of, 153–74
    Ephesians on, 61–103
    Gospel of Luke on, 128–39
    Gospel of Matthew on, 112–23
    Rauschenbusch on, 21–37
    Yoder on, 40–57
  unity in, 64–89, 99–103, 108, 140, 156, 162, 169, 182, 185–93, 210–12
  victory of, 10, 41, 46–47, 56, 71, 81, 92–95, 101, 141–48, 153, 229
Christendom, 181
church
  authority in, 161–62, 226
  common life of, 109–29, 137–48, 158–59, 166–76, 186, 204, 250–51, 261–66
  Ephesians on, 61–90, 99–103
  marriage in, 160, 211–14
  and political authority, 199–203, 225–26, 232, 234, 238, 246
  as political entity, 220, 243–45, 256–58
  union with Christ, 187–88
  vocation in, 184–85
  witness of, 154–55
  Yoder on, 39–57
citizenship
  Christian, 256–58, 263
  early Christian, 220
  political, 203
Constantine, 225
consumerism, 178, 182
contemplation, 6, 8–9
conversion
  and the church, 155
  of the nations, 146
  personal, 12, 159, 163, 169
creation
  forces opposed to, 91, 141, 146
  fulfillment of, 56, 110
  God as ruler of, 229
  God's provision for, 261
  God's purposes for, 62, 65–66, 70, 72, 78, 98, 128, 142, 154, 168, 224, 231
  intervention of God within, 36–37

manifestation of God to, 17
marriage and, 212
and the meaning of history, 42
political authority in, 199
and redemption, 75, 216
redemption of, 12, 30, 62, 67, 156, 226–27
unity of, 69, 103
and worship, 70, 142

democracy, 84, 128, 208–9, 261
desert fathers, 3, 10
devil, 14, 92, 126–27, 131, 141–43, 147. *See also* Satan
divorce, 116–19, 168n6, 186, 211–13, 251
duty, 111, 113, 123, 136, 173, 177
  Christian, 52, 155, 219, 221, 251, 261, 266
  moral, 128, 268
  political, 221
  religious, 120, 128

Eastern Orthodoxy, 74–75, 110, 168, 176, 194n22, 224, 226, 228
Enlightenment, 21, 48, 212–13, 222
equality, 33
  Christian, 28, 204–5
  democratic, 25, 32, 221, 232–37, 241, 247–50
  in the New Testament, 88n9
  Rauschenbusch on, 32–37
  social, 87
  Yoder on, 54
ethics
  Christian, 129, 139, 142
    authority in, 162
    basis of, 112, 157
    Cassian on, 7
    ecclesial focus of, 121, 156, 172–73, 176, 179, 182–83, 185, 194–98, 215, 218, 233
    Ephesians on, 61, 67, 69, 74, 77, 81, 102
    goal of, 155–56
    Rauschenbusch on, 19–21, 24–30, 36
    Yoder on, 38, 41–43, 45–46, 51, 53–57
  social, 172, 201
Eucharist, 99, 191
eudaimonia, 4, 8, 11, 14, 111, 145
evil
  age, 83, 86, 92, 94, 101, 195
  Christ's victory over, 141, 145–48
  Christian response to, 118–19, 219, 259
  in the church, 266
  exposing, 172
  forces of, 128–30, 141, 156–57
  God's battle with, 171

Subject Index

governance and, 125
nonresistance to, 167
political authority and, 245–47
Rauschenbusch on, 19, 23–28, 35
resisting, 261
Satan and, 126–27
Yoder on, 40, 42, 45, 47, 49, 52
evolution
biological, 21, 30
social, 36

forgiveness
God's, 70, 130, 166
human, 18, 31, 45, 65, 83, 92, 102, 121, 123, 133, 137, 162, 169–70, 191, 193, 206, 210, 239

gifts (spiritual), 71–74, 81, 83, 90, 128, 184, 189, 233
gnosticism, 75, 99
governance (human), 125, 198–200, 202, 216, 220–34, 238–39, 247, 256, 258, 260

Holy Spirit
and biblical interpretation, 68
Cassian on, 7, 9, 16–17
and Christ's conception, 110
grieving, 89
in the Gospel of Matthew, 112
reception of, 71
work of, 74, 76, 100, 103, 138–39, 148–49, 153, 156–58, 194, 204, 216, 219
Yoder on, 41, 49–51
humility, 12–18, 28, 31, 33, 79–83, 88–89, 92–94, 102, 115–18, 137, 162, 169–70, 184–85, 206, 210, 239

idolatry, 144, 257
individualism, 54, 206, 235, 240, 248–49
industrial revolution, 20–21
injustice, 25, 238
political, 246–47, 263–64, 266
structural, 56
Israel (biblical), 30, 49–50, 62–65, 70, 109–16, 120, 126–34, 137, 168, 229

justice
attributive, 259–61
authority and, 162, 264
as cardinal virtue, 171
Christ and, 28, 126
and the church, 119–20, 251

God's, 229
human governance and, 199, 221, 233, 246–48
and the kingdom of God, 22, 232
New Testament conception of, 109, 118
political concept of, 221, 227
Rauschenbusch on, 31, 34–35
and rights, 233–41
Yoder on, 41, 43–44

Kant, Immanuel, 20–23, 36, 215, 238
Kierkegaard, Søren, 17, 87, 89, 160
kingdom of heaven
Cassian on, 5–9, 12, 16
and Christian ethics, 69–70n8
and marriage, 116–17
in the Gospel of Luke, 130–36, 159
in the Gospel of Matthew, 123–26, 159
Rauschenbusch on, 19, 21–37
Yoder on, 43, 55

law
biblical, 225, 229, 233
of Christ, 24, 30, 35
Christ on, 62, 86, 109, 111, 113–16, 119, 158, 166
church, 40, 251
God's revealed, 239
inability to save, 63
and mercy, 266
moral, 29, 215
natural, 40, 215, 251
O'Donovan on, 234–37
and rights, 240–43, 249
liberalism
political, 240
theological, 43
liberation theology, 31–32, 36, 125
liberty
in the church, 89
concept of, 221–23
governance and, 234
Jesus on, 125
kingdom of God and, 232–33
O'Donovan on, 235, 237
policy and, 221
Rauschenbusch on, 32–34, 37
in World War II, 208
Yoder on, 49

marriage
as analogy for Christ and church, 86
and the church, 186–88, 199, 211–14

and the kingdom of God, 116–17, 134, 160, 167–68
patriarchy and, 86–87
Roman Catholic Church on, 251, 254
as social contract, 204, 214–15
martyrdom, 108, 144–48, 165, 230, 263

neoorthodoxy, 36, 40–41
North America
churches, 173, 181, 215, 269
consumerism, 178
and democracy, 32, 209
and individualism, 203
marriage, 186
moral education, 178, 267–68
political struggles of, 256
religion, 182
and secularism, 200
society, 177–78, 200–201

O'Donovan, Oliver, 159n2, 202, 204n14, 205, 216, 228, 229n11, 230n12, 231, 233–38, 246n1, 258

pacifism, 262–63
in Mennonite tradition, 39
Yoder on, 43, 52
philanthropy, 163–64, 188–90
Platonism, 12, 18, 216, 227, 247
pluralism
democratic, 128, 178
postmodern, 68
religious, 74
Protestantism, 181, 201
and marriage, 212, 251
and morality, 253–56
and secularism, 252–53
providence, 11, 28–30, 34, 37, 47, 138, 149
and the church, 64, 69, 74, 112, 142, 192, 196, 202–3
and the political state, 42–43, 45, 56–57, 224–31, 243, 245–46, 256–58, 262–63

Rauschenbusch, Walter
on Christian ethics, 30
on the corporate nature of salvation, 21
on the human condition, 19
on Jesus, 22, 26–29, 35
on justice, 34
on the kingdom of God, 19, 23, 35
and the social gospel, 21, 33
on virtue, 31–32

reason
Enlightenment views of, 222
and the image of God, 240
and passions, 4–5
practical, 242, 261
and revelation, 239
and rights, 239
Stoicism on, 69
repentance, 44, 79, 123, 131, 133, 137, 155, 159, 166, 183, 191–94
resurrection (of Christ), 46–47, 55, 62, 70, 74, 81, 95, 131, 136, 138, 147, 157
Revelation (biblical book)
and idolatry, 141
and liberation from oppression, 140
and memory, 183
and suffering, 141, 147–48, 165, 210
and the victory of Christ, 148, 156
and worship, 146, 263
revelation (divine), 26, 40, 81, 96, 126
of God's rule, 266
and reason, 239
in Scripture, 157
righteousness
as armor of God, 92–94
of the disciples, 113, 119–23, 166
of God, 140, 229
personal, 31
in the Sermon on the Mount, 113–16
rights, 188, 214–15, 226, 237, 239
Christian approach to, 243, 248–51
civil, 235
conferred by the state, 254
Enlightenment views of, 222–23
human, 234
individual, 240
legal, 240
and marriage, 213
according to the Roman Catholic Church, 241–42
universal, 239
Roman Catholic Church
and European royalty, 201
and marriage, 212
social and political teaching, 224
view of rights, 240–41
Roman Empire, 33, 130, 141–44, 165, 217, 229

sacraments, 13, 39, 191
salvation, 72, 135
as armor of God, 91, 93, 95
Cassian on, 14

Subject Index

in history, 158
and human governance, 199, 232
individual, 11
God's plan of, 126, 130, 138
Rauschenbusch on, 21, 26
universal character of, 133
of the world, 126
Yoder on, 55
sanctification, 159, 228
Satan, 126–28, 131, 133, 138. *See also* devil
sectarianism, 30, 38, 45, 95, 202, 216
secularism, 200–201
Sermon on the Mount, 7, 52, 109, 111–13, 125, 129, 132–33, 138–39, 170, 261–62
sexuality, 4–5, 168–69, 186–87, 211–13, 251, 254
sin, 10, 16, 23, 54, 74, 96, 100, 130, 147, 169, 203, 227, 256
social contract, 222, 224
social gospel, 21, 27, 56, 129
socialism, 34, 36, 45
St. Benedict, 180–81, 187–88

theoria. *See* contemplation
totalitarianism, 125, 183
Trinity, 51, 56, 74, 77, 111, 148

Vatican, 251
vices, 10–17, 80, 88, 102, 176, 179, 184

violence, 23, 41, 47, 52–53, 56, 116, 118, 167, 226
virtues, 31
in ancient ethical theories, 97
Aquinas on, 195
in the Beatitudes, 114
cardinal, 171
Cassian on, 5–15
political, 266
Rauschenbusch on, 31–33
theological, 171

wealth, 189–90, 260
worship, 50, 65, 75–76, 107, 109–10, 112, 127, 142–43, 145–47, 154–56, 165, 181–85, 196, 225, 229, 232, 257, 263, 267

Yoder, John Howard
Barth's influence on, 40
on the church, 45, 53
on the goal of Christian ethics, 42–43, 55
on history, 46
on Jesus, 49–52
against neoorthodoxy, 41
on nonresistance, 47
on pacifism, 39, 262

www.ingramcontent.com/pod-product-compliance
Lightning Source LLC
Chambersburg PA
CBHW021803220426
43662CB00006B/162